CASTLES and LANDSCAPES

Studies in the Archaeology of Medieval Europe
Edited by: John Schofield

This series brings together new archaeological studies of medieval Europe (1100 to 1600). We want to describe life in medieval Europe and to show how archaeology does this. It is a new form of history. There will be studies of regions such as the North Sea, of subjects such as towns or castles, and of relevant areas of study such as ceramics. To what extent was Europe a cultural, economic and religious entity? Understanding leads to appreciation, and that leads to a concern for conservation of our common European past. The authors will be drawn from Britain and other European countries.

Forthcoming books in the series:
Medieval Towns:
The Archaeology of British Towns in their European Setting
John Schofield & Alan Vince

Medieval Europe Around the North Sea
Brian Ayers

CASTLES and LANDSCAPES

*Power, Community and Fortification
in Medieval England*

O.H. CREIGHTON

LONDON   OAKVILLE

Published by

UK: Equinox Publishing Ltd
Unit 6, The Village,
101 Amies St.,
London, SW11 2JW

US: DBBC,
28 Main Street,
Oakville, CT 06779

www.equinoxpub.com

First published in hardback by Continuum International Publishing Group Ltd in 2002. This paperback edition with enhanced photographs published by Equinox Publishing Ltd. in 2005 by arrangement with Continuum International Publishing Group Ltd.

British Library Cataloguing-in-Publication Data
A catalogue record for this book is available from the British Library.

ISBN 1 904768 67 9 (paperback)

Printed and bound in Great Britain by Antony Rowe, Chippenham, Wiltshire

Contents

Foreword

This series brings together new archaeological studies of medieval Europe. We want to describe and explain life in medieval Europe, between the late eleventh and seventeenth centuries, and to show how archaeology does this. It is a new form of history.

The series sets out to be a major review of recent achievements and of future directions for the subject. Each book is based on new archaeological research, often arising out of work made necessary by urban and rural redevelopment. Each volume will assess new and profitable methods of analysis. It will encourage debate and not avoid controversy.

The choice of subjects is deliberately wide. There will be studies of regions of Europe, such as individual countries or the North Sea, where a geographical or cultural zone will provide the scope or framework. Others will be of features of medieval life, such as towns or castles in their landscapes. A third kind will review recent work on certain classes of artefacts, to show how archaeological work is revolutionizing our view of medieval living standards, trade or religious experience. Yet others will be devoted to new and challenging methodologies instead of surveying areas of results.

The series will address important questions: to what extent medieval Europe was a cultural, economic and religious entity, how western Europe rose to be a centre of civilization, and how the present countries of Europe should manage and enhance their medieval heritage. Understanding leads to appreciation, and appreciation leads to a concern for the conservation of our common European past. This series will constitute a formidable array of handbooks to explain why the past and its products, from artefacts to great buildings and historic landscapes, are important for enriching life in Europe today.

John Schofield, series editor

Figures

Acknowledgements

My greatest thanks in the writing of this book are owed to two individuals: Dr Robert Higham, who provided the initial inspiration for this work while the author was an undergraduate student at the University of Exeter; and Dr Neil Christie, of the University of Leicester, for his help and encouragement. I am also grateful to a number of other academics who have been encouraging and generous with their advice, including Prof. G. Barker, Dr H. Fox, D. Gore, Dr T. Kirk, G. Longden, Dr S. Rippon, D. O'Sullivan and Dr R. Young. Thanks are also due to other researchers, including J. Freeman, M. Gillard and S. Prior.

Outside academic establishments, the research for this book would have been impossible without the personal help of staff during many study visits to sites and monuments record offices and county record offices across the country. Personnel at a number of other organizations are also duly credited for help during study visits, in particular Chris Chandler and Lyndsey Jones at the National Monument Record, and the staff of the Cambridge University Aerial Photograph Collection. I would also like to thank those individuals who have provided help in surveying and recording sites in the field, including Dr J. R. Seguí and Dr G. L. P. Walker.

My sincerest thanks also go to Mike and Sue Rouillard and Barbara Garfi, who produced many of the line drawings, and various other institutions and individuals for providing me with photographs or permitting me to make use of illustrations, including the Archaeological Journal; University of Cambridge Committee for Aerial Photography; Dr A. E. Brown; BKS Air Surveys; Clwyd-Powys Archaeological Trust; Prof. T. Darvill; F. M. Griffith (Devon County Council); Dr R. Higham; Dr R. Liddiard; Dr T. McNeill; Northumberland County Council; Nicholas Palmer (Warwickshire Museums); N. Osbourne (Phillimore); The Royal Commission for Historical Monuments (England); and Peter Weddell (Exeter Archaeology). The sources of illustrations previously published elsewhere are acknowledged within the accompanying captions. Thanks are also due to many others who have provided support or inspiration for this work, including Lynn, Richard and Lauric Creighton, Marcus Horsfall, Peter Waterman, Chris Young, Ian Astbury and the Glare family. Finally, I wish to acknowledge the Humanities Research Board of the British Academy for a one-year MA studentship, a three-year PhD studentship and an academic research grant that, combined, allowed much of this research to be undertaken.

Exeter, September 2001

To Ramona

1 *Introduction*

Castles were among the most characteristic features of the European medieval landscape, and many remain imposing structures to the present day. While popular perceptions of medieval castles are often dominated by their presumed military significance and rôle in contemporary warfare, the defining feature of the medieval castle was, rather, that it served a number of diverse needs. All castles were built, at least to some degree, to serve as high-status private residences and estate centres as well as military strongpoints. As judicial centres and seats of local government, castles were commonly the venues of manorial or honorial courts, while many royal strongholds were also armouries, jails and treasuries. On a day-to-day basis, castles, whether left in the custody of appointed officials or with their royal or aristocratic owners in residence, were bustling centres of social and economic activity, generating commerce and forming central places and natural nucleation points in the landscape. They would have attracted, and periodically accommodated, an exceptionally large and varied human concourse including miscellaneous officials such as auditors, lawyers and stewards; traders and craftspeople; guests and their retinues; and, of course, military personnel of various types. But castles were also built to impress; they were superimposed on earlier landscapes and often located at highly visible or otherwise significant places, overawing nearby communities and always proclaiming the status of their aristocratic builders, owners and inhabitants (Fig. 1.1). The particular functions of castles varied greatly, both through time and between different types of lordship and region; what was consistent, however, was that the castle always represented the essential apparatus of seigneurial (or lordly) power and territorial control.

The impact of castles on the landscape has been profound. As evocative symbols of lordship, they represented a powerful ideological force, and their construction must have re-shaped the landscape in the minds of contemporaries. Perhaps of even greater significance was the influence that the owners of castles exerted over territories under their jurisdiction. A castle did not exist or function in isolation from its surroundings. Most lay at the hub of a wider network of estates rendering services and rents that sustained the seigneurial centre. Castles thus placed demands on the resources of the land and radiated political and administrative control over their surrounding hinterlands; their lords, whether kings, barons or lords of the manor, were often important agents of landscape change who managed dependent estates to further their own social and economic interests. This symbiotic link between castle and hinterland was an enduring feature of the medieval period, and a theme that recurs time and again in the history of fortification. In the late Saxon period, for instance, it is well known that the defences of *burhs* (defended towns) were garrisoned and maintained by labour drawn from their surrounding rural territories, as illustrated in the Burghal Hidage. Indeed, it is only with the Tudor period and the construction of coastal artillery

Figure 1.1   Corfe Castle (Dorset), showing the impressive location of the castle on a steep-sided hill within a natural gap through the Purbeck Ridge (photograph: Oliver Creighton).

fortifications designed for the defence of an emerging nation state that we see the nexus between fortified sites and their dependent territories finally broken.

   The academic writings of both archaeologists and historians, especially those with a strong militaristic or architectural focus, have, however, generally tended to discuss castles in isolation from their surroundings (see Austin 1984). While a number of important studies of castles in their wider social and economic contexts have been carried out, there is little doubt that this way of studying castles has been severely under-represented in the past. This book is therefore an attempt to remedy this imbalance in study and put medieval castles back in their places. The central aim of this study is to re-examine medieval castles by looking at their settings within, and their contribution to, the medieval landscape. It attempts to draw together the results of wide-ranging research conducted on castles and their environs, including the contributions of historical geographers, documentary and architectural historians, and archaeologists. The underlying tenet is that, by widening our frame of reference and adapting a 'landscape approach' to castles, we achieve a more holistic and balanced understanding of these most characteristic but frequently misunderstood features of the medieval world. This work is not, then, intended solely as a book about castles. In its own broader context, it is also a study of the impact of medieval power and lordship upon the landscape of England that, it is hoped, will prove of interest to students of the English landscape as well as those with an interest in medieval archaeology and castle studies.

Castles in the landscape

The interrelationship between any given castle and its surroundings can essentially be understood from two perspectives: the impact of the landscape on the castle, and the impact of the castle on the landscape. First, the physical and human landscape provided a setting that influenced decisions of castle siting, development and function. For instance, the character of pre-existing settlement patterns and administrative structures as well as physical geography had a vital part to play in influencing the choice of site for a castle. The topographical setting of a castle certainly influenced the way in which it was seen and experienced by contemporaries; it perhaps also imposed certain restrictions on the site's structural evolution. Second, the construction of castles and the policies of their lords could have many long- and short-term consequences for the development of their surrounding cultural landscapes.

In addition to an undoubted psychological impact on the nearby human population, castle construction was often accompanied by other changes, perhaps including the re-orientation of field systems or the planning or re-planning of settlements. The importance of the castle as a nucleation point for rural settlement is particularly well known in southern Europe. Here, the phenomenon of *incastellamento* (where a fortified hilltop village nestled within or beneath a fortified seigneurial site) was a common feature of the medieval Mediterranean landscape. Although the influence of castles on settlement patterns in Britain and northern European was perhaps less obvious, a surprising number of towns and villages nonetheless owe their origins or plan-forms to the existence of a castle.

The immediate physical setting of a castle site could also be manipulated, for instance through the diversion or damming of nearby streams and rivers for aesthetic, defensive and other practical reasons, while changes could be made to the local communications network of roads and tracks. The presence of a castle and a powerful seigneurial force in the locality could have other less immediately obvious effects. For instance, estate frameworks and patterns of land tenure could be reorganized. Through patronage and endowment, castle lords and their families could also make an enduring mark on the ecclesiastical landscape through the establishment of chapels, churches and religious houses. It was not unknown, however, for the construction of a castle to obliterate an existing cemetery or cause the removal or relocation of an earlier ecclesiastical site.

At one level, the setting of a castle comprised a zone under private own-ership that lay immediately beyond the defensive perimeter. This area would typically contain appurtenances with trappings of lordship that might be found elsewhere in close association with a non-defended status site such as a palace or important manorial residence. Prominent among these were gardens, fishponds, mills, orchards, and perhaps a dovecote, vineyard, rabbit warren and deer park. Around many rural castles also lay outbuildings and agri-cultural facilities that reflected their place in the local manorial economy. Beyond the defences of very many rural castles lie earthwork or other remains that represent precisely these types of activities, although such features can remain poorly recorded and little understood (Aston and Rowley 1974: 145–6). This immediate landscape was very often nested within a series of others.

Within the context of a parish or township, a castle was embedded within a local settlement pattern and, being a manorial centre as well as a residence, was often linked to a hinterland of agricultural resources, usually including areas of arable, pasture and rough grazing, and perhaps managed woodland. But the jurisdiction of castles could range well beyond the surrounding parish. Many castles were important places in the medieval landscape on a far wider scale, being also the *capita* (or heads) of more extensive units of lordship in which holdings could be scattered across a number of separate shires or, indeed, on both sides of the English Channel. Any castle could also have interesting spatial relationships with other castle sites. Some larger units of landholding were administered by networks of castles of different status, some held by sub-tenants, in addition to other lordship sites. Other patterns of castle building arose out of more directly martial circumstances, including the construction of siege castles.

Besides the various types of territorial unit that were in one way or another dependent upon the castle, each site was also simultaneously part of a very different type of landscape. The work of local historians has shown that that the landscape of medieval England comprised a series of regions – or *pays* – with their own particular social structures, agricultural systems, settlement patterns and physical resources (Everitt 1977, 1979). Although the boundaries of these units were not fixed, the available evidence suggests that this type of regional diversity was well established by the Norman period, as apparent in Domesday Book (Darby 1977). Castles were therefore built in medieval landscapes with their own distinctive regional cultures. Here we can make an important point. Medieval castles were, at one level, the symbols and products of an élite aristocratic culture – 'polite' forms of architecture that in many ways transcended regionality. At another level, however, the English castle was adapted to a wide range of different landscape contexts and invariably functioned within the context of local manorial economies. The availability of local resources, including labour and building materials, could also influence the physical designs of castles. While the owners of castles could be prominent figures on the national political scene, or indeed kings, and the buildings themselves could occasionally play a part in important historical events, most medieval castles had mundane everyday lives as farms and manors linked inextricably to the management of surrounding resources.

Something of this great variety of landscapes in which any castle was set is captured in Gerald of Wales's famous description of the castle of Manorbier (Pembrokeshire), the family seat where he was born in *c.* 1146. This affords a tantalizing glimpse of how a medieval mind viewed the castle (here in a Welsh rather than English context) in its broader physical context, emphasizing that a 'landscape approach' to castles is not a modern concept:

> It is excellently well defended by turrets and bulwarks, and is situated on the summit of a hill extending on the western side towards the sea-port, having on the northern and southern sides a fine fish-pond under its walls, as conspicuous for its grand appearance as for the depth of its waters, and a beautiful orchard on the same side, inclosed on one part by a vineyard, and on the other by a wood, remarkable for the projection of its rocks, and the height of its hazel trees. On the right hand of the promontory, between the castle and the church, near the site of a very large lake and

mill, a rivulet of never-failing water flows through a valley, rendered sandy by the violence of the winds. Towards the west, the Severn sea, bending its course to Ireland, enters a hollow bay at some distance from the castle; and the southern rocks, if extended a little further towards the north, would render it a most excellent harbour for shipping. (quoted in Wright 1863: 407)

Castle studies and landscape history

Despite the growing popularity of landscape archaeology and landscape study since the 1950s, the study of castles in relation to their surroundings has remained a curiously neglected area of research. This is emphasized by the proliferation of studies that have sought to examine other characteristic features of the medieval landscape in their wider contexts. Prominent among these are *Villages in the Landscape* (Rowley 1978), *Churches in the Landscape* (Morris 1989) and *Monasteries in the Landscape* (Aston 2000). Castles, in contrast, have often have remained beyond the horizons of landscape historians. W. G. Hoskins's *The Making of the English Landscape* – a seminal work representing the foundation of modern landscape studies – devoted a single nine-line paragraph to the subject of castles, drawing attention to their impact on urban settlements and uneven distribution across the shires, but neglecting their contribution to the rural scene (1955: 91). Among later texts, the consideration of castles as contributors to their surroundings by Muir within a treatment of 'defence in the landscape' (2000: 223–44) is a rare but welcome exception. While the Deserted Medieval Village Research Group and Moated Sites Research Group merged in 1986 to form the Medieval Settlement Research Group (MSRG), in recognition of the fact that high-status sites also formed part of the settlement pattern, castles have remained beyond the remit of the amalgamated group. Overall, landscape historians have rarely viewed castles as part and parcel of the full medieval settlement pattern.

A number of deeply rooted historiographical traditions within castle studies have combined to ensure that the academic writings of castellologists have tended to sever castles from the landscapes within which they were built and functioned. Castles, along with cathedrals, have been viewed as the pinnacle of contemporary society's architectural achievement. Primarily, it is the very wealth and architectural splendour of upstanding masonry remains that has deflected attention away from associated earthworks and other features in the landscape – what has been termed the 'Orford syndrome', in reference to the famous and innovative polygonal keep in Suffolk, whose landscape context remains rather more obscure (Welfare *et al.* 1999: 53). Many popular and academic texts have focused principally on the evolution of castle design, examining the subject through analysis of some of the more prominent masonry castles in order to present a somewhat Darwinian sequence of increasing technological sophistication. This type of account was pioneered in Hamilton Thompson's *Military Architecture in England During the Middle Ages* (1912), the essential framework of which has remained substantially unaltered by subsequent authors, including Brown (1954, 1976) – amounting to what Coulson (1996: 203) has termed a 'prolonged adolescence' for English castle studies.

Another enduring tradition has been the pre-occupation of archaeological field studies of castles with the classification of surviving structural remains and earthworks into categories and sub-categories, to the detriment of our understanding of their wider contexts. This was exemplified by Müller-Wille's (1966) division of the mottes of the Rhineland into different classes depending upon their height – a scheme subsequently applied to the mottes of England and Wales (King 1972). Numerous later studies have treated the classification of castle sites as an objective as opposed to a step towards further analysis. We can also note that militaristic interpretations of castle function have often completely overshadowed their 'peacetime' rôles as élite residences and estate centres. From some of the earliest academic studies of castles an orthodoxy emerged that saw the castle as an essentially warlike phenomenon. Studies such as Viollet-le-Duc's mid-nineteenth-century writings on functionalism within Gallic military architecture drew a firm link between the evolution of castle architecture and developing techniques of warfare – a view later epitomized by Clark's *Mediaeval Military Architecture in England* (1884–5). Analysis of particular features of defensive architecture – machicolation, crenellation, arrow loops and barbicans – has often broken castles down into discrete, component parts, giving little idea of how they functioned *in toto*. Further, military determinism has influenced our understanding of castle siting. Nowhere is this illustrated better than in the approach of Beeler (1956, 1966) who interpreted the map of English castles as the product of the same type of strategic master planning that influenced the distribution of Roman forts and frontier works. Views such as these cast a long shadow over twentieth-century studies, greatly retarding any ambition towards a more holistic understanding of castles. Yet other early studies show a greater recognition that castles were indeed part of the medieval landscape. In particular, the work of Ella Armitage – a rare female castellologist – as embodied in *The Early Norman Castles of the British Isles* (1912) paid considerable attention to the siting and distribution of mottes in support of her contention that they were, indeed, Norman fortifications as opposed to Saxon *burhs* (see also Counihan 1990).

From the late 1970s, however, the field of British castle studies witnessed a gradual change in emphasis. A number of general syntheses rejected the formulaic military-architectural approach to castle study, most important among them Thompson (1987, 1991) and McNeill (1992). Other significant new studies have adopted a more narrowly focused or thematic approach. These include Kenyon's welcome account of the archaeology of medieval fortifications (1990); Higham and Barker's definitive survey of earth and timber fortification (1992); and Pounds's remarkable (although primarily non-archaeological) study of the social and political roles of castles (1990). Another important trend has seen greater recognition given to the social functions of castles as expressions of social status and chivalric culture. Through documentary study, Coulson (1982, 1993, 1994a) has radically re-appraised the meanings of licences to crenellate, stressing their importance as badges of seigneurial status as opposed to attempts by the Crown to control and regulate centrally the fortification of the realm. Architectural analyses of individual sites, meanwhile, have sometimes drawn attention to military deficiencies in castle design and highlighted the sophistication of domestic planning. Key studies include Knaresborough in North Yorkshire (Dixon 1990); Norham in Northumberland (Dixon and Marshall 1993) and Orford in Suffolk (Heslop 1991) as well as comparative studies (Dixon 1998). Other innovative studies have applied increasingly sophisticated techniques of spatial analysis to examine access patterns and room functions within masonry castles (Faulkner 1963; Fairclough 1992; Mathieu 1999). Landscape archaeologists and garden historians have had a rôle to play too, through a number of studies showing that medieval castles as well as palaces could be accompanied by designed ornamental settings, as at Bodiam (East Sussex), Kenilworth (Warwickshire) and Ravensworth (North Yorkshire) (Taylor 2000).

Developments such as these have prompted a widespread debate within castle studies that has sometimes polarized 'militaristic' interpretations of castle function against 'social' interpretations (cf. Stocker 1992; Thompson 1994; see also Coulson 1996). Overall, however, we must bear in mind that the defining aspect of medieval castles was, indeed, their truly multifaceted nature. All castles had a wide range of functions – military, domestic and residential, social and symbolic, administrative, economic and judicial – that varied not only through time, but also regionally and in response to different demands of lordship, in a manner so complex as to almost defy classification.

The need to study castles holistically and to explore their wider interrelationships with medieval economy, society and environment was enshrined within the foundation statement of the Castle Studies Group:

1. to promote the study of castles in all their forms and by all possible means: documentary studies, architectural history, fieldwork and excavation.
2. to promote the study of castles as resources for a more widely-based appreciation of medieval society, emphasising their social and political history, their defensive and domestic evolution, their role in settlement development and their value as a source for the reconstruction of landscapes and economic environments.

(Castle Studies Group 1987: 2)

Structure of the text

The text of this book is arranged into four sections. The first section (Chapter 2) examines the many and varied ways in which previous studies have attempted to understand the context of castles within their landscapes. The second (Chapters 3–5) focuses on the multifarious relationships between castles and their surroundings by examining in turn the military, symbolic and administrative rôles of castles in respect to their hinterlands. The third section (Chapters 6–8) examines the interrelationships between castles and the medieval church; the impact of castle-building on urban settlement; and the contribution of castles to the development of the countryside. The fourth and final section (Chapter 9) provides an overview that draws attention to some central themes and highlights a number of avenues for future research.

This study is intended to be generously inclusive in its definitions, and covers a wide range of castle sites of differing date, form and function. Many major studies of British castles have tended to put emphasis on those sites which are, in some way, at the 'cutting edge' of contemporary architectural achievement and which preserve striking physical remains – classic examples being Colchester (Essex), Conisborough (South Yorkshire) and Dover (Kent) – at the expense of castles with designs of lesser technical sophistication. It is the aim of this study to treat these less spectacular sites with equal respect as that given to the architectural gems, and, in particular, to pay full attention to the numerous but neglected earth and timber fortifications which form an equally important part of the total distribution (Higham and Barker 1992). Modern inventories of castle sites make it impossible to overlook the sheer number of private fortifications that dotted the landscape. King (1983) records a figure just short of 1500 castles in the English counties (a number that far outstrips the total number of monasteries), with densities in excess of one site per 10 square miles in certain border areas (see Chapter 3).

This study deliberately avoids complex debates concerning what exactly constitutes a castle. Here, the classic definition of a castle as the fortified residence of a lord is used flexibly, although late-medieval tower houses, fortified manors and artillery fortifications are generally excluded. The concept of 'landscape' is likewise interpreted in a broad sense, to include patterns of land ownership, agricultural exploitation, administration and human settlement as well as those less tangible, though equally important, symbolic and aesthetic dimensions. The definition of landscape is also extended to the urban scene (or townscape), while in the countryside the contribution to castles in many different types of terrain is reviewed, including, upland, lowland, wold, fen and moor.

The geographical scope of this work is restricted to England, although material from elsewhere in the British Isles, and in particular Wales, is referenced where appropriate for comparative purposes. It should of course be borne in mind that many present-day administrative and political boundaries had little or no significance in the medieval period. For instance, the site of Hen Domen – by some measure the most thoroughly investigated earth and timber castle in Britain – currently lies in the Welsh county of Powys (formerly in Montgomeryshire), but at the time of its foundation lay on the western fringes of the English county of Shropshire (Higham and Barker 2000).

The study also aims to show no geographical bias towards a favoured region. Inland counties where the traditions of private fortification often fell into decline at a relatively early date have, unsurprisingly, not received the same attention from castellologists as the border regions, where castles are perhaps a more familiar part of the heritage. The interrelationships between castles and landscapes in the central lowland regions of England are, however, no less worthy of analysis than areas more prone to the ravages of border warfare. Finally, it should also be noted that modern (as opposed to pre-1974) counties are used to locate sites.

2 Castles and Their Contexts

In attempting to understand the interrelationships between medieval castles and their surroundings, undoubtedly the most important source of information available to us is the landscape itself. The English landscape can be understood as a palimpsest upon which successive generations have left their imprint but simultaneously erased some of the marks left by earlier societies (Hoskins 1955; Hooke 2000). Castles were but one contributor to the development of the particularly rich and complex palimpsest that was the medieval landscape, and the key challenge of the landscape historian in this context is to strip away layers of earlier and later evidence in order to assess their contribution to its overall evolution. Archaeologists too have an important contribution to make. Besides the use of excavation in its various forms, modern British archaeologists are able to apply a vast array of less destructive methodologies, ranging from the traditional (such as the recording of earthworks and other surface remains) to the more scientific (such as aerial photographic analysis and sub-surface geophysical survey). The most effective studies of medieval landscape will usually couple techniques such as these with analysis of a wide range of historical source material including maps and written records. This chapter highlights some of the problems and possibilities for research into the landscape contexts of castles, and stresses in particular the fundamental importance of a multifaceted and integrated approach. The final part of the chapter critically assesses the contribution of combined fieldwork, excavation and documentary research to our understanding of two very different medieval castles in contrasting landscape settings.

Excavation, survey and fieldwork

The contribution of archaeological excavation to the study of fortified sites in medieval Britain has been thoroughly discussed elsewhere (Kenyon 1990). The vast majority of these excavations have focused, unsurprisingly, on the plans, residences and defences of castles. From one perspective, the spatial limitations of archaeological excavation have further compounded a rather inward-looking view of castles. A broad trend is now, however, evident within castle archaeology, away from investigation of the more 'attractive' features such as keeps, defences and halls, and towards more peripheral zones such as outer wards and baileys (Coad 1994: 218). The archaeological investigation of such areas can provide welcome information on the everyday lives of fortified sites, as indicated by large-scale open-area excavations of baileys or outer wards, as at Barnard Castle (Co. Durham) (Austin 1979, 1980) and Hen Domen (Powys) (Barker and Higham 1982; Higham and Barker 2000).

But this development has occurred slowly, and our data set remains biased towards defensive features, while the further goal, of looking beyond the defences of castles and examining their context within, and linkages to, their hinterlands, has remained rather elusive. An interesting parallel here is our comparatively advanced understanding of the functions of monastic precincts and outer courts relative to castle baileys. While monastic archaeology has, since the 1960s, focused increasingly on the precinct as the key to a monastic site's economic life (Greene 1992; Aston 2000), castle archaeology has, by comparison, lagged behind.

Many excavation reports have contained little mention of a castle's landscape context other than a summary of its location in relation to physical topography and presumed strategic significance, and only rarely has the castle's position with relation to contemporary human and physical geography considered adequately. Austin (1984) has, however, laid important theoretical foundations for re-interpreting castles in their wider contexts, demonstrating that their study can be enriched through the application of the theories and methodologies of landscape studies, as those offered, for instance, by the *Annales* school. A small but growing number of excavation reports have carried this ideal towards reality. Munby (1985) has set the standard with a remarkably integrated analysis of the royal castle of Portchester (Hampshire) within its local and regional context, examining the different interrelationships between the royal stronghold and associated settlements, field systems and nearby forests, among other aspects of the countryside. Another area with immense potential has been the systematic archaeological survey of the hinterlands around excavated castles. This is exemplified at Hen Domen (Powys), where field recording and earthwork survey within the parish, coupled with extensive archival research, has shown the motte and bailey to lie within an enormously rich palimpsest (Fig. 2.1) (Higham and Barker 2000: 141–57). Comparable examples of fieldwork and castle excavation complementing one another include important projects at Middleton Stoney (Oxfordshire) (Rahtz and Rowley 1984), and Ludgershall (Wiltshire) (Ellis 2000). A worrying trend, however, is that these remarkable results were achieved within the context of the type of long-term, evolving archaeological project that became increasingly rare in British archaeology towards the end of the twentieth century.

The field archaeology of early castles has been further developed in other, more specialized studies concerning the identification and distribution of related earthworks. These include studies of mottes (Renn 1959; King 1972) and ringworks (King and Alcock 1969), in addition to King's indispensable inventory of castles in English and Wales, which forms an essential starting-point for future field studies of castles, *Castellarium Anglicanum* (1983). Surveys of field monuments in counties and other regions represent another type of study that has furthered in a different way our understanding of the landscape settings of castles. The tradition of producing inventories of castle sites was pioneered by *The Victoria History of the Counties of England* (VCH) launched in 1899, which published important annotated lists of castle earthworks for most counties, usually supported by useful accounts of their siting and their ownership histories. A good example is the account of earthworks in Suffolk (VCH Suffolk 1911: 583–603). Alongside accounts of impressive castle earthworks such as Clare and Framlingham, this work also paid attention to many more minor mottes and 'lesser' sites including examples at Ilketshall St John, Otley and Milden, and formed the first systematic survey of castle remains in the county.

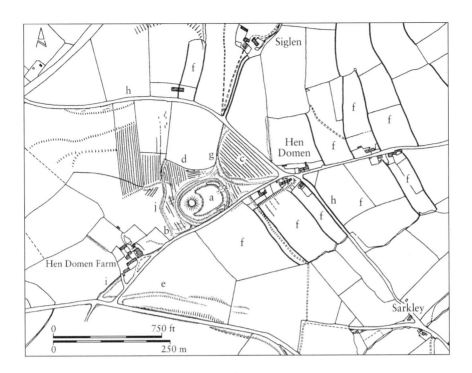

Figure 2.1 The topographical setting of the motte and bailey castle at Hen Domen (Powys). The castle (*a*) was imposed within a pre-Norman field system, traces of which survive as relict ridge and furrow (features *c* and *d*). The site is also surrounded by the earthworks of sunken hollow-ways (*e*, *g*, *i* and *j*) and house platforms (*b*), roads (*h*), and other fields whose boundaries are probably medieval in date (*f*) (Barker and Higham 1982).

The Royal Commissions on Historical Monuments for England, Scotland and Wales (RCHM), founded in 1915, established new standards for the identification and recording of field monuments, as reflected in county inventories that contain a wealth of information on individual castles and their surroundings (e.g. RCHME Dorset 1952–75). Some of the more recent thematic volumes produced by the Royal Commissions continue this tradition, as exemplified, for instance, by the work on West Lindsey, Lincolnshire (Everson *et al.* 1991), which includes detailed surveys and descriptions of some important castle earthworks and their relationship with other features of the medieval landscape.

The production of detailed and accurate large-scale surveys of the above ground remains of castle sites can be of particular value in showing the relationship between a castle and other topographical features, including roads and the earthworks of deserted settlements or garden features (Bowden 1999: 78–80). Produced by the RCHME, the plan of the surviving earthworks associated with Stafford Castle gives an excellent indication of the types of information that can be revealed by systematic survey (Fig. 2.2). Here, as is the

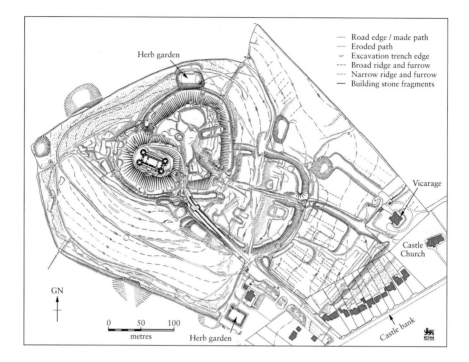

Figure 2.2 Plan of Stafford Castle (Staffordshire) and surrounding earthworks. The site has both an inner and outer bailey and is surrounded by other complex and multi-phase earthworks including hollow-ways, field boundaries, ridge and furrow, and garden features. The parish church is also located close by and a medieval community may have lain in the immediate vicinity, although the physical remains of a village or small borough cannot be identified positively (© Crown copyright NMR).

case with so many other castles, upstanding masonry structures represent only the tip of the iceberg of a far more extensive field monument, while more still have no surviving masonry or were never built in stone at all. The dismantled folly built on the foundations of Sir Ralph Stafford's rectangular turreted keep of 1348 lies at the heart of a multi-phase complex of earthwork remains (Jecock and Corbett 1997). For instance, the site had two baileys: a small inner bailey that seems, perhaps surprisingly, to partly overlie and post-date the large outer rectangular unit where barns, granaries and a large complex of stables are recorded in documentary sources. Non-defensive earthworks are well represented too. At least two suites of gardens were laid out: a series of terraces created on the west slopes below the keep, from which they were apparently intended to be admired, and a later formal garden created within the outer bailey after it otherwise fell into disuse. In the immediate environs of the site can be identified ridges and furrows representing the vestiges of arable cultivation of different periods and various boundary earthworks, including some marking the limits of the 'Great' and 'Little' Parks that embraced the entire west side of the complex. On a wider scale, the castle site was clearly an important node on the local communications network, and its construction seems to have generated new roads, as indicated by the three sunken hollow-ways that converge on the castle earthworks from the north, east and south-east. Finally, the proximity of the parish church and arrangement of further hollow-ways between it and the castle suggest the presence of a dependent community or even a small failed borough, although house plat-forms and property boundaries can not be identified positively in the earth-works (Hill and Klemperer 1985).

Aerial surveys of medieval Britain in general, and castles in particular, have also leant themselves to the portrayal of surviving field monuments in relation to their surroundings (e.g. Simpson 1949; Brown 1989; Beresford and St Joseph 1979: 142–58). An oblique view of the motte and bailey at Bishopton (Co. Durham), for instance, draws attention not only to the impressive pro-portions of the defensive earthworks, but also to the context of the site in various ways. It lies within the remains of an artificial lake, possibly incor-porating fishponds, is surrounded by the vestiges of field systems that both antedate and post-date its construction, and was also related to nearby human settlement, being linked umbilically to the nearby market village via an earthen causeway (Fig. 2.3).

Another fruitful means of setting castles within their broader contexts is represented by archaeological studies of groups of castles in defined geo-graphical areas. A large number of county-based surveys have been produced, covering a good sample of the shires. Important studies of this type include accounts of the castles of Devon (Higham 1980, 1982b), Cumbria and Lancashire (Higham 1991), Hampshire (Hughes 1989), Herefordshire (Shoesmith 1996), Leicestershire (Cantor 1978; Creighton 1997), Norfolk (Liddiard 2000a, 2000b), Nottinghamshire (Speight 1994, 1995), Rutland (Creighton 1999b, 2000b), Staffordshire (Cantor 1966) and Wiltshire (Creighton 2000a). Comparable surveys in Wales include Breconshire (King 1961), Cardiganshire (King 1956), Glamorgan (Spurgeon 1987a; RCHMW 1991) and Montgomeryshire (Spurgeon 1965–6). Other published studies have examined the context of castles within topographical units; significant examples include studies of the mottes of the Vale of Montgomery (Chitty 1949; King and Spurgeon 1965), the Golden Valley (Marshall 1938) and the Lune Valley (Bu'Lock 1970). More broadly based accounts of the field archaeology of counties or regions can also throw up a wealth of data con-cerning the status of castles as landscape features; good examples include studies of Exmoor (Riley and Wilson-North 2001) and North Derbyshire (Hart 1981). Finally, a number of historical atlases also contain valuable geographically based studies of castles, including surveys of south-west Eng-land (Higham 2000a), Norfolk (Rogerson 1994) and Sussex (Jones 1999). Accounts such as these often lend themselves to the analysis of castle siting and distribution, in particular, of those sites with little or no supporting doc-umentary evidence, although some studies have unfortunately proved better at collecting rather than analysing data. Comparisons between different areas can, however, reveal intriguing contrasts in patterns of castle building: between upland, lowland, and coastal plains, between compact lordships and areas where estates are more dispersed and between regions characterized by non-nucleated and nucleated rural settlement patterns.

Figure 2.3 Bishopton Castle (Co. Durham) from the air. This fine example of a motte and bailey is surrounded by a low artificial lake crossed by two causeways that survive as earthwork features. The site is also surrounded with ridge and furrow cultivation of different dates, and appears to have been closely related to the adjacent village (© Crown copyright NMR).

Environmental archaeology

It is worth considering in more detail the contribution of environmental archaeology to our understanding of castles in their wider palaeoenvironmental and palaeoeconomic contexts. Important types of environmental material that can be recovered through the excavation of castle sites include plant microfossils (e.g. pollen) and macrofossils (e.g. seeds), as well as molluscs, insects and animal bones (Alcock 1987). Analyses of these types of material can provide us with valuable insight into the animal and plant resources available in a castle's hinterland, and the way in which they were managed, potentially elucidating modes of cultivation, patterns of husbandry and practices of woodland management. Archaeological studies of castles have, however, been slow to recognise the value of environmental archaeology, reflecting wider attitudes within medieval archaeology generally, whereby environmental evidence has often been viewed as of comparatively lesser value than in a prehistoric research context (Grant 1984: 179; Bell 1989: 271). In particular, research designs geared towards the recovery of structural data have meant that surprisingly few excavation reports contain environmental analyses, and the findings are rarely given the attention they deserve. This is unfortunate because castles often provide a plethora of archaeological contexts favouring the accumulation, preservation and recovery of environmental data, including, for instance, deeply stratified and/or waterlogged wells, ditches and cisterns (Fig. 2.4 and 2.5). Considerable care is, however, needed in identifying and interpreting environmental samples gathered from contexts such as these. Common problems include the fact that defensive ditches are likely to be periodically cleared; the motte ditch at Hen Domen (Powys), for instance, was re-cut no less than six times (Grieg *et al*. 1982: 71). Deposits within outer ditches may relate to episodes of dumping from within the site, but could also derive from nearby settlements using them as refuse tips. For instance, Newcastle's castle ditch was used as an official urban tip, with 3.85 m of rubbish accumulating in one sampled area during the century before 1600 (Harbottle and Ellison 1981: 93; Harbottle 1982: 412).

At Baile Hill, York, other site-formation processes compromised the value of environmental evidence. Differences in bone assemblages derived from occupational levels on the motte top and others from the base of the feature indicate that larger bones had been cleared selectively from occupied areas. The high preponderance of smaller bones derived from sheep/goat, pig, fish and birds did not therefore reflect aristocratic dietary preferences nor functional differences between the two zones, but complex taphonomic processes (Rackman and Wheeler 1977: 146–7). The sampling of deposits within internal features such as wells, drains, pits and garderobes can sometimes provide a wealth of qualitative data on aristocratic diet, as indicated by the remarkable evidence of a medieval feast within a blocked drain at Barnard Castle (Co. Durham) (Donaldson *et al*. 1980; Kenyon 1990: 178–80). Some of the less well represented species within animal bone assemblages provide particularly good insight into the often privileged diet of castle inhabitants. The sample of bird bones from the early phases of Launceston (Cornwall), for instance, featured crane, lapwing, grey partridge, golden and grey plover, swan and woodcock (Albarella and David 1994: 65–6). Such data can also indicate from how far afield food items were obtained, providing an important source of information regarding the integration of castles within regional as well as local economies and, in particular, linkages to distant maritime resources (Ervynck 1991). At Okehampton (Devon), for example, the sample of excavated fish remains, comprising approximately 3,000 fragments representing 27 species (most prominently hake, herring, plaice and whiting), broadly paralleled the sample from medieval Exeter (Wilkinson 1982). That the castle lay on the northern fringes of Dartmoor, in the centre of the county

Figure 2.4 Wet sieving of archaeological deposits from pits and drains during excavations at Okehampton Castle (Devon) (photograph: R. Higham).

and some 40 kilometres from the coast, demonstrates the influence that the social status of a site could have on its ability to draw food resources from an extensive hinterland.

Environmental sampling can thus illuminate the relationship between a given castle and its hinterland at a variety of levels. At a localized scale, assemblages of molluscs from excavated contexts sometimes show that artificial microhabitats had been created by the construction of a castle. At Middleton Stoney (Oxfordshire), the changing composition of molluscan fauna through time reflected small-scale environmental changes bought about by castle building, such as changes in soil type, rather than indicating changes in the management of its wider environs (Evans 1972: 129; Rahtz and Rowley 1984: 3). At Okehampton (Devon), the range of mollusc species was again overwhelmingly conditioned by synanthropic factors such as the shady microenvironment provided by the castle walls and refuse dumping in the

Figure 2.5 Dump of antler and deer bone at the foot of the motte of Okehampton Castle (Devon) (photograph: R. Higham).

castle ditch (Bell 1982: 146). At Castle Acre (Norfolk) the timber impressions associated with masonry bridge abutments provided another microenvironment colonized by certain mollusc species (Murphy 1987: 303). A particularly important type of microenvironment that could be created within a castle bailey resulted from the deposition of animal fodder, as demonstrated at Rumney (Glamorgan) (D. Williams 1992: 156) and Hen Domen (Powys) (Barker and Lawson 1971: 70). This almost certainly indicates the presence of live animals within the defensive perimeters of castles. Although environmental archaeologists have developed increasingly sophisticated methodologies for recognizing the signatures left by fodder (Charles *et al.* 1996), it is difficult to differentiate fodder destined for war horses from that intended for farm animals. We may also note the interesting distinction in faunal assemblages between intra-site units at Castle Acre. Whereas the upper ward was dominated by sheep/goat, deer and cattle bones, the lower ward demonstrated a greater preponderance of rabbit and chicken, indicating perhaps social differences, but also perhaps the penning of animals within the lower unit (Lawrance 1982: 289–91; 1987: 300).

Another particularly important category of environmental evidence derives from contexts that demonstrably antedate the construction of a castle, such as land surfaces sealed beneath defensive earthworks. Such evidence can potentially aid reconstruction of the local environment immediately prior to a castle's construction and has immense value in providing a benchmark against which to compare subsequent environmental change in the functional lifetime of the site. Although conditions of preservation may be excellent, as deposits can be sealed anaerobically, logistical factors ensure that excavation on this scale is rare indeed. At Hen Domen, the profile of a buried soil horizon beneath the bailey bank revealed compacted ridge and furrow that extended

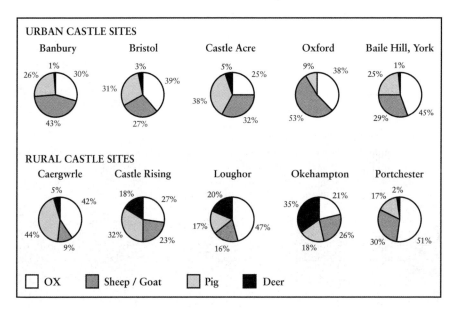

Figure 2.6 Relative proportions of major animal species from urban and rural castle excavations. Figures are based on numbers of identifiable bones and exclude pre-Conquest deposits. Sample sizes: Banbury, 159; Bristol, 3468; Caergwrle, 488; Castle Acre, 4833; Castle Rising, 2194; Loughor, 3655; Okehampton, 5348; Oxford, 623; Portchester, 2444; York, 394 (sources: Noddle 1975; Marples 1976; Wilson 1976; Grant 1977; Rackman and Wheeler 1977; Lawrance 1982; Maltby 1982; Berg 1994; Jones 1997).

beyond the site's defences (Fig. 2.1). Pollen samples taken from these levels showed an open pre-castle environment with few trees but an abundance of weeds and bracken. The clear implication is that arable cultivation had been abandoned shortly before the castle was built, although whether this was due to an episode of devastation or other factors remains open to question (Barker and Lawson 1971; Freeman 2000). Environmental evidence from other sites indicates, in contrast, the placement of castles in locations which have seen no recognizable arable cultivation, as at Lismahon (Co. Down, Ireland) (Proud-foot 1959: 172), and Middleton Stoney (Oxfordshire) (Evans 1972: 129).

Comparisons of environmental evidence between different castles (inter-site analysis) can, however, only be carried out at a relatively crude level. Non-standardized sampling strategies, variations in preservation and taphonomy and inconsistent modes of faunal analysis mean that we must compare different environmental reports with extreme caution. Fig. 2.6 draws together data from a representative range of rural and urban castle sites and illustrates the relative percentages of animal bones recovered through excavation for key species. These assemblages are the clearly the result of a wide range of factors including the operation of animal husbandry in a site's hinterland and aristocratic patterns of food consumption, as well as reflecting the specific circumstances of on-site archaeological sampling. Nonetheless, two broad trends can be distinguished within the data set.

First, collectively and individually, rural castle sites demonstrate markedly

Figure 2.7 Barnard Castle (Co. Durham). This important baronial castle occupies a rocky river cliff above the Tees, overlooking the site of an ancient ford. The faunal bone assemblage from the site contains an exceptionally high proportion of deer bones, indicating a close association with surrounding hunting resources (photograph: Oliver Creighton).

higher percentages of deer bones relative to urban sites. As well as indicating élite dietary preferences, in part this must also be a reflection of the association of rural seats with managed hunting resources, whether private parks and chases (e.g. Okehampton), or royal forests (e.g. Portchester). An interesting variation on this model is Loughor (Glamorgan), where the exceptional size of deer bones has been taken as indicative of hunting within virgin forest (Noddle 1975: 253). A common trend is the increasing proportion of fallow relative to roe and red deer bones in faunal assemblages derived from castle sites, especially from the thirteenth century. This seems to be a direct reflection of the suitability of fallow deer for intensive management within parks and the progressive clearance of woodland habitats more suited to the other species. At Launceston (Cornwall) and Okehampton (Fig. 2.5) the processing of deer carcasses seems to have occurred predominantly outside rather than within the castle, and prime joints, particularly haunches, were imported (Maltby 1982: 135; Albarella and Davis 1994: 32–4). At Hen Domen the converse appears true, with deer clearly butchered inside the site having been bought back from the hunt whole, as indicated by the recovery of jawbones, teeth and antlers among other parts of the carcass (Browne 2000: 129). Whether these differences reflect contrasts in status or, perhaps more likely, in the availability of deer in local hunting parks and further afield, remains to be tested, while archaeological sampling strategies may be another factor. The characteristics of the medieval animal bone assemblage from excavations at Barnard Castle (Co. Durham) (Fig. 2.7) suggest processing of deer carcasses within the castle at a quasi-industrial scale (Austin 1984: 75). The exceptional proportion of red deer in the total assemblage, combined with the large size of beasts and high incidence of non-meat bones, indicates the intensive exploitation of deer at a level far exceeding domestic requirements. This may seem surprising given the conventional belief, based on a lack of documentary references, that venison, as a highly prized élite foodstuff, was not sold on the open market (Rackham 1986: 126), although horn and hide by-products presumably were. The bone assemblage from Castle Acre (Norfolk) indicates that remains of fallow deer were widely used in a small-scale bone- and antler-working industry (Lawrance 1982: 282).

Second, we may note the broad correspondence in species representation between urban castle sites and other urban assemblages, and fortified rural seats with other domestic rural assemblages. It has been noted that sheep/goat bones commonly outnumber cattle bones in excavations within medieval towns, whereas the converse is true of most ordinary rural sites (Grant 1988: 151–3). Notably, this distinction is mirrored within bone assemblages derived from urban and rural castle excavations. This might well suggest that faunal assemblages within urban castle sites are indicative not only of élite dietary patterns, but also close linkages with local economies. For instance, butchery data from Banbury suggests that joints of beef and mutton were probably obtained direct from the local market (Wilson 1976: 146). Elsewhere, the preponderance of juvenile specimens from Bristol Castle and Baile Hill, York, mirrors the slaughter patterns recognized within other medieval urban market economies (Noddle 1975: 257; Rackman and Wheeler 1977: 152). We may thus note that, behind the superficial similarity of their defensive structures, rural and castle sites were enmeshed within fundamentally different economies and may show divergent patterns of consumption.

Case Studies: Castle Excavations and the Medieval Landscape

In the following section two case studies are reviewed in order to illustrate the different ways in which modern interdisciplinary study can illuminate the interplay between a castle and its hinterland, The examples (Goltho, Lincolnshire and Sandal Castle, West Yorkshire) are selected principally because of the marked contrasts they offer in terms of castle siting, both relative to physical topography and the human landscape. In particular, while one castle (Goltho) lay within a medieval agricultural community, the other (Sandal) was an isolated site of lordship, but with close connections to the nearby urban centre of Wakefield. Moreover, while Goltho was the fortified manorial residence of a series of local lords, Sandal was one of a network of castles built and initially held by a great aristocratic family (the de Warennes) and later became a royal castle. Although both sites were, to different degrees, élite residences and defended estate centres, while the concerns of the lords of Goltho were purely local, the horizons of Sandal's owners extended well beyond the regional scene. Both castles were thus responses to different demands of lordship, built and maintained by lords with access to different levels of resources to administer and control different types of hinterland. Crucially, it is only with reference to this wider context of the structure of lordship that each castle's status within, and impact upon, the medieval landscape can hope to be understood. Finally, both sites have been extensively excavated and fully published, and the results supplemented and sometimes challenged by other academic papers and publications.

The rural castle and its parish: Goltho, Lincolnshire

The site of Goltho is of unique significance to an archaeological study of castles in their landscape contexts because it is the one instance where large-scale excavation of a deserted village has been coupled with the excavation of an associated castle. These excavations, conducted by Guy Beresford in the late 1970s, cast considerable light on the community of a medieval clay-land village, but also revealed a remarkable and unanticipated history of occupation on the seigneurial site. The sequence of aristocratic occupation here stretched back to the late Saxon period, comprising a succession of increasingly powerfully defended residences that culminated in the construction of an earth and timber castle of more than one phase. Despite the fact that the castle and village were basically parts of the same site (Fig. 2.8) and clearly had interlinked histories, the excavations were published in two parts, one report focusing on the deserted village (Beresford 1975), and another on the manorial site (Beresford 1987; see also Beresford 1977, 1981). Although this has tended to artificially sever the castle from its rightful context, subsequent studies have reassessed the site in its entirety and within the context of the surrounding parish (Basset 1982; Stocker 1989; Everson 1988; Everson 1990). In addition, the medieval settlements of West Lindsey have been the subject of a broader archaeological survey (Everson *et al.* 1991). Although there is still much that remains unclear about Goltho, studies such as these have allowed us a greater understanding of the context of the castle within its surrounding landscape, and it is upon these that the following account is largely based.

Our understanding of the place of Goltho's castle within its local landscape has been altered since the original excavation reports in two important ways. First, the context of the site within the administrative history of the area has been re-assessed (Everson 1988, 1990). This has demonstrated the extreme likelihood that the excavated manorial site and village actually represent the remains of medieval Bullington as opposed to Goltho. A great anomaly within the original excavation report is that the manor of Goltho was not documented until the early thirteenth century. Everson has argued that it is inconceivable that the excavated site, evidently a settlement of considerable size and status, was not recorded earlier and resolves the problem by suggesting that the documented entity known as 'Goltho' only came into existence when the manor site was relocated to the edge of the parish. This seems to have caused the original parish of Bullington to fragment into two portions: Bullington, which incorporated the western part of the parish and centred on the medieval priory, and Goltho, incorporating the decayed village and relocated manorial *curia* (Fig. 2.9). Second, the original dating of the site has been challenged (Hodges 1988; Stocker 1989). The precise arguments behind this are beyond the scope of the present work, but the upshot is that the enclosed Saxon manorial complex of Phase 3 (originally dated to *c.* 850) seems to have

Figure 2.8   Aerial view of Goltho (Lincolnshire), showing the site of the manor/castle (bottom left-hand corner) adjacent to the chapel (tree-covered) and the earthworks of the associated medieval village (Cambridge University Collection of Air Photographs: copyright reserved).

been dated *c.* 50 years too early. This revised chronology also pushes forward the dating of the site's later phases, so that the Phase 5 ringwork (dated to *c.* 1000) may well be Norman or even span the Conquest, while the Phase 6 motte and bailey (*c.* 1080) could be a twelfth-century castle of the Anarchy. The revised dating sequence, with immense implications for the site's context within the surrounding landscape, is summarized in Table 2.1.

The physical site chosen for the castle had no observable strategic significance of any description; located on low-lying clay lands approximately 15 kilometres north-east of Lincoln, the castle was remote from important settlements and routes of communication. Constructed upon a thin natural lens of sand and gravel, it did, however, occupy the most visible topographical position in the immediate vicinity, elevating it slightly above the grassed-over earthworks of the adjacent medieval village that survived until the entire site was levelled by bulldozing and deep ploughing. The castle earthwork, comprising in its final phase a sub-rectangular mound surrounded by a ditch and

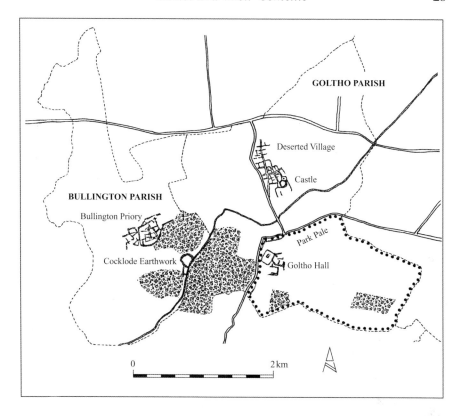

Figure 2.9 The topography of Goltho and Bullington parishes (Lincolnshire), depicting the principal medieval earthworks and areas of historic woodland (based on Everson 1990, with additions).

other less prominent earthworks, formed a distinct feature in the south-west corner of the village plan (Fig. 2.8). Castles in these types of physical settings were invariably also manorial centres; what makes the case of Goltho of particular interest, however, is that here the castle represented the final stage within a longer sequence of aristocratic occupation already well established by the time of the Norman Conquest. Rather than reflecting any military consid-erations, the location of this particular rural castle was determined by a practi-cal need for continuity in estate centre. Continuity of another sort and at an altogether different scale is indicated by the fact that the castle and village were embedded within a field system containing vestiges of a rectilinear network of boundaries of considerable antiquity, indicated by the fact that it is partially overlain by a Roman road (Bassett 1985).

The excavation report relating to the village adjacent to the castle reflects the priorities of medieval rural archaeology in the 1970s in its focus on the settlement's desertion, tending to overlook the questions of village economy, nucleation and morphological change that now dominate the academic agenda (see Wrathmell 1994: 180–7). What can we gauge of the relationship between the seigneurial site and its attendant village?

The excavations show beyond doubt that a nucleated community existed

Table 2.1   Revised dating of Goltho manor/castle site

Phase	Description	Original dating (after Beresford 1987)	Revised dating	Comments/manorial descent
2	Middle Saxon village	*c.* 800–850	*c.* 850–900	Two ninth-century farmsteads cleared to make way for Phase 3 enclosure
3	Fortified manor	*c.* 850–950	*c.* 900–1000	Defended complex of hall, bower and weaving shed
4	Fortified manor	*c.* 950–1000	*c.* 1000–1050?	Hall and ancillary internal buildings rebuilt within the same fortified enclosure
5	Enlarged ringwork	*c.* 1000–1080	*c.* 1050–1140?	Fortified enclosure rebuilt in larger form. In 1066 two of the three Domesday manors of Bullington in the possession of the Saxon lord Lambecarl; in 1086 the three manors held by individual tenants
6	Motte and bailey	*c.* 1080–1150	*c.* 1140–1150?	Motte raised within enclosure of greatly reduced size, possibly during the Anarchy; manor of Bullington reunited under the Kyme family in the mid-twelfth century
7	Platform castle	*c.* 1150	*c.* 1150–1235?	Castle rebuilt as a hall on top of an enlarged castle mound; manorial focus shifts to Goltho Hall early in the thirteenth century

Source: Hodges 1988; Stocker 1989

here at the time of the Conquest, with a focus of settlement somewhere in the south-eastern part of the later village. Several factors point towards the village attaining its later form not through haphazard growth, but through at least one episode of deliberate planning, probably prompted by seigneurial intervention. The irregular arrangement of crofts in the south-eastern part of the village is morphologically distinct from the regular north–south row of crofts, which has the appearance of a regular, planned two-row addition to an earlier organic core. Yet excavation shows the specific constructional history and design of each croft was different and individual, outwardly seeming at odds to the largely formalized layout of the village. While the initial occupation of Croft C, the only excavated village property within the northern row, was dated structurally to the twelfth/thirteenth century, the excavated peasant houses in the southern part of the settlement (including those removed to make way for the Saxon manor) were occupied appreciably earlier. Limited field-walking has also indicated that a substantial settlement in the north part of the village area was established by the twelfth century (Beresford 1975: 7, 20). The documentary evidence is of less value in indicating likely periods of expansion, as the physical evidence clearly shows an intervening population maximum between 1086, when a maximum population of 27 is recorded in Bullington, and 1327–8, when the declining settlement had 14 tax-payers (Everson 1988: 96). Combined, the evidence suggests a planned extension to an extant 'magnate core' in the functional lifetime of the castle site. Field survey within the region certainly favours the hypothesis of lordly intervention in settlement change, as indicated at sites such as Kingerby, Linwood, North Ingleby and Rand, all of which seem to have been reorganized in regular form by landlords in the eleventh or twelfth century (Everson *et al.* 1991: 16). At Goltho, the mid or late twelfth century is, circumstantially, the likely period of settlement planning, when the manor of Bullington was reunited under de Kyme lordship following sub-division into three minor holdings from 1066 (Table 2.1). Village planning may only have formed one component of an integrated and conspicuous programme of seigneurial redevelopment also evident in the Kyme's patronage of the Gilbertine priory as well as the reconstruction of the old site of lordship in a manner more suited to a small but ambitious baronial family.

We can only speculate as to how the villagers would have perceived the manor site in its various phases. What archaeology makes very clear in the light of the manor's re-dating is that very little changed in terms of observable material evidence as a result of the Conquest, the old site of lordship being maintained basically as before. Certainly, if one were viewing the site with a prehistorian's gaze – stripped of all knowledge or preconceptions of castles and their significance – there is little or nothing to suggest that an event such as the Norman Conquest bought about a major change in the site at this time. When the finds from the castle and village are compared, it is also notable that there is relatively little to distinguish the presence of an aristocratic family. For instance, spurs, arrowheads and javelin heads are common to both village and castle in some numbers. Such finds within the village may have ultimately been derived from the castle, but the essential point remains that there is little in such material terms to separate one institution from the other. The most marked change in the castle's physical appearance came in Phase 6 (motte and bailey) where the residential zone contracted to a cramped and poorly drained residential cell comprising a single hall – in all probability the accommodation for a bailiff rather than the residence of the owners. This phase was significantly also marked by the re-orientation of the principal point of access to the site *away* from the village to the east, the village hollow-way having led up to the entrance in earlier phases. In addition, the surface of the motte was revetted with pebbles set in a layer of clay, leading the excavator to suggest that this represented an attempt to give the external appearance of a shell keep (Beresford 1987: 103). Much about this phase of the site suggests a gulf between its impressive external appearance and the squalid reality of internal domestic occupation. It was probably the very inconvenience of this castle – most likely a short-term response to the turbulence of the Anarchy – that prompted the Kymes to rebuild it as a platform on which was set an enlarged hall.

The relationship between the aristocratic site and adjacent chapel is a feature of Goltho's topography largely overlooked in the original excavation reports but which may be of particular importance in the settlement's development. While the small brick-built chapel of St George's, built no earlier than the fifteenth century, was clearly not coexistent with the seigneurial site, its site perpetuated that of an earlier ecclesiastical building. Excavations conducted during the installation of drains in the redundant chapel in 1986 revealed that it overlay the foundations of a far larger earlier medieval church, whose nave presumably lay to the west (Youngs *et al.* 1987: 150). While this church was not dated independently, a time lapse between the demolition of this building and the erection of the chapel was demonstrated, making it very likely that this structure represented the lost parish church of medieval Bullington, St James's. Vestiges of earthworks around the castle, meanwhile, suggest that the church was at some stage enclosed within a substantial embanked precinct that defined the zone of lordship. Close physical relationships between lordship sites and parish churches are common feature of many medieval landscapes and are unlikely to be coincidental. It is entirely likely that the church at Goltho represented the estate church – or *Eigenkirche* – of a Saxon lord constructed close to his residence, along with which it was appropriated by an incoming Norman lord. In its late Saxon phases this complex may well be the physical embodiment of the *bell-house* and *burh-geat* that were the pre-requisites of Saxon thegnly status, as indicated in a well-known law-code, although a more symbolic, quasi-legal interpretation of the phrase cannot be ruled out (A. Williams 1992: 230). The Norman lord would have inherited the status that the possession of a church implied. The morphological arrange-ment of lordship site, church and village was also, no doubt, deliberate – the ecclesiastical building standing at the junction between the seigneurial and communal zones, and emphasizing the lord's status as patron.

While the relationship between the church and seigneurial site was therefore probably well established by the time of the Conquest, the Norman lords bought a new type of ecclesiastical presence to the parish in the form of the Gilbertine priory of Bullington established by Simon, son of William in 1148–54. This site, now traceable only as a confused series of earthworks, lay in the west part of the parish approximately two kilometres from the castle (Fig. 2.9). That it was positioned at a point in the landscape intervisible not only with the Kyme's castle, but also the towers of Lincoln's new cathedral emphasizes its position within a network of patronage and influence that linked together élite secular and ecclesiastical sites (Everson 1988: 98). The priory's initial foundation grant indicates that it was also located within the Kyme's seigneurial deer park of *Lindeleya* (Lindley) which, seemingly carved partly from woodland, appears to have been another introduction to the local scene by Norman lords. The original boundaries of this feature may be reflected in the curving profile of part of the parish boundary, although its integrity was disrupted by further grants of land to the priory. The enigmatic earthwork nearby at Cocklode, set within a block of historic managed woodland, may well have been an associated parker's lodge. The notion of an intensification of hunting exploitation after the Conquest is also supported by the bone assemblage from the castle site, demonstrating a marked increase in the presence of deer in Period 5. Lamentably, however, non-standardized sampling strategies make further analysis of the assemblage virtually mean-ingless, which is unfortunate given the favourable conditions of preservation and the site's clear links with the management of woodland resources (Jones and Ruben 1987: 197). An interesting trend is, however, the remarkable rise in the proportion of sheep/goat and less marked fall in the proportion of deer during Phase 6, seemingly reflecting a downgrading of the site as an aristo-cratic seat and its detachment from the management of surrounding resources.

The eventual abandonment of the Kyme's castle in the early decades of the thirteenth century did not represent the cessation of lordly presence within the parish; instead, the seigneurial focus shifted to a new site near the edge of the parish, breaking centuries of continuous aristocratic occupation. A new manorial residence was laid out approximately one kilometre to the south on a fresh site uncluttered by the village (Fig. 2.9). This continued as the principal high-status residence within the locality, as represented by a succession of gentry houses and the earthworks of post-medieval formal garden remains on the site now known as Goltho Hall (Everson *et al.* 1991: 98). The new manorial site was secluded further by the creation of a new deer park, whose boundary earthwork still survives in sections and follows the parish boundary. This feature probably replaced the earlier park on the opposite side of the parish, which was by this period eroded by grants to the priory. This physical separation of lord from community is symptomatic of a more general trend towards the seclusion of lordship sites and is paralleled elsewhere within the region, as at Lea, where a manorial residence was similarly re-located away from the principal settlement (Everson *et al.* 1991: 117–19). At Goltho, the manor certainly appears to have been one of the first elements of the village to be deserted, although it would be over simplistic to suggest that the removal of seigneurial presence contributed in any way to the settlement's decline. The village's desertion was not atypical, but part of a far broader trend of depopulation in West Lindsey resulting from the increasing profitability of pastoral as opposed to arable farming, exacerbated perhaps by climatic deterioration that was particularly severely felt on the clay-lands.

The honorial castle: Sandal Castle, West Yorkshire

The formidable remains of the great castle of Sandal (Magna) (Fig. 2.10) represent a complete contrast to Goltho. This site, constructed by the de Warenne earls of Surrey at the very beginning of the twelfth century, was a seat of one of the wealthiest and most influential families in post-Conquest Britain. The castle's status was maintained until 1317, when it came under an extended period of Lancastrian and then royal possession, under whose absentee lordship it generally stagnated, despite a brief renaissance under Richard III. Nonetheless, the castle remained an administrative centre and occasional residence until its ultimate demise following the Civil War siege of 1645. The site's residential and defensive structures were extensively investigated during ten seasons of research-led excavation from 1964. While the published report (Mayes and Butler 1983) focuses principally on the structural evolution of the site, many aspects of the excavated evidence (not least the environmental report) are of immense significance in reconstructing the inter-relationship between the site and the resources of its hinterland. In addition, other published archaeological and documentary studies allow the site to be examined within the context of the tenurial and administrative landscape (e.g. Clay 1949; Moorhouse 1979; Faull and Moorhouse 1981).

Unlike Goltho, Sandal Castle was built as a fresh seigneurial site, located in response to the demands of a new type of lordship in the area. Excavation has shown no evidence of antecedent occupation on the site save slight traces of

Figure 2.10   Aerial view of Sandal Castle (West Yorkshire), prior to excavation. The present settlement near the castle earthworks is modern; for much of the medieval period the castle was an isolated feature in the landscape, entirely surrounded by a deer park (Cambridge University Collection of Air Photographs: copyright reserved).

prehistoric activity. Instead, this castle was raised literally on a greenfield site – the ridges and furrows of a pre-existing field system running under the ramparts – and not on the estate centre of a Saxon lord. The castle was not, however, positioned solely in response to military needs, but relative to a wide range of factors that marked Sandal out as the most suitable location for the *caput*. Sandal Castle was built as the new administrative centre of the manor of Wakefield, an extensive and complex territorial entity focused on a major urban centre, granted to William de Warenne by Henry I shortly after 1106. The borough was thus administered without the direct presence of a castle and focused instead on an ecclesiastical site; the manorial court (formerly the Moot Court within the borough) and focus for estate management (Sandal) were thus discrete units. This contrasts sharply with other major early castle

Castles in the Manor of Wakfield

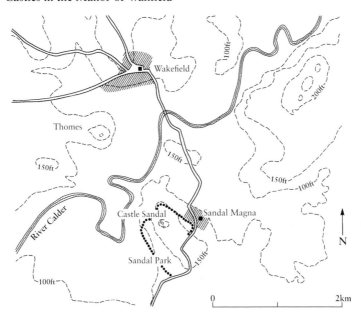

Figure 2.11 The wider topographical setting of Sandal Castle (West Yorkshire), showing the location of another motte and bailey castle at Thornes (based on Mayes and Butler 1983, with additions).

sites in the region. For instance, whereas the otherwise comparable Saxon royal manor of *Tanshelf* was overawed and ultimately displaced by Ilbert de Lacy's fortified *caput baroniae* of Pontefract, Wakefield lacked a castle. Part of the reason for this must be the circumstances of Sandal Castle's foundation, not as part of the initial wave of Norman colonization, but more than forty years after the Conquest.

Sandal's physical setting was nonetheless striking, being raised just over two kilometres south of the town in an isolated position (Fig. 2.11). The castle's topographical position at the end of a prominent spur projecting from the south side of the Calder valley gave it excellent advantages of visibility as well as obvious military and constructional benefits. The de Warenne's new castle was sited at a point within the landscape that incorporated most of the borough of Wakefield within its viewshed, to whose inhabitants it provided an obvious statement of new Norman lordship. The castle also lay close to other less obvious manorial resources or sites of significance within the local landscape: the ancient meeting place of the hundred lay nearby at Asbrigg, while on the bend of the Calder below lay the manorial mill. The castle's seclusion from human settlements was, however, further emphasized by the creation of a deer park that entirely surrounded it – a rare occurrence, as nearly all other deer parks associated with castles were appended to one side of the seigneurial site (see Chapter 8). If it did not lie in the geographical centre of the manor of Wakefield, the Warenne's impressive new fortification lay at the very heart-land of the territory in terms of the distribution of arable and population resources. Of the outlying berwicks appurtenant to Wakefield at Domesday, Sandal was the only lowland constituent, lying within the fertile Coal Measures in the east of the manor, in contrast to the pastoral economy of the gritstone slopes that formed much of the portion to the west of Wakefield.

The parish church of St Helen lay just over half a kilometre east of the castle within the village of Sandal Magna, whose open fields were disrupted by its construction and subsequently the creation of the park whose boundary it lay against. This substantial church probably had pre-Conquest origins, as reused masonry in the south transept is likely of late Saxon date, while two churches and three priests are mentioned in the composite Domesday entry for Wakefield (Ryder 1993: 171). Whereas many Norman castles in Yorkshire were sited deliberately to dominate important Anglo-Saxon churches, sometimes also probably taking over – or arrogating – the residences of Saxon thegns (as at Laughton-en-le-Morthen, South Yorkshire: see Chapter 6), here the castle was more remote from the parish church. Nonetheless, a conspicuous programme of remodelling under the patronage of the de Warenne lords is indicated by the earliest *in situ* fabric, the bases of twelfth-century crossing piers. Another highly characteristic type of linkage between the lords of a castle and a nearby parish church is indicated by the transfer, pre-1147, of Sandal Magna church to the Cluniac priory of St Pancras at Lewes, founded beneath the fortified caput of the de Warenne's Sussex estates (Clay 1949: 87).

At Domesday, Sandal was one of nine berwicks dependent upon Wakefield, which also had an extensive jurisdiction of sokeland. Following the manor's acquisition by the de Warennes, Sandal Magna township was, unlike large portions of the land unit, unsurprisingly retained in demesne. By *c.* 1300, the administrative geography of the surrounding area had been radically re-cast by the appropriation, through coercion or forfeit, of the adjacent former sokelands of Alverthorpe, Crigglestone, Horbury, Ossett and Stanley, to create a substantially enlarged demesne estate held with Sandal as its gravitational centre. Archaeology provides us with many interesting insights into how the castle functioned as an estate centre. The inventory of recovered artefacts includes a distinctly limited assemblage of military artefacts relative to a high proportion of household items (e.g. kitchenware and needlework apparatus), agricultural tools (e.g. spades, pitchforks and axes) and personal items (e.g. non-military brooches and rings), providing a reminder of its everyday life. Detailed studies of the pottery assemblage, meanwhile, suggest that tenurial linkages between the widely scattered de Warenne estates had an important influence on the distribution of ceramic products (Moorhouse 1981, 1983). Some 40 vessels from the Conisborough locality were identified, in addition to over 100 from kilns in the Doncaster area, and, most notably, others from West Sussex and Buckinghamshire, all in the vicinity of other important de Warenne assets. Rather than reflecting commercial trade, the likely scenario is that this pattern reflects the physical movement of individuals such as estate officials and their families over relatively long distances between disparate parts of the lordship.

The report on the environmental archaeology of Sandal Castle is remarkable not only for the sheer variety of evidence that it incorporates (including animal bones, charcoal, sea and land molluscs and pollen) but also the manner in which these data complement one another (Mayes and Butler 1983: 341–59).

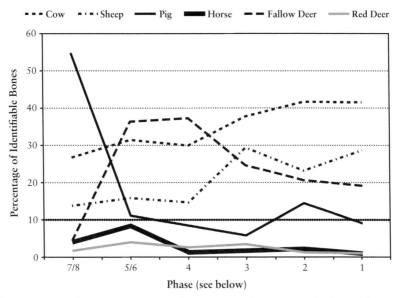

Figure 2.12 Relative proportions of major animal species in the faunal bone assemblage from excavations at Sandal Castle (West Yorkshire). The figures are based on numbers of identifiable bones. Key to phasing: 7/8, *c.* 1106–1130; 5/6, *c.* 1130–1400; 4, *c.* 1400–1450; 3/2, *c.* 1450–1485; 1, *c.* 1485–1600 (Based on Griffith *et al.* 1983).

Overall, we have a remarkably detailed understanding not only of the physical environment surrounding the medieval castle, but also how it changed through the period of the site's occupation. At one level we have insight into the immediate setting of the castle site and, in particular, certain microhabitats created by its construction and functions. For instance, the range of land-based molluscs sampled in the barbican ditch reflects the colonization of a damp and sheltered, food-rich environment created through refuse dumping rather than indicating any pattern of aristocratic consumption. Pollen and seed samples from peat cores within the outer moat, meanwhile, show a successive colonization of vegetation in and around the castle's defences, with nettles, thistles and shrubs such as hawthorn gradually replaced by willow and eventually oak as it fell into disuse. At a slightly broader scale, the castle was placed within a local landscape free of tree cover for a surrounding distance of perhaps around one kilometre, as suggested by the proportion of weed species and cereal indicators in pollen samples taken from the ridge and furrow system sealed beneath the bailey. Cropmarks to the north of the castle visible on aerial photographs seem to represent vestiges of field boundaries and tracks associated with this system, the castle seemingly being placed in the infield (Jones 1983, 70).

It is the faunal bone assemblage, however, that is most informative about the management of the surrounding estate (Fig. 2.12). Changes in the management of the demesne estate seem to have bought about an intensification of cattle and sheep farming at the expense of the exploitation of woodland through the farming of swine. This sequence is substantiated by the species representation in charcoal samples, suggesting a change in the character of surrounding woodland during the occupation of the castle. If, as seems likely, the samples provide a reliable indication of species in the area, then the woodland around Sandal Castle was gradually opening up to create an increasingly diverse woodland habitat (Bartley 1976: 233–4). The changing representation of deer bone through time is also of great interest. While the low proportion of deer bones in the earliest castle may be attributable to an initial period of primarily military activity, in later periods a gradual transition in site function is apparent as the castle increasingly became an aristocratic centre of consumption. From c. 1130 until the middle of the fifteenth century, deer bones (especially those of fallow deer, particularly suited to extensive management within deer parks) are proportionally the most important within the entire faunal assemblage. The subsequent decline in their importance probably indicates less intensive deer management under royal absentee ownership rather than changing dietary preferences.

Of course, the progressive clearance on the woodland fringes around Sandal was not unusual in the region or elsewhere within the manor. Indeed, analysis of toponymic surnames and manorial documentation, in particular the printed and unpublished court rolls of the manor of Wakefield, indicates a more general pattern of assarting and clearance in the region, reaching a peak of intensity in the early decades of the fourteenth century (Moorhouse 1979: 47), as exemplified by detailed study of the graveship of Scammonden (Redmonds and Hey 2001). Given the absorption of sokeland to enlarge the demesne estate at Sandal, the conditions of tenure on this land, and the intensity of deer management in the area, the sequence may have been more rapid and concentrated in the territory immediately surrounding the de Warenne's *caput*.

However, Sandal was not the only Norman castle in the manor of Wakefield, nor the de Warenne's principal castle in the kingdom. Just under two kilometres to the north-west lay another motte and bailey ('Lowe Hill') at Thornes, occupying another natural eminence on the opposite bank of the Calder, and separated from it in the medieval period by low-lying marshland. The site's name may indicate that the nucleus of the motte was formed by a prehistoric barrow, the first element of the place-name deriving from the Old English element *hlāw* ('mound/burial mound'), which commonly denotes the presence of such a feature (Cameron 1961: 122; Smith 1961b: 170). In the vast majority of cases where two castles lie this close, one site usually seems to have succeeded the other (see Chapter 3). There are good reasons, however, to suggest that Lowe Hill was not a precursor of Sandal built either by the Crown prior to 1106 or as the de Warenne's first estate centre, while its degree of structural development and topographical position suggest that it was not an undocumented siege castle. Although the precise origins of this enigmatic site remain uncertain, a likely hypothesis is that it was a subsidiary fortification to Sandal, built under the same lordship as part of a local strategy. Both sites are intervisible and together overlook an important crossing point of the navigable River Calder. Limited excavation on the site has dated its construction to c. 1150, perhaps implying a foundation of William, third Earl Warenne (d. 1148), a known participant in the Civil War of 1138–49 (Hope Taylor 1953: 13). Both Sandal and Wakefield (Thornes) castles are documented as late as 1324 in a royal edict of Edward II, when committed to the hands of Richard de Mosely (Walker 1939, 45). The Lowe Hill site thus seems to have been a secondary focus of de Warenne lordship in the area, more closely associated with the borough, and complementing Sandal militarily and perhaps administratively; it is no coincidence that it is Thornes rather than Sandal that is documented as Wakefield Castle.

While these two castles lay at the administrative heart of the manor of Wakefield, the spatial extent and non-contiguous nature of the holding required the provision of other subsidiary castle sites as outlying centres of lordship. Two undocumented earthworks elsewhere within the manor probably fulfilled such functions. A small, bailey-less motte at Rastrick (West Yorkshire) lay in the semi-detached block of estates forming the western portion of the manor, Rastrick being a demesne graveship and important manorial meeting centre (Faull and Moorhouse 1981: 739). Another minor castle site at Sowerby (West Yorkshire) was an outlying hunting seat, lying in the vicinity of Erringden Park and situated in one of only a handful of upland townships in Sowerbyshire to be retained in demesne by the earls (Kendall 1926: 97–9).

Yet the manor of Wakefield was a subsidiary, even peripheral concern within the total holdings of the de Warenne lords in the twelfth century. Within Yorkshire, acquisition of the manor added to the extensive and valuable soke of Conisborough, which William de Warenne held in lordship at Domesday. Excavation has shown the famous polygonal keep at Conisborough (South Yorkshire) to surmount the remains of a less well known motte that was the de Warenne's first castle (Johnson 1980: 77). Despite Conisborough's clear importance as a central place in the late Saxon landscape, it never obtained a market or urban privileges. The settlement retained an irregular, organic plan, with the seigneurial parkland appurtenant to the castle enveloping it to the south and effectively blocking its expansion (Magilton 1977: 28; Hey 1986: 34). A secondary seat of lordship in the area was built at Thorne (South Yorkshire), close to the hunting grounds of Hatfield Chase within a large and detached part of the land unit (Hey 1979: 44). Along with the manor of Wakefield castles, these sites are quite unlike others erected within post-Conquest Yorkshire fiefs in that none spawned a seigneurial borough in the manner of otherwise comparable *capita* such as Pontefract (West Yorkshire), Richmond (North Yorkshire), Skipsea (West Yorkshire) and Tickhill (South Yorkshire) (see Chapter 5). Other important royal and baronial castles elsewhere within the shire were erected within extant towns, as at Doncaster (South Yorkshire), Tadcaster and York (North Yorkshire). In explanation, we may point to the wider distribution of de Warenne estates as the key variable; this is the scale at which decisions of seigneurial policy can be most appropriately understood. In addition to their Yorkshire estates, the de Warennes, as the earls of Surrey, held their principal urban seats elsewhere (Castle Acre, Norfolk; Lewes, Sussex; and Reigate, Surrey), in addition to substantial holdings around Varenne, near Dieppe in Normandy (Coad and Streeten 1982: 139–40). In the north, the castles of the de Warennes were clearly centres for consumption as well as administrative and military sites, intended as isolated seats of rural lordship with good access to hunting resources.

Summary

The case studies of Sandal and Goltho, while illustrating sharp contrasts in the ways in which castles were interlinked with their hinterlands, together emphasize the importance of a multifaceted but integrated approach to castles and their settings. Traditionally, the zone within the defensive perimeter has remained the concern of castellologists while the area beyond has been the territory of the landscape archaeologist. Similarly, while above-ground masonry structures have received the attentions of architectural historians, below-ground remains have been the domain of the archaeologist. One of the most pressing challenges for future studies is to break down these divisions in order to recognize that all these sources of information are, in reality, part of a far broader data set.

3 Castle Siting and Distribution

Surprisingly little has been written about the factors that governed the placement of castles in the landscape. This can be attributed partly to a lack of documentary evidence concerning the decision-making processes behind castle siting, but also to an often implicit assumption that military considerations were paramount in the minds of castle builders. Given the exceptional investment of resources that the construction of a castle entailed, choice of site was clearly not taken lightly, but made relative to a wide range of factors. The pattern of castle-building can essentially be examined at three scales: across the country as a whole; within individual units of lordship; and at the local level, in relation to fields, houses and physical terrain. Analysis of the pattern and process of castle-building at these three levels makes one thing very clear: military considerations were only one of many variables that influenced the decision of where to build a castle.

The military functions of castles were many and varied, and summarized well by King (1983: xvii–xxiii). An essential part of the castle's rôle in periods of warfare was as a base from which a force could rapidly deploy for a counterattack or foray into the surrounding hinterland. The military needs of castle builders were certainly not necessarily best served by naturally defensible, inaccessible hilltop positions (although some were occasionally chosen: e.g. Beeston, Cheshire and Peak, Derbyshire), and it is striking quite how many medieval castles were directly overlooked by higher ground in their immediate localities. While this may seem surprising to the modern military mind, we should consider that a distance of only a couple of hundred metres put a castle beyond the range of bowshot and siege weaponry. The sites of castles should not therefore be examined as if they were military structures of the post-medieval or modern age. In lowland districts, castles are principally found in the same sorts of position where we might find other medieval lordship sites such as manors and palaces.

Although in terms of immediate setting, a castle may appear located relative to particular geographical features, such as a river crossing, fording-place or crossroads of communications routes, in a wider sense, the building of a castle was related, first and foremost, to the ownership and control of territory. Indeed, the reinforcement of territorial control was usually the central motive in the decision to construct a castle. We must also take care not to neglect that certain topographical positions with apparent defensive qualities could also have been selected, at least in part, for their natural visibility, making the seigneurial site a prominent landmark and a conspicuous symbol of power with a panoptical viewshed over the surrounding territory.

Castles and their sites

There was, emphatically, no ideal site for a castle; all were responses to different demands of lordship within the context of different physical and human landscapes. Castles were so multifaceted in terms of their functions, built at such a range of levels within society, and applied to such a variety of landscapes, that in fact no overall trend is apparent. For instance, those landholders building more than one castle selected different types of site for different purposes. A prime case in point is the pattern of castle-building within the estates of William de Warenne in the immediate post-Conquest years. William's key stronghold in the south was at Lewes Castle, raised on a prime military site comprising a steep-sided chalk promontory overlooking a crossing point of the tidal Ouse where it flows through a gap in the Sussex Downs (Drewett 1992: 69–70). In contrast, the key de Warenne castle in East Anglia lay at Castle Acre (Norfolk), a position evidently located for administrative convenience at the gravitational centre of his other holdings in the region (Liddiard 2000a: 28–31). Another clear example of a Norman castle sited for its centrality and convenience relative to surrounding estates rather than for any military strategic reason was Helmsley (North Yorkshire). Built as the *caput* of Walter Espec in the early twelfth century, Helmsley was, remarkably, the only Yorkshire manor in this extensive lordship that contained a Norman castle (L'Anson 1913: 352–3). Generally, the process of castle siting embodied a level of interplay between two essential, and somewhat contradictory, motives: the practical and economic advantages of raising a seigneurial site close to manorial resources, and those pragmatic military/defensive needs often best served by other more isolated geographical positions (Bur 1983: 132; Eales 1990: 64).

It is instructive to examine the placement of castles in the landscape in a military sense in relation both to tactical considerations and strategic factors. While the former imply the significance of the site's immediate physical surroundings, the latter denote the place's significance relative to wider patterns of communication and territorial control. Notably, while the immediate setting of a castle could reflect a need to meet a wide range of threats ranging from full-scale siege warfare to civil insurrection and banditry, in a strategic sense the castle could be an offensive tool of warfare, as vividly illustrated by William's initial programme of castle-building in 1066 designed to secure bases on the East Sussex coast, as at Hastings and Pevensey, which was constructed within the Saxon Shore fort partly to protect the invasion fleet and control access to it.

If any notion of strategy in castle siting can be discerned, it lies in the distribution of royal castles. The policies of the Norman kings ensured a relatively even spread of royal fortresses throughout England through a systematic programme of castle-building in the principal urban centre within each shire, many of which were maintained as seats of local government (see Chapter 7). This policy of urban castle-building had two essential objectives: to suppress centres of population, administration and wealth, and to seize control of important routes of inland communication. Crucially, the geographical circumstances of urbanization up to 1066 ensured that William I's programme of castle-building in major urban foci achieved both aims simultaneously. William's policy also emphasizes the two-fold importance of castles as tools of conquest: on the one hand urban castles were instruments of an offensive military campaign, while on the other, they were defensive strongpoints which served to isolate and contain potentially rebellious districts. Here we may mention Nottingham Castle (Fig. 7.5), raised, unusually for an urban castle some 0.5 km west of the earlier urban defences upon a precipitous rocky sandstone river cliff, but overlooking a ford over the River Leen, a tributary of the Trent (Drage 1989: 15–19). At a strategic scale Nottingham Castle lay at the very junction of highland and lowland England, on a key node on the communications grid at a point where the Trent was navigable but also fordable. With ready access to its extensive hinterland, the castle was used as a convenient repository for royal siege machinery and a centre for the gathering of taxes, while also lying close to the hunting resources of Sherwood (Pounds 1989: 11). Of the principal royal castles documented in the eleventh century, only a tiny proportion were rural; the remainder were imposed within the urban centres of Anglo-Saxon England. Anomalies included the quasi-palatial Windsor (Berkshire), set above the Thames on a steep chalk escarpment a convenient distance from London; Wisbech (Cambridgeshire), an expedient fenland campaign fortress; and Rockingham, built as a rural retreat in a heavily wooded and sparsely populated part of Northamptonshire.

Other Norman castles built in the immediate wake of the Conquest may owe their sites primarily to military considerations. One such example is Castle Neroche (Somerset), an enormous enclosure castle built within earlier defences on a scarp of the Blackdown Hills. This phase has been interpreted as a base for a striking force of Norman troops, perhaps in response to the disturbances of 1067–9. The site had great strategic significance in that it overlooked the important route into the south-west peninsula along the Langport Ridge and enclosed an area large enough for stabling horses and quartering a substantial field force (Davison 1972: 23–4). Other Norman sites that may have fulfilled similar rôles include the substantial early enclosure castles at Deddington and Rochester, which formed the gravitational centres of the Honour of Odo of Bayeux in, respectively, the areas of Oxfordshire/ Buckinghamshire and Kent (Ivens 1984: 113–14).

The surviving earthworks of many early castles show that mottes and ringworks were skilfully tailored to local topography in order to enhance defensibility and minimize the time and labour necessary to raise ramparts and dig ditches. This is demonstrated well by the numerous motte and bailey castles formed by scarping the point of a natural promontory (very often an interfluvial ridge) to form the base of a motte, and the construction of a series of transverse earthworks to define a series of baileys. Other than providing benefits in terms of construction, this type of site also gave advantages of visibility, the motte usually being intervisible with an extensive hinterland. Excellent examples include Beaumont Chase (Rutland), Bicknoll Castle (Wiltshire) and Mount Ferrant, Birdsall (North Yorkshire). The motte at Okehampton (Devon) was another that was partly natural, being carved from natural rock, as was the motte of the Norman castle at Hickleton (South Yorkshire), prior to its destruction by limestone quarrying. Here we may also mention those 'partial' ringworks where the defensive earthworks do not

Figure 3.1 Aerial view of Old Sarum (Wiltshire), showing the defences of the iron-age hill fort containing a Norman ringwork and the foundations of the cathedral (Cambridge University Collection of Air Photographs: copyright reserved).

entirely surround the site but are built to form a crescentic rampart and ditch that backed against a river (e.g. Stapleford, Wiltshire), the edge of a cliff (e.g. Easby, North Yorkshire and Gisburn, Lancashire) or isolated the tip of a promontory (e.g. Lydford, Devon). In low-lying marshy areas a castle was very often raised on a natural eminence, typically a glacial knoll, as at Fenny Castle, Wells (Somerset) and Branceholm Castle, Swine (East Yorkshire).

Other castles adapted sites whose defensive potential had been recognized much earlier. Some of the most striking examples of castle builders reusing extant defensive works are those mottes and ringworks inserted into iron-age hillforts. This mode of antecedent activity influenced decisions of site, but also planning of intra-site units. Conceivably, it also hints at an underlying, if interrupted, functional continuity in the use of a site not only as a defensible nucleus, but also as a focus of centralized authority. Only rarely were these castles built centrally within pre-existing defensive circuits, as seen most dramatically at Old Sarum (Wiltshire) – where the defences of the great Norman ringwork are roughly concentric with those of the hillfort (Fig. 3.1) –

but also at the Herefordshire Beacon. The defences of the univallate hillfort of Mount Caburn, Glynde (East Sussex) were also reconditioned to form in effect a massive ringwork. Usually, however, a motte or ringwork occupied a peripheral position within the interior of a hillfort, as at Almondbury (West Yorkshire: see Fig. 7.17), Barwick-in-Elmet (West Yorkshire), Caus (Shropshire) and Hembury (Devon). This pattern is particularly well-illustrated by the earthworks known as 'The Rings' at Loddiswell (Devon). Here, a ringwork and bailey was inserted into the north-western part of the hillfort, effectively converting the remainder of the prehistoric enclosure into a vast outer bailey, although signs of medieval activity are obscured by post-medieval plough ridges (Wilson-North and Dunn 1990). We remain quite uncertain, however, of the activities contained within outer enclosures such as these, and indeed outer baileys in general, although they could certainly be large (the outer enclosure at Loddiswell, for instance, occupied an area of approximately 2 hectares). Others are more extensive still; the vast horseshoe-shaped enclosure appended to the cliff-edge ringwork at Harewood (West Yorkshire), and again seemingly a reused prehistoric earthwork, occupied over 7 hectares. Likely hypotheses are that these units embraced dependent communities or else were left largely open, perhaps as a secure area of pasture or as the assembly point for a military force. But not only larger late-prehistoric defended sites were adapted as castles. For instance, the motte at Bury Castle (Somerset) was built to surmount the inner rampart of a smaller iron-age domestic enclosure (known in the Exmoor region as a 'hillslope enclosure'), the prehistoric defences being refurbished to form a bailey *c.* 60 m across (Riley and Wilson-North 2001: 65, 104–5). Remote from other settlements, and overlooking an important crossing point of the Exe as well as commanding the valley-based routes of communication on the fringes of the moor, this undocumented site was probably an Anarchy-period fortification.

Military factors must have conditioned the siting of these castles, with existing defences proving a ready-made defensive circuit that could be quickly and efficiently converted into a strongpoint. But not all castles raised in hillforts were built in periods of military crisis or as campaign bases. While the iron-age ramparts of Beeston Castle (Cheshire) were sufficiently preserved to dictate the circuit of the medieval outer curtain wall, the site of the castle, built in the 1220s, was selected during a major reorganization of Earl Ranulf's estates upon his return from the Crusades (Ellis 1993: 211). It was apparently not designed to protect the earldom from Llywelyn, as the process of association was well under way with a treaty in 1218. Raised on an impressive rocky eminence looming high above the plain and left as rough grazing between the iron age and the early thirteenth century, the choice of site was clearly influenced by non-military factors.

The close association between Norman castles and the network of Roman roads has been long recognized (Armitage 1912: 84), indicating that in the medieval period these routes survived as visible landscape features and still formed the backbone of the communications system. In Hampshire, for instance, approximately 80 per cent of castles are sited on or in the immediate vicinity of a known Roman road (Hughes 1989: 34). While this pattern could superficially give the impression of fortifications sited to control the communications network for military reasons, it must also reflect the needs of lords to

Figure 3.2 Brough Castle (Cumbria). The Norman keep stood within a triangular enclosure inserted into one corner of the Roman fort of *Brocavum*, commanding a strategically important trans-Pennine route (photograph: Oliver Creighton).

move between estates that were often widely scattered (see Chapter 5). Skipton (North Yorkshire) is an excellent example: a genuinely strategic foundation lying at the head of the Ribble and commanding the passage of a Roman road through the Aire gap. Of course some castles also re-occupied Roman civilian or military sites located on the former Roman communications grid: for example, while the austere Norman keep at Bowes (North Yorkshire) now appears to be an isolated structure, it in fact stood within an angle of the defences of the Roman fort of *Lavatrae*, which were reconditioned to form a bailey (Wright and Hassall 1971: 251). But again, this was also a site with natural strategic significance, situated on the key east-west route and former Roman road through the Stainmore Pass, as was Brough Castle (Cumbria), that lay within another Roman fort to the west (Fig. 3.2). A similar observation can be made about the Norman readaptation of a castle as part of the Roman fort of *Deventio* at Malton (North Yorkshire), which overlooked an important crossing of the Derwent (Robinson 1978: 31). We must remember, however, that castles were built to hold and control territory rather than to block lines of communication and prevent the movement of hostile forces. Indeed, from another point of view it is surprising to find that many key strategic river crossings or crossroads of major communications routes lacked castles, or had one only briefly, as at Reading and Coventry (King 1988: 11).

At a local level, castle-building could result in major changes to the road network. This is especially evident in the urban context, where Saxon streets were buried beneath defensive earthworks and either diverted or replaced by new road networks, as at Bedford, Lincoln, Wareham, Winchester and York and elsewhere. Excavation on the outer castle defences at Wallingford

(Oxfordshire) has provided remarkable insight into the site's impact on the communications network. The earliest Norman castle must have interrupted the gridded Saxon street pattern in the north-eastern part of town but not the cardinal north-south and east-west thoroughfares. The addition of a third (outer) moat in the thirteenth century, however, resulted in the re-routing of the principal north-south route which formerly lay *c.* 90 m to the east of the present line of Castle Street, which today still sweeps around the castle defences. Both the road surface and remnants of the town's dismantled north gate were buried during the moat's excavation, while the town rampart and wall were reduced at the point where they intersected with the castle's upgraded defences (Brooks 1965–6: 20). It was also not unusual for the presence of a new castle to generate new roads, or for pre-existing routes to be re-routed through an attendant settlement, often for commercial reasons, as at Devizes (Wiltshire) and Pleshey (Essex). Those castle earthworks closely associated with deserted settlements invariably also preserve the remains of sunken hollow-ways, which might converge from several directions on the seigneurial site (e.g. Stafford: Fig. 2.2), or else be diverted around defensive earthworks (e.g. Kingerby, Osgodby, Lincolnshire: Fig. 8.21), or through the defences themselves (e.g. Pilsbury, Derbyshire: Fig. 3.10).

The desire of Norman castle lords to exercise control over the movement of road traffic is reflected particularly well at Mileham (Norfolk), where an important east–west road ran directly through a large rectangular enclosure attached to the north side of the castle's defences (Fig. 3.3). This route was undoubtedly in existence by the late Saxon period, as fieldwalking has established the street village that lay east of the castle to have shifted to this new position from an earlier site near the parish church by this time (Wade-Martins 1975: 147–9). The changes to the local communications pattern bought about by the construction of another important Norfolk castle at Castle Acre may have occurred for other reasons altogether (Liddiard 2000a: 60–2). Here, the route of Peddars Way, a former Roman road and the principal north-south route through west Norfolk, was diverted circuitously to create a carefully contrived approach that drew attention to an élite Norman landscape comprising the castle, town and priory, all set against the backcloth of a deer park. Another way in which the medieval mind would have viewed castles is as points on itineraries. This concept is expressed particularly well on Matthew Paris's mid-thirteenth-century maps of Britain, which clearly used itineraries as a source of information. One of these depicts a conspicuous line of castles and/or fortified towns on a north-south axis stretching between the border stronghold of Berwick in the north to Dover in the south, including many sites on major river crossings, such as Pontefract (West Yorkshire) (Delano-Smith and Kain 1999: 45–6).

Changes in river networks since the medieval period often mean that it is difficult to appreciate the topographical significance of nearby castle sites. The alteration of surface run-off patterns as a result of human landscape modification, combined with the canalization of some rivers and the artificial diversion of others, means that many modern rivers are a shadow of their medieval equivalents. Indeed, it can be surprising quite how many apparently inland castles were associated with settlements that functioned as small ports or landing places in the medieval period; some of the many examples include

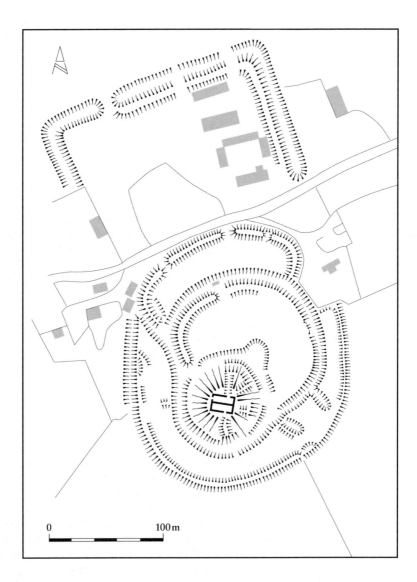

Figure 3.3 Earthwork plan of Mileham Castle (Norfolk). This substantial motte and bailey castle seems to have been positioned to overlook the movement of traffic along the east–west road that still runs through the large rectangular enclosure attached to the north side of the defences (Liddiard 2000a).

Downend and Dunster (Somerset), Plympton (Devon), Skipsea (East Yorkshire) and Tregony (Cornwall). Very many castles overlooked points where rivers were traversed by other communications routes, whether by ford, ferry or bridge. The siting of Norham Castle (Northumbria), for instance, was clearly related to the location of an ancient fording point over the Tweed, as were the border fortresses of Wark-upon-Tweed to the west and Berwick to the east. The strategic significance of some of these sites was long established.

A great many castles built within the defences of Roman or early medieval towns lay close to fording points of long-term strategic significance. A classic example is Wallingford Castle (Oxfordshire), whose great Norman motte lay on a gravel terrace by an important ford over the Thames, north of the Goring Gap where the river ran through the Chilterns – a position that made the town a natural junction of route-ways. Another such site was Thetford, where the Norman motte was raised within the defences of an iron-age enclosure that dominated not only the Saxon town but also the points where the Icknield Way crossed the Thet and Little Ouse. Other fording points were formerly traversed by Roman roads that remained arterial routes of communication in the medieval period, as at Goodrich (Herefordshire) where the castle overlooks from a high spur the ancient fording place where the Wye was crossed by the Roman road from Gloucester to Caerleon. Later changes in communications networks could, however, obscure the original significance of such sites: for instance, the Norman castle at Restormel (Cornwall) commanded the major crossing point of the Fowey until the construction of a bridge downstream at Lostwithiel in the later medieval period. The place-name 'Fairies Hill' given to a small motte near a bend of the River Calder at Whitwood (West Yorkshire) is almost certainly a corruption of 'Ferry Hill', the site being an outlying fortification of the Honour of Pontefract (Armitage 1912: 84). Other Norman earth and timber castles built near ferry crossings include the motte at East Bridgford (Nottinghamshire) overlooking a crossing of the Trent, and the ringwork at Barrow Haven (Lincolnshire) on the south bank of the Humber.

The important honorial castle of Bramber (West Sussex) was associated with an unloading quay on the River Adur, to which it was linked via a wooden causeway. Evidence from a sewer trench excavated in 1974 suggests that the quay, constructed from beech piles and backed with cobbles, was constructed in the last quarter of the eleventh century, perhaps initially for the unloading of materials needed for the castle's construction (Holden 1975: 116). Documentary evidence also indicates that the first Norman lord of Bramber, William de Braose, exerted his seigneurial influence through the erection of a timber bridge over a second deep stream to the east of the castle, where tolls were levied on river traffic. Construction of the bridge restricted the passage of ships that had been able to freely pass upstream to Steyning before the Conquest. Warkworth (Co. Durham) was located at the narrow neck of a pronounced meander of the Coquet, with a fortified bridge positioned to protect the natural point of access to its attendant town. Durham Castle and the precinct of the adjacent cathedral priory church similarly stood on a narrow isthmus within a tight loop of the Wear. Corfe Castle (Dorset) occupies one of the most striking physical situations of all, perched on a natural but artificially scarped eminence in the gap where the River Corfe flows through the Purbeck Ridge (Morley 1983: 53) (Fig. 7.12).

England has suprisingly few truly coastal castles; rather, those located close to the shore were invariably sited in relation to rivers, estuaries, ports and other anchorages, as were the Roman Saxon Shore forts, some of which were adapted as castles, as at Pevensey (East Sussex) and Portchester (Hampshire) (Gale 2000: 74). Some royal castles were, however, certainly built to be supplied from the sea, as epitomized by several of Edward I's great fortresses in North Wales, such as Caernarvon and Rhuddlan, which both embraced within their defences small quays or artificial channels linked to the coast. In other areas of Britain, of course, many castles on the seaboard and those on islands were associated with maritime hinterlands, no more so than on the west coast of Scotland and in the castle-building of Gaelic lords and kings in Ireland (Cruden 1960: 38–49; McNeill 1997: 157–64). Medieval castles in England were not sited, nor of course designed, for national coastal defence. It is only with Henry VIII's great programme of coastal artillery fortification that vulnerable invasion shores and landing beaches were defended in an integrated manner, as exemplified, for instance, by the three Henrician 'castles' of the Downs: Deal, Sandown and Walmer (Kent) (Hale 1983). Henry II's Orford, for instance, built from 1165, was certainly not designed for coastal defence, as has sometimes been claimed, although it certainly formed a prominent landmark visible to shipping. The keep's nostalgic symbolism and the political circumstances of its construction indicate that its principal purpose was as a conspicuous assertion of royal authority in the face of the growing influence of the Bigods, who held power bases in the county at Bungay, Framlingham and Walton (Brown 1952; Heslop 1991). Previous to this, Suffolk had lacked a royal castle and Norwich remained the sole royal stronghold in East Anglia. Fostered by the Crown, the settlement linked to Orford Castle prospered as a port (although the growth of the spit known as Orford Ness has since obscured this former role), so that by the early thirteenth century it generated a greater volume of trade than Ipswich (Poole 1955: 96).

Those castles built in or near the key channel ports, such as Folkestone (Kent) and Southampton, were not so much a scheme of national defence as a policy designed to control routes of communication and trade with Normandy. The significance of many of these sites was, however, greatly reduced following the breakdown of the Anglo-Norman union in the early twelfth century. The importance of Pevensey declined even more significantly given physical changes to the coastline in the area, so that by 1288 the castle accounts indicate difficulties in unloading goods destined for the site (K. Thompson 1997: 217; Dulley 1966: 42). The royal stronghold built within the Saxon Shore fort of Portchester (Fig. 8.1) lay on a promontory at the head of Portsmouth harbour, the most secure and strategically important anchorage west of Dover. Again, the castle was not intended primarily as a bulwark against foreign invasion. Readily accessible from its inland hinterland, close to the Forest of Bere and situated conveniently for travel between Winchester and Normandy, Portchester was frequently used as a royal departure point and its enormous open bailey as a mustering place for offensive military operations overseas (Cunliffe and Munby 1985: 296). While Dover castle, the 'key and redoubt of England', loomed conspicuously above the coastline and lay close to the important Roman road to Canterbury, it also overhung a small harbour (Coad 1995: 12). Exceptions are found on the coast of Northumbria, where Bamburgh Castle (Fig. 3.4), perched on a great outcrop of the Whinsill, per-petuated the site of the ancient seat of the kings of Northumbria and was periodically used as a communal shelter against Scottish raids (Brown 1989: 41–4). William le Gros's promontory castle at Scarborough (North Yorkshire) was another that perpetuated a site of prior significance: the steep-sided natural eminence was the site of an iron-age settlement, Roman signal station,

Figure 3.4 Vertical aerial photograph of Bamburgh (Northumberland), showing the coastal position of this immense border fortress and refuge, and its relationship with the adjacent settlement (BKS Air Survey Ltd: copyright reserved).

and more problematically, the *burh* established by Skardi *c.* 966 (Binns 1966; Farmer 1988: 124). Remarkably, excavation of the Roman signal station has revealed the twelfth-century castle chapel of Our Lady to overlie a tenth-/eleventh-century church with associated cemetery, indicating the presence of a substantial population in the vicinity (Hamilton Thompson 1931: 51–2). Dunstanburgh Castle (Fig. 8.2) was built for Thomas of Lancaster in 1313 on tall basalt cliffs overlooking the North Sea as a border refuge and temporary cattle pound, as indicated by its vast outer ward, embracing a bare headland of nearly 4 hectares (St Joseph 1950: 12–13). As with Dover and Scarborough, the exceptional size of this castle was influenced directly by the nature of its topographical site.

Castle distribution

A distribution map of castles, like a plot of any category of archaeological site, can be as misleading as it is illuminating. Such a map subsumes a wide range of building processes, including sites of radically different date and function, and we have remarkably little notion of which were occupied contemporaneously. Whereas all royal fortifications and many of the more prominent baronial or other private castles have some documentation, the vast bulk of rural earth and timber castles have no conventional ownership history, being mostly founded in the notoriously sparsely documented period between 1066 and the mid-twelfth century, with a probable peak around *c.* 1100 (Stenton 1932: 198–201; Eales 1990: 54–63). The late eleventh century witnessed an unrivalled boom in private defence, when lords of relatively humble means but high aspirations were able to fortify their estate centres (the closest comparison is the proliferation of towers on the Anglo-Scottish border in the later medieval period). A large proportion of these works must have been raised with reference to the networks of estates they were intended to secure and sometimes dominate, and were also built as manors. Further, while castles can be defined as élite structures, there was great temporal and spatial variation in the classes of people able and willing to construct them. In certain contexts, castle-building remained essentially a royal prerogative, as in the royal forests, while at the opposite end of the spectrum, castle-building could sometimes proliferate among the ranks of minor tenants and sub-tenants, as along the Welsh Marches in the late eleventh and early twelfth century.

Much remains obscure about motte building, yet some interesting spatial patterns are evident. It is abundantly clear that the distribution map of castles is not a simple index of levels of insecurity at various times, nor merely an indicator of concentrations wealth or population, but the result of a complex combination of all these factors, and more. Analysis of motte distribution (Fig. 3.5) indicates these constructions were not simply a reflection of those areas exposed to warfare, but denote a particular type of insecurity. The marked thinning out of mottes along the northern part of Anglo-Welsh border where the earldom of Chester faced the kingdom of Gwynedd, and their relative scarcity in the east portion of the Anglo-Scottish border suggests that many of the smaller mottes were a response to small-scale raiding and perhaps banditry and not designed to cope with full-scale warfare (McNeill and Pringle 1997: 222). Another socio-political context encouraging the erection of mottes by petty landlords was the civil war of Stephen and Matilda. The events of this period largely explain high densities of rural mottes and ringworks in Oxfordshire and other surrounding counties such as Wiltshire that formed the focus of the struggle during this period (Bond 1986: 149).

A further interesting type of distribution map compares the proportions of mottes and ringworks (or enclosure castles) in different parts of Britain, indicating where one type of earthwork is more likely to occur than the other (Fig. 3.6). This indicates that the proportion of mottes to ringworks across England and Wales is certainly not evenly spread. The pattern of ringwork building cannot, however, be related convincingly to any chronological, geographical, historical or even ethnographic variable, and instead seems simply to be the product of the idiosyncratic preferences of castle-builders

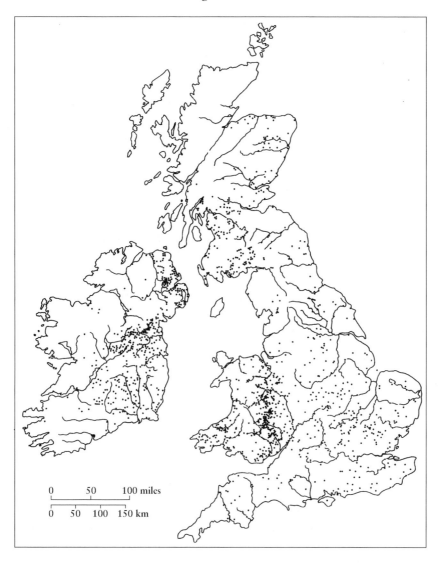

Figure 3.5 Distribution map of mottes in Great Britain (McNeill and Pringle 1997).

(King and Alcock 1969: 103). That concentrations of ringworks are usually small and localized perhaps indicates seigneurial emulation at an essentially local level, while the manner in which ringworks, relative to mottes, may have sometimes been economical in terms of time and labour points towards their employment as rapid and expedient forms of fortification. The importance of this second factor may be heightened by geological factors. That the distribution of mottes could be influenced in some way by the suitability of sub-soils for the construction of large earthworks was recognized in a study of castle distribution in North Wales (Neaverson 1947: 17). Later studies of early castle siting in Glamorgan refined this basic idea, suggesting that the presence or absence of glacial drift deposits can be a key determinant of whether a

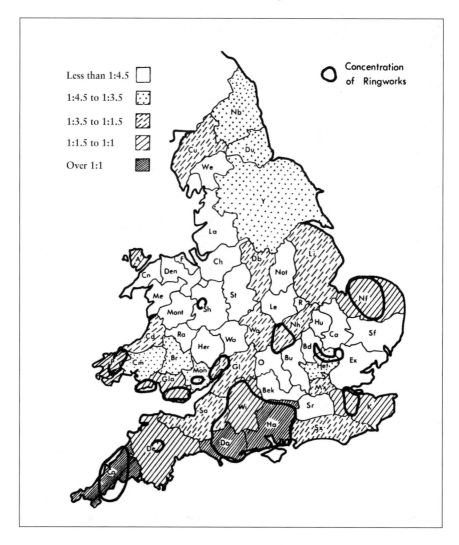

Figure 3.6 Map showing the proportion of ringworks to mottes in England and Wales and indicating principal concentrations of ringworks (King and Alcock 1969).

motte as opposed to a ringwork was built (Spurgeon 1987a: 206–7; Spurgeon 1987b: 32–6; RCHMW 1991: 34–6). Specifically, ringworks appear to cluster on those areas where shallow soil directly overlay rock, making these types of earthwork more practicable to build than mottes, which lay predominantly on areas with alluvium or overlying drift deposits. It will be interesting to test this hypothesis in other parts of Britain, although the particularly sharp division between sub-soil conditions both suitable and unsuitable for the construction of mottes in this part of Wales perhaps suggests that geological factors are less likely to be as important elsewhere. Geological and other conditions may coincide to explain the small but significant concentration of eight ringworks in the Derbyshire Peakland, including those at Hartington, Hathersage and

Hope. Most of these earthworks were probably rapidly built to oversee the agricultural management of the best available land in a region devastated by William's harrying in 1068–9 and to suppress the potentially rebellious hill-farming population (Hodges 1980: 32).

The construction of a ringwork may also have been more appropriate for the enclosure of extant structures, either where the need arose to defend a complex of domestic buildings in a time of crisis, or where an earlier manorial centre was fortified as an act of usurpation and conquest. Finally, we must remember that any clear-cut division between mottes and ringworks is ultimately misleading, as it neglects the sheer variety of early castle forms, their longer-term development and their reference to pre-existing landscape features, both natural and anthropogenic. In a study of the early castles of Devon, Higham has deliberately avoided classification of related earthworks as 'mottes' or 'ringworks', and raised the intriguing suggestion that in this area it may rather be the morphology of the summits of these features that provide an indication of status, as mottes with concave (rather than level) summits were seemingly built by those lower down the social scale (Higham 1982: 102). In addition, we must bear in mind that an initial ringwork might be converted into a motte, as at Goltho (Lincolnshire) (see Chapter 2). Certainly the classification of castle earthworks and related surface remains into categories and subcategories – typically: mottes, ringworks and 'other sites' of various sizes, with or without baileys – has a limited rôle and forms only a platform for further detailed study.

Intriguing regional trends in castle design exist, although they have been given less attention by medieval archaeologists than, for instance, variations in parish church architecture. The concentration of round castles in Cornwall, for example, has been long recognized (Toy 1933). In fact, the distribution extends into Devon and across the Bristol Channel, and must represent a fascinating blend of factors including seigneurial emulation along with limitations posed by the availability of resources including building stone, lime for mortar, and labour (Higham 2000b: 136).

Inventories of castles also throw up countless examples of disputed sites. The field archaeology of early castle earthworks can be complicated by the fact that features of alternative origin can be mistaken for defensive sites. Natural glacial features, barrows, windmill mounds, Civil War artillery emplacements and prospect mounds have all been mistakenly identified as mottes, and prehistoric domestic enclosures, Roman amphitheatres and stock enclosures as ringworks. Perhaps the greatest confusion exists where post-medieval prospect mounds have been misidentified as mottes. It is only in the last quarter of the twentieth century that the ubiquity of such garden earthworks has been fully recognized by field archaeologists, and many have been listed as mottes by earlier fieldworkers. The alleged motte at Scraptoft (Leicestershire) is a good example; here a large conical mound with an internal chamber and spiral pathway cut into its flanks was plainly part of the mid-eighteenth-century remodelling of the grounds around Scraptoft Hall, and described as such by Throsby (Hickman and Tew 1989: 62). Earthworks of similar origin that have also been erroneously listed as mottes include mounds known as 'The Mount', Oulston (North Yorkshire); 'Cat's Gruff', Gumley (Leicestershire); 'Clack Mount', Bradenstoke (Wiltshire); and the Morcott Spinney earthwork, Pilton

(Rutland), all of which are likely garden features. The key problem here lies, of course, in differentiating between such features and genuine castle earthworks that have been remodelled to form the basis of garden features (see Chapter 4). As well as viewing platforms, mottes could be readily adapted to form mill mounds, as revealed by excavation at Lodsworth (West Sussex) (Holden 1967). An advantageous site could mean that a castle earthwork could also be adapted for military reasons centuries after abandonment. The motte at Huntingdon, for instance, was converted into a gun platform in the seventeenth century, as indicated by the earthen ramp constructed against it and a depression on the summit where a gun-trail was dug in (Taylor 1974: 64).

Some studies have attempted to find evidence for an overall military strategy in the distribution of English castles. Most notably, Harvey (1911) and Beeler (1956, 1966) suggested that castle-building in Norman and Angevin England was carried out in a coordinated way to create a system of national defence. For instance, Beeler, through a somewhat over-simplistic scrutiny of the castle distribution map, has argued that London and Coventry, both key centres on the medieval road network, were surrounded by dense screens of fortifications guarding principal routes of communication (1966: 51–7). This view stands in sharp contrast to other early studies that recognized that castle-building can most appropriately be understood at the local scale, with manorial rather than military considerations invariably of greater importance (Armitage 1912: 83–4; Painter 1935). Perhaps the most penetrating critique of the notion that castles were constructed relative to a strategic master plan has been advanced by Warren Hollister (1965: 161–6), emphasizing both the lack of written evidence for any such scheme and the fact that limited geographical knowledge would have made its coordination utterly impractical. Behind the distribution map, castle-building was carried out not as part of any grand national strategy, but relative to the motives and aspirations of a multitude of individual decision makers. While the Crown may, in a broad sense, have been able to encourage castle-building in certain places and regions at certain times, and actively discourage it in other contexts, there is no evidence for any master plan of castle-building. Even if the creation of large but compact lordships in the north, along the Welsh border and along the south coast may, at the wider scale, have encouraged and in a sense delegated castle-building, there is no evidence that the Crown could dictate the location of individual castle sites built by barons and their tenants (see Chapter 5).

Some of these concepts are underlined well by a detailed case study of castle-building and English military strategy on the Anglo-Scottish border in the eleventh and twelfth centuries (Strickland 1992). While the pattern of medieval fortresses strung along the border – including Carlisle, Newcastle-upon-Tyne, Norham and Wark-on-Tweed – appear superficially to represent a chain of strongpoints constituting a coordinated defensive scheme, detailed scrutiny of their dates and their role in border warfare emphasizes that this was not the case. The various castles were founded, if not haphazardly, in a piecemeal fashion (Norham not until 1121); likewise, the border was itself not fixed but flexible and ill-defined. Furthermore, the relative ease with which the Scots penetrated deep into England, as evident for instance in the campaigns of 1138 and 1173–4, underlines that these border castles were not able to ever stop an army outright, but each built to operate in a largely independent and self-contained manner.

It is not until the Tudor period that we again see fortifications in England as products of a centralized authority and part of a national defensive strategy. Henry VIII's programme of coastal artillery fortification in the period 1539–43 was remarkable not only for its unprecedented cost, but also in marking the origins of a national defence policy (Saunders 1989: 34–52). Although many of Henry's forts and blockhouses, such as Deal (Kent) and Pendennis (Cornwall) are now called, mistakenly, castles, they were military strongpoints only, without the private residential character of their medieval antecedents. These forts may have had the architectural trappings of medieval castles – drawbridges, portcullises and crenellation – but they were also squat in appearance, lacking the visual impact of a lofty donjon or a motte-top tower. Their physical locations also indicate a centrally planned scheme rather than local aristocratic initiative. Typically, Henry VIII's 'Device' forts, were sited in isolated coastal positions to dominate anchorages, harbours or landing places; as such it was neither necessary nor desirable for them to have a village or town in attendance, nor even for the occupying authority to have legal jurisdiction over the surrounding area. Artillery forts such as these were thus instruments of statecraft rather than tools of medieval lordship, and were not entwined with the manor and local economy in the same way as medieval castles.

As well as attempting to seek logic in the physical positioning of castles in the landscape and explain their proliferation, it is also important to bear in mind that castles are rare or absent in certain areas, including particular lordships and types of physical terrain. This is illustrated well by the relative densities of castles within the English shires (Table 3.1). A marked sparseness or complete absence of castles in certain regions, such as areas of high moorland and fells, as well as low-lying fenland, is relatively easy to explain. While in some ways the resources available to local lords in such places were insufficient to support castle-building, perhaps more importantly, castles near these areas tended to be built at zones of interface between different types of landscape. The siting of royal or major baronial castles at the junction between areas of upland characterized by pastoral land-use and hunting resources and arable vales is a recurrent theme in the highland zone of England. Important Norman baronies in Cumbria display a particularly notable and doubtless deliberate division into upland and lowland components. In the barony of Cockermouth, for instance, the 'five towns of Cockermouth' and other lowland estates were held by free tenants, while the upland Derwent fells were forest or free chase under direct seigneurial control; the baronial castle, situated at the end of a ridge between the Derwent and Cocker, lay at the point of interface between the two resources (Winchester 1987: 19–22). Comparable patterns are evident in the location of castles at Barnard (Co. Durham), Pickering (North Yorkshire) and Richmond (North Yorkshire); a parallel site from south-west England is Okehampton (Devon).

Overall, medieval castles show little direct relationship with areas of pastoral land use, and, on a national scale, cluster more thickly on the zone of arable cultivation. This is particularly evident in the lowland Vale of York and the subsidiary Vales of Mowbray and Cleveland, which contain dense

Table 3.1   Numbers and overall densities of castles in pre-1974 English counties*

County	Density	Total castles	County	Density	Total castles
Northumberland	8.7	233	Hampshire/IoW	47.0	35
Herefordshire	9.05	93	Worcestershire	47.7	15
Shropshire	12.0	112	Wiltshire	48.2	28
Cumberland	18.5	82	Yorkshire	48.9	124
Bedfordshire	18.9	25	Cornwall	51.9	26
Westmorland	23.2	34	Huntingdonshire	52.3	7
Rutland	25.3	6	Suffolk	52.9	28
Buckinghamshire	29.9	25	Lancashire	53.7	35
Northamptonshire	30.4	35	Sussex	56.0	26
Kent	30.5	50	Cambridgeshire	57.6	15
Warwickshire	30.5	31	Surrey	60.1	12
Durham	32.7	31	Devonshire	60.7	43
Leicestershire	34.7	24	Derbyshire	62.9	16
Oxfordshire	35.7	21	Somerset	64.8	25
Gloucestershire	38.2	33	Lincolnshire	70.1	37
Hertfordshire	39.5	16	Nottinghamshire	70.8	12
Berkshire	42.6	17	Staffordshire	72.4	16
Essex	46.3	33	Norfolk	89.3	23
Cheshire	44.1	23	London/Middlesex	—	6
Dorset	46.5	21			

* Density figures give the number of square miles per site, so lower numbers indicate higher densities. The table provides a good general idea of the spread of castles across the shires, but should also be interpreted with caution. The totals include late-medieval tower houses and Tudor artillery fortifications, as well as sites that are documented but lost; other undocumented sites have doubtless vanished without trace (data compiled from King 1983).

concentrations of castles on the glacial and fluvio-glacial gravels, sands and clays that rendered it a readily cultivable zone which was settled from an early date. Kapelle has suggested that the 'oat bread line' (the division between areas of winter-sown and spring-sown cereals) was a crucial factor in the Norman settlement of the North (1979: 214). It is no coincidence that the thickest scattering of early castles in Yorkshire lie on the wheat-bearing lands, indicating the settlement of Norman tenants and sub-tenants within the arable heartland of Yorkshire in the wake of the harrying and associated large-scale reorganization of estate frameworks. This underlines the role of the Norman castle in an essentially colonizing venture, securing newly appropriated agricultural resources as an act of seigneurial economic policy as much as military conquest (see Dalton 1994: 116).

East Anglia, while containing some of the wealthiest and most populous parts of medieval England, had an exceptionally low density of castles. Norfolk had fewer per square mile than any other English county, attributable partly, no doubt, to military factors but also to a pattern of land-holding where a relatively small number of magnates commanded the resources necessary for castle-building (Rogerson 1994: 68). Detailed regional analysis actually indicates that castle builders in the county appear to have expressly avoided areas of dense population and, in particular, concentrations of freeholders, in planning the locations of residences associated with appurtenances such as deer parks and boroughs (Liddiard 2000b). Another conspicuous blank spot on the distribution map is the woodland and wood-pasture of the Kent and Sussex Weald, and in particular the High Weald, where a social structure of different character tended to discourage castle-building. The fenland districts of medieval England unsurprisingly demonstrate an extremely scarce distribution of castle sites on the low-lying and poorly drained peats, although those sites occupying settled pockets of this zone, predominantly on narrow silt belts, can be profitably related to the characteristically dispersed settlement pattern in these areas (Fig. 8.8). The boulder clay-capped wolds as found, for instance, in high Leicestershire and Rutland unsurprisingly feature few castle sites. Although the late eleventh century marked a period of continuing colonization (Fox 1989), these areas were usually lacking in the important long-established settlements and hunting resources which attracted early castles in other parts of the counties.

Other tracts of the landscape may have been free of castles due to deliberate policies of enforcement. In the wrong hands, castles could prove a political threat to the ruler and a very real danger to the population at large, and much debate has centred on the extent to which the pattern of castle-building could be contained and controlled by royal authority (Eales 1990). This factor must account for the open zone on the castle distribution map around London, where the nearest private castles (Bletchingley and Reigate, Surrey and Ongar, Essex) were some 30 kilometres away. Other towns with hinterlands similarly lacking in castles include Bristol, Hereford, Lincoln, Shrewsbury and Winchester. At a wider scale still, relatively low densities of castles in Cheshire and County Durham (Table 3.1) are doubtless attributable to a high level of political centralization exerted by palatine earls and bishops who appear to have been particularly unwilling to permit castle-building by their tenants. Similar factors may also partially explain the relatively low density of Norman castles within Cornwall, where at Domesday, Robert of Mortain enjoyed a virtual monopoly on landholding in a manner quite unlike the pattern of post-Conquest land tenure in neighbouring Devon (Higham 2000a: 140). Indeed, until the fortification by the Crown of St Michael's Mount in 1194, the peninsula contained only a single castle west of the Fowey estuary, and that an undocumented ringwork at Veryan (King 1983: 72–80). Hard evidence for the demilitarization of certain landscapes due to baronial policy is hard to find, though a certain capacity to regulate the proliferation of castles is indicated in the remarkable non-aggression pact between the earls of Chester and Leicester in 1148–53 (Coulson 1994). This precluded castle-building by either party in an extensive area forming a zone within a 30- to 40- km radius of Leicester as delimited by the positions of important urban centres (e.g. Coventry) and castles (e.g. Donington, Leicestershire and Rockingham, Northamptonshire), again underlining the essential link between territorial control and the possession of castles.

Decisions about castle siting were made within the constraints of available resources, of which the most important was wealth tied up in land and estates, but the local availability of suitable labour and raw materials were other key factors. We remain remarkably ignorant of where labour for castle-building came from and how it was organized, especially in the eleventh and twelfth centuries, although it is clear that monumental efforts were sometimes needed. For the most part, labour on castle-building was probably part and parcel of the labour services that tenants were liable for. Estimates of the time and labour required to construct an earth and timber castle are notoriously problematic given uncertainties over a multitude of variables including the character of local geology, the organization of the labour force and the volume of material to be moved. Nonetheless, some indication of the effort required is given by the calculation that the construction of the Norman motte at Castle Neroche (Somerset), a large but not exceptional earthwork some 6m high and 75m across, took a total of 13,780 man-days (Davison 1972: 56–7). Given the dispersed settlement pattern in the area, this represents an exceptional centralization of labour, which could not fail to impact on the locality. The immense motte at Bramber, meanwhile, is estimated to have taken 228,269 man-hours (Barton and Holden 1977: 69–70).

Finally, reference must be made to water supply. In contrast to monastic archaeology, where many studies have cast light on often remarkably complex systems for the supply of water to religious houses for domestic, industrial and agricultural purposes (Greene 1992: 109–32; Aston 2000: 24–5), relatively little research has been carried out into the water supply systems of castles (see Kenyon 1990: 161). Ease of access to a reliable source of clean water must have been an essential factor in the minds of those making decisions of where to build a castle. This is underlined by a statistical analysis of 423 castles across the United Kingdom, demonstrating that 82 per cent of those sites where the source of water is known contained wells located within the inner defences, while 24 per cent featured two or more wells (Ruckley 1990: 23–4). Identification of sites with potential for the sinking of wells clearly demanded a sophisticated understanding of geological characteristics including the relative porosity jointing of bedrock. The wells of castles built on lofty natural protrusions were often exceptionally deep. Few, however, match the feat of engineering at Beeston Castle (Cheshire), where the shaft cut through sandstone to a depth of 124m (Weaver 1987: 24), although the wells at cliff-top castles such as Dover and Scarborough bear comparison. Rather less frequently we have evidence that castles were supplied with cisterns fed by rainwater or natural groundwater seepage (e.g. Okehampton, Devon), or exceptionally through a piped system capturing water from a roof (e.g. Lydford, Devon), and these usually only to supplement a well. A well-documented system of piped water supply served Windsor Castle, which by the time of Henry III featured both primary and secondary cisterns, and conduits supplying kitchens and other domestic buildings, while Chester Castle had something approaching an integrated supply system (Pounds 1990: 191). Only rarely, however, were castles supplied by a source external to the defensive perimeter. An interesting exception is Restormel (Cornwall), where an hydraulic system of lesser sophistication supplied water from a natural spring under pressure to 'each house of office' through a lead conduit, as recorded in a survey of 1337 (Hull 1971: 41).

Multiple castles and siege-works

There are a surprising number of instances where two or more castle sites are closely spaced in the landscape, often within a few hundred metres of one another. Here we should not, however, confuse genuine examples of separate but closely juxtaposed castles with those Norman fortifications built with two

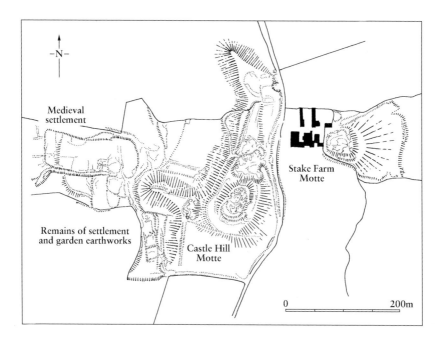

Figure 3.7 Earthwork plan of two closely spaced motte and bailey castles at East Chelborough (Dorset) (based on Lewis 1989, with additions).

mottes on the perimeter of a single bailey, as at Lewes (East Sussex) and Lincoln. The origins of what can be termed 'multiple castles' cannot be explained by any single common factor; instead, four possible scenarios can be identified. First, one castle may have been raised in opposition to another during a time of hostility, usually as a royal response to baronial insurrection. Second, the sites may have quite distinct ownership histories and have lain in separate lordships. Third is the possibility that a new site has replaced an old one. The fourth scenario is that the castles coexisted under the same ownership and complemented one another within a unified strategy.

The precise chronological and functional relationship between two or more nearby castle sites is, however, not always clear, especially where documentary evidence is minimal or lacking. Attempts to date, even crudely, the construction of earth and timber castles through archaeological excavation, meanwhile, often end in failure. Consequently, it is usually only by examining the respective topographical settings of these castles, in addition to morphological study and analogy with other sites, that we may gain some insight into their origins and relationship. Indeed, study of the many closely spaced medieval castles in the British landscape represents a fascinating yet little tackled avenue for research. For example, the instance of paired mottes at East Chelborough (Dorset) (Fig. 3.7) has traditionally been regarded as a case of re-siting, with one motte and bailey (Stake Farm) being superseded by a larger and more sophisticated version (Castle Hill) on a better drained ridgetop site (RCHME Dorset I 1952–75: 90). Neither motte is, however, documented and the nature of their relationship remains open to speculation. A more recent study (Lewis 1989) has suggested, on the basis of a re-survey of the earth-works, that the Stake Farm motte, located in a less commanding position downslope of the other site, from which its bailey tilts away, is in fact a siege-work. More complex still is the pattern of castle-building within the parish of Hamstead Marshall (Berkshire), where a full three undocumented castle earthworks can be identified (Fig. 8.6). Here, two virtually adjacent motte and baileys are best explained as a case of re-siting, whilst the small isolated motte on a strong natural site some 800 m distant may well be an unfinished siege-work (Bonney and Dunn 1989).

In war, a castle could make particular demands on its hinterland, which might also fall victim to the ravages of conflict. While through plunder a besieging force could systematically devastate the estates surrounding a castle, a garrison's aggressive foraging could have similarly grave consequences, as widely chronicled during the Anarchy. An illuminating example is provided by a remarkable charter of Roger de Mowbray, which granted rights in Nidderdale to Fountains Abbey in recompense for the actions of his men. Near the end of Stephen's reign, his forces had taken grain and extracted funds from the monastic estates while operating from his castle at Kirkby Malzeard (North Yorkshire) (Greenway 1972: lxi, 75–6). The consequences of such events are, however, difficult to examine through archaeological or other physical evi-dence. The surviving earthworks of medieval siege castles represent the most tangible evidence of the impact of siege warfare on the landscape.

Medieval siege castles are, however, little studied and often misunderstood, as so few have been examined archaeologically and surface remains are often minimal (Bradbury 1992: 86–7). As expedient and hurriedly built mottes and ringworks, many siege castles described in chronicles have vanished entirely, including sites at Rochester (Kent), Bamburgh (Northumberland), Castle Cary and Dunster (Somerset), and Downton (Wiltshire). Some of these were no doubt slighted soon after construction while others have been eradicated by the plough or obliterated by settlement expansion. A lost siege-work in Exeter (Devon) was only rediscovered in 1993, when excavations during the redevelopment of a reservoir recovered almost its entire plan (Nenk et al. 1994: 203–4). Although the Gesta Stephani makes no specific mention that King Stephen erected a siege-work during his three-month siege of Exeter in 1136, it seems beyond reasonable doubt that the tiny ringwork was built then, situated menacingly 275m north-east of Rougemont Castle on the opposite side of the valley (Fig. 3.8).

Renn (1959) has traced 31 instances of siege castles in England and Wales, which appear to have been raised an average of 200–300 yards (c. 180–270 m) from the site being besieged, apparently so that the fortification would be beyond effective bowshot. Excellent examples include the ringwork known as 'Pampudding Hill' raised against Bridgnorth (Shropshire), from which it lies 320 m distant, by Henry I in 1102, and 'The Rings', a ringwork and bailey built by Stephen on a low-lying site 270 m from Corfe (Dorset) in his unsuccessful siege of 1139. As an ideal, and where topography made it pos-sible, a siege-work would also be raised to overlook its target. The topo-graphical positions of other small mottes or ringworks close to important castles suggest that they are works relating to undocumented sieges; candi-dates include Beacon Hill, Pickering (North Yorkshire) and the ringwork in

Figure 3.8 Danes Castle, Exeter: a small twelfth-century siege-work under excavation in 1993 (© Exeter Archaeology).

Keeper's Wood near Castle Rising (Norfolk). Although works such as these are commonly listed as castles, we should bear in mind that as temporary military installations, most lacked the residential character that was an otherwise essential aspect of castle function, and do not display the same connections with the local economy and settlement pattern.

The exact purposes of these castles erected in military opposition to others must have been varied, yet two essential types can be identified. First, we may identify those siege castles built for the express purpose of providing a secure platform from which the other site could be attacked, either by armed assault, through the employment of siege engines, or by a combination of both. A distinction can be drawn between these sites and those in a second category, whose purpose was less outrightly aggressive and more long-term; namely those erected to observe their prey and contain the activities of garrisons. Medieval chronicles make it clear that these sites were often effective in preventing enemy forays into the surrounding landscape and strangling lines of reinforcement and re-supply, and they could be readily garrisoned with a subsidiary body of troops while the main force campaigned elsewhere (Morillo 1994: 96). We should also not overlook the psychological and intimidatory effect that these works would have had. Sites which fall into this category can be more appropriately termed 'counter-castles'. These two types of fortification can often be differentiated from one another by their physical settings. While the first type of site will tend to overlook or command the object of their aggression and occupy classic defensive positions, often on the rear of a slope facing the besieged site, the second will be more remote and often command key routes of communication, especially river crossings.

It was by no means unknown for more than one siege-work to be raised against a single castle, during single or multiple sieges, while some were reused on separate occasions. The small ringwork known as 'Cam's Hill' (Wiltshire) is almost certainly one of a series of three parasitic castles raised by Robert, Earl of Gloucester, against Malmesbury in 1144. The site, overlooking an important crossing of the Avon from high ground 1.5 km south of the town is a classic counter-castle, although its two companions cannot be identified positively (Creighton 2000a: 108). Wallingford Castle (Oxfordshire) was besieged no fewer than three times between 1139 and 1153, during which at least two counter-castles were raised, at Crowmarsh and Brightwell, while fieldwork has revealed other undocumented earthworks in the locality which may have played a rôle (Slade 1960; Spurrell 1995). The ringwork known as Barley Pound (Hampshire) is bracketed by two small mottes known as Bentley Castle and Powderham Castle, both no more than 600 m distant and almost certainly built during the siege of 1147 (Stamper 1984: 81). At least two works were raised to blockade Arundel (West Sussex) in 1102, at Lyminster and Rackham, and there may have been others besides.

Other small, impermanent earth and timber castles were erected to support the sieges of defended towns rather than private castles, although of course castles were often integrated within town walls and contributed to their defence (Turner 1970: 74–5). One such example may be the ringwork known as Studforth Hill at Aldborough (North Yorkshire), raised less than 150 m beyond the south-east corner of the Roman defensive circuit around this small medieval town some time before 1205–6 when it is recorded as disused (Myres *et al.* 1959: 5). A site that may be interpreted in a similar light is the motte known as 'Castle Hill' lying in the grounds of Tapton Park (Derbyshire), and overlooking Chesterfield from the opposite bank of the River Rother. Sites such as these present many difficulties in interpretation, as it is difficult to distinguish whether the fortification was constructed in opposition to, or to guard access to, the urban centre, as both scenarios could demand similar sites. Another site which deserves a mention in this sense is the small motte to the south of the market town of Melton Mowbray (Leicestershire). Overlooking a crossing of the River Eye on one of the main southern approaches to the town, this undocumented earthwork may well have been erected as a form of property protection at a time of crisis or uncertainty (Liddle 1989: 119).

Examples of nearby and contemporary castle sites that have not been constructed in direct military opposition to one another but built by separate lords in separate tenurial contexts are far less common. Perhaps the clearest example is the parish of Ascot-under-Wychwood (Oxfordshire), where a small early twelfth-century keep and a motte and bailey lie at opposite ends of the village, merely 550 m apart, but set respectively within the separate manors of Ascot Doilly and Ascot Earl (Jope and Threlfall 1946–7: 167; Jope and Threlfall 1959: 219). The two early castle sites within the modern parish of Catterick (North Yorkshire) – a motte ('Palet Hill') adjacent to the parish church and motte and bailey ('Castle Hills') located barely *c.* 1.5 km to the south-east near a ford over the Swale – similarly appear to have been built in separate tenurial contexts within the Honour of Richmond (Butler 1992:

73–5). A more tenuous example may be the castles of Winkleigh (Devon), where twin earthworks ('Croft' and 'Court' Castle), positioned on either side of the parish church no less than *c.* 250 m apart, were probably raised in two separate manors belonging to the baronies of Gloucester and Barnstaple (Higham 1982b: 105). Nonetheless, given the extreme proximity of the sites and the fact that the latter was far smaller than the former, the possibility that the juxtaposition results from a siege cannot be ruled out.

The scenario of two nearby castles being built to support one another in a tactical sense is better represented, although fortifications of this sort remained relatively uncommon until the era of artillery fortification, when the construction of two or more coastal blockhouses with interlocking fields of fire is exemplified by sites at Dartmouth (Devon) and Portland (Dorset). Complementary castles are represented in the larger towns, most notably by the two Norman castles in York and the three in London necessary to impress and subdue large and independent-minded urban populations (see Chapter 7). Rural examples are less well documented, although fieldwork has indicated some possible examples where specific topographical circumstances made this worthwhile. The small bailey-less motte known as 'Round Hill' at Carlton-in-Coverdale (North Yorkshire), for instance, appears likely to have been an outpost to Middleham, located on the ancient route-way to Kettlewell in an area where the lords had extensive pasturage (L'Anson 1913: 334).

Perhaps the clearest example of a group of castles being constructed in a short space of time as a coordinated policy to meet a single objective is the arc of sites north of Cambridge. Burwell Castle (Fig. 8.11) was built by King Stephen in an effort to contain the depredations of Geoffrey de Mandeville, Earl of Essex, the quintessential robber whose power base lay on the Isle of Ely and who, in 1144, was killed during a siege of the partly built castle (VCH Cambs. 1948: 38–9). This fen-edge castle forms one link in a chain of fortifications, placed 10 to 15 km apart, including Lidgate (Suffolk), which flanks the Icknield way, and three sites in Cambridgeshire: Rampton, commanding the causeway over the fens to Ely; Caxton, overlooking the old Roman Road of Ermine Street; and Swavesey. Another chain of fortifications whose origins are clearly linked which have been the subject of fieldwork and documentary analysis is the cluster of no fewer than twelve closely spaced mottes in the Vale of Montgomery (Fig. 3.9). Despite the small physical size of these earthworks, each site appears to have represented the deliberate settlement of a tenant as opposed to a temporary watchtower or signal station (King and Spurgeon 1965: 84–5; see also Chapter 8).

In the north-west of England mottes at Arkholme and Melling (Lancashire) were positioned on opposite banks of the River Lune near a crossing, while earthwork castles at Ashton (Lancashire) and Penwortham (Cumbria) flanked an estuary crossing (Higham 1991: 83). Another possible example of two complementary castles is represented by the two mottes in the parish of Hartington Town Quarter (Derbyshire). Here, a small ringwork known as Banktop appears to be an outlier of the larger and more complex motte and bailey at Pilsbury (Fig. 3.10), the two fortifications being intervisible and together controlling river crossings and the north–south corridor through the narrow Dove valley (Hart 1981: 146). The striking concentration of three motte and baileys disposed in a triangle around the village of Penselwood

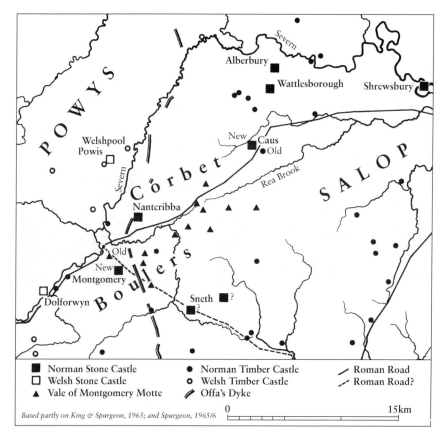

Figure 3.9 Castles in and around the Vale of Montgomery (Higham and Barker 1992).

(Somerset) represents another possible example of a local strategy of castle-building (Fig. 3.11). In the absence of any supporting documentation, the origins and ownership histories of these sites again remain a matter for speculation, although one intriguing possibility is that one or more represent a programme of Norman subjugation in the wake of the 1069 rising against nearby Montacute. A cluster of Domesday manors in the Penselwood-Bruton area show a drastic deterioration in value in the period 1066–86 which may owe something to these events (Welldon Finn 1971: 289–90; Creighton 2000a: 112). The siting of the Castle Orchard motte and bailey, near Gasper (Wiltshire) is of particular interest. Built along a prominent greensand ridge, the castle was closely associated with the millstone quarries known as the 'Pen Pits', some of which clearly antedated it, as demonstrated by excavations conducted by Pitt-Rivers (Winwood 1879, 1884).

The physical relocation of a castle from one site to another in the immediate locality is by far the most common reason for the juxtaposition in close proximity of two castle sites, good examples being the two castles at Lythe (North Yorkshire), St Briavels (Gloucestershire) and Sheriff Hutton (North Yorkshire). In a very few instances, a change of decision could have left one

Figure 3.10 Pilsbury (Derbyshire). View of the motte and bailey looking north-west along the Dove valley. The earthworks to the extreme left include part of a deserted medieval settlement and a hollow-way diverted through the bailey enclosures. The remains of a second early castle at Banktop, which may have been a subsidiary fortification, are located 2.5km further down the valley (photograph: Oliver Creighton).

castle partly finished and abandoned in favour of a superior alternative site nearby, as seems to explain the two nearby ringworks at Berden (Essex). The chronology of relocation and the reasons for such an expensive and time-consuming action vary widely. Although the slighting or destruction of one castle may occasionally have prompted the foundation of a replacement nearby, in the majority of cases the re-siting of a castle was in response to the changing demands of lordship. Possibly the most common trend was for a site in a naturally defensible position to be replaced by one in a more convenient location. This is demonstrated well at Bradfield (South Yorkshire), where the coincidence of two castle sites within 600 m of one another suggests the relocation of lordship from an earlier ringwork located on a exposed rocky promontory ('Castle Hill') to a powerfully defended motte and bailey ('Bailey Hill') adjacent to the parish church and forming a focus within the settlement (Birch 1980a, 1980b). Sometimes the transplantation of a site was coincident with the foundation of a new planned town or village, with the transferral of lordship part and parcel of a more extensive scheme of seigneurial aggrandizement. A well-known example is the movement in the mid-twelfth century of the principal Albini castle in Norfolk to New Buckenham from their earlier site at what became 'Old' Buckenham. The new seat of lordship was laid out some 2.5 km distant in close conjunction with a new grid-plan town (Fig. 8.7), on an open site in an area of former common land (Liddiard 2000a: 48–51).

In the towns, the transferral of lordship from one site to another is represented well by the two castle sites in Canterbury (Kent), Gloucester and Lydford (Devon) (Fig. 3.12), although the origins of other twinned urban

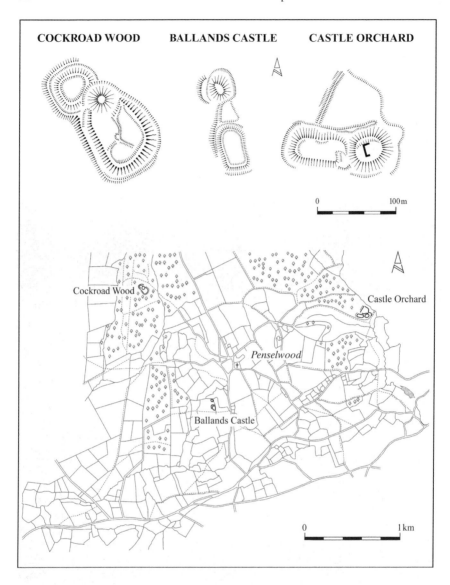

Figure 3.11 The landscape around Penselwood (Somerset), showing the plans and locations of three motte and bailey castles. All three sites are undocumented, but may well represent a coordinated Norman policy of subjection in the late eleventh century.

castles is unclear. For instance, the motte known as Boley Hill immediately adjacent to Rochester Castle has been variously interpreted as an earlier castle, a siege motte and an outwork built to reinforce the castle's vulnerable southern defences (Flight and Harrison 1978). Excavation in 1960 failed to date the earthwork's origins, and the issue remains unresolved. A similar range of explanations is possible regarding the origins of the undated, undocumented motte-like earthwork known as the 'Priory Mount' *c*. 400 m south of

Figure 3.12 Lydford (Devon) from the air. The earthwork of the Norman ringwork, located at the point of the Saxon *burh* defences, can be identified to the bottom of the photograph; the remains of the second, later, castle and prison lie in the centre, just above the parish church (photograph by F. M. Griffith. Devon County Council: copyright reserved).

Lewes Castle (East Sussex), although conceivably the feature is actually a misidentified formal garden feature (Rudling 1983: 69–72).

Summary

This analysis of castle siting has drawn attention to the sheer variety of functions to which castles were put and the broad range of topographical sites that they occupied. Although castles with spectacular and photogenic settings, such as Corfe or Peveril, represent a familiar part of our heritage, it is wrong to see these as 'classic' positions for castles. In reality, the sites chosen for many castles were essentially similar to those occupied by other manorial sites. Despite the production of inventories of castles and the development of schemes of classification, it is surprising quite how vague our overall understanding of castle distribution through time really is. Basic uncertainties over dates of foundation or periods of occupation mean that, in practical terms, a simple map of the distribution of castle sites in any given zone at any given time contains many assumptions. The many hundreds of undocumented earth and timber fortifications, which form an essential part of the overall pattern of medieval private fortifications but whose dates of foundation and periods of occupation remains so enigmatic, hold particular challenges. Overall, it is clear that analysis of the physical setting of a castle in terms of defensive strength and strategic value forms only a small part of any explanation as to why a particular site was built in a particular place. Of at least equal if not greater importance were considerations of a site's accessibility and viability as an estate centre and its visibility and even aesthetic qualities, and it is to these that we will now turn.

4 *The Castle as Icon: Landscapes of Status and Symbolism*

Any past landscape comprised far more than the physical 'nuts and bolts' of, for instance, settlements, roads, field systems and property boundaries, all of which interacted and communicated, but did so in varying patterns. In recent years landscape archaeologists, influenced by developments in history, geography and the social sciences, have paid increasing attention to the ways in which landscapes were perceived and experienced by past societies, and the impact of monuments on the human senses (see Tilley 1994). We are now very aware that past landscapes were more than templates against which everyday life was played out; to contemporaries they were panoramas full of social significance and symbolic significance, although of course different individuals will have perceived landscapes in different ways, depending on a multitude of factors including personal circumstances and social status.

Medieval castles, by definition, acted as residential, administrative and defensible foci within their landscapes; yet their iconic rôles as symbols of power and influence coexisted with, and sometimes transcended their military importance (Johnson 1996: 122–3). Unambiguously, the castle was a highly visible, physical manifestation of seigneurial authority; in an 'imitative age' (Lewis *et al.* 1997: 231), when lordship was reinforced by mechanisms of patronage and display, a castle represented a means of conspicuous consumption as well as a military strongpoint. What is central to this discussion is that the topographical setting of a castle could be selected and remodelled to emphasize this iconic status, often presenting the seigneurial site from the most favourable angles and perspectives against a backcloth of landscape features with élite connotations, such as deer parks and garden features. In addition, we should not neglect the fact that many castles, as large and often inordinately complex structures, constituted deliberately structured landscapes in their own right; in considering the 'castle in the landscape', it is important not to overlook the 'landscape in the castle'. This chapter examines some of the psychological impacts of castle-building on the landscape, exploring their significance as potent symbols of status, but also, in many cases, as elements within landscapes designed for aesthetic appeal and entertainment.

Castles and symbolism

It goes almost without saying that the physical appearance of castles, as visibly élite structures, must have reshaped the landscapes around them. Indeed, the physical fabric of castles may have encoded social values that we are scarcely aware of, as indicated, for instance, by a twelfth-century sermon of Ailred of Rievaulx:

> In a castle there are three things that are strong, the ditch, the wall and the keep... what is a ditch except deep ground which is humility. The spiritual wall is chastity, and you will have this ditch of humility and wall of chastity so must we build the keep of charity.
>
> (quoted from Thompson 1991)

One of the words most closely associated in the modern mind with the medieval castle is the term 'keep', usually thought to derive from the verb (to keep), and implying a building designed with the ultimate aim of holding out. The word may, however, ultimately derive from a late fourteenth-century coining of the Middle English word *kipe*, used to describe the pattern of weaving on a basket, here with reference to the appearance of banded masonry on a cylindrical tower (Kenyon and Thompson 1994). Nonetheless, the term was not used widely until the sixteenth century. Instead, the medieval French word to describe these structures was *donjon*, derived ultimately from the Latin *dominium*, meaning, significantly, lordship. Stocker (1992: 415–16) has usefully coined the phrase 'nailing the valley' to describe the essential symbolic functions of such masonry towers. Always forming the visual focus of the site, the physical form of the donjon proclaimed both the power and permanence of lordship. The gatehouses of castles were another focus for architectural elaboration that could express lordship to a wider community in the same way that a town gate might serve as a symbol of civic pride. Renn (1993: 183–6) has suggested that galleries in the upper levels of eleventh-century gatehouses at Exeter (Devon) and Ludlow (Shropshire) actually compromised defensibility and served principally as devices for public exhibition. At the opposite end of the chronological spectrum the gatehouses of Herstmonceux (East Sussex), licensed in 1441, and Cooling (Kent), licensed in 1381, were conspicuously embellished showpieces of 'military' architecture, while few sites match the late fourteenth-century gatehouse of Hylton (Co. Durham) for its chivalric symbolism, incorporating elaborate heraldic panels and multi-tiered battlements complete with statuettes (Morley 1976).

Perhaps the most vivid embodiment of the symbolism that could be ingrained in castle architecture is Edward I's showpiece of Caernarvon Castle (Gwynd). The combination of polygonal towers and turrets, the visual impact of the dominant 'Eagle Tower' and the conspicuous use of banded masonry on the castle's external faces is seen as a deliberate emulation of Byzantine Constantinople, and thus a powerful icon of royal power and quasi-imperial authority (Brown *et al.* 1963: 369–71; see also Mathieu 1998). What is particularly pertinent here is that this architecture of authority was apparent to the community at large rather than only to personnel admitted into the fortress. Polychrome banded masonry at sites including Dover (Kent) and Wareham (Dorset) may be interpreted in a similar light. That the external appearances of castles could be designed with particular reference to the organization of the surrounding landscape is less clear, although two examples demonstrate the possibility. At Chepstow (Monmouthshire), re-used Roman tile and brick is incorporated into the Norman donjon to form a string course running around all sides of the rectangular structure except to the east, where it terminates neatly. This architectural detail gives the distinct impression that the structure, with its echoes of Roman authority, faced quite deliberately into the unconquered lands of South Wales (Eaton 2000: 137–8). Okehampton Castle (Devon) demonstrates an alternative scenario. From its earliest eleventh-century phases, the castle's plan had taken an elongated form, squeezed onto a narrow east-west spur on the edge of Dartmoor. A grandiose scheme of rebuilding early in the fourteenth century, probably initiated by Hugh II Courtenay, resulted in a massive upgrading of the castle's domestic facilities (Higham *et al.* 1982: 63–74). After its refurbishment the castle's architecture presented two different faces to quite different audiences. Anybody approaching the site along the Old Okehampton Road, a highway that skirted the north side of the castle, was confronted with a martial façade provided by the imposing enlarged keep, barbican and curtain wall. On the south side, however, a suite of sumptuous new domestic lodgings with large windows and window seats presented an entirely different impression from the Courtenay's deer park, over which they enjoyed a splendid view uninterrupted by a curtain wall.

In a series of influential articles, Coulson (1979; 1982; 1993; 1994a) has stressed the essential sociological functions of medieval licences to crenellate and drawn attention to the metaphysical importance of crenellated buildings as potent vehicles for social expression. The possession of a licence had great symbolic significance in its own right, and it is highly significant that not all describe actual physical changes that were made to buildings (see also Price 1996). In addition, while a battlemented building was an evocative way of proclaiming lordship and status to rivals and a wider community, it should not escape our attention that many licences to crenellate formed only part of a larger package of seigneurial privileges. This was relatively commonplace by the late fourteenth century. For instance, William Lord Hastings received licence to crenellate his manor at Ashby (Leicestershire) in 1474, a year after a grant of two fairs and permission to enlarge his deer park to 3,000 acres; Sir Edmund Bedingfield's licence to crenellate Oxburgh Hall (Norfolk) was granted in association with the grant of a weekly market (Coulson 1979: 79).

Although it is often an implicit assumption that symbolism in castle architecture was only possible with the use of masonry, archaeological excavation of the traces left by timber superstructures that surmounted mottes and ringworks has, in recent years, revolutionized our understanding of the appearance of earth and timber castles (Higham and Barker 1992). It is important not to overlook that the construction of these sites could have equally profound symbolic impacts on their surroundings. In particular, excavation at Hen Domen (Powys) has demonstrated that a castle never rebuilt in stone could be a dominating and imposing structure, far removed from the more traditional reconstructions of sites such as Abinger (Surrey). In the late eleventh and early twelfth century, the impressive appearance of such sites (in particular those with towering mottes) served as cultural markers, proclaiming and legitimating territorial control and expressing the cultural identity of a new élite. It is interesting to note, however, that the social status implied from the archaeological evidence of powerful defences is not always reflected in the material finds from early castle excavations. Barker (1987: 54) has indeed suggested that the castle seigneury at Hen Domen in the late eleventh century would have had their wealth tied up in livestock rather than finery, as demonstrated in an almost total absence of rich, portable material culture.

To gain further insight into the visual impact of castles on their surroundings we may also turn to the artistic and literary evidence so often neglected by students of castle studies. *Sir Gawain and the Green Knight* is an alliterative poem written in the late fourteenth century by an unknown source. Although the subject of intense analysis for its literary value, the poem, written in an authentic native tradition, has enough realism to be an important source for architectural studies (Thompson 1989; 1997). The poem includes a remarkable description of the setting of Sir Bertalik's castle as viewed by the approaching knight:

> Thrice the sign of the Saviour on himself he had made,
> When in the wood he was aware of a dwelling with a moat
> On a promontory above a plateau, penned in by the boughs
> And tremendous trunks of trees, and trenches about;
> The comliest castle that ever a knight owned,
> It was pitched on a plain, with a park all round,
> Impregnably palisaded with pointed stakes,
> And containing many trees in its two-mile circumference.
> The courteous knight contemplated the castle from one side
> As it shimmered and shone through the shining oaks.
> (quoted from Stone 1959)

The claim that the fortress which the knight beholds can perhaps be equated with Beeston Castle (Cheshire) is a matter for debate. But what is absolutely clear is that the poet had in mind a fixed notion not only of the ideal castle, but also of its ideal context. From its sylvan setting to the spiky silhouette described later in the poem, the castle has a stunning visual impact on the senses. A further iconographic aspect of the castle's description is its portrayal as a centre of cultural refinement, in contrast to the untamed wilderness of the forest and open countryside. This depiction of castles as part of the civilizing process, putting their mark on their surroundings and symbolizing control over nature, is well represented elsewhere in contemporary romances, as for instance in Perceval's vision of Gornement de Gohort's castle in the *Conte de Graal* (Putter 1995: 41–50).

The iconographic significance of the medieval castle is also expressed well by medieval seals used to authenticate documents such as charters and grants. Cherry (1992) has demonstrated that whilst depictions of castles on seals are imperfect sources for the reconstruction of a castle's architecture, they emphasize well the importance of the buildings as tokens of authority. For instance, the thirteenth-century seal of Rochester (Kent) depicts the great tower keep not within the town walls, but artificially standing in isolation, closely associated with three lions symbolizing royal control. The stylized depiction of castles on a wealth of other seals used by local government officials such as sheriffs, and on customs seals, further underlines their association with concepts of justice and authority.

We can recall also that castle-building introduced new and alien place-names of Norman-French derivation, which must in some way have reshaped the surrounding landscape in contemporary minds, especially where a place was deliberately re-named. There are relatively few entirely original Norman place-names in the English landscape; rather, most names that show Norman influence demonstrate an alteration in pronunciation or spelling, or the addition of a French surname to an English or Scandinavian element, as at Kibworth Harcourt (Leicestershire). More striking is the strong association between new French names and important castles, and the tendency of these names to reflect topographical observations about the site (Reaney 1960: 193–4; Cameron 1961: 87–8). Hence we have Richmond, North Yorkshire ('strong hill'); Mountsorrel, Leicestershire ('sorrel-coloured hill'); Egremont, Cumbria ('sharp-pointed hill'); Montacute, Somerset ('pointed hill'); and Rougemont, in both Devon and West Yorkshire ('red hill'). Elsewhere, compounds of *bel* or *beu* show, at the simplest level, an awareness of the aesthetic qualities of castle sites and their settings: prominent examples include Beaudesert, Warwickshire ('beautiful wilderness'); Beaumaris, Anglesey ('beautiful marsh'); Beaufront Castle, Northumberland ('beautiful brow'); Belvoir, Leicestershire ('beautiful view'); and the three castles associated with the name Beaumont ('beautiful hill') in Cumbria, Oxfordshire and Rutland. It is quite possible, of course, that some of these names could have been transferred directly from places in France, perhaps as statements of a colonial settlement, but also, no doubt, for nostalgic or sentimental reasons. At Caus (Shropshire), the new Norman lord was more explicit about naming his newly planted castle and borough after his homeland in Caux, France (Beresford 1967: 334). There is little doubt, however, that most of these Norman-French introductions to the landscape described equally well the topographical settings of castles.

Castles and the past

Through survey, excavation and documentary analysis, it is becoming increasingly clear that many medieval castles were placed at points in the landscape that had been previously occupied, or else were the focus for other types of antecedent activity, such as agriculture or burial practices. The process of castle-building on a site of earlier occupation may embody a range of complex and interrelated motives. At one extreme, it may represent little more than coincidence, and in some cases an earlier site will have been derelict, abandoned, or even forgotten. In other cases, reoccupation of an earlier site may provide certain advantages and its appropriation could be more of a deliberately calculated process. Many castles reused antecedent structures with clear defensive potential, perhaps as an expedient way of rapidly raising a fortification that minimized the cost of labour and other resources. This type of pragmatism is reflected most obviously by the adaptation of extant town defences to define the perimeters of urban castles, as at Gloucester, London and elsewhere, and the adaptation of iron-age hillforts as vast bailey enclosures, as at Almondbury (West Yorkshire) (see Chapter 3). An even more remarkable example of this type of continuity is the refurbishment of

Silchester's decayed Roman amphitheatre through the addition of a timber revetment and palisade to form a pre-positioned ringwork (Fulford 1985: 77–8).

At times, we may suspect that a prehistoric barrow has been reused to form a conveniently placed ready-made motte, as at Brinklow (Warwickshire) – noticeably containing the Old English place-name element *hlāw* ('mound/ burial mound') (Gelling 1978: 134–5). A derivation of the same element may indicate that the enormous Norman motte at Marlborough, Wiltshire ('barrow of Maela') was formed from a similar feature (Gover *et al.* 1939: 298). The motte of Canterbury's first castle was unusually constructed by remodelling a substantial Roman burial mound (Lyle 1994: 57–8), while excavation at Driffield (East Yorkshire) has shown this motte originated as an early medieval sepulchral mound (Eddy 1983: 40). An altogether different type of barrow reuse is evident at Edburton (West Sussex). Here a small undocumented earth and timber castle ('Castle Ring') perched high on an extremely steep scarp of the South Downs and unusually remote from population, agricultural resources and water supply, incorporates two small barrows within the line of its bailey rampart. The intervisibility of this particular point in the landscape with the surrounding district presumably marked it out as a suitable location for a short-term fortification, just as it had provided an attractive site for the prehistoric barrow builders. Elsewhere, the incorporation of prehistoric funerary monuments within castle earthworks probably results from pure coincidence, the site being selected for alternative reasons – as at York, where early excavations showed the motte on the site known as Clifford's Tower to seal a small cist burial (Renn 1968, 351). But potential confusion also exists in the respective identification of mottes and burial mounds as field monuments, particularly barrows of Roman or Saxon date, whose size relative to prehistoric burial mounds makes them more motte-like in appearance. For instance, the large mound known as Ailcy Hill near Ripon Cathedral, while often listed in the past as a Norman motte, has now clearly been shown to be a natural glacial mound adapted as a cemetery in the early medieval period (Hall and Whyman 1996: 65–7).

Elsewhere, castles undoubtedly re-occupied sites imbued with regal, high-status or religious connotations in contemporary minds, none more dramatically than William I's palace-keep raised on the podium of the Claudian temple at Colchester (Essex) (see Chapter 7). This mode of reuse may have been particularly characteristic of the castles of the Norman Conquest and is essential in understanding something of the impact of castle-building on the late Saxon landscape. On the one hand, the Norman appropriation of élite Saxon sites represented high-status continuity, yet on the other hand was a statement of conquest to a wider audience. There is a rapidly expanding corpus of archaeological evidence showing Norman castles to have developed from late Saxon élite defended residences. Examples include Goltho, Lincolnshire (Beresford 1987); Portchester, Hampshire (Cunliffe 1976); Middleton Stoney, Oxfordshire (Rahtz and Rowley 1984); Stamford, Lincolnshire (Mahany 1977); Sulgrave, Northamptonshire (Davison 1977); and Trowbridge, Wiltshire (Graham and Davies 1993); and, less certainly, Eynsford, Kent; Castle Neroche, Somerset; Castle Bromwich, West Midlands; and Chalgrave, Bedfordshire (Higham and Barker 1992: 49–57).

The social and legal contexts of these high-status Saxon residences, many of

Figure 4.1 The medieval donjon at Warkworth, raised on an earlier motte (photograph: Oliver Creighton).

which were closely associated with small proprietary churches and probably the seats of Saxon thegns, is now better understood (Renn 1993; A. Williams 1992). Saxon thegns tended to have expansive residences, and their appropriation by new Norman landlords often meant their remodelling as more compact, heavily defended and visually imposing units that presumably had a strong local psychological impact, especially where a new motte towered over the tenants (Hinton 1990: 110). We must remain aware, however, that our sample of adequately excavated sites is tiny, even if fieldwork and scrutiny of other topographical and documentary evidence throws up countless examples where it seems likely that a Norman castle was preceded by a Saxon manor. Nonetheless, even where excavated evidence has revealed high status antecedent occupation, this need not constitute imposition in the true sense, with the implication of the assertion of coercive power and possibly violence and displacement. First, it is not always clear that occupation continued directly up to the point of castle foundation. Second, a sequence that may outwardly appear to represent martial imposition could inwardly reflect manorial continuity.

We should also be careful not to neglect that the builders of many later medieval castles sought to make propaganda from the past, both by perpetuating recognized high-status sites and through the aestheticization of military architecture. Indeed, the simple fact that many castles were rebuilt and continuously modified through the medieval period is, in itself, a reflection that they represented the perpetuity of lordship. The famous mid-fifteenth-century keep at Warkworth (Northumberland) (Fig. 4.1) can be interpreted in precisely this way. Conspicuously raised on a motte – by this time an archaic feature of the skyline more than 300 years old – the very siting of the keep symbolizes both the ancestry and identity of the Percy earls of

Northumberland (Johnson 1999: 75–7). Moreover, the great heraldic stamp of the Percy lion, forming the centrepiece of the keep's north elevation, faces outwards to loom above the town that was planned in an axial arrangement with the seigneurial site.

The structural development of Lydford Castle (Devon) (Fig. 3.12) is likewise informative. The present appearance of the site – a square tower apparently built upon a motte – is misleading, and conceals a more complex sequence. Excavation and structural survey reveal the earthwork as a late thirteenth-century addition at the same time as an earlier free-standing prison was partially demolished and the upper parts rebuilt more elaborately (Saunders 1980). The addition of a rock-cut ditch and miniature bailey completed the martial appearance of the site, although such renovations made little military sense in the context of late medieval Dartmoor. Furthermore, documentary evidence indicates that the site fulfilled a dual rôle as the administrative and judicial centre for the Forest of Dartmoor and the Devon Stannaries and, as such, as the venue for courts and a gaol, rather than a principally military site. The excavator has thus described the rebuilding programme as a deliberate and anachronistic conceit designed to express the lordship of its owner, Richard, Earl of Cornwall, clearly showing the symbolic associations of the castle with the concepts of lordship and justice (Saunders 1980: 162).

Even more intriguing was Richard's association with Tintagel and its glamorous past. Tintagel Castle can be regarded as a thirteenth-century folly, although built on the site of remarkable Dark Age activity. Geoffrey of Monmouth's famous mid-twelfth-century *History of the Kings of Britain*, in celebrating a link between Tintagel and Arthurian legend, clearly imbued the headland with a sense of grandeur and so established its regal connections in the minds of contemporaries (Doel *et al.* 1998: 95; Trezise 2000: 63–4). Tintagel's contemporary fame was also reflected in medieval romances, such as the story of Tristan and Iseult, as well, no doubt, in Cornish folklore. Shortly after being created Earl of Cornwall in 1227, Richard purchased the headland and obtained through exchange the surrounding manor of Bossiney from Gervase de Tintagel (Padel 1988: 64). This acquisition effectively allowed the earl to appropriate and exploit Tintagel's famed past through the physical act of castle-building, despite the site's absolute lack of military or other strategic significance.

Landscapes of pleasure and display

Study of the physical remains of parks and gardens, driven largely by the fieldwork of the Royal Commissions is one of the fastest growing branches of modern British archaeology (Taylor 1983a, 1996, 1998; Brown 1991; Everson and Williamson 1998). A by-product of this upsurge in interest has been the growing recognition that medieval landscapes could be created and manipulated for aesthetic reasons, in a manner essentially similar to our far better documented post-medieval parks and gardens. The most fruitful of these studies have combined the results of field survey with analysis of documents concerning the social context of medieval gardens as status symbols often loaded with romantic, religious and chivalric imagery (Everson 1998; Taylor 2000).

The majority of these medieval designed landscapes were physically associated with status buildings, including royal palaces, episcopal and archiepiscopal residences and important manorial sites, as well as castles. The number of these 'ornamental landscapes' known to have been associated with castles is growing rapidly as fieldworkers become increasingly aware of the ubiquity of earthworks and other physical traces left by garden features that have often been previously ignored or misidentified as defensive outworks, fishponds or even settlements. An ornamental setting provided not only recreational and aesthetic benefits but also proclaimed the social status and awareness of contemporary fashions of their aristocratic occupants. A consistently striking feature is the overall integrity of large-scale designs that very deliberately embedded buildings within contrived surroundings. Many were designed to provide a backdrop that visually enhanced the residential building, which formed a focal point. But, conversely, buildings could also provide places from which their surroundings could be admired, although other vantage points, such as elevated viewing platforms could also be incorporated in designs. These considerations underline that it is as wrong to study élite buildings such as these in isolation from their designed settings as it is to study the landscapes but ignore the buildings. In this sense considerable common ground clearly exists between castle studies and garden archaeology, with immense potential for future collaboration.

Castle gardens

The environs of a castle site could be designed for aesthetic reasons at two key scales: through the creation of small-scale enclosed gardens (the classic *hortus conclusus* type) in the immediate vicinity; or through large-scale redevelopment, typically including artificial water features, enclosed pleasure grounds and deer parks. There is, however, no rigid division between these two types of designed landscape; indeed, many schemes incorporated both, with small formal gardens lying adjacent to the castle but also projecting into and nested within a parkland setting. It is precisely this arrangement that is reflected in John Norden's picture map of Windsor Castle dated 1607, showing an enclosed garden and associated orchard lying beyond the castle's defences at the end of the Little Park (Taylor 1998b: 20). There is also a somewhat hazy division between medieval ornamental landscapes and deer parks. Many studies have created a false dichotomy between medieval parks and their supposed practical functions and post-medieval parks and their aesthetic functions. Private medieval parks must, to a certain extent, have had certain pleasing aesthetic qualities as well as being venues for aristocratic entertainment and a means of economic exploitation (see Chapter 8), and in many cases we may suspect that deer parks were designed to complement and complete a designed setting. We may well under appreciate the number of deer parks that were designed primarily as pleasure parks, containing, for instance, grandstands, pavilions and tilting yards, as occasionally indicated by place-name evidence or earthworks.

The small-scale enclosed medieval garden, commonly referred to in documentary sources as the *herbarium*, was usually square or rectangular in plan and enclosed by a hedge or wall, as often illustrated in manuscript pictures on the continent but less so in Britain. The interior typically comprised regularly or geometrically arranged areas of turf, raised beds of herbs, flowers or shrubs, and, occasionally, pathways (Landsberg 1996: 11–48). Although this type of medieval garden had utilitarian as well as aesthetic functions, those associated with castles must have also been designed largely as objects of pleasure rather than a means of supplying the kitchens with herbs. While enclosed gardens may have taken their inspiration, in part, from the monastic cloister, they were certainly not as common in castle baileys as they were in monastic precincts. Whereas medieval monastic communities sought, at least in principle, a degree of self-sufficiency, castle owners (perhaps only in occasional residence) and their retinues will have relied more heavily on renders and produce from surrounding estates.

The enclosed medieval garden's place in castle designs, was usually, like the vineyard and orchard, as a plot within or immediately beyond the bailey. Occasionally, castle gardens could form cloister-like spaces around which suites of residential apartments were planned, with chamber windows commonly looking out onto them, as with Henry II's garden at Arundel. The account rolls of Henry III suggest that Windsor Castle possessed at least two gardens. The King's garden lay beyond the walls and was surrounded with a ditch and hedge, while the King's herb garden formed an open space between the chapel and ranges of residential buildings, onto which the newly installed opening glazed windows in the Queen's chamber faced (McLean 1981: 94–5). Built entirely within the more secluded setting of the royal deer park, the castle garden at Odiham (Hampshire) was rather different. In 1332 the garden was extensively remodelled for Queen Philippa, when a boarding fence with five doors was added and other features described, including benches protected by turf roofs and a garderobe screened by a hedge (Harvey 1981: 87; MacGregor 1983: 102). Royal expenditure on enclosed castle gardens, including their construction and renovation, and the payment of gardeners, is also recorded at Gloucester, Nottingham and Winchester, among others (Brown *et al.* 1963). Even Edward I's newly built castles at Conway and Rhuddlan contained gardens for Queen Eleanor, for which great quantities of turves were transported by river at significant expense (Taylor 1998b: 24).

Despite a wide range of documentary evidence for castle gardens of this type, their physical survival is actually quite rare. A particularly good example is the walled garden at Tintagel Castle (Fig. 4.2). Excavated by Radford in 1935–36 and restored shortly after, the quadrilateral garden, measuring *c.* 20 × 14 m, in all probability dates to the castle's principal thirteenth-century phase. The garden is contained within the main castle complex, but clearly placed with consideration for its wider context on the dramatic headland. The formal and intimate enclosure provided an enchanting contrast to its otherwise wild natural setting, and its close juxtaposition with the chapel may have been a deliberate attempt to re-create a literary landscape that contained powerful and evocative references to popular medieval romances (Rose 1994: 176–9).

Figure 4.2 Enclosed medieval garden within Tintagel Castle (Cornwall) (photograph: Oliver Creighton).

Ornamental landscapes

At an entirely different scale, a series of important studies during the 1980s and 1990s have suggested that the entire settings of castles could be purpose-fully manipulated through the creation of vast and ostentatious water features and the planning of walkways, terraces and artificial observation platforms. Among the first of this type of designed landscape to be recognized were those associated with the episcopal palaces of Somersham (Cambridgeshire), where a 14-acre garden complete with terraced walks and moats formed an orna-mental landscape in which the village was re-located, and Stow (Lincolnshire) (Taylor 1989). The realization that comparable schemes could have been designed around castles has been prompted principally by radical revisionist studies of Sir Edward Dalyngrigge's castle of Bodiam (East Sussex), licensed in 1386, and with a place in many minds as the quintessential 'picture book castle'. Our understanding of the site has been revolutionized by two impor-tant contributions that have complemented one another and opened up entirely new ways of understanding the settings of élite medieval buildings. First, analysis of the standing structure, coupled with a re-assessment of the documentary evidence, has suggested that the castle was an 'old soldier's dream home' as opposed to a military installation in any real sense, and certainly not the bulwark against French raiding that is suggested by a superficial reading of the licence (Coulson 1990, 1992). Second, a survey of the complex earthworks surrounding the site by the RCHME in 1988 (Taylor *et al.* 1990; Everson 1996a, 1996b) has shed light on the sheer scale at which a castle's setting could be designed for aesthetic effect. The castle lay at the heart of a series of shallow lakes constituting a carefully contrived ornamental landscape through which visitors could be steered via a circuitous route in order to present the structure, which on approach appeared to suddenly rise above its surrounding moat, from the most favourable of angles (Fig. 4.3). Furthermore, an earthwork known as the 'Gun Garden' on the crest of the ridge 300 m north of the castle has been interpreted as a viewing platform from which the castle could be observed, visually enhanced by its fantastic setting (Fig. 4.4). What makes the designed setting of Bodiam especially remarkable is its intactness, due, in part, to the abandonment of the castle as a principal residence at a relatively early date. Earthworks in the vicinity of the Kentish castles of Coldbridge (licensed 1314) and Cooling (licensed 1381) bear some comparison to Bodiam's, although in neither case are conditions of preservation nearly as favourable. A later site with comparable evidence is Bronsil (Herefordshire) (1460), a quadrangular castle surrounded by a double moat with an intervening flat terrace that seems to have carried a walkway. Nonetheless, the intensity of research carried out at the fascinating site of Bodiam has made it seem almost unique. Indeed, so ambitious was this scheme of medieval landscape design, and at such a scale, that it requires a change of perception to acknowledge that it is, in essence, another form of medieval garden.

Kenilworth Castle (Warwickshire) has perhaps the most sophisticated system of water features found at any castle in England, and among the most extensive of any medieval site in Britain. In essence, the system comprised a suite of ponds formed by constructing a series of dams across a shallow valley draining from west to east, including several associated with the nearby priory (Fig. 4.5). The principal feature was the Great Mere, a vast artificial lake over 40 hectares in area, fed by the Inchford Brook and held back by a large earthen dam (the 'Tiltyard') that also served as a causeway providing access to the castle's inner and outer courts (Fig. 6.12). A section excavated through the causeway revealed evidence of an earlier dam, suggesting the level of the mere had been raised by over 3 metres, and its area greatly increased, either in the reign of King John or Henry III (Thompson 1965: 160–1). On the south side of the Tiltyard lay a crescentic outwork (the 'Brays') around which a mill-race ran, feeding two of the castle's three mills. Immediately downstream lay another dam holding back the smaller, rectangular, Lower Pool, while further to the north-east additional dams indicate the presence of at least another five pools, including the Abbey Pool and Bakehouse Pool (Drew 1963). A later addition to the system was 'the Pleasance in the Marsh' – an isolated banqueting house containing a hall and chambers constructed on waste ground at the north-west extremity of the Great Mere by Henry V, probably in 1414 (Brown *et al.* 1963: 684–5). This feature survives as a rectangular double-moated earthwork with evidence of corner turrets and possibly flower beds. It also contained a miniature harbour that linked it to the mere via a short canal, and was clearly intended to be accessed principally by water, perhaps from the west side of the castle, where a postern known as the King's Gate provided access to another small dock (Thompson 1964). That the Pleasance was situated at a point visually removed from the castle must have further added to its qualities as a place for secluded entertainment.

While Kenilworth castle formed the centrepiece within a fantastic water-scape, the surrounding water-management system also served a number of

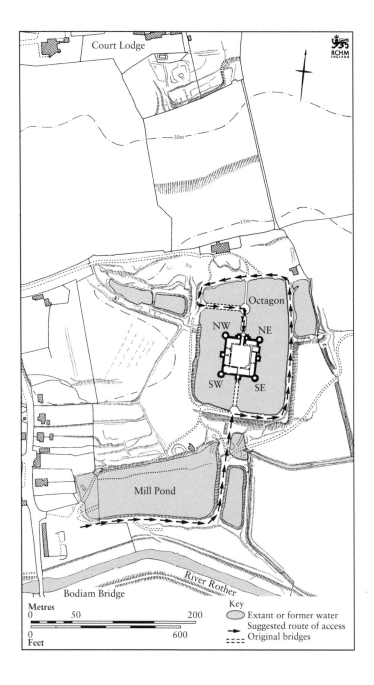

Court Lodge

30m

15m

Octagon

NW   NE

SW   SE

Mill Pond

River Rother

Bodiam Bridge

Metres
0   50   200

0   600
Feet

Key

⬭ Extant or former water
⇢ Suggested route of access
- - - - Original bridges

Figure 4.3 Plan of Bodiam Castle (East Sussex) and surrounding earthworks, showing the circuitous approach route to the castle through a complex series of water features. North of the castle can be identified the earthworks of a medieval viewing platform from which the designed landscape could be admired (© Crown copyright NMR).

Figure 4.4 Bodiam Castle (East Sussex) and its setting, as seen from the medieval viewing platform north of the castle (photograph: Oliver Creighton).

Figure 4.5 Kenilworth Castle (Warwickshire), viewed from the south-west across the area of the artificial mere drained in the mid seventeenth century (photograph: Oliver Creighton).

more utilitarian needs in a remarkably integrated manner. A substantial pool containing fish was certainly in existence in the early twelfth century, when a charter granted to the priory by the castle founder, Geoffrey de Clinton, permitted the canons to fish with 'boats and nets' on Thursdays (Aston and Bond 1988: 422). A stream flowing into the Abbey Pool also fed a large suite of fishponds, perhaps related to fish breeding. While large expanses of water clearly had an aesthetic appeal in their own right, with the castle splendidly reflected in the mere to anyone approaching, the fish and even swans that water features such as these supported could imbue the landscape with additional religious and romantic imagery that we remain little aware of (Everson 1988: 32–3).

At Hereford Castle the inhabitants had the luxury of a large detached water garden and orchard amidst the meadows on the opposite bank of the Wye. The earthwork in this area, known as Row Ditch and sometimes thought to be defensive in nature, may well have been built to enclose the gardens, which were conveniently situated along the route linking the castle and the Royal Forest of Heywood (Shoesmith 1982: 19). A similarly detached but smaller pleasance associated with Gloucester Castle occupied a small island within the Severn known as 'Naight' (Harvey 1981: 86).

Ravensworth Castle (North Yorkshire) (Fig. 4.6) is another site formerly set within a large artificial lake (now a marshy depression) whose function may have been largely ornamental (Ryder 1979: 97–9). Aerial views demonstrate the earthen causeway linking the castle to the village green to have been flanked by the terraces and enclosures of a small formal garden. A substantial deer park, in existence by the fourteenth century and occupying the slopes on the opposite side of the castle, provided a scenic backdrop that completed a carefully designed landscape. Extensive water gardens have also been recognized below the motte at Kilpeck (Herefordshire) (Fig. 7.14: centre), where an artificial lake retained by an earthwork dam formed part of an ornamental setting incorporating an enclosed orchard and elevated walkway (Whitehead 1995: 199–200). Clun (Shropshire) is another castle where adjacent low-lying water meadows contain ornamental garden features (Remfry 1994: 19). Some of the many other castles associated with substantial artificial meres or suites of ponds with an ornamental aspect include Framlingham (Suffolk), where the vestiges of two former lakes and an associated wharf can be traced; and Bredwardine (Herefordshire), where the castle overlooked a complex of fishponds, orchards and a small lake from a platform above the Wye; in addition to Sauvey (Leicestershire), Shotwick (Cheshire), Whittington (Shropshire) and Whorlton (North Yorkshire) (Fig. 4.7).

Elsewhere it can be both difficult and hazardous to disentangle the physical vestiges of medieval ornamental landscapes from episodes of post-medieval remodelling. For instance, sixteenth- and seventeenth-century formal gardens that may well overlie earlier arrangements such as the 0.4 hectare enclosed garden known as 'The Wilderness' at Ashby-de-la-Zouch (Leicestershire) (Jones 1985: 13). Although the present landscape around Leeds Castle (Kent) has the appearance of an eighteenth-century landscape park, the setting of this royal castle seems to have been carefully designed from at least the late thirteenth century, when Edward I had built a detached gloriette (Brown *et al.* 1963: 695–702). This feature overlooked a suite of artificial lakes and ponds

Figure 4.6 Aerial view of Ravensworth (North Yorkshire). In the centre of the photograph, immediately below the castle, lie the earthworks of a small formal garden. The castle lay within a shallow artificial lake visible as a depression (Cambridge University Collection of Air Photographs: copyright reserved).

set within a deer park, while a viewing platform may have provided another place from which the entire ensemble could be admired.

Many of these examples raise the intriguing question of whether the physical sites of castles could have been selected with an eye for natural aesthetic qualities and their potential for re-design. In other cases, castles were physically transplanted from naturally defensible positions to more convenient and expansive sites. This was certainly the case at Old Bolingbroke (Lincolnshire), where an earlier hill-top fortification was abandoned in favour of a moated hexagonal castle of stone built in a low-lying position merely 400 m distant (Fig. 4.8). The remarkable and extensive suite of earthworks associated with the castle indicate the presence of a large enclosed water garden, now criss-crossed by modern drainage ditches and disrupted by the insertion of a pond for stock in what was later known as the 'Rout Yard' (animal pound). In North Yorkshire early Norman castles at Middleham and

Figure 4.7 The ditch in front of Whorlton Castle (North Yorkshire). Rather than representing a defensive feature, this large flat-bottomed depression is probably an ornamental water feature that was part of a deliberately designed landscape around the castle (photograph: Oliver Creighton).

Sheriff Hutton, both sited on natural eminences, were similarly replaced by masonry castles on flatter sites, both surrounded by large moated precincts.

While aerial photographic analysis is an essential tool for the recognition of ornamental landscapes associated with castles, we must always bear in mind that oblique aerial views provide a perspective that would have been entirely alien to the medieval mind. This is not to say, however, that the physical fabric of castles did not provide opportunities for viewing their surroundings. At the simplest level, the geometric designs of medieval enclosed gardens could be appreciated from overlooking towers and domestic buildings. Elsewhere we may speculate as to whether windows in elevated structures were positioned to enable occupants to appreciate panoramic views from window seats. A clear example is Kenilworth (Warwickshire), where the enormous artificial mere created in the thirteenth century was clearly visible from John of Gaunt's remarkable first-floor hall. The elaborate suite of garden features at Stokesay (Shropshire) (Fig. 4.9), including a substantial artificial lake and associated suites of ponds, seems also to have been laid out to be viewed from the windows of the late-thirteenth-century tower (Taylor 1998a: 5). The terraced gardens beneath the mid-fifteenth-century keep at Stafford are other features that seem to have been created to be observed from above, against the backdrop of a deer park (Fig. 2.2). The cylindrical, two-storey great tower inserted into the shell keep at Launceston (Cornwall) may have been another structure designed for similar reasons. The building was sufficiently restricted to have few other practical functions but enjoyed spectacular views over surrounding parkland and completed a remarkable and particularly con-spicuous three-tiered design that proclaimed lordship over the surrounding

Figure 4.8 Aerial view of Old Bolingbroke (Lincolnshire). In the centre of the photograph lies the early-thirteenth-century hexagonal castle, adjoined by an enclosure that preserves the earthworks of ponds and ornamental water features linked to the site's moated defences, although disrupted by drainage ditches and other later features. This enclosure was later used as an pound for stray stock rounded up from the surrounding commons, and the large rectangular feature seems to be a related watering pond. To the north (left of the photograph) lies the parish church, overlooked by the earlier fortification of Dewy Hill (off photograph). To the east (in the background) lies a separate unit of settlement focused on a medieval marketplace now partially in-filled by housing development (Cambridge University Collection of Air Photographs: copyright reserved.)

countryside (Fig. 7.13). Other late-medieval towers or keeps may have even featured roof-top walkways. Sir William Aldeburgh's rebuilding of Harewood Castle (West Yorkshire) in 1367 probably incorporated such a feature, as may the early fifteenth-century modernization of Middleham Castle (North Yorkshire) (Taylor 2000: 42–3).

Another site of particular interest in this regard is the royal castle and hunting lodge of Ludgershall (Wiltshire). Situated near the dense belt of royal forest along the Hampshire/Wiltshire border, the site was developed from the

Figure 4.9 Stokesay (Shropshire). More a defended manor house that a castle, this picturesque residence was accompanied by a designed landscape that incorporated an artificial lake and other water features as well as an orchard (photograph: Oliver Creighton).

twelfth to the fourteenth century as a sophisticated royal residence designed increasingly for comfort and privacy. Indeed, plan analysis of the adjacent medieval borough suggests that a large banked and ditched enclosure was appended to the castle and superimposed over part of an earlier settlement in the mid-fourteenth century in an extension of the king's park (Everson *et al.* 2000: 109–12). This sequence marks a notable contrast to the situation in many other later medieval castle-towns where urban property encroached onto the castle rather than vice versa (see Chapter 7). Also significant is the interpretation of part of the large, flat-topped outer bank of the site's northern enclosure not as a rampart but as a garden walk accessible directly from the royal lodgings (Fig. 4.10), and from which staged activities in the surrounding park could be observed (Everson *et al.* 2000: 101–3). The marked difference between this site and other medieval ornamental landscapes is that it lacked the large-scale manipulation of water for aesthetic effect. Comparable examples doubtless remain to be recognized, although potential candidates include Restormel (Cornwall), where the flat-topped profile of the outer bank again suggests remodelling as a garden walk.

Nonetheless, the study of medieval ornamental landscapes is still in its infancy, and some major challenges exist in recognizing and interpreting those associated with castles. Most fundamentally, it is often intensely difficult to date the creation of a designed landscape and link its chronological development to the structural and ownership history of the castle. In many cases documents are uninformative about garden features, or provide only incidental references, while future excavation is likely to be unrewarding. The

Figure 4.10 Part of the earthworks associated with Ludgershall Castle (Wiltshire), showing the flat-topped outer bank that is probably a garden walkway or viewing platform from which activities in the adjacent park could be seen (photograph: Oliver Creighton).

identification of designed landscapes associated with sites such as these has, however, highlighted some new ways of looking at castles and opened up many exciting avenues for future research.

In particular, three important questions remained to be answered concerning these landscapes of pleasure designed around castles. First, and perhaps most importantly, how far back in time we can push the notion that castles could be associated with landscapes designed for pleasure? Without supporting documentation, it is difficult to see how gardens and related features can be dated, nor how the concept diffused through the social hierarchy. Second, these foregoing observations raise interesting questions regarding the extent to which aesthetic considerations influenced original decisions of site. Third, our present data set is limited, and we remain unsure as to how widespread the phenomenon was. It is only due to exceptional conditions of preservation that formal gardens and pleasure grounds can be identified and surveyed. We may only speculate as to how many other sites were associated with contemporary designed landscapes that have been obliterated by agricultural or building development, or else re-fashioned as landscape parks in the post-medieval period. But while it is fascinating to try and imagine how contemporaries would have perceived medieval castles, it is currently difficult to see how future archaeological research can contribute.

Post-medieval designed landscapes

Given the proportion of castle sites where high-status occupation continued into the post-medieval period, it is certain that many medieval designed landscapes have been destroyed by later phases of remodelling, particularly by the eighteenth-century fashion for landscape parks. The picturesque movement saw something of a fashion for exhibiting dilapidated castles, as well as other medieval ruins such as abbeys, in landscapes designed around gentry houses, as exemplified in Humphry Repton's scheme of 1792 for Mulgrave Castle (North Yorkshire) (Bowden 1998: 25). The eighteenth-century cult of ruins sometimes meant that abandoned castles could be themselves be remodelled and romanticized to create the broken, soft silhouettes and decayed, rough appearance suited to contemporary tastes, while simultaneously casting medieval glamour on the families who owned them. Often forming the foci of carefully designed vistas, these re-invented castles acted as touchstones to an idealized medieval past. For example, Sir John Vanbrugh's original design for the landscape around the new Palladian mansion of Castle Howard (North Yorkshire) deliberately drew attention to the ruins of its predecessor, Henderskelfe Castle, partially destroyed by fire in 1693 (Hunt 1992: 22–4). Vanbrugh's involvement in the dramatic remodelling of other castles including Kimbolton (Huntingdonshire) and Grimsthorpe (Lincolnshire), as well as the theatrical rebuilding of Bolsover (Derbyshire) by Smythson and others, embodied a similar desire to give a castle-like 'gothick' appearance to country houses.

At Old Wardour (Wiltshire) (Fig. 4.11), the outer ward of an unusual late-fourteenth-century hexagonal castle was laid out as a garden and its surroundings landscaped in the picturesque style by Lancelot 'Capability' Brown to enliven the scenery around New Wardour Castle, built between 1769 and 1776 (Keen 1967: 69). The ruined walls of Harewood Castle (West Yorkshire) were repaired and reinforced in iron when it became a focal point in the designed nineteenth-century landscape of Harewood Park, although the earthworks of a small symmetrical fourteenth-century garden laid out in conjunction with the medieval castle survive (Moorhouse 1986; Gaimster *et al.* 1990: 222–3). The eighteenth-century remodelling of Dunster Castle (Somerset) and its environs for Henry Fownes Luttrell included the erection of a ruin, Conygar Tower, that was visible from the castle, some of whose towers were reconstructed as follies, while newly-erected bridges, around the castle added to the mock medieval ambience (Riley and Wilson-North 2001: 135).

While the incorporation of medieval castle ruins into later designed landscapes is relatively well known, less widely recognized is the remodelling of mottes, ringworks and associated earthworks as garden features. Recent fieldwork, especially detailed regional surveys by the RCHME in Northamptonshire (1975–84, vol. II: lxiv) and Lincolnshire (Everson *et al.* 1991: 54), is only now beginning to show how common – and how little understood – abandoned garden earthworks are. Perhaps most common of all is the transformation of mottes into prospect mounds. The proportions of these often immense medieval earthworks (making their removal a considerable task) combined with their typical location at points in the landscape enjoying excellent visibility, meant that this type of re-use is surprisingly common.

Figure 4.11 Old Wardour Castle (Wiltshire). The broken silhouette of John, Lord Lovell's ruinous late-fourteenth-century castle with its unique hexagonal plan was remodelled within the context of the eighteenth-century designed landscape around the gentry house of New Wardour Castle. Elements of the parkland landscape, such as the ornamental lake, may, however, have medieval origins (photograph: Oliver Creighton).

Winding spiral pathways or 'screw walks' were cut into the flanks of many mottes, as at Hamstead Marshall (Dorset) (Keevill and Linford 1998: 14). Another particularly clear example of this process is the immense motte at Marlborough (Wiltshire), which formed an imposing feature in the corner of a seventeenth-century formal garden later incorporated into the grounds of Marlborough College (Field *et al.* 2001). Similar examples of mottes with later spiral walkways include Dunham Massey (Cheshire) and Holdgate (Shropshire), while others were terraced back severely to give an artificial stepped appearance on one side, as at Egmanton (Nottinghamshire) and Topcliffe (North Yorkshire). The gardens and orchards around the great quadrangular castle of Wressle (East Yorkshire) as observed by Leland in the 1530s contained two substantial prospect mounds with terraced spiral walks that were apparently part of a post-medieval remodelling of the castle environs (Toulin Smith 1907: 53). But not all terraces cut into castle earthworks were necessarily associated with formal gardens. At Beeston Castle (Cheshire) two large rectangular terraces in the outer ward are thought to be platforms for temporary tents used during the nineteenth-century Bunbury Temperance Fairs, as indicated by the presence of stone-set iron rings detected during geophysical survey (Ellis 1993: 2:E3-9).

Structures such as pavilions, summer houses and belvederes were also occasionally added to the summits of mottes, as at Groby (Leicestershire), where the castle was remodelled as a landscaped feature in the grounds of Groby Old Hall (Woodward 1984). Exceptionally, mottes were cut down and

Figure 4.12 Medieval motte at Laxton (Nottinghamshire). The smaller mound on the flat summit of the motte is likely to be an observation platform that post-dates the castle's military phases (photograph: Oliver Creighton).

their ditches partially filled in to form level earthen platforms that served as bowling greens, as is documented as Dunster (Somerset), Leicester and West Dean (Wiltshire). Of course, a considerable danger exists that this type of post-medieval adaptation can easily be taken as evidence of a site's original appearance. For instance, a small rounded mound on the summit of the motte at Laxton (Fig. 4.12), often interpreted as the base of a tower, can more confidently be identified as a prospect mound associated with a later manor house that occupied part of the bailey (Speight 1994: 61). The earthworks of other early castles have been remodelled in more complex ways still. The motte and bailey at Aughton (East Yorkshire) was adapted first as a moated manor and later as a garden feature, with the motte converted into a squared and terraced prospect mound and a brick-faced ha-ha later inserted into the bailey rampart (Le Patourel 1973: 18, 109; Loughlin and Miller 1979: 41). At Aslockton (Nottinghamshire), a motte was again scarped to give it a square plan, and the bailey modified as a series of ornamental ponds to form 'pleasure grounds' (Chalkley Gould 1907: 60–1). All these examples serve to show an active, ongoing negotiation of the landscape as social structures, fashions and perceptions evolved.

Summary

This chapter has illustrated that the physical appearance of castles, as conspicuously élite structures, influenced the ways in which contemporaries experienced the landscapes around them and, moreover, that their surroundings could be manipulated for aesthetic effect. While the clearest examples of designed landscapes created around castles date from the later medieval period, we should be aware that the planning of deer parks, settlements and roads around Norman castles could also create landscapes with very deliberate connotations of status as well as other functions. While one challenge for the future is to identify other castles of all dates associated with designed ornamental landscapes, another is to ensure that the pendulum does not swing too far towards the social interpretation of such features and deny or misinterpret more utilitarian explanations. Another recurring theme is that the iconic status of the castle was enhanced by the fact that so many occupied sites of prior significance, with episodes of rebuilding symbolizing the continuity of power and lordship.

5 The Castle as Estate Centre: Tenurial Landscapes

Castle and land, and in particular the key resources of human population and agricultural production, went hand in hand. Control, if not outright ownership, of land was, if nothing else, a necessary pre-requisite for castle-building, so that character of landholding was always an important factor that influenced the circumstances of castle siting. Any individual castle was suspended within a web of tenurial relationships and ultimately part of a hierarchy of other castle sites ranging in function from instruments of royal authority to minor fortifications built to secure the estates of petty sub-tenants. As central places within the medieval landscape, castles were also usually the focus of surrounding networks of estates rendering rents, taxation, services and produce, and most were simultaneously manors. Castles were thus invariably sited with reference to a pre-existing pattern of land ownership, but, once founded, the seigneurial presence could have a marked impact on tenurial geography. For example, holdings in the surrounding territory could be acquired, sold or exchanged in order to mould the pattern of surrounding estates relative to the physical position of the *caput*. The status of castles as estate centres has, however, often remained understated. These administrative functions may seem mundane relative to the rôles played by castles during wartime, yet are absolutely essential if we are to develop a mature understanding of the castle.

Castles and land tenure

Interesting patterns of variation are apparent in the relationship between castles and lordships. At a very simple level, two distinct patterns of landholding can be identified in England after the Norman Conquest: those large and valuable but compact blocks of land under unified lordship known variously as earldoms, honours, palatinates or rapes; and scattered patterns of mixed estates under independent feudal control. What is important here is that the size and integrity of these fees had a profound influence on the decisions of castle siting. In smaller lordships, the topographical choice of castle site may reflect compromise between various military, domestic and economic requirements. Yet in spatially extensive lordships a wide range of potential sites could present themselves, while different castles could be built for different purposes, through the delegation of military and administrative authority to tenants or estate officials.

We must also remember that while most castles were related to units of lordship, the converse was not necessarily true: many fees could be, and often were, administered perfectly effectively without the presence of a castle. Certain types of lordship certainly tended to preclude or limit castle-building;

most notably, castles are extremely rare, if not absent, on church land, while a
fee had to be sufficiently large or valuable for the lord to muster sufficient
resources to support the construction and maintenance of a castle. A multitude
of social and tenurial factors thus meant that not all lords able to do so created
strongholds within their estates. For instance, of a total of fifteen
Northumbrian baronies, while eight contained castles before 1189, seven did
not (Hunter-Blair l944: 119).

Here we must make an important distinction: castle-building was, in the
overwhelming majority of cases, carried out subsequent to the receipt of land
rather than vice versa, although occasionally the processes of land acquisition
and castle foundation may be sufficiently linked for the events to have
occurred almost simultaneously. Evidence of the converse process – i.e. castle-
building foreshadowing land seizure – is comparatively rare, although the
systematic programme of royal castle-building in late-Saxon urban centres
probably embodied similar motives (see Chapter 7). In addition, siege-works
and other impermanent castles of war must have been constructed in the
absence of any tenurial rights to the site. The first wave of post-Conquest
castle-building by Norman tenants-in-chief and under-tenants was principally
a process of consolidating, legitimizing and expressing symbolically existing
territorial claims, as opposed to a military spearhead pre-empting and
enabling secondary confiscation of estates. Very occasionally, documentary
sources provide direct evidence that a manor was obtained specifically for the
reason of castle-building, whether through purchase, exchange or coercion.
The site of the royal castle of Odiham (Hampshire) was obtained when John
dispossessed his tenant, Robert the Parker, of 20 acres of meadow and
destroyed his mills, as a result of which his rent was reduced to 1d (Mac
Gregor 1983: 22). Corfe (Dorset) was built on its prime site only after the
Crown exchanged property in Gillingham with the nunnery of Shaftesbury (as
recorded in Domesday Book) in order to obtain the manor within which the
castle was raised (Armitage 1912: 135). Similar transactions are known to
have preceded the construction of royal and baronial castles including Lewes
(East Sussex), Montacute (Somerset), Warwick and Windsor (Pounds 1990:
57, 68).

Another important way in which a castle and its dependent estates might be
bound together was through the arrangements that could be made for the
garrisoning of the fortress. Castle-guard was a specialized form of feudal
tenure through which particular tenants settled on outlying estates were
obliged to periodically contribute to a castle's defence and maintenance,
although its commutation for money by mutual agreement became frequent
from as early as the mid twelfth century (Round 1902). King (1988: 15–19)
has traced documentary evidence for castle-guard arrangements at a total of
104 sites in England and Wales. The system seems to have been relatively
widespread in the late eleventh and early twelfth century, as epitomized by
those holdings documented as 'castleries' – especially compact groups of
dependent fees with responsibility for providing a garrison, including
Berkhamsted (Hertfordshire), Dudley (West Midlands), Pontefract (West
Yorkshire) and Richard's Castle (Herefordshire). Dedicated accommodation
for these knights sometimes lay within the castle's defences, as recorded at
Newcastle-upon-Tyne, while at Dover the identities of the various baronies

that owed castle-guard service were remembered in the names of individual towers (Ballard 1910: 713–14). A good example of the impact such arrangements could have on the tenurial landscape is the case of Portchester (Hampshire), where in the late eleventh or early twelfth century portions of the appurtenant royal estate were carved off to create five small manors held of the Crown by castle-guard service (Rigold 1965: 9).

We can identify five essential ways in which a castle might have been tied to the tenurial landscape. Of course, this relationship was not fixed, as a castle may have originated to serve a certain administrative purpose or to fulfil a particular, limited, military rôle, yet subsequently assume greater or lesser significance in line with wider political developments. It is sobering to note, however, that in some areas it is the minority of castles that have any form of contemporary documentation. Bedfordshire, Buckinghamshire, Herefordshire and Shropshire are examples of the many English counties where the proportion of castles unknown to history exceeds 50 per cent (King 1983). In such cases it is usually only through analysis of manorial descents that insight into the tenurial history of a site can be gained, although correlating such data sources with sites on the ground can prove intensely problematic.

First, we may identify those castles either built originally by the Crown or taken into royal ownership at a later date. The first generation of royal castle foundations were by far the most numerous and important. These were primarily fortifications sited within pre-Conquest urban centres functioning as seats of civil administration and stamps of centralized Norman authority (see Chapter 7). In contrast, later royal castles were invariably sited within easy reach of hunting resources or other important residences, and can be seen as part of a wider pattern of royal houses that included palaces and hunting lodges. Windsor Castle, for instance, was surrounded in the later medieval period by a ring of at least five subsidiary hunting lodges and other royal houses (Steane 1999: 83). The royal castle of Odiham (Hampshire), one of only four built by the Angevin kings in England, conveniently lay mid-way between Windsor and Winchester, and thus served as a useful stopping-off point on royal itineraries, being also located in an area with plentiful opportunities for hunting (Hughes 1976: 100). Many of those earlier royal castles in shire towns, meanwhile, declined at an early date (e.g. Gloucester: see Chapter 7), or else received less lavish upgrades than their rural counterparts because of their inconvenient positions relative to hunting resources. Overall, royal castle sites thus have less of a spatial relationship with patterns of landholding per se than castles in private hands, and tended to have small appurtenant estates rather than forming the hubs of more extensive land units. In addition, as they were not permanent seats of residence, royal castles were usually entrusted to the custody of an appointed castellan or hereditary constable, often meaning that the distinction between royal and baronial castles can be less than clear-cut (Brown *et al.* 1963: 34).

While important urban castles such as Leicester and Warwick were initially built as instruments of royal policy and subsequently became baronial centres, other royal strongholds such as Tickhill (South Yorkshire) and Peveril (Derbyshire), were baronial in origin but came under the control of the Crown following forfeit or escheat. Occasionally, we may suppose that such sites were upgraded or even acquired for their particular geographical advantages.

Tickhill was appropriated from *c.* 1100 and employed principally for its strategic significance, forming an important node on the nationwide network of communications routes on the northern edge of the midland plain (Warren Hollister 1989: 193; Pounds 1990: 27–9). Peveril, in contrast, was not utilized primarily for its military value, but functioned from *c.* 1155 as the key centre for the administration of Peak Forest following its expansion through the addition of Longdendale and division into three administrative districts (Barnatt and Smith 1997: 85). As such, Peveril Castle is representative of the physical association between royal castles and forests; other examples include Knaresborough and Pickering (North Yorkshire), Rockingham (Northamptonshire) and St Briavels (Gloucestershire) (Steane 1999: 79–80).

Second, we may identify castles built as the heads – or *capita* – of baronies, or as the centres of archiepiscopal estates. These sites were typically the principal, if not permanent, seat of seigneurial residence, and periods of absenteeism would see the site entrusted to an administrative official such as a bailiff or constable. Many such castles were located in a central position relative to the surrounding estates that comprised the barony or honour and often gave their name to the land unit. Substantial outlying portions of the dependent territory might be sub-infeudated (i.e. managed by tenants, the more important of whom may themselves have occupied castles). The estate within which the fortified *caput* lay, and perhaps others in the immediate hinterland, were, however, invariably retained in the hands of the tenant-in-chief (e.g. Sandal, West Yorkshire: see Chapter 2), although the leasing of demesne estates became increasingly common in the later medieval period.

Castles in the hands of feudal vassals and tenants form the third group. These sites acted as subsidiary centres of devolved seigneurial authority, often within spatially extensive fees. These were thus satellite centres of lordship, serving to administer widely scattered estates held from the tenant-in-chief as economic concerns or, more rarely, to maintain a seigneurial presence in areas used as hunting resources.

The fourth category comprises a range of more minor fortifications, including watchtowers and sentinel posts built as subsidiary fortifications to those above, usually fulfilling a specific tactical rôle, such as commanding a ferry crossing or pass. Castles such as these were characterized by impermanent or non-residential status, yet, crucially, located with reference to a wider lordship, usually as a means of protecting seigneurial assets and reinforcing claims of territorial control.

A miscellany of impermanent fortifications forms the fifth and final category. These were short-term fortifications of ephemeral and entirely military character, thrown up for reasons of immediate tactical benefit in time of conflict, usually as predatory sites or siege-works (see Chapter 3) and sometimes termed 'field castles'. In terms of surviving field evidence and location, these sites may be difficult to differentiate from those described in the category above. This type of site was distinct, however, in that the castle builder did not necessarily hold the land upon which the fortification was raised, although a degree of prior territorial control is implicit. Here the term 'adulterine' is perhaps best avoided; it has become commonplace to dismiss many undocumented earth and timber castles as short-term fortifications of the civil war between Stephen and Matilda, when a large proportion may be more accurately interpreted as castles of the immediate post-Conquest period. Many so-called 'castles of the Anarchy' were rather refurbished eleventh-century fortifications, or else products of the further expansion and consolidation of Anglo-Norman settlement (Coulson 1994b: 67). Indeed, of the 27 castles in England positively documented as having been built in the reign of Stephen, 56 per cent are entirely vanished (King 1983: xxxii), demonstrating such sites to be generally transient landscape features.

Castles and Domesday

Domesday Book is a much under-exploited resource for understanding the tenurial contexts of many otherwise undocumented Norman mottes and ringworks. By reconstructing the frameworks of estates recorded in 1086, it becomes possible to see how some early castles fitted into the landholding pattern, while the information which Domesday provides on land tenure before the Conquest crucially also allows us to relate newly imposed castles to the late Saxon landscape. Domesday does not help, however, with those sites in areas such as Northumbria and County Durham, which were beyond its horizons. A number of other methodological issues arise in attempting to relate an early castle site to the pattern of landholding recorded in Domesday Book. In particular, considerable problems arise in attempting to equate Domesday holdings with present parishes and townships, especially where place-names are lost or where a discrete settlement within the present land-scape was sub-divided manorially in 1086. In addition, we must recognize that a number of undocumented earth and timber castles will have been raised some time after Domesday and, if there have been radical changes in tenurial geography, will have little or no spatial relationship with the pattern of land ownership recorded in 1086. This is illustrated well by the case of Abinger (Surrey) – the small but famous motte that was the subject of a pioneering excavation showing the earth and timber fortification to have been built *c.* 1100 and re-occupied during the Anarchy after a period of disuse (Hope Taylor 1950). The tenurial context of the site's early phase remained obscure, however. The Domesday manor was held in demesne by William Fitz Ansculf, who, holding estates widely scattered across many counties, is unlikely to have chosen Abinger as an estate centre. Detailed analysis of the manorial descent has apparently resolved the issue, showing that the manor became the *caput* of a tiny lordship that took shape soon after Domesday. A small group of estates including Abinger was sub-infeudated to Robert of Abinger in the 1090s or 1100s, and subsequently his son William, one of whom appears certain to have raised the motte next to the estate church (Blair 1981).

It is also extremely rare for a castle to be mentioned in Domesday; they were sources of expenditure as opposed to taxable assets, and thus beyond the concerns of William's commissioners, although a total of 48 castles are mentioned directly and a further two by inference (see Harfield 1991). Most prominent among these were those royal urban castles that caused wide-scale disruption to taxable resources such as fishing rights, urban property or agricultural land (e.g. Lincoln and York). Remarkably, only two castles are mentioned in Domesday as economic assets: Chepstow (Monmouthshire), where a toll was due for boats crossing the Wye near the castle, and Eye (Suffolk), where a seigneurial market was held.

Over much of central and southern England, medieval tenurial geography was characterized by endowments of land held in small, locally based and loosely grouped parcels of estates, with a number of widely dispersed holdings typically constituting the combined fee of a major tenant in chief. This type of estate structure might have arisen for a number of reasons. Quite often, Domesday Book indicates that the holdings of a single Saxon antecessor had been transferred (or sold), more or less wholesale to a Norman tenant-in-chief, the tenant generally holding the combined lands of several pre-Conquest thegns (Golding 1994: 72). This may well have been a deliberate attempt by William to ensure that key magnates were prevented from holding large contiguous blocks of territory so as to limit their authority. Other factors have to be taken into consideration, however. Notably, existing estates were sometimes already widely scattered by 1066 through processes of division and amalgamation, with the lands of a single thegn often spreading across a number of separate shires. In addition, while the precise chronology of land redistribution in the period 1066–86 remains little understood, it is reasonable to assume that the process will have been piecemeal, with tenants receiving land as Saxon lords were displaced and land became available.

Nonetheless, certain undocumented castle sites can be clearly related to the patterns of estates appropriated by the incoming Norman aristocracy in the immediate post-Conquest period. In Wiltshire, for instance, at least two rural mottes can be confidently correlated with newly created blocks of estates that had little relationship with the pattern of pre-Conquest landholding (Creighton 2000a: 114–15). At Sherrington, a large motte standing next to the manorial mill and with an attendant estate church lay, at a wider scale, in the centre of a group of nine closely spaced manors held in chief by Osbern Giffard, a Norman lord who held comparatively little land outside the county. Bicknoll Castle similarly formed the core of a small fee comprising five contiguous manors all held in chief by Gilbert of Breteuil, of whose four other outlying Wiltshire manors all but one were in the hands of sub-tenants. But by no means all compact fees recorded in the Wiltshire Domesday contained castles; for instance, Ralph Mortimer held six neighbouring manors in the Grittleton-Hullavington area, but none of his estates contained a castle. Part of the explanation here is that this particular Norman aristocrat held substantial properties in eleven other shires. In Bedfordshire, a comparable regional analysis has also shown a close spatial relationship between several early castles and compact groupings of Domesday manors, including the large motte and bailey at Yielden and the undocumented ringwork known as 'Quince Hill', Old Warden, (Baker 1982b: 41–3). Some of these small compact fees were certainly created for security reasons in the immediate post-Conquest decades. A prime example is the solid lordship centred on the Isle of Axholme (Lincolnshire) that was in the hands of Geoffrey de la Guerche at Domesday, but which survived intact well into the twelfth century. This land unit was carved from the lands of eight pre-Conquest tenants and almost certainly created in response to the use of the area by a Danish army in 1069. The motte and bailey castle of Kinaird (Owston Ferry), first recorded in the mid twelfth century but presumably much earlier, formed the power base within the fee, positioned near an important crossing of the Trent to oversee the principal route between Lindsey and the Isle (Greenway 1972: xxi; Loughlin and Miller 1979: 156).

A more localized study of the pattern of late eleventh-century land tenure in the locality of the motte and bailey castle of Rayleigh (Essex), however, provides a cautionary warning that an apparent concentration of estates around a Norman castle can be misleading (Loyn 1989: 238–41). At first glance, the Domesday evidence suggests that the castle formed the focus of a concentration of vills in the hundreds of Rochford and Barstable, all in the hands of Suen of Rayleigh and apparently indicating the existence of a small castlery. More detailed scrutiny of the Domesday entries reveals, however, that these estates were actually interspersed with the holdings of other powerful magnates, while Suen was actually tenant-in-chief in only two of his other six vills in the area surrounding the castle. This provides a reminder of quite how complex and fragmented the tenurial geography of such areas could be in the late eleventh century and beyond, so that castle lords did not necessarily enjoy a monopoly of lordship on a surrounding hinterland.

Castles and Domesday estates: case-studies from Leicestershire

The different ways in which a Norman castle could relate to the pattern of landholding in the surrounding locality are illustrated well by two examples taken from the county of Leicestershire (Fig. 5.1). The superb earthworks of Hallaton Castle represent by far the best preserved motte and bailey in the county. Located at a prominent point on an interfluvial ridge that commanded a view over the village, the site was also positioned next to the 'old Leicester way', a formerly important east-west route of communication linking the area to Leicester (Fig. 5.2). Being undocumented and never re-built in stone, the site has often been thought to represent a short-lived Anarchy-period foundation (e.g. Hoskins 1970: 55). Examination of the pattern of eleventh-century tenurial geography recorded in Domesday Book suggests, however, that the castle was constructed soon after the Conquest as a seat of Norman lordship built to administer surrounding estates.

In 1086 Hallaton was part of a remarkably compact estate that also comprised the manors of Billeston, East Norton, Goadby, Keythorpe, Rolleston and Tugby, while Allexton and Skeffington were probably part of the same land unit at some stage – the Eye Brook forming an obvious northern boundary (Fig. 5.1: bottom). The nucleus of this estate had come through the Conquest essentially intact, and was held in 1086 by the great magnate Geoffrey Alselin and sub-infeudated to his tenant, 'Norman'. The owner of the estate in 1066 was the Saxon Toki, perhaps recalled in place-name Tugby, upon which Keythorpe and East Norton were dependent ecclesiastically and which probably formed the estate centre (Bourne 1988: 13–14; Hoskins 1957: 8–11). After the Conquest, however, Tugby was retained by the Crown and carved from the estate to become part of the soke of Rothley, an area set aside as a royal hunting area (Squires 1995: 94). The motte and bailey at Hallaton thus seems to have been built as a new estate centre before or very soon after 1086, as Alselin's lands were subsumed within the Peveril estate shortly

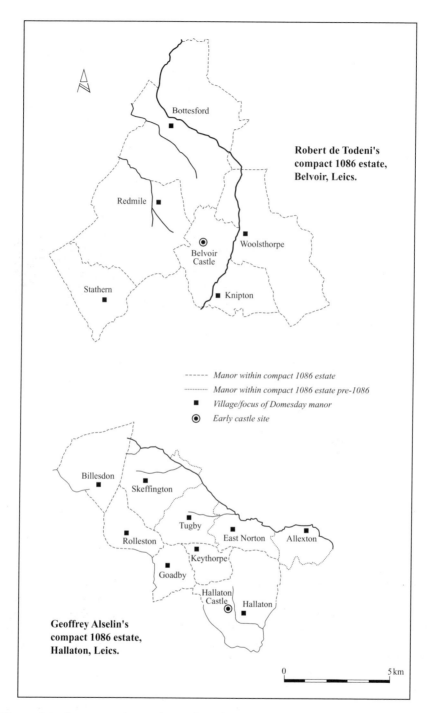

Figure 5.1 Reconstructions of two late-eleventh-century estates in Leicestershire, showing the likely relationship between Norman castles and estate frameworks both before and after the Norman Conquest. The information is based on Domesday Book.

Figure 5.2 Aerial view of Hallaton (Leicestershire), showing the well-preserved earthworks of an isolated motte and bailey thought to represent the centre of a small compact estate recorded in Domesday Book (Cambridge University Collection of Air Photographs: copyright reserved).

after Domesday, before the manor of Hallaton eventually escheated to the Crown in 1155 (VCH Leicestershire 1964: 121). The choice of castle site thus reflects the relocation of lordship to the most appropriate physical setting within the geographical constraints of the estate framework – a defensible but also accessible and visible site that proclaimed the new seigneurial presence to the tenantry.

The late-eleventh-century tenurial landscape around Belvoir, the site of an important baronial castle 37 km to the north of Hallaton, represents a sharp contrast (Fig. 5.1: top). Although Belvoir is not mentioned in Domesday, the site of the castle seems to have lain at the hub of a small yet compact estate that straddled the border between Leicestershire and Lincolnshire, forming the local power base of the Norman tenant Robert de Todeni, a standard-bearer of the Conqueror. In Leicestershire the manor of Bottesford and its dependencies of Redmile and Knipton flank the site, while Stathern was appended to the south-west. The Lincolnshire Domesday records that Woolsthorpe, flanking Belvoir to the east, was also in the hands of de Todeni, completing the unit. This tenurial pattern indicates that here redistribution of land in the late eleventh century was intended specifically to support a castle, the estates that formed the small fee around Belvoir having been taken largely from the holdings of the Saxon lord Leofric, whose extensive estates were scattered across midland England. At Belvoir the pattern of tenurial geography – with subsidiary manors arranged around the central *caput* in the manner of spokes around a wheel – is, unlike the rather different arrangement at Hallaton, entirely a post-Conquest creation. Clearly interesting patterns of variation are thus apparent, which we can only hope to explain when further studies have been undertaken.

That the manor of Bottesford was unusually sub-infeudated to ten *francigenae* may well indicate the deliberate settlement of a body of retainers to support the castle, as may a similar reference relating to nearby [Castle] Bytham (Lincolnshire) (Round 1907: 508). Here, seven *francigenae* with two ploughs are also mentioned. Although translated literally as 'Frenchmen', Stenton (1932: 44) argues that the term may have connotations of 'sergeants and household officers', perhaps suggesting small communities associated with the running of a castle. Empirical analysis of the distribution of other Leicestershire 'Frenchmen' in 1086 demonstrates an interesting correlation. Of the total of seventeen manors containing Frenchmen, eleven are in the hands of three tenants-in-chief (Hugh Grantmesnil, Robert de Todeni and Robert de Vessey), and four are associated with the earthworks of early mottes (Bottesford (Belvoir), Gilmorton, Ingarsby and Kibworth Harcourt). The latter three mottes are of identical dimension and it seems likely, if impossible to prove, that the sites were the seats of early groups of colonist sub-tenants, introduced to cultivate the demesne of newly acquired estates.

Castles and honours

More extensive but compact lordships were predominantly found in areas that were in one way or another strategically important for the security of Norman England: in particular along the northern and western borders, but also on vulnerable or otherwise significant parts of the east and south coasts. The classic explanation is that these lordships were created by royal authority in response to, or as a deterrent against English insurrection and the threat of Scottish, Northumbrian, Cumbrian and Scandinavian raiding or invasion. In the north, the Palatinate of Durham, Honour of Richmond and other large blocks of estates formed a buffer zone, while the east coast of Yorkshire was dominated by the Honour of Holderness (Fig. 5.3: bottom).

Perhaps the clearest example of the strategic settlement of favoured magnates in compact lordships with a castle as each unit's administrative centre is, however, the division of post-Conquest Sussex into a series of six contiguous land units known as 'rapes.' Yet the rôle of these land units in national defence may be overstated; while the Sussex coast was, in common with the marcher

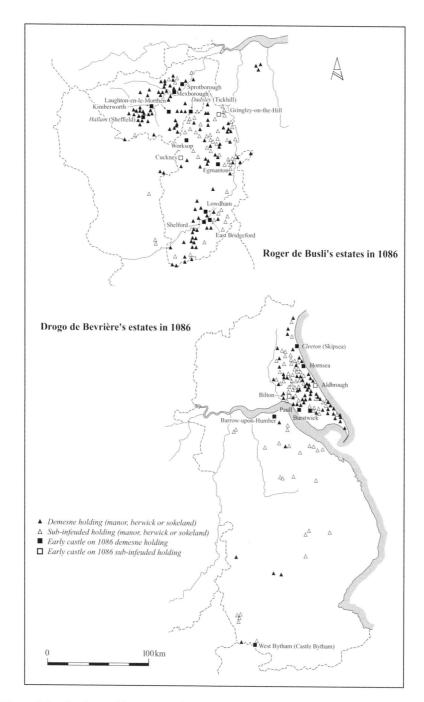

Figure 5.3 Castles and honours in the north of England. The map depicts the location of eleventh- and twelfth-century castle sites in addition to Domesday manors both held by the tenant-in-chief and by sub-tenants. It should be noted that not all the castles were necessarily in existence at Domesday (based on Dalton 1994, with additions).

regions, effectively a border zone, the rapes also served to secure access between Normandy and London. The integrity of each unit was particularly exceptional given the absence of a royal sheriff in the region (each rape had its own), and the lack of royal demesne (Cownie 1998; Adams 1999). The origin of the word rape is not Norman, but probably derived from the Saxon *rap* ('rope') with implications of measurement and the demarcation of territory, highlighting the origins of the units as fresh entities carved out to support the castles within them (Mason 1964: 92). Besides the principal castles, all of which formed the administrative and economic as well as military centre of each unit and lay on or near the coast, each rape was supported by a network of subsidiary fortifications established to control resources further inland. One typical such fortification was at Knepp, an outlying motte which later doubled as a hunting lodge in the northern portion of the Rape of Bramber (Jones 1999).

Five rapes are recorded in Domesday either directly by name or by implication: (from west to east) Arundel, Bramber, Lewes, Pevensey and Hastings. Several factors suggest that this pattern was not the product of a single action, but the result of more complex territorial changes. In particular, William de Braose's Rape of Bramber seems to be a later insertion, as indicated by the alignment of deanery boundaries, apparently created more or less coincident with the creation of the other rapes, but with which the boundaries of Bramber did not coincide (Hudson 1912; Salzman 1931). Bramber was also distinct in that the honorial centre was not an established port and borough, although Steyning, which lay within its jurisdiction, essentially fulfilled the same functions. The Rape of Chichester was even more of a latecomer: it did not emerge as a separate entity until the twelfth century and not documented by name until as late as 1275 (VCH Sussex IV, 1973: 1–2), at which time the castle in the north-east corner of the city wall was actually redundant. This unit seems originally to have been part of the Rape of Arundel, which incorporated within its jurisdiction the former Roman city of *Noviomagus* – from *c.* 1075 the new diocesan seat, replacing Selsey Bill, where a ringwork was built close to the former ecclesiastical centre at Church Norton (see Chapter 6).

This arc of coastal fees was completed to the west by Carisbrooke, where the castle and its compact lordship was granted to Baldwin de Redvers by Henry I, while in Kent to the east a series of lordships that, while not forming contiguous blocks, also had the appearance of strategic settlements; these include the lands of Odo of Bayeux (centred on Rochester) and Hugh de Montford (Hythe) (Pounds 1990: 35). On the Devon coast, meanwhile, the concentration of estates around Totnes formed the comparable power base of the Breton magnate, Judhael.

Compact fees in militarily sensitive zones in other parts of the newly conquered Anglo-Norman realm comprised the three earldoms on the Welsh marches of (from north to south): Chester, Shrewsbury and Hereford (Whiteman 1962; Mason 1963; Walker 1967; Alexander 1970). Simultaneously sealing the border and providing a platform for offensive action, these massive land units, sometimes called palatines, were distinctive historically in the level of sun-infeudation and the delegation of castle-building. This gave rise to prominent marcher families such as the Corbets and Mortimers, the castle-building activities of whom, along with their under-tenants, gave rise to a proliferation of private defence that created some of the highest densities of castles in England (Table 3.1).

William Peveril's Domesday estates in Nottinghamshire and Derbyshire constituted a less well-recognized compact fee closely related to a pattern of castle-building. Peveril's manor of *Pecheters* ('Peak's Arse') and the castle that it contained headed a list of seven Derbyshire manors retained in demesne. The Castle of the Peak was complemented by a small ringwork at Hope that overlooked the Hope-Castleton route of communication, located midway along the same valley and, in 1066, a royal estate centre associated with seven outliers (Hodges 1980, 32). The manor of Hope was in the hands of the Crown in 1066, and, as was customary, passed to William I, who, rather than retaining it in lordship, sub-infeudated the manor to Peveril, thus completing a contiguous block of Peakland estates focussed on Peveril castle. This concentration of estates and the two castle sites represented a coherent and deliberate settlement designed to subjugate this zone of the marginal Pennine uplands as a focus for resistance in a manner analogous to the great northern honours, but on a less extensive scale (Hart 1981: 48). Of Peveril's seventeen holdings in Derbyshire, the value of only two had increased in the period 1066–86: 'Peak's Arse' (1040–50s), and Bolsover (1040–60s), probably reflecting the rapid foundation of small castle boroughs (see Chapter 7). It is no surprise that an early castle was raised at Bolsover, which heading the list of Peveril's ten additional Derbyshire manors in the hands of five sub-tenants, formed another compact estate block in the east of the county. Peveril's Nottinghamshire estates, meanwhile, were concentrated around Nottingham, dominating its immediate hinterland and flanking approaches to the urban centre via the Great North Road through possession of key manors such as Clifton and its outliers (Roffe 1997: 36). William Peveril was installed at Nottingham as royal castellan, the castle forming his principal residence and effectively the *caput* of his fee, while the honorial court also lay within the town (Owen 1945: 18).

Case study: the honours of Norman Yorkshire

A number of conditions, internal and external, marked Yorkshire out for the strategic settlement of key magnates in a series of compact fees. At Domesday, the northern limits of Yorkshire constituted not a static border but a fluid frontier zone, forming a buffer against perceived military threat from Scotland and a semi-independent Northumbria. On the east coast, meanwhile, Yorkshire faced a still active Danish threat, indicated not only by the events of 1069–70, but by threatened invasion as late as 1085 (Brown 1985: 168–73). Le Patourel has also argued that part of the Norman intention in the creation of these compact lordships may also have been offensive, as they were not situated directly on the Scottish frontier (1971: 14–15). The Norman settlement of Yorkshire, and the castle-building that accompanied it, was thus as much a means of internal pacification, re-settlement and economic intensification and an attempt to secure effectively the means of production and control, as it was a matter of deterrence and defence. The creation of compact fees may have been further encouraged by the level of socio-economic dislocation in the wake of the Harrying of 1070–71, which in many ways 'paved the way' for Norman settlement in the northern zone, ensuring that the policy of redistributing the lands of a single pre-Conquest land-holder to a Norman, was impractical given imperfect knowledge of earlier tenure (Williams 1995: 40; see also Palliser 1993).

These northern honours in particular represented the settlement of Norman magnates and their tenants in the twin rôle of 'an army of occupation and a border force' (Brooks 1966: 56); but despite martial origins, most of these units survived as baronial franchises well into the later medieval period. Whereas the Honour of Tickhill failed to survive the twelfth century in its original form, the structural integrity of the Honours of Holderness, Pontefract and Richmond was more enduring. Two of these units are styled as castleries in Domesday: Count Alan the Red's castlery centred on Richmond, while land at Thorner was disputed as being 'within the bounds of Ilbert's castlery' (later Pontefract) in the Yorkshire claims. Wightman demonstrates, however, that late-eleventh-century references to castleries may not necessarily imply the pre-existence of a castle, as the phraseology of later documents implies that the term was equivalent to the word 'honour' before the latter became accepted widely as a legal term (1966: 24). The spatial extent, internal structures and origins of these different land units show many interesting contrasts. How did this influence the pattern of castle-building within them?

Richmond

The Honour of Richmond straddled the key border territory south of the Tees, occupying the key route of approach from the north to the Vale of York and ultimately lowland England, as well as the pivotal crossing of the Pennines through Stainmore to Carlisle. At Domesday, Count Alan (the Red), a Breton, was in possession of an especially compact lordship comprising no fewer than 199 manors and a further 43 outlying holdings. In addition to its key border location, the honour was one of most enduring of the great Domesday fees, retaining its territorial integrity until 1399 (Mason 1968: 704). But despite its border context, we see little in the distribution map of fortifications within the honour to suggest that the programme of castle-building was designed specifically for defence. Certainly there is nothing of the thick clustering of mottes on the exposed borders of certain Anglo-Norman lordships noted in Ireland (McNeill 1997: 68–9). Rather, the settlement of sub-tenants and construction of early castles as their estate centres went hand in hand.

Butler (1992) has emphasized through an examination of twelfth- and thirteenth-century lists of knights fees that the lordship was welded together via a closely integrated network of enfeoffment and military service. The honour was studded with a high density of castles of varying functions and ownership, forming a web of sites with a clear hierarchy (L'Anson 1913). The honorial *caput*, comprising the familiar Norman triumvirate of new castle, borough and religious house was located on a fresh site at Richmond (Figs 5.4 and 7.10). The Honour of Richmond was distinctive in that its territorial integrity can be traced back to the pre-Conquest period – the name

Figure 5.4 Richmond Castle (North Yorkshire). Occupying a dramatic cliff-top site above the River Swale, this castle formed the *caput* of the Honour of Richmond (photograph: Oliver Creighton).

'Richmondshire' probably indicating a re-naming of pre-Conquest Gillingshire (Palliser 1992: 25). An interesting parallel in Yorkshire was the territory of Hallamshire, focused on Sheffield, which again seems to have been a pre-Conquest land unit that re-emerged as a Norman honour with a castle (Sheffield) as its gravitational centre (Hey 1979: 26–9). But far from perpetuating an existing centre, the foundation of the *caput* at Richmond (Fig. 5.4) replaced the pre-Conquest centres of Catterick and Gilling with a single pre-eminent focus. Richmond's position was carefully selected for its location not only at the approximate geographical centre of the territory, but also between its highland and lowland components, as much as for its military advantages (see Chapter 7).

The former estate centre of Catterick was fortified with a motte ('Palet Hill'), while an early castle built at Pickhill suggests a deliberate policy of siting early castles as central places within the three Hundreds of the Honour ('Gilling': Richmond; 'Hang': Catterick; and 'Hallikeld': Pickhill). All these manors were retained in demesne at Domesday, indicating the systematic nature of castle building and its relationship to the late Saxon administrative landscape. Another tier of castles originated as the residences of the principal sub-tenants and knights and lay on manors sub-infeudated in 1086, comprising: Killerby, Kirkby Fleetham, Middleham and Ravensworth, many of which are associated with villages of planned appearance. Notably, these castles dominated the pacified Vale of York rather than the troublesome Pennines that were the heartland of anti-Norman unrest. Such a colonial settlement of Breton sub-tenants was indicative of a systematic and controlled Norman policy ensuring effective management of agricultural resources.

Clearly, economic sustainability, as much as military security, was the key to retaining social and political control in the north. Other less substantial fortifications were sited for more specific tactical reasons: mottes at Cliffe and Low Dinsdale, for instance, overlooked the point where a Roman roads crossed the Tees, while another at Scotch Corner commanded a junction of routes (Butler 1992: 71–4).

Holderness

The relationship between castles and post-Conquest land tenure in Holderness, East Yorkshire (Fig. 5.3: bottom), is of particular interest in that it represents an extreme form of aristocratic Norman settlement, attributable largely to the strategic significance of this area. The Holderness peninsula was consistently referred to as an island throughout the Middle Ages – its isolation attributable not only to the Humber estuary to the south, but the marshes on the peat and alluvium of the River Hull flood plain that defined its western limit. Prior to the Conquest, Domesday Book shows that Holderness comprised a series of modest scattered holdings in the hands of minor lords, interspersed with a small number of more valuable manors held by important Saxon magnates including Morcar, Tostig and Harold. Within a few years of the Conquest this tenurial pattern had been swept away to create a compact fee, later known as the Honour of Holderness, in the hands of Drogo de Bevrière, that, following forfeit, descended through the Counts of Aumâle (English 1979). In the north-west, Roger of Poitou's lands in Lancashire between the Ribble and Mersey formed a comparable settlement designed seemingly for coastal defence (Tait 1904: 152).

The personal names of Drogo's Domesday tenants indicate a high level of Flemish colonization (Drogo was Flemish origins), reminding us that the Norman settlement of the North was part of an expansionist and colonial enterprise. The importation of Flemish *locatores* has been noted in south-west Wales (Kissock 1997: 129–31); a key difference was that the Norman lords in Holderness did not establish new planned villages as in Pembrokeshire and, indeed, elsewhere in Yorkshire. Rather, the rural landscape remaining dominated by irregular, attenuated settlements related to the characteristic economy and manorial structures of the region (Harvey 1982: 65–6).

The post-Conquest redistribution of lands, while ensuring *territorial* integrity, cut across pre-existing *tenurial* patterns, leading to severe socio-economic dislocation, as reflected in the distribution of Domesday waste. The relationship between this remarkable pattern of tenurial geography and the siting of early castles is of great interest. First, there is a notable correlation between manors in the hands of Saxon magnates in 1066 and the location of key fortified sites. *Cleeton* was in the hands of Harold in 1066, and had the powerful motte and bailey of Skipsea raised in its immediate locality to form the central *caput* of de Bevrière's fee (Figs 5.5 and 7.17). The strategic importance of Skipsea is self-evident, guarding the key route through the Hull marshes that linked Holderness to the rest of the East Riding, whilst remaining closely in touch with maritime communications. Both Aldbrough and Burstwick were also clearly key pre-Conquest estate centres, being in 1066 in

Figure 5.5 The motte of Skipsea Castle (East Yorkshire). Formerly marking the *caput* of the Honour of Holderness, this immense earthwork rises above marshy ground that indicates the site of a mere drained in the nineteenth century. The parish church, formerly separated from the motte by the mere, can be seen in the background (photograph: Oliver Creighton).

the hands of, respectively, Ulf and Tostig, with extensive jurisdictions and high values. Although the site of Aldbrough Castle, documented in 1115, is lost, the natural eminence of 'Castle Hill' overlooks the parish church of St Bartholomew's, which contains early Norman work and an eleventh-century sundial recording 'Ulf' as ordering the church's construction (Twycross-Raines 1920). If the church is indeed a Saxon *Eigenkirche*, it is likely that a manorial residence lay nearby. While a manorial centre at Burstwick is not documented until the thirteenth century, when it became the successor to Skipsea as the *caput* of the Aumâle fee in the early thirteenth century, field evidence suggests the prior existence of a motte and bailey on the site of the later residence (Denholm-Young 1934: 401; VCH ER Yorks. 1984: 9–10). The raising of castles in these estates thus reflects a systematic appropriation of the more valuable holdings and the management of their associated agricultural resources under new lordship, but also the location of military sites near key pre-Conquest administrative/manorial centres. In addition, these three key sites were sited respectively within the three Hundreds of Holderness ('North': Skipsea; 'Middle': Aldbrough; and 'South': Burstwick), as in Richmondshire. Although, as a whole, the Honour was thus an artificial Norman creation, the specific circumstances of castle siting hark back to the late Saxon geography of Holderness. Other early castle sites on Holderness appear sited with specific reference to military need. The small motte at 'Swan Hill', Bilton, on the western fringes of the Hull marshes, may have guarded a southern approach into the peninsula, while the tiny bailey-less motte at Hornsea may have been a subsidiary lookout post or signal station.

Although Holderness formed the key to Drogo's possessions in 1086, a

Figure 5.6 Aerial view of Castle Bytham (Lincolnshire). The massive earthworks of this motte and bailey are flanked by the ridges and furrows of a medieval field system and a series of fishponds that lie to the extreme left of the photograph. The curving line of the village street in the top left-hand corner probably fossilizes the perimeter of an embankment that embraced the parish church and linked the settlement to the castle (Cambridge University Collection of Air Photographs: copyright reserved).

series of more scattered estates lay beyond Yorkshire. Drogo held 24 Lincolnshire estates in 1086, including major holdings at Barrow-upon-Humber and Carlton le Moorland, with the gravitational centre at West (Castle) Bytham (Fig. 5.6) – a valuable manor of Morcar in 1066 retained in demesne in 1086. In addition, early castle sites at Paullholme and Barrow-upon-Humber (East Yorkshire) lay respectively within Drogo's estates on the north and south banks of the Humber and seem complementary elements within the late-eleventh-century estates fortification, linking portions of a fee which were otherwise isolated from one another by the Humberhead marshes. The situation of the motte and bailey at Barrow is indicative of maritime links, lying on an island of boulder clay and surrounded by former marshland to overlook water traffic at the mouth of Barrow Haven (Atkins 1983: 93; Loughlin and Miller 1979: 183).

Blyth-Tickhill

The Honour of Blyth-Tickhill, formed from the core of estates held by Robert de Busli at Domesday, was another land-unit created *de novo*, carved from a multitude of pre-Conquest estates to create a coherent entity (Fig. 5.3: top). Variously in the hands of powerful magnates and the Crown from *c.* 1100, this land unit did, however, lack the territorial and tenurial continuity that characterized other Yorkshire-based honours. The creation of the fee was of undoubted strategic value in the late eleventh century. Bracketed by the Pennines to the west and the Humberhead marshes to the east, while the Nottinghamshire portion of the Honour bordered on Sherwood Forest, the fringes of the fee were strategically troublesome weak spots in the newly conquered north (Kapelle 1979: 145). As such, the honour effectively blocked the northern entrance to Nottinghamshire and the Midland plain via the Roman road south from York. Nevertheless, the honorial *caput* at Tickhill (South Yorkshire) did not lie on a frontier, and the fee's creation seems as much attributable to the pacification of a troublesome region as defensive necessity per se.

The honorial castle at Tickhill (South Yorkshire) lay on a newly selected site not named in Domesday, although the castle and borough are likely concealed within the composite entry for *Dadsley*, Stainton and Hellaby, and probably superseded a nearby vill (see Chapter 7). The economic intensification of *Dadsley* manor in the immediate post-Conquest decades is evident in the fact that the composite holding is the only instance of a de Busli estate in Yorkshire increasing in value (increasing from £12 to £14 in the period 1066–86). The motte and bailey at Laughton-en-le-Morthen (South Yorkshire) was not so much a secondary administrative centre within the honour as an element within an tripartite stamp of Norman authority on the region, comprising two complementary military/administrative sites (Laughton and Tickhill) and a new priory (Blyth) that lay somewhat unusually distant from the honorial castle. The motte and bailey occupied a seat of evident pre-Conquest administrative importance forming the centre of the ancient territory of Morthen (Parker 1986). In 1066 the manor, including a berwick and extensive jurisdiction of sokeland, was in the hands of Earl Edwin; in 1086 it formed de Busli's most valuable holding in the shire and headed his list of demesne. Whilst the baronial *caput* thus occupied an essentially *de novo* site, well served by communications routes and with the potential for economic investment, the selection of Laughton as a subsidiary centre harked back to the pre-Conquest past (see Chapter 6).

Elsewhere, we may be less certain that castles lying on de Busli's 1086 estates originated in the late eleventh century, but a number of candidates offer themselves (all now in South Yorkshire). The motte and bailey of Mexborough overlooks the important ford of Strafforth Sands, lying on a demesne manor where a subsidiary court of the honour was later held (Glassby 1893: 16–19; Hey 1979: 44). Mottes at Kimberworth and Sprotborough may be interpreted in much the same light as outlying sites necessary to oversee a spatialy extensive honour.

The cliff-top castle at Sheffield is generally assumed to date from the early twelfth century, when the pre-Conquest territory of Hallamshire re-emerged

to form the heart of William de Lovetot's barony following the royal confiscation of the Honour of Blyth (Hey 1986: 31; Speight 1995: 66). Nonetheless, re-examination of archaeological evidence at Sheffield suggests that de
Lovetot's fortification may have been preceded by an earlier Norman castle
built to dominate the valuable Domesday manor of Hallam, the main
administrative centre of pre-Conquest Hallamshire (Hey 1979: 29). Other
than Laughton, Hallam was the only other manor within de Busli's Yorkshire
estates to have been in the hands of a key Saxon magnate in 1066 (Earl
Waltheof had a hall here), and an early castle seems likely. In Nottinghamshire
other sites apear to have been built as early fortifications on an outlying part of
the Honour of Tickhill: principal among these were Lowdham, lying on a
demesne de Lacy manor north of the Trent, while a small motte and bailey at
East Bridgford was elevated above an important ferry crossing over the Trent,
thus securing access with the detached portion of the honour to the south
(VCH Notts. 1910: 17).

Pontefract

Unlike Blyth-Tickhill, the territorial integrity of the Honour of Pontefract,
originating in the Domesday holdings of Ilbert de Lacy, largely survived the
Middle Ages, being incorporated within the Duchy of Lancaster from the mid
fourteenth century (Faull and Moorhouse 1981: 250). That this lordship was
again a deliberate creation – and an artificial one in terms of a pre-Conquest
administrative geography – is emphasized by the fact that William took the
unusual step of granting all *terra regis* within the area, with the single
exception of the great manor of Wakefield, to Ilbert (Wightman 1966: 30). In
geographical terms, the fee occupied a nodal position at the intersection of two
arterial routes of communication: the north-south Roman road between
Durham and Doncaster, and the natural crossing of the Pennines through the
Aire Gap. Stretching continuously from the Pennines in the west to the low-
lying marshes around the Aire, Don and Ouse to the east, Ilbert's castlery
occupied a key block of territory, both in tems of pacifying existing trouble-
spots and blocking potential invasion routes from Cumbria and Scotland.
That Pontefract castle was referred to as the 'key to Yorkshire' in a letter to
Henry III in 1264 (Shirley 1866: 255) is due more to its geographical position
than the castle's military strength per se.

  Bishop (1948: 13–14) draws attention to thirteenth-century documentary
evidence implying an unusually high level of obligation including week work
in Pontefract and its immediate environs. Week work was otherwise uncommon in Yorkshire, perhaps indicating conditions inherited from the late
eleventh century and relating to a period of intense and forced demesne cultivation at the hub of the honour. The considerable spatial extent of the
honour suggests a pattern of decentralized administration based on a number
of separate foci dominated by castles, one overseeing the eastern portion of the
honour (Kippax, later Barwick-in-Elmet), and another the southern eastern
portion of the honour (Kippax, later Barwick-in-Elmet), and another the
southern estates held in demesne (Almondbury). The motte and bailey at
Saxton (North Yorkshire) may be another such site, located at the heart of an

outlying number of estates in the north-east of the honour, whilst the demesne estate of *Tanshelf* (Pontefract) lay to the south, on the site of a former *villa regia* (see Chapter 6).

Topographical analysis of castles within late-eleventh-century Yorkshire honours thus suggests many common features – in particular the systematic siting of Norman castles within the vicinity of sites of pre-Conquest secular and religious importance, both as an appropriation of the machinery of manorial administration and a statement of conquest. But there are variations too, particularly in the location of honorial *capita*. Overall, the creation and organization of new Norman lordships in Yorkshire appears to have been a policy geared towards inward economic stability and sustainability as opposed to external threat. But at the moment we are insufficiently aware of how these patterns varied across Britain, depending upon different circumstances of lordship and in different physical landscapes, and comparative studies of castle siting in different lordships are urgently needed.

Summary

Private fortifications were built and owned by such a broad range of people within the upper echelons of medieval society that only the most general observations can be made about the interrelationships between castles and landholding. While in certain contexts lordships were administered without castles, most lords able to mobilize the resources necessary for castle-building appear to have raised fortified centres within their estates. But while some lordships were administered from a single castle, others were studded with multiple fortifications, some in the hands of tenants and others of more temporary character. Of particular importance among the many factors that influenced the pattern of castle-building within lordships was the relative compactness of estates as well as their economic potential, while few castle-building strategies were entirely unrelated to earlier patterns of tenurial geography and the location of related administrative centres.

6 Power, Patronage and Parish: Castles and Ecclesiastical Landscapes

Given the manner in which religion permeated almost every aspect of medieval life in a way now almost unimaginable, it comes as no surprise that castles had close connections with the ecclesiastical landscape. The church was, alongside the castle, another important pillar of feudal lordship and a similarly powerful force for change in the landscape and townscape (Morris 1989). Churches and castles were the focus of enormous investment by the medieval élite; the foundation or patronage of an ecclesiastical institution by a castle lord could be an important social statement and an expression of wealth as well as piety.

Wherever castle and church are closely juxtaposed in the English landscape we may suspect common patronage and very often the foundations will have been closely linked. Even where the two structures do not lie adjacent, a parish church will invariably have received the investment of the castle lord. Quite often we may suspect that major episodes of church re-building will coincide with modifications to the seigneurial site, perhaps using the same masons or craftspeople and giving rise to interesting stylistic parallels between church and castle architecture. Nowhere are these links more apparent than in those medieval cities where castle and cathedral lie adjacent, as at Durham, Old Sarum (Wiltshire) and Rochester (Kent) (Fig. 6.1). Sometimes, castle and cathedral exhibited secular and ecclesiastical interpretations of the same architectural forms. At Norwich, for instance, ranks of blind arcading on the cathedral's north transept mirror those on the keep, while at Lincoln, the new Norman cathedral's west front contains conspicuous features of military architecture and the structure lay directly opposite the castle (Gem 1986; Heslop 1994). The patronage of castle lords also found expression in the foundation of chapels for their households and garrisons, and, often at a different scale altogether, in the endowment and support of collegiate churches and houses of various monastic orders. This chapter explores some of the chronological, spatial and functional relationships that existed between castles and different ecclesiastical sites, underlining in particular their significance as complementary tools and symbols of medieval lordship.

Castles, churches and chapels

The framework of parishes in England was already relatively well established by the middle of the eleventh century, so that most castles were imposed within, and often located in relation to, an extant pattern of parochial topography. Only very rarely was a new parish created concurrent with, or shortly

Figure 6.1 Rochester (Kent), showing the juxtaposition in close physical proximity of the cathedral and bishop's castle (photograph: Oliver Creighton).

following, the foundation of a castle. The most obvious examples of this process are where a new Norman castle borough was founded on a green-field site, attracting population that required additional ecclesiastical provision, as at Belvoir (Leicestershire) and Castle Carlton (Lincolnshire). Here and elsewhere, new parishes were carved *de novo* from earlier entities and new parish churches built on fresh sites. Devizes (Wiltshire) is an excellent example (Fig. 6.2), the place-name being derived from the Norman-French *le devises* ('the divisions') and reflecting the foundation of Bishop Roger of Salisbury's new castle and borough between the hundreds of Potterne and Cannings, thus disrupting an extant pattern of parochial topography (Gover *et al.* 1939: 243).

The relationship between castles and parish churches is a theme often alluded to, both in ecclesiastical studies (Morris 1989: 250–74) and castle studies (Pounds 1990: 222–4; Pounds 1991; Fawcett 1998). That castles in the English landscape, especially those established in the Norman period, lie so frequently close by and often immediately adjacent to parish churches was recognized by Addy (1913: 104–37) in his book *Church and Manor*, and various other studies have indicated the strength of the link between the two institutions. For instance Le Maho (1976) has shown that almost 50 per cent of all eleventh- and twelfth-century earthwork castles in the Grand Caux peninsula, Normandy, lie within 500 m of a church, with a clear implication of linked histories. In an analysis of castle sites in a sample of ten English counties, over 40 were demonstrated to lie within 50 m of the parish church (Pounds 1991, 12). What is especially important is that a seigneurial residence and estate church formed a 'magnate core' that very often constituted the nucleus of a settlement and a distinct zone of lordship (Roberts 1987: 73–5); the example of Aughton (East Yorkshire) is perhaps typical in this regard (Fig. 6.3). Some of the countless other English castles of all sorts which lie in this

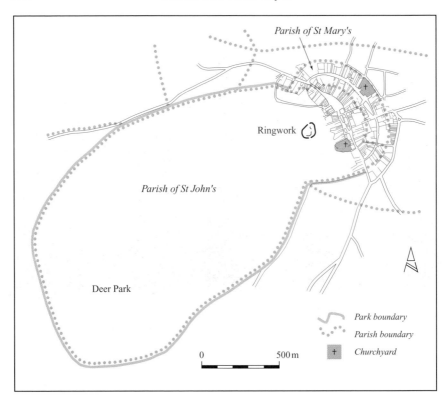

Parish of St Mary's

Ringwork

Parish of St John's

Deer Park

Park boundary

Parish boundary

Churchyard

0   500 m

Figure 6.2 Devizes (Wiltshire), showing the relationship between the medieval ring-work, town, deer park and parish boundaries.

type of position include mottes at Almeley (Herefordshire), Burton-in-Lons-dale (North Yorkshire), Gilmorton (Leicestershire), Isfield (East Sussex) and Penwortham (Lancashire), and ringworks at Beaudesert (Warwickshire), Benington (Hertfordshire), Essendine (Rutland) and Hathersage (Derbyshire). The precise physical relationship between a castle and a nearby church could, however, take one of many forms, while a number of different scenarios can explain the association (Fig. 6.4). Certainly the association between parish churches and adjacent castles is unlikely to have originated much after the twelfth century nor to be coincidental; castles with later dates of foundation that lie adjacent to parish churches may perpetuate earlier manorial residences with associated ecclesiastical sites. Exceptions are few: at Groby (Leicester-shire), for instance, the present parish church next to the large motte is entirely a Victorian creation without medieval ancestry. Elsewhere, a barrow on the edge of a churchyard could be mistaken as a motte, as at Ogbourne St Andrew (Wiltshire) and Ryton (Co. Durham) (Young 1980: 10; Creighton 2000a: 116).

We must also remember that many non-defended high-status medieval residences are also found in close association with parish churches. At Raunds (Northamptonshire), excavation has revealed the manorial site and adjacent proprietary church to have lain perpendicular to one another within linked

Figure 6.3 All Souls' parish church, Aughton (East Yorkshire). This small parish church lies adjacent to a motte (tree-covered in the background) located on the edge of the marshes around the River Derwent. The church contains a Norman chancel arch and south doorway and was probably a foundation of the castle lord. Both features stand at the west end of a linear village that grew up outside the seigneurial focus (photograph: Oliver Creighton).

embanked and ditched enclosures on higher ground than the rest of the settlement, from which the complex was deliberately segregated (Saunders 1990: 187–8). The clear implication is that the juxtaposition of castles and churches represents part of a broader association between the residences of medieval power-holders and churches, most of which will have originated in a proprietary capacity.

Quite how closely linked castle and church could be is demonstrated well at Castle Camps (Cambridgeshire), the site of a large but partially levelled ringwork and bailey of the de Vere family (Fig. 6.5). What is unusual is that here both the church and part of its churchyard overlay the ditch of a small rectangular inner bailey that seems to have been an earlier feature. The likely sequence is that the church, which contains re-set thirteenth-century fabric, was constructed contemporary with, or immediately after, the planning of a second, larger outer bailey that entirely embraces the earlier enclosure, the ditch of which was filled in (Taylor 1973: 41). We should not overlook that the church was, at one level, integrated within the defensive perimeter but also lay at the very junction between the zone of lordship and community beyond. This type of relationship is duplicated in many other places, including Skelton (Cleveland) where the parish church again simultaneously formed a bridge and barrier between lord and community (Daniels 1995: 89).

By physically associating a private place of residence with a place of worship, the church founder or patron received spiritual benefit as well as social status from his action. Seigneurial influence over a church could be heightened

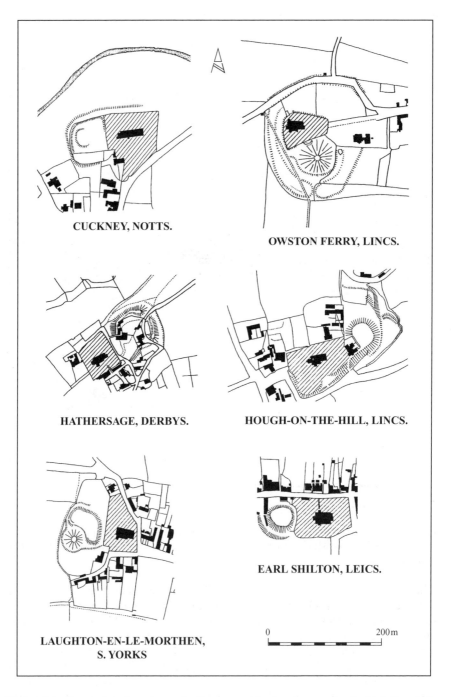

CUCKNEY, NOTTS.

OWSTON FERRY, LINCS.

HATHERSAGE, DERBYS.

HOUGH-ON-THE-HILL, LINCS.

LAUGHTON-EN-LE-MORTHEN, S. YORKS

EARL SHILTON, LEICS.

0   200m

Figure 6.4 Examples of castles and adjacent parish churches, some of which lie within bailey enclosures. While a number of these churches probably originated as castle chapels, others certainly antedate the castles, including the examples at Laughton-en-le-Morthen and Hough-on-the-Hill, which contain Saxon architectural features.

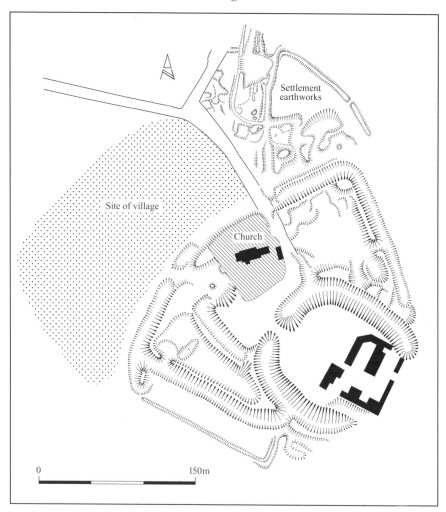

Figure 6.5 Castle Camps (Cambridgeshire), showing the relationship between the motte and bailey, parish church and deserted medieval village (based on Taylor 1973, with additions).

where the lord held the advowson, allowing personal appointment of a favoured priest. At Owston Ferry (Lincolnshire) charter evidence demonstrates precisely this type of linkage. By *c.* 1145, the Mowbray lords had installed a cousin (Samson d'Aubigny) as the parish priest, as at a number of their other castles, including Burton-in-Lonsdale and Thirsk (North Yorkshire) (Greenway 1972: lxv–lxvi, 138–9; Speight 1994: 63). At Owston, the churchyard again occupies a sector of the bailey, the church being sited somewhat asymmetrically within the enclosure (Fig. 6.4). Here and elsewhere, whether the church preceded or post-dated the castle site, its physical setting within the castle bailey ensured that access to it was controlled and 'spiritual space' effectively appropriated, as populations will have had limited access to the enclosed zone. Furthermore, through rentals, incumbency payments and other customary dues, the church could actually act as a long-term source of financial return for a lord, despite the initial outlay. The combination of castle and church thus represented an integrated unit of lordship sending powerful signals of social, military and, indeed, spiritual control to a neighbouring community. But while the foundation and occupation of many early castles occurred at a time when the private foundation and control of churches was acceptable, the church reforms of the twelfth century came to see this as politically ill-advised. Private rights came to be entrusted to religious institutions, which received tithes and appointed priests. A typical example of this process is the transferral of All Saints, the 'church of the castle' of Skipsea (East Yorkshire), to the monastery at Albermale by Stephen, Earl of Albermale, *c.* 1098–1102 (L'Anson 1897: 58) (Fig. 5.5). To some extent this saw the link between castle and church weakened or indeed broken, although seigneurial influence continued to find expression in the endowment and promotion of monasteries (see below).

While castles spawned churches, the reverse process was rather less common. Bishops could fortify their residences and palaces (e.g. Liddington, Rutland), monasteries could be defended with curtain walls and gatehouses (e.g. Lindisfarne Priory, Northumberland), and it was not unknown for ecclesiastical precincts to be crenellated under licence (e.g. St Augustine's, Canterbury). But by and large castles were rare on church land. Occasionally, a documentary source such as a monastic foundation charter makes it clear that the site of an abandoned or slighted castle was given over to a religious house, making permanent its decommissioning. The Premonstratensian abbey of Newhouse (Lincolnshire), established *c.* 1143, was raised on such a de-militarized zone, being built on the actual site of the castle of its benefactor, Peter of Goxhill, as specified in the foundation charter (Colvin 1951: 41–2). This was also the case with the first Albini castle of Old Buckenham (Norfolk), the site of which was granted, along with 80 acres of the park, to the Augustinian canons of the nearby priory *c.* 1146 (Rutledge 1980: 352). The site of Montacute Castle (Somerset) and its appurtenances was granted by William, son of Robert of Mortain to the Abbey of Cluny *c.* 1093–1104, and despite the close morphological relationship between castle, priory and settlement plan, the commercial development of the manor, including the addition of a marketplace and borough extension, occurred long after the seigneurial site had been abandoned (Aston and Burrow 1982: 123). Later but otherwise comparable examples include the sites of castles at Abingdon (Berkshire) and Barnwell (Northamptonshire), which were acquired by nearby abbeys in 1247 and 1276 respectively, and Mettingham (Suffolk), left to a college of priests in 1387 (King 1983).

Antecedent churches

The chronological relationship between closely juxtaposed castles and churches can be difficult to unravel, as their foundations are rarely documented while present field monuments and structures may seal or otherwise obscure evidence of earlier origins. It is only through exceptional clarity of evidence, or through topographical guesswork, that we may hope to gain further insight into the likely sequence. For instance, the date of the ecclesiastical building partially buried within the rampart of Castle Rising (Norfolk) remained unclear until excavations on the site suggested that it was not of late Saxon date, as had often been proposed, but was built around *c.* 1100 (Morley and Gurney 1997: 24, 133). With its tripartite plan, the building appears not to have been a private church, but probably originated as a chapel of ease associated with an expansion of the village, part of which was removed to make way for William d'Albini's castle of *c.* 1140.

The physical fabric of the many other parish churches within or adjacent to castles sometimes contains clear evidence of pre-Conquest origins, as with All Saints, Hough-on-the-Hill (Lincolnshire), which features a remarkable Saxon west tower with external stair turret and a triangle-headed doorway (Pevsner and Harris 1989: 399). This was another parish church contained within a bailey (Fig. 6.4); immediately to the south lie earthwork traces marking the site of Hough Priory, an Augustinian cell founded in 1164 (VCH Lincs. 1906: 242–4). Elsewhere, the mention of a church and/or priest in Domesday provides a tentative hint that a church next to a Norman motte may well have pre-Conquest origins, as at Catterick (North Yorkshire) and Earl Shilton (Leicestershire). That a great many Norman castles were built next to earlier churches is particularly well illustrated by the case of the Lune Valley. Of the nine mottes that cluster within the catchment, no fewer than four lie adjacent to parish churches containing pre-Conquest architectural fabric, while four more are found in close proximity to other churches, leaving only one site (Castle Stede, Lancashire) that is remote from an ecclesiastical site (Bu'Lock 1970). Another particularly interesting case is the small ringwork at Week St Mary (Cornwall), which the plan of surrounding property boundaries and other topographical evidence suggests was set with its associated earthworks, adjacent to the parish church but also inside a much larger curvilinear enclosure. While this feature appears to pre-date the castle, church and churchyard, it is unclear whether this was an early ecclesiastical enclosure, like others known in the county, or had secular origins (Preston-Jones and Rose 1986: 170).

In these cases and others, the physical juxtaposition of castle and church may well perpetuate earlier arrangements. How often was the association of a high-status seat of lordship and ecclesiastical structure established before the Conquest? The construction of private churches (*Eigenkirchen*) by early medieval power holders was perhaps the most important motor behind the proliferation of churches in the pre-Conquest centuries (Gem 1988: 23). Early medieval law codes reveal the social value of church possession, with the ownership of a 'bell and a burh-geat' an essential criterion differentiating a thegn from a ceorl (A. Williams 1992: 226–7). Could some of these twinned castles and churches overlie the earlier sites of Anglo-Saxon high-status residences with private churches that had been appropriated and rebuilt by new landlords? Of those Norman castles shown by excavation to overlie late Saxon defended residences, many indeed lie adjacent to parish churches or chapels, including most prominently Goltho (Lincolnshire) and Sulgrave (North-amptonshire) (Morris 1989: 250–74). The Saxon manorial compound at Trowbridge (Wiltshire) was another that featured a small private church or chapel effectively appropriated by Norman castle-building (Graham and Davies 1993).

The parish church of All Saints at Laughton-en-le-Morthen (South Yorkshire), renowned for its fine spire, is another likely case. The church lay within a large outer bailey, the profile of which is indicated by partially surviving earthworks and the alignment of roads and property boundaries (Fig. 6.4). The volume of high-quality pre-Conquest masonry, including the remains of a late Saxon *porticus*, that the church contains, indicates beyond doubt that here a motte and bailey were imposed adjacent to an earlier church of some significance (Ryder 1982: 71–83). Moreover, the fact that Domesday records that Earl Edwin had an *aula* (hall) in Laughton in 1066 (though the church is omitted) raises the distinct possibility that the Norman castle perpetuates the site of a late-Saxon high-status residence with a proprietary church (Hey 1979: 41). Although only large-scale excavation could ever provide the answer, the plan of the earthworks make it feasible that that the motte and bailey have been inserted into a large oval enclosure which could have enclosed the Saxon manorial site, as at Goltho (Lincolnshire, see Chapter 2). The Saxon church was virtually eradicated by a radical Norman rebuilding within a generation or so of the Conquest, involving its wholesale re-planning around a new nave to the east of the Saxon crossing, thus altering the ground plan in line with the position of the new castle (Ryder 1980).

It is vital not to overlook the essential symbolic dimension to this Norman takeover of parish churches. Where castle was imposed upon a pre-Conquest residence, the appearance of the fortification, in particular of a towering motte, must have appeared an alien and aggressive symbol to the pre-existing population. Yet this was often balanced by the fact that the castle was occupying an existing, recognized seat of power. At one level this was an act of conquest, but at another a form of continuity. Some pre-Conquest churches with nearby castles were clearly important places, and not merely parish churches. For instance, the undocumented ringwork in Church Norton on Selsey Bill (West Sussex) stands hard by St Wilfrid's chapel, the structure of which protrudes slightly into the defensive ditch. Despite its present appearance, the chapel is the sole remaining fragment of the parish church of Selsey, partly dismantled in 1865, but until 1075 the cathedral church of the diocese, prior to the movement of the bishopric to Chichester (Aldsworth 1979).

The parish church of St Mary's, Kippax (West Yorkshire) is another that seems certain both to have pre-dated the adjacent Norman castle and to have been of particular ecclesistical importance in the surrounding district. The morphological relationship between the church and adjacent ringwork known as Manor Garth Hill suggests that here the (earlier) ecclesiastical site lay immediately against a bailey, or feasibly within an appending outer enclosure (Fig. 6.6: inset). The church incorporates a considerable volume of transitional herringbone masonry and at least two fragments of late tenth-century Saxon work (Collingwood 1914–18: 200–2; Holmes 1883–4: 380), suggesting that the structure may have been substantially re-built shortly after the Conquest, presumably around the time the ringwork was built. Three entries in the cartulary of Pontefract Priory suggest that the three parish churches of Swillington, Garforth and Whitkirk, were dependent upon a mother or minster church at Kippax (WYAS 1991: 11). Furthermore, reconstruction of the

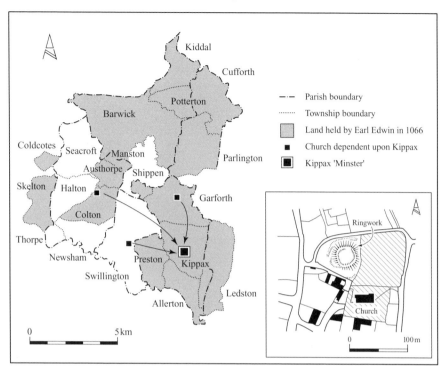

Figure 6.6 Kippax (West Yorkshire). Conjectured topography of a late-Saxon multiple estate and (inset) plan of the ringwork castle sited adjacent to the parish church of St Mary's (based on WYAS 1991, with additions).

late-eleventh-century tenurial geography of the surrounding area from the evidence of Domesday Book suggests that Kippax formed the *caput* of a compact, if decayed, pre-Conquest multiple estate (Fig. 6.6) (Faull and Moorhouse 1981: 420). In 1066 the surviving portion of this land unit was in the hands of Earl Edwin, but by 1086 it had been granted to Ilbert de Lacy and became part of the Honour of Pontefract. Kippax's pre-Conquest status was reflected in the construction of the ringwork next to the church, and ultimately in the fact that the honorial court was held here. Whether or not the ringwork is another that perpetuates the site of a Saxon thegn's residence remains a matter for speculation, but given the evidence from elsewhere, seems to be a distinct possibility.

Another way in which castle-building and the patronage of new Norman lords could influence the ecclesiastical landscape is demonstrated by the case of Pontefract (West Yorkshire) (Figs 6.7 and 6.8). This honorial castle, built by Ilbert de Lacy shortly after the Conquest in or near the Saxon settlement and *villa regia* of *Tanshelf*, had an initially disruptive impact. A pre-Conquest two-cell church with underlying burials has been excavated on the Booths site, with an associated cemetery that extended as far as Tanner's Row and Ass Hill, while other early medieval burials have been located within the bailey banks (Wilmott 1985, 1986, 1987a, 1987b; Youngs *et al.* 1987: 172). The church and its graveyard were thus displaced by the construction of the Norman

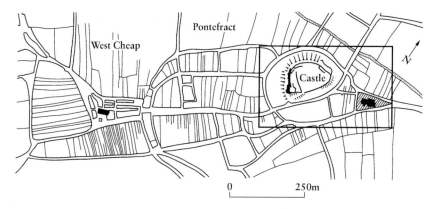

Figure 6.7 Urban and ecclesiastical topography at Pontefract (West Yorkshire), showing the street plan of the medieval castle-borough and the secondary borough of West Cheap, with a separate church. The area within the rectangle is mapped in more detail in Fig. 6.8 (based on Aston and Bond 1976, with additions).

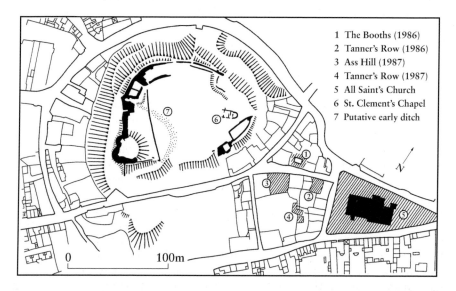

1 The Booths (1986)
2 Tanner's Row (1986)
3 Ass Hill (1987)
4 Tanner's Row (1987)
5 All Saint's Church
6 St. Clement's Chapel
7 Putative early ditch

Figure 6.8 Pontefract Castle (West Yorkshire), showing the location of All Saints' church and nearby excavations (after Wilmott 1987a).

castle, representing a massive assertion of seigneurial authority and a deliberate Norman intrusion into, and manipulation of, settlement and ecclesiastical topography. The town's ecclesiastical provision was radically altered by the end of the eleventh century through the foundation of the new Norman parish church of All Saints, while the collegiate church of St Clement's was constructed within the bailey to serve the spiritual needs of the castle household's inner core. The religious patronage of the de Lacy family found further expression in the endowment of a Cluniac priory (founded *c.* 1090) on a more secluded site beyond the town but within sight of the castle (Knowles and

Hadcock 1971: 102, 102, 435). That this structure represented the stamp of a powerful aristocratic family on the landscape as well as an expression of piety is reflected by the fact that Robert's parents were moved from their original place of rest to be re-interred in his new foundation (Hadley 2001: 142). Finally, the church of St Giles (earlier St Mary *de Foro*: 'in the market'), originating as a dependent chapel of All Saints but elevated to the status of parish church in 1789, was planned at the west end of the medieval town to serve the second borough of West Cheap.

Fortified churches

Occasionally a parish church could itself be converted into a fortification. As repositories of considerable portable wealth, medieval churches were prone to robbery and could be designed as extremely secure structures (Addy 1913: 89–98; Oman 1979). The rapid transformation of churches into defensible strongpoints by organized bodies of armed men is, however, quite different. This represented a response to another type of insecurity and is especially well chronicled during the Anarchy of Stephen's reign by the *Gesta Stephani* (Potter 1976). The common factor in these examples is extreme military necessity: the fortification of churches only occurred during periods of acute social and political stress, when the conservation of labour and time was at a premium and concerns about breaching the sanctuary of a church at a discount (Strickland 1996b: 86–90). This activity seems to have generally been opportunistic and short-lived, but has left little physical evidence. In Oxfordshire, for instance, the church tower at Bampton was fortified with a timber superstructure by the Empress as an outpost to Oxford, while in Wallingford, St Peter's, near the town's east gate, was converted into a siege-work by royal forces besieging the castle (Slade 1960: 36–7). Comparable Anarchy-period transformations of other ecclesiastical sites include the circumvallation of Southwell Minster (Nottinghamshire) in 1142 and the conversion of Bridlington Priory (North Yorkshire) into a fortification in 1143 after the canons had been evicted (King 1983: 382, 531). More important ecclesiastical buildings were also not exempt; the cathedrals of Coventry, Hereford and Lincoln were all employed as temporary military bases or 'counter-castles' during the Anarchy. No site in England, however, rivals the martial adaptation of the church at Meelick (Galway, Ireland), where the shell of the building was filled to the gables with spoil to form the nucleus of a motte (Renn 1968: 242). A possible parallel is the Norman motte at Great Somerford (Wiltshire), where excavations on the castle mound in 1910 revealed evidence of a buried earlier building with Romanesque windows that could be interpreted in a similar light (Goddard 1930: 88–9).

But castle-building could also result in the wholesale removal of churches and changes to the funerary landscape that could on occasion obliterate burial grounds, particularly in the urban context, where pressures on space could mean that church land was not immune to fortification (Hadley 2001: 40–1). At Barnstaple (Devon), the graveyard of a Saxon church, possibly a minster, was disrupted by the raising of castle earthworks shortly after the Conquest and the associated cutting of an enormous tidal moat (Fig. 6.9). Here,

Figure 6.9 Barnstaple (Devon) from the air. The large clump of trees to the centre-right of the photograph marks the position of the medieval motte whose construction disrupted an earlier cemetery; the perimeter of the Saxon town defences are perpetuated by the curving street pattern (photograph by F. M. Griffith, Devon County Council: copyright reserved).

archaeology indicated at least a degree of respect for the cemetery, as a minimum of nine graves were exhumed shortly beforehand, probably indicating de-consecration and the subsequent removal of high-status individuals or a family group for re-burial elsewhere (Miles 1986: 68). The ringwork known as Red Castle, Thetford (Norfolk) was constructed, rather unusually, astride the Saxon town ditch, in doing so also sealing a small church and associated cemetery outside the town defences, from which 85 burials have been excavated (Knocker 1966–9: 125–8, 130–1). Another Norman military infringement onto church property is documented at Worcester, where the bailey ditch cut off part of the cathedral priory cemetery (Brown *et al.* 1963: 888). Similar disturbances to urban burial grounds through castle-building are known archaeologically from Cambridge (Renn 1968: 128) and Taunton (Leach 1984: 26–36). In few of these cases, however, is archaeological evidence unequivocal that cemeteries were in use immediately prior to castle-building.

Those Anarchy period fortifications built within towns appear to show particular disrespect for burial grounds as castle builders sought to occupy open sites within the lines of town defences. Most notably, the graveyard of Hereford Cathedral was desecrated in 1140 when a rampart was built within it, as recorded in the *Gesta Stephani*. This provides a gruesome account detailing the unceremonious exhumation of decomposed bodies to the horror of the community (Speight 2000: 270–1). The erection of a castle in the precinct of Reading Abbey in 1150 prompted a papal bull forbidding future castle-building in the abbey's land (Astill 1978: 80), while the encroachment of a castle at Malmesbury (Wiltshire) onto the monks' cemetery prompted similar outrage (Haslam 1976: 35). These examples again underline that, in a time of perceived crisis, urban property – ecclesiastical as well as secular – could be rendered disposable due to the need to build on a preferred site.

Enclosed churches

We must distinguish between these aforementioned examples where castles were physically imposed upon extant church sites, and other cases where a church was embraced within the defended area, most usually lying inside the earthworks of a bailey or other appending enclosure, as at English Bicknor (Gloucestershire) and Lidgate (Suffolk). Occasionally, parish churches are contained within medieval ringworks, as at the sites of Hanslope and West Wycombe (Buckinghamshire) (VCH Bucks 1908: 26–7). Even where a church lies immediately adjacent to the castle site, perhaps sharing a common boundary, we may suspect that it formerly lay within outer defences that do not physically survive. This appears to be the case at Sherrington (Wiltshire), where the curving alignment of the road east of the motte and bailey seems to fossilize the outline of an outer bailey that embraced the small Norman parish church with its unusual dedication to Sts Cosmas and Damian (Creighton 2000a: 114–5). The parish church of St Nicholas in the small market town of Thorne (South Yorkshire) is another that seems to have been established in a former castle bailey appended to the motte known as 'Peel Hill'. The rectangular outline of this enclosure is again preserved in the surrounding street pattern, which also shows the castle and church to have lain adjacent to a marketplace, together forming the medieval core of the settlement (Ryder 1982: 97). Elsewhere, the plans of a churchyards as well as roads and properly boundaries may indicate the former alignment of bailey or outer bailey defences that are fully or partially eroded, as at Earl Shilton (Leicestershire) (Fig. 6.4), Palet Hill, Catterick (North Yorkshire) and Haughley (Suffolk). A key point here is that these churches – if they indeed coexisted with the castle in some form – would have occupied considerably less space in their eleventh- and twelfth-century forms. Many of these small, early churches within bailey enclosures may have been intended originally to serve the lord's household and its dependants only, and the tower may well have had some significance in proclaiming the lordly status of the site. These sites may thus perpetuate an earlier tradition, as indicated by the number of important Anglo-Saxon churches associated with high-status late Saxon residences, including good examples at Barton-upon-Humber (Lincolnshire) and Earl's Barton (North-amptonshire) (Williams 1992: 234–5; Audouy *et al.* 1995: 87–90). Renn (1993: 182) has coined the term 'towers of display' in the recognition that many late Saxon churches such as these were badges of secular status as well as ecclesiastical authority, as reflected in the emblematic architecture of their towers. Possession of a church conferred similar status on a Norman castle lord.

We should also not neglect that the presence of a church in a bailey could also have military advantages, with a stone tower perhaps acting as a strongpoint in an earth and timber fortification (Cronne 1970: 2). In a few instances a church may have effectively formed a gatehouse, as seen in the D-shaped Viking-age fortification at Repton (Derbyshire) (Biddle 1986: 16). Yet most enclosed churches sit predominantly in the centre of bailey enclosures, a notable exception being Redbourne (Lincolnshire), where the church of St Andrew is situated on the western perimeter of a moated outer ward (Loughlin and Miller 1979: 207). The parish church of St Mary, Cuckney (Nottinghamshire) stands entirely within a rectangular outer bailey associated with a low motte built on marshy ground within a bend of the River Poulter (Fig. 6.4). Here we have an unusual scenario in that the foundation date of a minor rural motte and bailey is well established: the cartulary of Welbeck identifies Thomas de Cuckney as the builder of the new castle during the 'old war' of 1139–45 (Stenton 1932: 199). Underpinning work beneath the church has revealed a large mass burial, comprising *c.* 200 male individuals, packed haphazardly into a minimum of three trenches that clearly antedated the church (Barley 1951). Its mid twelfth-century reconstruction may well be an act of seigneurial penance: de Cuckney was also the founder of the Pre-monstratensian house of Welbeck, whose foundation charter of *c.* 1153–4 includes St Mary's at Cuckney as a gift, and records the remarkable dedica-tion, '. . . for my soul and the souls of my father and my mother, but also for all those whom I have unjustly plundered' (Colvin 1951: 64–5). Here the present church may well therefore actually post-date a short-lived Anarchy-period castle. A far later example of a castle complex enveloping a parish church is Farleigh Hungerford (Somerset), where Walter Lord Hungerford's addition of a new outer ward to his father's fortified manor in the 1420s embraced the church of St Leonard (Morley 1977: 357). The building was retained, along

Figure 6.10   The unusual battlemented circular castle chapel at Ludlow (Shropshire). The standing structure represents the nave; only the foundations of the chancel survive (photograph: Oliver Creighton).

with its dedication, but converted into a castle chapel, and a replacement built within the village. Similar sequences have been recognized at Hereford, where an Anglo-Saxon church was enclosed within the defences of the first Norman castle and later abandoned, and Dover and London, where earlier churches were embraced following the extension of the castles' defences.

Castle chapels

The current archaeological data set relating to castle chapels is synthesized elsewhere (Kenyon 1990: 151–7) and the key historical material summarized (Pounds 1990: 224–31). A castle chapel was an essential feature of spiritual provision within most of the more important castles (Fig. 6.10), which could be squeezed into the design in many ingenious ways. Chapels or oratories could be incorporated into square or rectangular keeps (e.g. Colchester, Essex), shell keeps (e.g. Restormel, Cornwall) and round or polygonal keeps (e.g. Orford, Suffolk). They could also be built into mural towers (e.g. Framlingham, Suffolk) and gatehouses (e.g. Goodrich, Herefordshire) or against curtain walls (e.g. White Castle, Monmouthshire), while others were constructed as free-standing structures within courtyards or baileys (e.g. Carisbrooke, Isle of Wight). The growing sophistication of domestic castle planning, especially from the beginning of the thirteenth century, ensured that chapels became increasingly secluded institutions within the castle, reflecting the observation that it is often the more infrequent social activities which become disproportionately formalized in building plans (Hillier and Hanson

Figure 6.11 The parish church of St Mary Magdalene, Essendine (Rutland). The church is embraced within a large ditched enclosure appended to a ringwork castle, and probably originated as the castle chapel (photograph: Oliver Creighton).

1984: 235; Fairclough 1992: 362–4). In this sense, the growing privatization of spiritual space within castle planning may well be a direct manifestation of the withdrawal of increasingly aloof castle lords from the community. This trend was matched by progressive erosion of seigneurial rights over parish churches, including proprietary customs and hereditary priesthoods, so that by the end of the twelfth century private churches had become rare (Platt 1995: 9). Essentially, while in the late eleventh century parish church and proprietary castle chapel may often have been virtually indistinguishable, the later medieval period witnessed a fragmentation between, on the one hand, internalized castle chapels, and, on the other, the transferral of parish churches into the hands of monastic houses.

Often, a parish church close by, or integrated within a castle will have originated as a private castle chapel that, having received a grant of glebe-land from the lord, subsequently assumed parochial functions – a typical example of this process being Clitheroe (Lancashire) (Pounds 1990: 230). The parish church of St Mary de Magdalene Essendine (Rutland) (Fig. 6.11) is another that probably originated in this way. Positioned not only within the castle bailey, but sited explicitly at the interface between the inner and outer enclosures, the site is documented in a manorial extent of 1417 as a chapel in association with the capital messuage, which is presumably how it was founded and why it is curiously dislocated from the rest of the village (Creighton 1999a: 25–6). That the castle chapel within the bailey of Pleshey (Essex) was associated with a cemetery may seem unusual, given that burial rights were usually guarded jealously by medieval parish churches. Here it seems that the considerable distance between the original parish church at

Easter and the newly established Norman settlement ensured that the dependent chapel was exceptionally granted burial rights (Williams 1977: 14). Sometimes, the upgrading of castle chapel to parish church may well have occurred after the functional lifetime of the fortified site. The church of St George's, Doncaster, was another that originated in the capacity as a castle chapel. It long outlived the Norman castle which was levelled as early as *c.* 1200 and was rebuilt in Early English style over part of the former motte (Magilton 1977: 34).

Religious houses

The religious patronage of Norman castle lords contributed to the upsurge in monasticism in the generation after the Conquest, as new religious establishments, and, in particular 'alien' houses that owed allegiance to mother establishments in the homeland, were established on freshly acquired estates (Aston 2000: 74–5). Through an initial gift of land, seigneurial control could be exerted on the physical location of a monastery, while influence could be expressed through the appointment of personnel with strong linkages to the family. Important Benedictine foundations of this time associated with castles include houses at Belvoir (1076–8), Chester (1092–3), Dunster (1090) and Wallingford (1077–97). More marked still was the relationship between houses of the new Cluniac order and the *capita baroniae* of their founders, who invariably came from the front rank of the Norman aristocracy (Matthew 1962: 55–8). Prominent among the many Cluniac foundations in this mould is St Pancras, Lewes (East Sussex), established at the foot of the de Warenne's castle in 1077; others include Barnstaple (1107), Castle Acre (1089) and Northampton (1093–1100). Through an examination of grants made to the abbey of St-Florent de Saumur, Martindale (1992) has demonstrated the foundation of castle-priories in England perpetuated a trend already well established in Aquitaine, Brittany and Normandy, including well-documented eleventh-century establishments closely associated with the castles at Aumay, Dol and Pons. The essentially colonial nature of this enterprise is illustrated well by the fact that two of the earliest and most important grants made to St-Florent in England were for priories either founded within, or on estates appurtenant to, the castles of Bramber (West Sussex) (*c.* 1073–80, then moved to Beeding), and Monmouth (*c.* 1076–86). In later years, however, such twinned foundations came to be frowned upon by the more austere reformed monastic orders.

The reasons why monasteries accompanied so many castles, especially important ones, are many and varied. The foundation of a religious house could reap social and economic, as well as spiritual rewards for a lord who could gain comfort from the intercessory prayers and often elaborate commemorative practices offered by the religious community for their benefactors (Mortimer 1978). The stimulus that a monastery gave to the local economy could also indirectly prove lucrative to a landlord whose holdings increased in value. But by no means all monasteries founded by castle lords were built close to their residences; indeed this was virtually precluded for grants to orders such as the Cistercians and Carthusians, whose rules

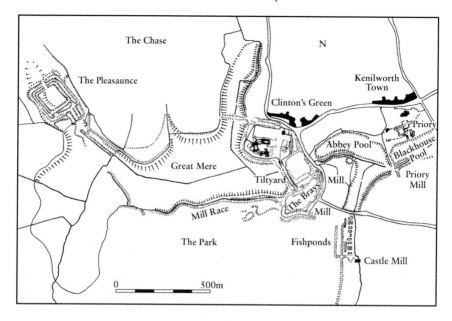

Figure 6.12 Kenilworth (Warwickshire), showing the medieval castle and priory and their relationship with water features including a large artificial mere and a series of fishponds (based on Aston and Bond 1988, with additions).

demanded a high level of seclusion. Nonetheless, the close physical juxtaposition of the two institutions could have additional practical benefits for a lord, including the local availability of legal, financial and secretarial expertise. Representatives of the monastic community could provide services in the castle chapel, which may partially explain the disproportionately large number of Augustinian houses found close to castles, as these canons were also ordained priests. A nearby monastery could also provide overspill accommodation for the households and retinues of visiting personnel. Finally and perhaps most importantly, the association of high-status residence and monastic house was a symbol of immense prestige – a notion that can be traced back to royal continental traditions of the tenth and eleventh centuries (Thompson 1991: 137). The type of élite landscape created by the combination of a castle and nearby religious house – which if not always directly adjacent were invariably intervisible – is illustrated particularly well in Gloucester. Here, in 1277 a bridge was thrown up over the castle ditch so that Eleanor of Provence and members of her household could gain access to the extensive gardens of Lanthony Priory that lay between the castle and monastic house (Harvey 1981: 84–6).

A twinning of monastery and castle could thus serve as a conspicuous monument to the founding family and their successors, especially when it simultaneously functioned as mausoleum for a dynasty whose principal seat of residence lay close by. Usually, the foundation of a monastery will occur subsequent to the establishment of the castle, often representing the apotheosis in the development of a wider seigneurial landscape. At Kenilworth (Warwickshire) (Fig. 6.12), however, the two institutions were planned

Table 6.1 Monastic foundations in England and Wales related to castles, by century

Order	11th	12th	13th	14th	15th	16th
Benedictine	14	13	—	1	—	—
Cluniac	7	6	—	—	—	—
Alien	15	8	—	—	—	—
Augustinian	2	26	2	3	—	—
Premonstratensian	—	6	—	—	—	—
Cistercian and Savignac	—	13	1	1	—	—
Secular colleges	6	5	3	16	8	2
Other orders	1	2	3	2	3	1
Totals	45	79	9	23	11	3

Source: Thompson 1986

together and built simultaneously, as indicated in the priory's foundation charter and evident in the remarkably integrated nature of the castle's and monastery's fishponds and other associated water features (VCH Warwicks 1908: 86; Thompson 1977: 4–5). Only in the later medieval period, and then only very exceptionally, do we see the castle as successor, as at Maxstoke (Warwickshire) and Wingfield (Surrey), where licences to crenellate closely followed the establishment of collegiate churches in the mid-fourteenth century.

A list of those monastic houses in England and Wales founded and promoted by castle lords has been compiled by Thompson (1986), comprising a total of 170 sites (Table 6.1). The pattern of foundation obviously reflects, in a wider sense, the prevailing fortunes of the various rival monastic orders, but also indicates that castle lords displayed preferences for certain types of houses. The scale of these monastic foundations varied immensely, ranging from tiny colleges of canons, to wealthy religious houses that rivalled the castle lord as a landholder and the castle itself as a focus of investment and economic activity. For example, the great Cistercian house of Rievaulx, founded by Walter Espec less than 3 kilometres away from his castle at Helmsley (North Yorkshire) emerged as the key economic institution within the locality, almost overshadowing the castle-town as a commercial centre. Overall, the physical link between the castle and monastery was not as strong as with the parish church, and there is evidence that the two were not always happy bedfellows. The case of Tynemouth (Northumberland) was certainly unusual, the Benedictine priory and castle here being virtually indivisible and together occupying a wild promontory, as with St Michael's Mount (Cornwall), originally a monastery but from 1194 also an island fortress of the Crown. Particularly short-lived was Henry I's foundation of a new house of Augustinian Canons at Portchester (Hampshire), located in the opposite corner of the Roman Saxon Shore fort to the castle. Established in 1133, the monastery was transplanted to Southwick between 1145 and 1153, and part of the abandoned building was re-used as the parish church (Cunliffe 1977: 3, 97–120). The Cluniac house that Hugh de Leicester established next to his castle at Preston Capes (Northamptonshire) in 1090 was also later moved, this time within a mere 18 years to Daventry, the monks having suffered from their proximity to the castle as well as a shortage of water (Golding 1980: 68).

The association between castles and colleges of secular canons, comprising associations of priests attached to a church and adhering to a common rule,

Figure 6.13 The parish church of St Nicholas, Bramber (West Sussex). This little church was established on the steep slopes below the entrance of the castle by William de Braose in *c.* 1073, not originally as a parish church but as the chapel of a body of secular priests (photograph: Oliver Creighton).

was a more enduring trend of the medieval period (Hamilton Thompson 1917: 153). The earliest of these sites were often small in scale, some being located within baileys, while others survive as parish churches, as at Bramber (Fig. 6.13). The small college of St Mary Magdalene founded in Quatford by Roger de Montgomery in 1086, was transplanted 12 years later by his son Robert to the bailey of his castle at Bridgnorth (Shropshire) (Clark-Maxwell and Hamilton Thompson 1927: 1). The collegiate church of St Mary de Castro in Leicester always lay in the bailey of the castle. Its establishment by Robert of Meulan in 1107 was probably a re-foundation on the site of a Saxon minster, and the church also had parochial status (Radford 1955: 156–8). Another enclosed collegiate church that may have pre-Conquest origins is the establishment crammed into the north side of the bailey of Hastings Castle (Sussex). Here, a late-thirteenth-century petition from the canons implies that Robert d'Eu, first lord of the Rape of Hastings, may have re-founded an earlier church, perhaps the enigmatic structure represented in stylized form in the well-known scene of Hastings on the Bayeux Tapestry (Taylor 1985: 233–40). After a steady stream of foundations, this tradition climaxed in the fourteenth and fifteenth centuries with the establishment of a series of vast and expensive collegiate churches associated with particularly important castles. Some of these again lay within baileys, such as St George's, Windsor, Berkshire (1348), which may have been an model for others, and Henry Percy's ambitious cruciform church at Warkworth (Northumbria), begun late in the fourteenth century but left unfinished. Other examples were built on plots beyond the defensive perimeter, including Fotheringhay (Northamptonshire) (1411), and Ralph Lord Cromwell's Tattershall (Lincolnshire) (1439–40).

Castle and monastery could have an important combined impact on town plans. Sometimes the two institutions formed a unified cell that could act as a stimulus to urban growth. Nowhere is this better represented than at Durham, where the precinct of the great Benedictine cathedral priory and the castle of the prince-bishop together occupy the entire area of a narrow peninsula within a bend of the Wear. The medieval topography of Belvoir (Leicestershire) also embodied the three-fold association of castle, borough and priory, and circum-stantial evidence points towards all three institutions being founded in a very short space of time by the same Norman lord, Robert de Todeni (Beresford 1967: 461–2). Situated on a spur of the Leicestershire wolds overlooking the Trent valley, the borough was, however, remote from routes of communica-tion, ensuring its eventual failure. At Bourne (Lincolnshire), the precincts of the castle and the abbey of St Peter and Paul, a house of Arrouasian canons established c. 1138, formed an integrated unit on the southern edge of the town. The creation of the large precinct that linked the two features resulted in the re-routing of the former Roman road King Street to form the axis of the medieval town that sprung up at their gates (Hayes and Lane 1992: 140). At Hinckley (Leicestershire) the castle and Benedictine monastery again form a unified cell under the patronage of the earls of Leicester (Thompson 1986: 313), the monastic institution flanked on one side by the castle and on the other by a deer park, as at Pontefract (West Yorkshire). The planning of deer parks in this manner may have been a very deliberate means of preserving the isolation of monasteries from the urban scene while physically associating them with the castle of their patron to create an élite landscape. The town plan of Dunster (Somerset) is another strongly related to its priory as well as the castle and appended deer park, the monastic precinct being an important topographical feature that both limited and dictated the course of the settlement's expansion into the post-medieval period (Riley and Wilson-North 2001: 120).

Perhaps more commonly, monastery and castle were separated in the town plan, as at Worksop (Nottinghamshire), where commercial activity focused on a small marketplace adjacent to the priory promoted by the castle lord, rather than concentrating near the motte and bailey (Holland 1826: 64; Speight 1995: 68). At Castle Acre (Norfolk), the Cluniac Priory lay in a generous precinct immediately beyond the defences of the planted castle-town (Fig. 6.14), although having originally being situated within the castle itself, probably in the lower ward (Beaumont 1997: 11). Here and elsewhere, seigneurial policy clearly favoured a separation of functions; clearly admin-istrative/defensive and ecclesiastical considerations demanded different opti-mal sites.

Summary

This chapter has explored the often complex networks of patronage that linked castles and their lords to the ecclesiastical landscape. While evidence for the interrelationships between castles and cathedrals, monasteries, parish churches and chapels has been reviewed separately, sometimes the distinction between these various ecclesiastical institutions could be blurred. For instance,

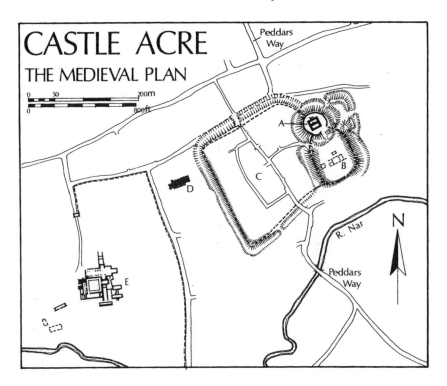

Figure 6.14 Castle Acre (Norfolk), showing the relationship between the medieval castle, town and priory. Key to numbering: A, castle upper ward; B, castle lower ward; C, medieval enclosed town; D, parish church; E, Cluniac priory (Coad and Streeten 1982).

it has been demonstrated that many parish churches began their lives as castle chapels (e.g. Doncaster), while other parish churches within or adjacent to castles were monastic in origin (e.g. Portchester). While monasteries seem to have generally followed castles, a great number of parish churches appear to pre-date the seigneurial site. Links between castles and the church were in many ways strongest in the late eleventh and early twelfth century. It was in this period that, at the upper end of the spectrum of castle building society, great magnates founded major monastic houses within sight of their *capita* (e.g. Lewes), and many lesser lords or tenants founded their castles adjacent to parish churches (e.g. Hough-on-the-Hill). While changing religious sensibilities and fashions saw some of these linkages weakened or broken, the fourteenth century saw a revival of sorts in the foundation of magnificent collegiate churches in association with some major castles (e.g. Warkworth). In all these cases, the power of religious patronage was another way in which castle lords and their families made their mark on the landscape.

7 Castles and Urbanism

Castles, along with those cathedrals transplanted to towns by the Norman regime, were newcomers to the urban scene, representing a type of private fortification that stood in marked contrast to the communal defensive traditions of earlier periods. What effect did the act of castle plantation and the new high-status presence have on the fortunes of an urban community, and, more importantly, what were the consequences, both long- and short-term, for the development of the townscape itself? Drage (1987) has defined two essential chronological relationships between castle and town: the 'urban castle', where the castle intrudes into an extant town, and the 'castle borough', where a primary castle attracts a secondary borough or the two are planned as an integrated unit. Both of these relationships are associated with distinctive spatial patterns: while an urban castle was commonly inserted on the periphery of a town, the plan of a castle borough usually gravitates around the dominant castle. In addition, while the plantation of an urban castle would transmit social signals of conquest and domination to the urban community, the foundation of a castle borough implies seigneurial economic ambition and investment (Drage 1987: 117, 128). But the division between the urban castle and castle with castle-borough was not always clear-cut. For instance, some Norman castle-towns were, in reality, Saxon villages re-cast as boroughs, while the imposition of new castles in Saxon urban centres could also result in the creation of separate boroughs.

Despite these various interrelationships between castles and towns, we must remember that castle-building in medieval England was predominantly a rural phenomenon. For complex social and political reasons that have yet to be fully explained, the medieval élite tended to build their defensible residences in the countryside rather than in urban settings (Higham and Saunders 1997: 122). In England, those castles built in major urban settlements (as opposed to castles to which towns were attached) were predominantly royal in origin, re-enforcing an enduring link between the monarchy and the towns. This is in contrast to other parts of Europe, and, indeed, elsewhere in the British Isles, where the construction of private fortified residences within medieval towns is well attested. In parts of Ireland, for instance, private tower houses built by members of the mercantile classes were not an uncommon feature of the late medieval townscape (e.g. Taafe's Castle, Carlingford, Co. Louth, Ireland), and some towns had more than one such site (McNeill 1997: 209–10).

Urban castles and the Norman Conquest

Castles built within the urban centres of late Anglo-Saxon England form a coherent group, in terms of their settings, initial functions and the date of their foundations. These sites, including some of the most imposing mottes and largest ringworks in Britain were raised, with very few exceptions, in the

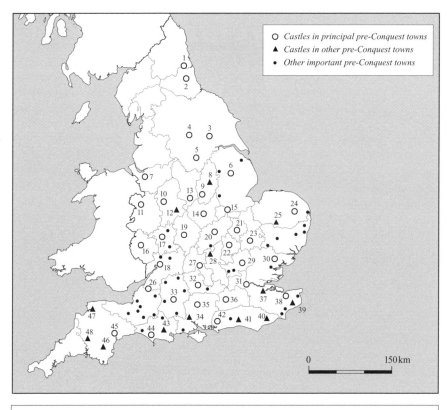

1 Newcastle	12 Tamworth	23 Cambridge	34 Southampton	45 Exeter
2 Durham	13 Derby	24 Norwich	35 Winchester	46 Totnes
3 York	14 Leicester	25 Thetford	36 Guildford	47 Barnstaple
4 Tadcaster	15 Stamford	26 Bristol	37 Rochester	48 Lydford
5 Doncaster	16 Hereford	27 Oxford	38 Canterbury	
6 Lincoln	17 Worcester	28 Buckingham	39 Dover	
7 Chester	18 Gloucester	29 Hertford	40 Hastings	
8 Newark	19 Warwick	30 Colchester	41 Lewes	
9 Nottingham	20 Northampton	31 London	42 Chichester	
10 Stafford	21 Huntingdon	32 Wallingford	43 Wareham	
11 Shrewsbury	22 Bedford	33 Old Sarum	44 Dorchester	

Figure 7.1 Location map of urban castles in England (based on Drage 1987, with additions).

unique socio-political context of the immediate post-Conquest years (*c.* 1066–80), and the majority sited in Saxon *burhs*. The net result of this castle-building programme was that, in a very short space of time, the majority of towns acting as major centres of regional administration in the first half of the eleventh century had castles imposed within them or in their immediate hinterlands (Figs 7.1 and 7.2). Most of these towns had royal connections: many contained mints and operated as centres for the gathering of taxes, collectively representing the machinery of political control. With the towns of England on the eve of the Conquest containing an estimated 5 to 7 per cent of the population, William's policy thus suppressed not only population centres, but also wealthy and powerful enclaves with the potential to challenge royal

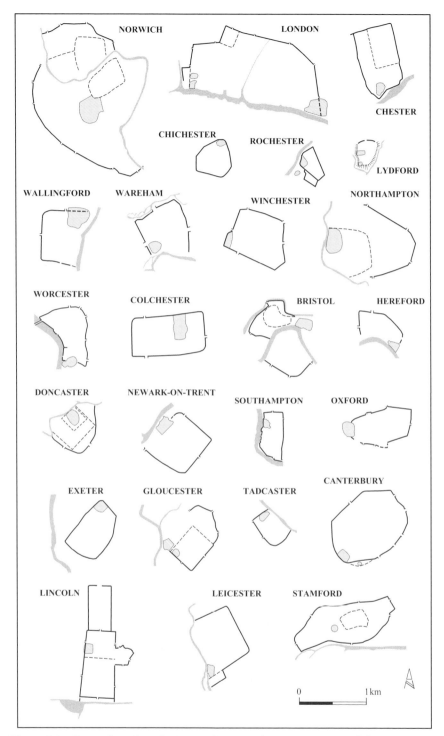

Figure 7.2 Examples of castles inserted into earlier towns. Town defences are indicated with solid lines and earlier defensive perimeters with dashed lines; the areas of the castles are indicated by shading.

authority (Hinton 1990: 115). Equally significant is the large proportion of the total number of early Norman castles raised in towns, with almost 50 per cent of all castles documented positively before 1100 having urban settings (Armitage 1912: 94–6; Drage 1987: 117). In an altogether different category are those few twelfth-century urban castles raised during the Anarchy, including examples at Shaftesbury (Dorset), and Cricklade, Malmesbury and Wilton (Wiltshire), all of which were built within towns of Saxon origin but were extremely short-lived and have left few discernible traces.

The systematic nature of eleventh-century urban castle-building also indicates Norman acceptance and perpetuation of an extant system of administration based upon the shire. Moreover, in the North, castles built in established centres of significance formed the administrative centres of new shires, as with Bamburgh (Northumberland), built on the ancient seat of the Northumbrian kings, and later Newcastle-upon-Tyne, and Carlisle (Cumbria). In the Midlands and the South, a high proportion of those Saxon centres containing urban castles emerged as medieval county towns. Those Saxon towns which escaped castle-building were primarily non-defended commercial and industrial foci, especially ports on the east coast (e.g. Torksey, Lincolnshire), or towns under ecclesiastical authority (e.g. Bury St Edmunds, Suffolk), as opposed to key military and political centres.

Derby was unique among the Five Boroughs of the Midlands in lacking a major castle. That said, a minor and impermanent Norman fortification appears to have been raised shortly after the Conquest: the *Copecastel* ('the castle near the market') is recorded in 1085, and a motte, depicted in pseudo-Bayeux style, is featured on Speed's map of 1610, although all evidence was obliterated by the late eighteenth century (Williamson 1942: 6). In explaining the unusual absence of an important urban castle within this shire it may be significant that in the eleventh century Derby was paired administratively with Nottingham, with which it shared a sheriff. The Domesday entry for the borough follows as opposed to precedes the folios relating to the rest of the shire, and Derby is thus associated in the text with Nottinghamshire (Martin 1987: 56). A royal castle at Derby may well have been superfluous, especially given the establishment of a new French borough at Nottingham in preference to its neighbour, whose fortunes after the Conquest declined in comparison. A parallel situation existed in East Anglia with regard to Norwich and Ipswich: the former with a major royal castle, the latter with a castle eradicated entirely from the townscape following demolition in the twelfth century (Barley 1976: 70).

The two principal urban centres of southern England – the old English capital of Winchester and the pre-eminent commercial centre of London – were singled out for castle-building in 1067, when new fortified enclosures were established in the corners of existing town defences of Roman origin. William the Conqueror's subsequent campaigns of conquest studded the towns of late Saxon England with castles which were likewise invariably built as intra-mural fortifications. The first major campaign resulting in and supported by the construction of urban castles was the repression of the south-western uprising of 1067–8. Following the resistance of Exeter's civilian population to a Norman siege of the city for no less than 18 days, a massive ringwork was established in the northern corner of the city, providing testimony of the effectiveness of the *burh* defences. Historical events such as

William's protracted siege of Exeter underline the point that urban castle-building was sometimes carried out in the face of very real native resistance. Such opposition was not coordinated across the newly conquered territory, but manifested itself in the form of fierce regionalist uprisings that necessitated the suppression of key power bases. The following campaign presumably involved the foundation of Devonian urban castles at Lydford, Totnes and, possibly, Barnstaple (Higham 1987: 35). The most important of William's subsequent military operations was the great northern campaign of 1068. In this year the Norman chronicler Orderic describes the construction of castles at Nottingham, Warwick and York as royal foundations in the first phase of the campaign; fortifications at Cambridge, Huntingdon and Lincoln were raised on William's return journey from York (Chibnall 1969: 218). The statement within the *Anglo-Saxon Chronicle* that castles were built 'everywhere in that district' (Whitelock *et al.* 1961: 148) provides the likely historical context for a series of other urban sites in the Midlands and the North (likely candidates include Leicester and Stamford, both of which lie on major communications routes probably used in the campaign); other urban castles built shortly after include Chester and Stafford (1070) and Durham (1072) (Brown *et al.* 1963: 20–1).

While significant in the late eleventh century, royal castle-building in the towns was anathema relative to the wider pattern of medieval castle plantation. As discussed in Chapter 3, most castles formed no part of a national defensive strategy, but were built relative to the aims, ambitions and motives of individual lords. Urban castles were the prominent exception to this rule: the rapidity and coherency of this castle-building programme points towards a unified programme of Norman repression. Here also emerges a central paradox: this unique generation of early urban castles, constructed under the express orders of William as tools of military conquest and in a sense the most 'Norman' castles of all, sometimes resemble earlier traditions of Anglo-Saxon fortification in terms of their social and landscape contexts. Indeed, the earliest Norman urban castles and latest Saxon *burhs* may not have been fundamentally dissimilar in function. This is especially so with respect to the last generation of tenth-century English *burh* building, when Edward the Elder and Ethelflaed built Saxon fortifications at places such as Stamford and Nottingham in support of offensive campaigns, as distinct from the classic conception of the Wessex *burh* (Strickland 1996a: 370). Later *burhs* such as these took the form of fortified enclosures for the containment of garrisons, built to dominate centres and control communications routes, rather than enclosing population and centralizing the means of production in the manner of Alfredian *burhs* such Wallingford and Wareham. In addition, in the years immediately following the Conquest, urban castles were not seigneurial residences in any real sense. Built under royal control these sites were nearly always entrusted to appointed officials such as castellans, stewards or sheriffs, including Baldwin de Meules (Exeter), Eudo Dapifer (Colchester) and William Peveril (Nottingham); it is only later that sites emerged at the head of feudal baronies or as episcopal seats. The specific sites chosen for some urban castles also hark back to earlier English defensive traditions, as exemplified by the twin castles of York, which straddle an important riverine route of communication in a manner reminiscent of the 'double-*burhs*' of the pre-Conquest period (Brooks 1971: 72).

As potent symbols of a newly established Norman regime, urban castles were also reminders to the indigenous population of who the power holders were in the new order. Nowhere was this more necessary than London, where William of Poitiers commented that the early Norman fortifications raised in 1067 (presumably on the sites re-built as the Tower of London, Baynard's Castle and Montfichet Castle), were '. . . completed in the city as a defence against the inconstancy of the numerous and hostile inhabitants' (Davies and Chibnall 1998: 161–3). The raising of three contemporary fortifications in a single city is unprecedented in Britain, reflecting the particular need to keep the population of London under subjection but also, perhaps, political motives, as while the Tower remained in royal hands, the other two castles were always under separate, private, occupancy (Watson 1992: 336). As Vince (1990: 39) has pointed out, it is not coincidental that the strongest, most impressive and best maintained defences of the White Tower (built around 1078) faced towards, rather than away from, the Saxon city and its resentful citizens. Only very rarely did the principal point of access to an urban castle face away from the town, although Winchester is one exception; invariably the gatehouse faced into the town. The psychological impact of the immense White Tower on London's late-eleventh-century cityscape must have been even more pronounced given the rather unimpressive appearance of the Saxon palace of Westminster, located west of the city on a low-lying site sandwiched between the abbey and banks of the Thames (Steane 1999: 72). The Norman palace-keep was, in contrast, a conspicuously elevated structure that loomed over the Thames estuary as an unmistakable feature to river traffic entering the capital from continental Europe.

Many of these early urban castles of the Norman conquest, built initially to serve very particular military purposes, fell into sharp decline from as early as the early twelfth century. At Gloucester, for instance, the original Norman castle, squeezed into the south-west corner of the Roman walled circuit (Fig. 7.3), was replaced by a new foundation on a fresh waterfront site to the north-west in the first decades of the twelfth century. By the late twelfth century the early motte and bailey was recorded as *vetus castellum* ('old castle') in the deeds of St Peter's Abbey (Hurst 1984: 76). Medieval towns could also expand internally, and there is much late medieval documentary evidence for piece-meal reclamation of castle sites by urban communities, most often for grazing, but occasionally for other purposes. The animal-bone assemblage from Launceston Castle (Cornwall) charts in particularly fine detail the site's decline in status as it was progressively used as an urban tip. This transition is apparent in the decreasing range of animal species and, in particular, the sharp decline of fish and birds in the assemblage from the sixteenth century onwards (Albarella and Davis 1994: 20). Other possible uses for neglected or abandoned castle sites are indicated by the incorporation of Baile Hill, York into the urban defences by the early fourteenth century (Addyman and Priestley 1977: 121), and the colonization of Oxford Castle's heavily silted moat with the plots of late medieval town houses (Hassall 1976: 254).

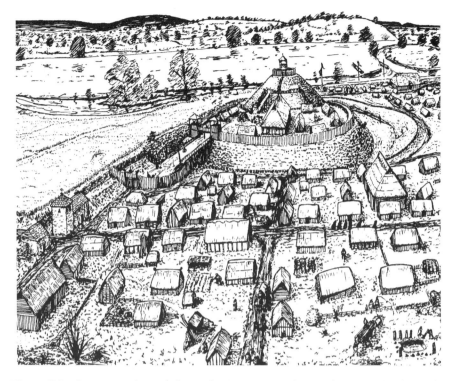

Figure 7.3 Reconstruction of the early Norman castle at Gloucester in the early twelfth century, showing the position of the motte and bailey relative to the town defences and urban settlement pattern (Darvill 1988).

Urban castles and Domesday Book

Domesday Book mentions the destruction of property and dwellings due to the construction of castle sites in eleven separate instances (Table 7.1). The vast mottes, baileys and ringworks that formed the earliest phases of these fortifications certainly took up large areas of urban space, and houses were doubtless flattened in order to prepare their sites. We should also not overlook the likelihood that substantial areas beyond a castle's perimeter defences would also have been cleared in order to create a surrounding *cordon sanitaire*, both for military reasons and to separate urban community and garrison. There are, however, two very good reasons why the statistics in Domesday should not be taken literally. First, some of the numbers of cleared properties are undoubtedly estimates rather than reliable figures; the entry for Lincoln, for example, shows a tendency to count properties in multiples of five or six, rather than representing the precise extent of damage (Hill 1965: 53–5). Second, terms such as *mansiones* (residences) and *mansurae* (dwellings) are used in a quasi-legal as opposed to a physical sense. This means that the number of wasted properties need not correlate with the number of actual households displaced. Indeed, in certain cases Domesday may severely underrepresent the destruction of property. This seems to have been the case at Stamford (Lincolnshire), where the castle may have lain beyond the custom-

Table 7.1 The destruction of urban property by Norman Castles mentioned in Domesday Book

Town	Description in Domesday Book
Cambridge	'This single ward was accounted as two before 1066 but 27 houses (*domus*) have been destroyed for the castle.' (189a)
Canterbury	'Of 32 others who were there have been destroyed, 11 in the city ditch, the Archbishop has 7 of them, the Abbot of St Augustine's another 14 in exchange for the castle.' (2a)
Gloucester	'Where the castle is sited there were 16 houses (*domus*) which do not exist now.' (162a)
Huntingdon	'On the castle site there were 20 residences (*mansiones*) liable for all customary dues, which paid 16s 8d a year to the King's revenue. They are not there now.' (203a)
Lincoln	'166 (*mansiones*) were destroyed because of the castle' (336c).
Norwich	'17 empty dwellings (*mansurae*) which are in the occupation of the castle' (116b).
Shrewsbury	'the earl's castle has taken over 51 dwellings (*mansurae*)' (252a).
Stamford	'5 (*mansiones*) are unoccupied because of the construction of the castle' (336d).
Wallingford	'8 sites (*haguae*) were destroyed for the castle' (56b).
Warwick	'4 (*mansurae*) are waste, because of the castle site' (238a).
York	'One of these (*shires*) has been laid waste for the castles' (298a).

paying boundaries of the borough and within a former Saxon royal estate, thus accounting for the exceptionally low figure of five displaced properties (Roffe and Mahany 1986: 6). The curiously low figure of eight properties destroyed to make way for the castle at Wallingford (Oxfordshire) indicates either that this part of the Saxon town was already depopulated by the time of the Conquest or, more likely, that it was the site of previous high-status occupation: Domesday Book records that Miles Crispin, the Norman lord of Wallingford and probable builder and castellan of the castle, holds 'the land where the housecarls lived' (Keats-Rohan 1986: 312). The impact of Norman lordship on the Saxon townscape was particularly conspicuous given that the Holy Trinity Priory was established adjacent to the castle by the end of the eleventh century, the precincts of two new sites taking up the entire northern part of the *burh* (Airs *et al.* 1975).

In addition, as a primarily rural survey, Domesday's account of the number of towns where property was wasted due to castle-building is not exhaustive, as archaeological evidence at, for instance, Newark (Nottinghamshire) has revealed (see below). In a number of other Domesday boroughs wasted property is mentioned, yet castle-building is, perhaps unsurprisingly, not singled out as the causal factor. Examples include Exeter (48 houses), Oxford (478) and Wareham (73); in all three cases it is likely that castle-building at least contributed to the displacement of property. But it is important to view the evidence of property wasted due to castle-building in the context of the destruction that could be wrought in boroughs for other reasons. Something in the region of 3,500 properties are documented as lying waste in 30 of the total 112 Domesday boroughs (Darby 1977: 364–8; Harfield 1991: 373), many for reasons not associated with castle-building. For instance, in Canterbury 27 dwellings were cleared for the archbishop's residence, while at Ipswich, 328 dwellings were recorded as waste in a town where no castle was ever built.

Urban castles and the townscape

The siting of castles within late Saxon towns highlights the often disruptive impact of Norman royal authority on the townscape, although in many cases a brief episode of devastation was followed closely by urban renewal. This Norman appropriation of extant urban centres is exemplified by an aerial view of Totnes (Devon) – the profile of the motte clearly imposed within earlier defences and its bailey projecting into the hinterland beyond (Fig. 7.4). Such re-use and adaptation of pre-existing defensive topography was at one level a pragmatic means of rapidly raising a defensive strongpoint in potentially hostile territory, but also represented a deliberate intrusion into urban space in order to keep the civilian population in check. Imposition of an urban castle could clearly transform a Saxon townscape radically. In the short-term, settlement could be flattened, communications networks disrupted and water courses diverted in order to level and defend a site, while, in the longer-term, properties and streets could be re-planned as the townscape adjusted to a castle's presence. The initial military rôles of urban castles ensured that optimum sites would be chosen almost regardless of consequences, and it was not unknown for castle-building to destroy churches, chapels and monasteries, and to swamp urban cemeteries. Excavations on the Castle Mall site in Norwich have provided remarkable insight into the consequences of a castle's imposition within a late Saxon town. The area known as the Castle Fee occupied an immense zone of over 9 hectares, with the construction and expansion of the royal castle causing immense disruption to the townscape; the appendage as early as 1075 of a borough for the *Franci de Norwic* on a greenfield site to the west, meanwhile, influenced the future course of Norwich's urban expansion (Ayers 1994: 74; Hutcheson 2000: 64–5). Beneath the south bailey evidence of some 26 timber pre-Conquest buildings has been identified, along with storage and refuse pits indicating craft production and grain storage (Shepherd 1997: 187; Shepherd 2000: 54). The southern bailey rampart sealed part of a cemetery in use until the time of the castle's construction while the north-east bailey disrupted a second graveyard and a pre-Conquest church; still more burial areas lie under the north part of the site (Ayers 1985: 63–6).

Even in the absence of detailed excavation, topographical analysis of surviving medieval street networks has much to tell us of disruptive impact of urban castles. At Wallingford (Oxfordshire) the castle takes up the entire north-east quadrant of the rectangular *burh*, obliterating all evidence of the grid-plan Saxon street network which is otherwise well preserved in the southern part of the town (Astill 1984: 73–6). Even after urban castles fell into disuse, as relict features their imprint on street networks and the pattern of later urban development could be enduring. At Wareham (Dorset) the Norman castle was similarly superimposed in one quarter of the Saxon *burh*, where a rectilinear street network and intramural route in the south-west corner has been replaced the curving lines around Pound Lane and West Street, fossilizing the perimeter of an inner and outer bailey (Hinton 1977: 131–2; Penn 1980: 111–12). The conspicuous gap in the gridded street network of Bedford, occupied by the castle earthworks, indicates a similar sequence: a conspicuous bulge in the road immediately to the east of the

Figure 7.4 Aerial view of Totnes (Devon). The street pattern clearly fossilizes the plan of Saxon *burh* defences, into which has been imposed a Norman castle (photograph by F. M. Griffith, Devon County Council: copyright reserved).

former castle site suggests the re-alignment of a pre-Norman road and other streets fossilize the outline of a lost bailey (Baker 1973: 15; Bigmore 1979: 98). At Lydford (Devon), the same relationship is duplicated, yet on a tiny scale, with the very tip of the Saxon promontory *burh* occupied by a small crescentic ringwork (Newman 2000). Part of the perimeter of the Norman fort was formed by the substantial Saxon defences, comprising a bank 40 ft (*c.* 12.2 m) wide, with an inserted granite revetment wall (Wilson and Hurst 1965: 170–1; Wilson and Hurst 1966: 168–9, 196–7: Wilson and Hurst 1967: 263). It seems inconceivable, however, that the construction of an earthwork occupying a site of merely *c.* 55 × 60 m could account for the 40 destroyed houses mentioned in Domesday (Saunders 1980: 127). Here, we may suspect the clearance of a far more extensive zone of the *burh*, perhaps an entire cell of the town plan to form a precinct associated with the ringwork.

In all these examples, and elsewhere, the Normans clearly favoured a policy of siting an urban castle in the corner of an extant defensive circuit of early medieval origin. A similar relationship between castles and pre-existing defences is apparent with regards to civil defences built in the Roman period. Outwardly, military pragmatism and economy of effort would seem to be the principal factors conditioning such a topographic relationship – the corner of the defensive circuit forming the structural basis for a motte or ringwork, and the right angle constituting two sides of a bailey. At Gloucester (Fig. 7.3), the early Norman motte, now obliterated by urban development, was squeezed exactly within the right-angle of the city wall, with the Roman town ditches incorporated into its defences on the south and west sides (Atkin 1991: 21). The motte and bailey at Leicester, sited in the south-west corner of the Roman defences, appears outwardly to have a similar setting. Limited excavations of the Roman civil defences immediately adjacent to the castle have, however, revealed the earlier rampart and wall to have been completely disrupted by the cutting of the Norman bailey ditch (Buckley and Lucas 1987: 45), indicating the castle defences as not respecting antecedent defensive topography in detail. Here the angle of Leicester's town defences may have been occupied for overall strategic value rather than economy of effort, with the castle sited to dominate communications routes from a prominent position raised high on the east bank of the River Soar.

The Norman Conquest's imprint on the townscape of York was particularly pronounced. With the sole exception of London, the city is unique in the imposition of multiple castles as elements within a unified strategy of urban domination: one erected in 1068 and garrisoned with 500 knights; the other raised in 1069 in response to a successful Viking attack on the first fortification (Armitage 1912: 242–3). What is abundantly clear is that complementary castles were clearly essential to achieve both effective subjugation of a city with two clear foci either side of the Ouse, and to seize and dominate the vital intersection of north-south and east-west routes marked by the river crossings (Figs. 7.5: top and 7.6). It remains uncertain, however, whether the Domesday evidence of urban devastation reflects destruction wrought on the city due to Norman ravaging and retribution following the events of 1068–9, or solely the physical clearance of tenements to make way for the two castles. At Durham, for instance, excavation has raised the possibility that medieval tenements in Saddler Street may have been deliberately fired during the harrying which

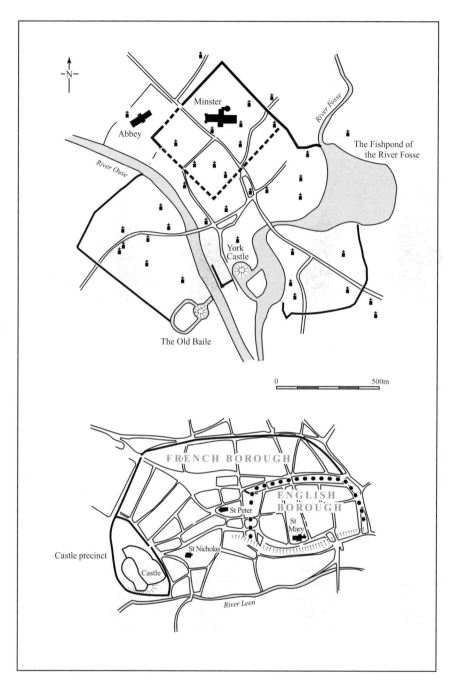

Figure 7.5 Urban castles at Nottingham and York.

Figure 7.6 Part of the city wall of York. The site of Baile Hill, York's second Norman castle located in the southern part of the city, lies in the background, partly obscured by tree cover (photograph: Oliver Creighton).

preceded castle-building (Carver 1979: 71). Both sites at York appear to have occupied relatively undeveloped areas of the cityscape in order to take advantage of commanding natural positions (RCHME York 1962: 107; 1972: 60, 87), and it seems likely that the devastation was attributable to other factors beyond the immediate preparation of two castle sites. The damming of the Foss to create the King's Pool, which flanked York castle, resulted in the inundation of part of six carucates of agricultural land belonging to the archbishop's hall and two newly built mills worth 20 shillings, as also recorded in Domesday Book (Rollason *et al.* 1998: 183–4). Furthermore, the erection of the great motte and bailey in the angle between the Foss and the Ouse resulted in a radical re-planning of communications routes: the arterial route in and out of the city via Fishergate was impinged upon by construction of the castle, splitting one of the city's main commercial districts in two. This resulted in a new route being created to skirt the defences of the castle, crossing the Foss over an enormous artificial dam (RCHME York 1972: 60). The number of eleventh-century church redundancies in Fishergate suggests a consequent shift in the focus of communications patterns to the new route via Walmgate north of the castle, in turn conditioning a major re-orientation of suburban development (Andrews 1984: 182).

Norman urban castles such as York's were invariably peripheral features of the townscape that, while located within the urban area and usually within the perimeters of town defences, tended to occupy sites remote from other foci such as marketplaces or episcopal palaces. This policy made obvious military sense, with the castle overlooking and overawing the civilian population, yet close to and occasionally embracing the town gates. Many other sites, such as

Tadcaster (North Yorkshire), Wallingford (Oxfordshire) and Wareham (Dorset) also commanded important bridges or fords. As such, a castle could effectively control access in and out of the city in order to secure ready access to the urban hinterland, while enabling the rapid reinforcement of the garrison. But later organic urban growth could mean that castles were overtaken by development. By the late twelfth century the built-up area of many English towns extended for several hundred metres beyond town walls (Keene 1976: 76), while defensive perimeters could be extended, as at Norwich, where a massive expansion of the walled circuit to the west of the city left the castle occupying a central position (Barley 1976, Fig. 36).

The most prominent exception to the general rule that urban castles were built within the line of earlier defences is Nottingham (Fig. 7.5: bottom). Here the royal castle was founded, in 1068 on a strong natural site west of the former Scandinavian *burh*, presumably for military reasons (see Chapter 3). While castle-building appears not to have infringed directly on urban property, diversion of the River Leen to feed the castle's water defences extinguished the fishing rights of the population of Leen, as mentioned in Domesday (Stevenson 1918, 73). Although the castle was distanced physically from the *burh* (later known as the English Borough), a castle-gate settlement (the French Borough) grew up soon after the Conquest, and a deer park to the west completed a classic piece of Norman town and country planning comprising of castle, borough and hunting park. The rise of the French Borough radically changed Nottingham's townscape, with the new castle-gate nucleus emerging to compete with, and eventually supplant the *burh* as the commercial focus (Barley 1969: 2). These changes to Nottingham's townscape also had an ethnic dimension. In common with Hereford and Norwich, a substantial immigrant French population in Nottingham is recorded in 1086 and legal distinctions between the two communities were preserved through different traditions of inheritance and the possession of separate sheriffs and bailiffs until the fifteenth century (Owen 1945; 1946). The rapidity of development at these three centres may be attributable to Norman economic initiative, and inducements may well have been offered to Norman merchants. For example, favourable judicial terms were designed to attract Norman colonists to the castle borough at Hereford, where settlers were granted the free customs of William Fitz Osbern's native Breteuil (Williams 1995: 202). Yet while legal distinctions remained between English and French communities at Nottingham, they were physically united within integrated town defences by the middle of the twelfth century.

The topographical relationship between a new Norman castle built to control one of the other Five Boroughs, Stamford, bears some comparison with Nottingham. The castle was similarly raised beyond the limits of the defended Anglo-Scandinavian borough, located on a natural spur elevated slightly above the town and overlooking an important crossing of the River Welland as well as occupying an earlier high-status defended site (RCHME 1977: 2–3; Mahany *et al.* 1982: 6–9). Both units were, however, embraced within the later town defences, and, furthermore, castle building seems to have brought about a radical re-orientation of Stamford's administrative geography. The Saxon royal estate within which the castle was built (previously lying in Rutland) was brought within the bounds of Stamford (and appended to the shire of Lincoln) shortly after the Conquest, and the town re-emerged as a regional centre as a consequence of the castle's presence (Roffe and Mahany 1986: 5).

At Chester too, the Norman castle was situated beyond the town wall. William's chosen site for his new castle lay beyond the south-west corner of the Roman city defences, overlooking the bridge over the Dee and the town's quay, although the circuit was extended in the twelfth century to incorporate the castle. By the later medieval period it was flanked by suburban development, including several monastic precincts (Carrington 1994: 64–8; Brown 1999: 10). Stafford Castle lay approximately 2 kilometres south-west of the *burh*. This site appears to have originated as the *caput* of Robert de Tosny's Honour of Stafford, replacing a short-lived royal fortification within the Saxon town abandoned by the end of the eleventh century (Darlington and Jecock 2001: 9). Like the de Warenne's *caput* near Wakefield at Sandal (West Yorkshire), while physically separated from an urban important centre, the castle, raised on a prominent ridge, was nonetheless a menacing presence on the horizon, visible to the townspeople and with an undoubted psychological impact.

Another possible ethnic dimension to the interrelationship between the castle and the medieval town is the evident link between royal urban castles and the settlements of Jewish communities. Richardson (1960: 110–11) has traced abundant documentary evidence throughout the twelfth and thirteenth centuries for the sheriffs and constables of royal castles being held responsible for the protection of Jewish populations, and suggested that many Jews will have dwelt in close physical proximity to castles. That sanctuary from persecution was sought in royal fortresses is evident not only in the horrific events in York of 1189, but also in accounts of refuge being sought in Lincoln and Northampton castles. Many Jewish properties in London certainly clustered close to the Tower (Roth 1964: 124), while the proximity of Jewry Street to Winchester Castle, with its Jew's Tower, has been noted, along with the fact that the Jewish cemetery lay immediately outside the castle gate (Keene 1985: 386). In medieval Bristol the land between the city wall and barbican of the royal castle appears not to have been held by borough tenure and to have similarly been a Jewish enclave (Leech 1989: 240–3), while Oxford and Norwich castles also lay close to Jewish areas.

Lincoln Castle occupied the south-west quarter of the Roman upper city in an intrusive manner 'like a cuckoo in the nest' (Donel 1992: 380), embracing the city's Upper West Gate within its bailey defences. Again, topographical evidence suggests a re-orientation of route-ways in the wake of castle founding, the incorporation of Upper West Gate resulting in the laying out of a new east–west route that skirted to the north of the castle. In addition, while the linear suburb of Wigford, to the south of the Roman city, was apparently well developed and enclosed by 1066 (Keene 1976: 76–7), the growth of the Newport suburb to the north appears to immediately post-date the construction of the castle (Barley 1976: 57; Colyer 1975: 31–5), and probably accommodated settlement displaced by its construction. Following the transfer of the episcopal see from Dorchester-on-Thames to Lincoln, the great tower of Bishop Remigius's cathedral was built facing the castle, with its west front incorporating conspicuous aspects of military architecture so that it may even have appeared from a distance to be the *donjon* (Gem 1986; Morris 1989: 252). The cognate result of these changes was the emergence of the Roman upper city, already raised naturally on a limestone ridge, as a tightly focused nucleus of Norman ecclesiastical, military and administrative power. The upper town thus formed in effect a vast outer bailey subsequently known as the 'Bail', not integrated legally with the rest of the city until the nineteenth century (Jones 1993: 19; Stocker and Vince 1997).

At Winchester the peripheral position of the castle relative to the city was emphasized by its construction within a large outwardly projecting salient of the Roman defences measuring 244 m north–south by 61 m east–west. The Norman fortification was further isolated from the town by a large ditch. Excavation has provided vivid evidence of the scale of disruption to the townscape, the castle earthwork obliterating a former north–south street forming part of the city grid, as well as an intra-mural route (Biddle and Hill 1971: 82; Keene 1985: 50). In total, archaeology has revealed evidence for the demolition of some four dozen houses, including masonry buildings, in order to create an artificial raised platform for the castle (Beaumont James 1997: 52). What is particularly interesting is that these consequences of castlebuilding for settlement within the town walls are barely reflected in the documentary record, while the ramifications of the events for extra-mural settlement are documented clearly. While the Winton Domesday remains silent on destruction within the town walls, clear reference is made to extra-mural settlement beyond the west gate destroyed due to the re-cutting and enlargement of the city ditch, and perhaps the establishment of an open zone beyond (Biddle 1976b: 303).

Physical evidence for the destruction of town properties has also been recovered from excavated contexts beneath Oxford Castle. Excavations under the south side of the castle mound in 1952 revealed a series of late Saxon pits accompanied by building debris (Jope 1952–3), while further investigations on the north side of the motte uncovered sealed occupation levels dating back to the tenth century (Hassall 1976: 253–4). Together, this evidence suggests the imposition of the castle on a developed street frontage, and the consequent diversion of the route south of the castle along medieval Westgate, although it remains unclear whether the pre-castle settlement lay within or beyond the *burh* defences. In the case of Gloucester's first castle too, traces of settlement sealed by the castle have been examined archaeologically. Remarkably, a late Roman building beneath the bailey surface had been occupied intermittently from the sixth until the eleventh century, when it was demolished and levelled in advance of castle-building (Darvill 1988: 45–6). Evidence for cleared pre-castle settlement beneath Canterbury Castle comprised a number of late Saxon pits and two wicker-lined well shafts (Bennett *et al.* 1982: 23, 48–50).

Although there is thus abundant evidence that domestic dwellings were swept aside to make way for royal castles, their peripheral positions within late Saxon townscapes usually argues against any previous high-status activity on their sites. Wallingford has already been mentioned as a possible exception to this rule, although the clearest case by far is the great Norman fortress-palace at Colchester (Essex) (Fig. 7.7), which was an atypical urban castle in many respects. The largest Norman keep in England occupies a central position within *insula* 22 of the former Roman town, raised on the immense

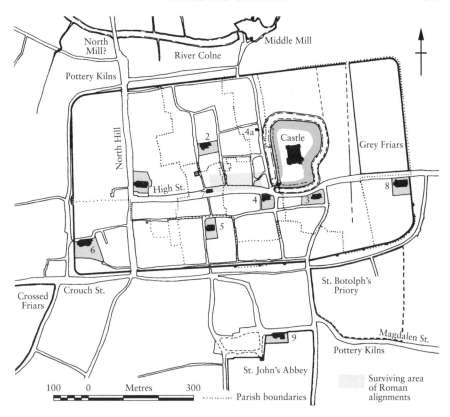

Figure 7.7 Colchester, showing the relationship between the castle and the medieval townscape. Key to numbering: 1, St Peter's church; 2, St Martin's church; 3, All Saints' church; 4, St Nicholas's church; 4a, St Helen's chapel; 5, Holy Trinity church; 6, St-Mary-at-the-Walls church; 7, St Runwald's church; 8, St James's church; 9, St Giles's church (Drury 1982).

podium of the classical temple of Claudius Caesar, while the bailey defences caused High Street to be diverted, probably causing the clearance of houses (Crummy 1981: 71). Excavation, combined with architectural analysis of the keep (which incorporates much Roman masonry) has indicated that the monumental structures formerly surrounding the temple survived to a considerable height immediately prior to castle-building, perhaps even as a complete circuit (Drury 1982: 397). Yet the Norman decision to raise the keep on this site was more than simply an example of military opportunism; indeed, the location of the castle just east of the centre point of the town, and thus hemmed in on all sides by property, makes little military sense. Instead, Drury (1982) has argued that *insula* 22 was the core of a late Saxon *villa regalis* (royal manor) within which the royal castle was raised for symbolic and political reasons. Drury's thesis centres on excavated evidence demonstrating the Norman castle chapel to be a reconstruction of two earlier chapel-like structures, the earliest of which featured plastered panels with elaborate painted decoration, and other documentary evidence of Saxon royal associations (Drury 1982: 390). It is certainly not without coincidence that the

Colchester Chronicle, a document composed in the mid-thirteenth century, tells us that William's steward Eudo Dapifer built the castle in 1076 on the foundations of the palace of Coel 'formerly king' (presumably a reference to Cunobelin, the pre-Roman king) (Hull 1958: 162). The great keep, one and a half times the size of the White Tower of London, and with clear architectural links to the great Carolingian palaces of northern France (Brown *et al.* 1963: 31–2), was thus a conspicuous symbol of William's imperial ambitions. In terms of its siting, the castle harked back to Colchester's regal past, no doubt impressing the Norman Conquest on the minds of contemporaries, but also as a means of legitimizing the claim to power of the new regime.

The work at Colchester Castle raises the intriguing possibility that other urban castles are raised on sites of previous significance, as were many of their rural counterparts (see Chapters 3 and 8). Nonetheless, it is difficult to see how definitive proof of this can be obtained in the absence of the large-scale urban digs that became so rare in British archaeology from their heyday in the 1960s and 1970s. At Southampton, however, the castle's position not within an angle of the defences but well within the late Saxon town may tell a similar story. The excavation in 1980 of a substantial Saxon hall beneath the bailey surface, circumvallated by a single, or, possibly, a double ditch, may also indicate Norman appropriation of an established seat of power (Holdsworth 1984: 340–1). Excavation at two other urban castles has raised, although has not fully answered, similar questions regarding high-status continuity on urban castle sites. A series of excavations and watching briefs at Newark Castle have shown that, far from originating as a twelfth-century episcopal castle, as often supposed, the first castle was built in the immediate post-Conquest decades (Kinsley 1993; Marshall and Samuels 1994). More remarkable is the evidence of antecedent activity, including a Saxon cemetery and contemporary curved ditch, apparently delimiting the zone of the Saxon town later occupied by the castle (Marshall and Samuels 1994: 53–4). When viewed in tandem with evidence of a probable late Saxon church in the vicinity of Bar Gate (to the north of the castle), this might indicate the site of an early medieval monastic, or more probably a high-status residential site (Kinsley 1993: 57–8). In addition, earlier excavations on the east rampart of the castle revealed a 'peasant hut' sealed by the defences, perhaps, in view of the later evidence, a product of an undocumented Norman clearance (Marshall and Samuels 1997: 10; see also Barley and Waters 1956: 30).

At Stamford, the castle may again have perpetuated an earlier seat of authority. Although archaeology has shown the zone later occupied by the castle to have been a primarily industrial zone in 1066, this area seems to have had prior high-status connections. Excavations on the castle site have revealed an earlier double ditched and ramparted enclosure defining the circular knoll, and what was. in all probability, a substantial high-status defended Saxon residence (Mahany 1977: 232–3; Mahany and Roffe 1982: 204). In administrative terms this area was further distinct as the hub of an extensive royal multiple estate and part of the liberty of Rutland, held in 1066 by Queen Edith, wife of the Confessor (Roffe and Mahany 1986: 718). Other than the Norman motives of dominating an important urban centre, the act of re-occupying the knoll, with its regal connotations, may have held a certain symbolic resonance.

Overall, we should certainly not overlook the immense psychological impact of castle-building in late Saxon power bases, as exemplified by the Norman motte at Thetford (Norfolk). This colossal earthwork – commonly recognized as the second largest artificial mound in Britain, second only to Silbury Hill – stands almost 20 m high and has a base diameter in excess of 100 m. Crowned by a correspondingly impressive timber superstructure, this earthwork must have towered above the double ramparts of the pre-Conquest D-shaped enclosure in which it was imposed shortly after the Conquest. This earlier enclosure in all probability formed the royal and administrative nucleus of Thetford, and its effective subjection was doubtless essential for the Norman conquerors to maintain an effective grip on the prime inland trading centre of East Anglia (Everson and Jecock 1999: 105).

Clearly town plans could be re-cast radically in the wake of castle-building, yet despite a wealth of archaeological, documentary and topographical evidence for the imposition of castles within late Saxon towns, there is nothing to suggest that castle-building resulted in wholesale urban collapse. To a certain extent this must be a reflection of the vibrancy of urbanism in mid-eleventh-century England. Those urban centres that subsequently failed (e.g. Lydford), suffered inherent geographical disadvantages or were already in economic decline, and decayed further after 1066 just as other marginal Domesday boroughs without castles did (e.g. Tilshead, Wiltshire). In other cases castle-building positively enhanced urban fortunes. Of Carlisle the *Anglo-Saxon Chronicle* describes that in 1092 William Rufus 'restored the city and erected the castle', indicating a positive impact that involved the re-foundation of Roman *Luguvalium* or at least the refurbishment of earlier defences (see McCarthy *et al.* 1990: 118–9). At Wareham, archaeological evidence indicates that the *burh* defences were completely refurbished at around the time of the erection of the castle (Radford 1970: 86), while earlier civil defences at towns such as Colchester and Tamworth may also have undergone Norman phases of re-building (Bond 1987: 112). All these examples underline the fact that Norman kings perpetuated the royal ties with major towns established by their Saxon predecessors.

Castle-boroughs

Far more common than the urban castle was the physical association of a private castle with a nascent town bearing the hallmarks of deliberate planning in the form of a regulated street network and burgage plots (Fig. 7.8). In this sense the castle has been described as a 'midwife' that bought into being numerous towns as offshoots of the seigneurial site (Thompson 1991: 145–6). An illuminating parallel for this phenomenon is the way that a Roman fort might have attracted a dependent *vicus* or civilian settlement (Carver 1987: 61).

In many cases castle lords were both willing and able to follow aggressive and interventionist policies of urban promotion, offering favourable conditions for new tenants and superseding earlier centres with new foundations. To an extent the relationship between castle and town was also symbiotic: while the seigneurial site provided obvious commercial benefits and perhaps

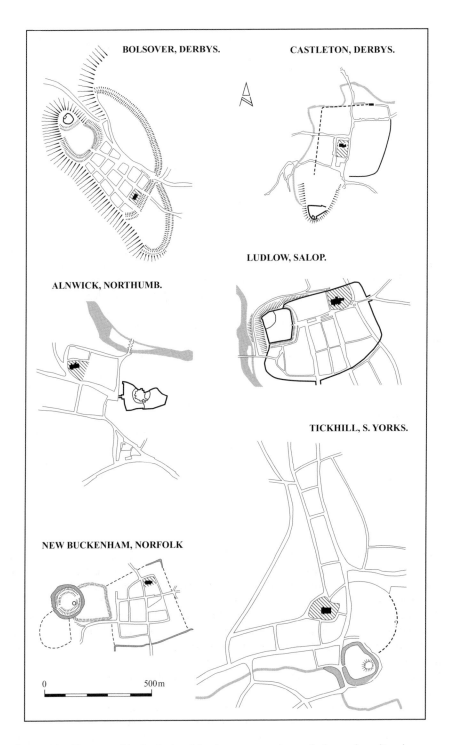

Figure 7.8 Topographical relationships between castles and planned medieval towns.

defensive advantages for the community, the settlement provided a ready source of labour, services and a market for the maintenance of the castle. These castles also contributed to the defence of urban communities, and were invariably integrated carefully within town walls (Palliser 1995: 107; Hopkinson 2000: 55).

The rise of castle-towns can and must be related to the national, and indeed pan-European, upsurge in urban expansion from the late eleventh century. In England, as elsewhere, the essential motor behind this boom in urbanism was the ambition of landlords – lay, ecclesiastical and royal – to indulge in schemes of town planning, initially as part and parcel of the Anglo-Norman consolidation, and later as economic investments and sources of revenue (Higham and Saunders 1997, 121). Indeed, the impact of castles and castle lords on medieval urban growth can be understood in terms of these two broad processes. Initially, the dual plantation of a castle and town combined military and commercial considerations in order to attain and enhance political and territorial control; these settlements may usefully be termed 'castle-dependent' towns. In late eleventh- and twelfth-century England, and later in Wales and Ireland, the castle-town was also an expression of Norman ideology used not only to enable and enforce, but to legitimize an essentially colonial settlement (Graham 1988; Lilley 2000). Subsequently, however, castle lords created, manipulated or expanded town plans increasingly as economic ventures and opportunities to amass revenues from their estates through the collection of rents and taxes. These schemes of urban promotion invariably involved more complex plan forms and major changes to communications networks, including bridge-building and road diversion. We may readily identify towns that embody one process or the other; more commonly, however, both are reflected within a composite plan resulting from multiple episodes of growth. The key problem for archaeologists and historical geographers is disentangling these two processes in town plans that are often blurred, decayed and unevenly documented.

Borough origins

Maurice Beresford's masterful *New Towns of the Middle Ages* (1967) has allowed the importance of castles to urban growth to be appreciated in a wider context. Of English towns planted in the period 1066–1100, 80 per cent contained a castle; from 1101–35 the figure drops to just over 50 per cent and declines sharply thereafter (Beresford 1967: 334–5). In England the period of castle-town foundation was thus short-lived but intense. The phenomenon also had a geographical pattern: while the process was essentially complete in most parts of lowland England by the time of Anarchy, in more exposed border regions and beyond, castle-towns remained important tools of colonization. For instance, Edward I's capture of Berwick-upon-Tweed from the Scots in 1296 precipitated a radical re-planning of both castle and town to form an integrated bastide-type arrangement on the crucial crossing of the Tweed (Brown *et al* 1963: 563–4). In contrast, Edward's other important town foundations at Kingston upon Hull (East Yorkshire) and New Winchelsea (Kent) did not include castles.

Perhaps typical of the small seigneurial castle-boroughs that were such a common feature of the landscape of Norman England are Bolsover and Castleton (Derbyshire) (Fig. 7.8: top). Although documentary sources do not indicate the existence of a town at either place until at least the late twelfth century, there is little doubt that both were early seigneurial foundations under Peveril lordship in the period before 1155, after which the estates escheated to the Crown, under which the centres were promoted further and their urban status formalized (Beresford and Finberg 1973: 85; Hart 1981: 139–40). Both town plans characteristically feature parish churches with demonstrably Norman origins that occupy primary positions within the plan. The town plan at Castleton comprises a mono-cellular grid plan embraced within a larger embanked enclosure suggestive of a partially successful plantation with a number of plots failing to be taken up (Brooksbank 1929). Bolsover took an essentially similar, although slightly more ambitious form as a linear town with developed back lanes, the site being planned along the spine of the Magnesian limestone ridge on which the castle also lay. The same spatial relationship of castle, in-filled marketplace and church is in evidence, although in more elongated form in response to limitations of site, with outer earthworks marking a secondary expansion from an original defended core (Symonds *et al.* 1995).

The distinction between medieval boroughs with recognized legal status and other market-based settlements is a notoriously grey area. While many medieval settlements had 'urban' functions, they could, in physical terms, be no larger than villages, as was often the case in Devon, where medieval nucleations of very small proportions could be boroughs – a good example being Winkleigh, which featured two early castles. Later changes could also cause a former castle-town to shrink or contract to village proportions, as at Lydford. What is essential here is that this urban/rural settlement divide is even less clear-cut when examining settlements which in some way owe their origins to the existence of a castle (Barley 1976: 59). Besides classic large castle-boroughs such as Arundel, Ludlow and Windsor there were a great number of more minor castle-dependent communities with urban pretensions, whose social and economic functions, at least initially, tended to be more limited and specialist in nature. Many of these sites were marginal and had limited commercial potential; following the abandonment of the castle they could fall into decline and eventually become completely deserted, although some survive as modern villages. At Downend (Somerset), for instance, the plan of the small village adjacent to a motte and bailey reflects the skeleton of a medieval borough. Constructed within an embanked precinct adjacent to the castle and a tiny inland harbour, the borough (founded *c.* 1159) lay on the end of the Polden Ridge to take advantage of a junction of sea, river and road traffic routes (Aston and Leech 1977: 39–41). The settlement was, however, eclipsed ultimately by its better-sited rival, Bridgwater, which itself grew up in conjunction with a new castle from the beginning of the thirteenth century.

The origins of castle-towns can be far more complex than may first appear to be the case, with a spectrum of potential scenarios evident, attributable to a wide range of variables including the nature of lordship and the character of a region's landscape and economy. At one end of this spectrum is the *de novo* castle borough, often identified by foundation at the boundaries of extant parishes, by Norman nomenclature and the absence of the place-name in Domesday, as at Devizes (Wiltshire). Yet castle-boroughs on virgin sites are rare, and even where this is the case, their foundation might have a serious consequences for nearby settlement. For instance, at Tickhill (South York-shire), while the L-shaped medieval town grew as an appendage of the great honorial castle on a fresh site, the establishment of this new plantation resulted in the desertion of an earlier settlement focus at *Dadsley, c.* 1.5 km to the north, as indicated by field names and the location here of the original parish church (Smith 1961a: 55; Hey 1980a: 420). The 31 burgesses at Tickhill mentioned in Domesday were almost certainly situated within the present town, indicating a rapid transplantation of population to the vicinity of the castle, while the street pattern of the new Norman town cut across the field and road system of the earlier settlement. A comparable case is Cockermouth (Cumbria), where the establishment of a market settlement near the baronial castle left the former parish church isolated as a chapel of ease in Brigham parish (Winchester 1987: 127).

It is often wrong to assume that the many towns which grew up around castles were 'new' settlements; indeed Beresford's classic work (1967) has done much to create a false dichotomy between the 'new town' and the far more common scenario of an extant village transformed into an urban set-tlement as an act of seigneurial initiative. A great many castle-towns evolved in precisely this fashion, either through the addition of a planned appendage to a pre-urban village that contained a castle (e.g. Downton, Wiltshire), or through the grafting of an integrated castle-borough unit to an earlier settlement (e.g. Nether Stowey, Somerset). In many cases the early core will survive in the form of an observable plan unit. At Clun (Shropshire), for instance, a pre-urban village nucleus containing the parish church is clearly differentiated in the settlement plan from the loosely gridded castle-gate town built on the opposite bank of the river (Roberts 1987: 194–5). More problematic are examples where antecedent settlement is apparently obliterated through the creation of a new morphological frame for settlement, as at Saffron Walden (Essex), where excavation of the town bailey ditch revealed evidence of a Saxo-Norman village that preceded the planned medieval town (Bassett 1982).

A key methodological problem is that the status of early Norman castle-dependent urban settlements such as these remained undocumented, typically until the late twelfth or thirteenth century, when market charters served to make *de jure* what was already *de facto*. This issue is exemplified by the example of Plympton [Erle] (Devon). Although the town's earliest recorded borough charter dates to 1194 when the fifth Earl of Devon, William de Vernon, granted a market and fair, the castle was certainly in existence from at least 1130, and more probably around 1100 (Higham *et al.* 1985: 60). Castle, church and churchyard are unusually arranged in linear fashion along the entire north edge of the town plan (Fig. 7.9), the close physical relationship between the seigneurial site and urban settlement making it extremely likely that the units were planned contemporaneously. A back lane between these two elements of the town plan apparently marks the original limit of the castle ditch, and an area of settlement development immediately south-east of the church encroaches on the likely site of a marketplace. Plympton's significance as a port rapidly declined as the River Plym progressively silted up, yet it

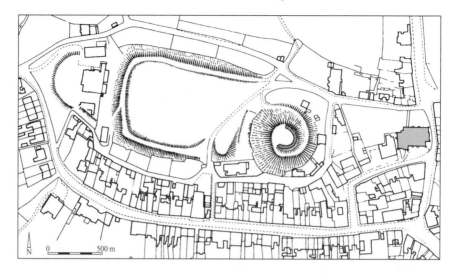

Figure 7.9 Plympton (Devon), showing the relationship between the medieval town plan, motte and bailey and parish church. The arrangement of all three elements suggests a high level of seigneurial planning (Higham *et al.* 1985).

remained the most profitable of the three Devon boroughs owned by the earls of Devon, the others being Honiton and Tiverton (Bearman 1994: 35–6).

The example of Richmond (North Yorkshire), allows us to explore the origins of a castle-borough in a little more depth. Often quoted as a classic example of Norman settlement (e.g. Brown 1989: 197–8), the town-plan is one of a small yet important number characterized by a semicircular configuration of burgage plots around the seigneurial focus (Fig. 7.10). The first borough charter dates to 1109–14, probably formalizing existing rights and privileges, as a later charter attributes the first liberties to some time in the period 1089–1136 (Beresford 1967: 518; Beresford and Finberg 1973: 187–8). Murage grants of 1313, 1337, 1341 and 1400, and the standing fabric of two portions of town wall demonstrate that this zone of settlement at the castle gate alone was walled, although the town had undoubtedly grown beyond its initial confines by the fourteenth century (Tyler 1976: 9). The likely explanation is that the later medieval town defences perpetuated the alignment of an earlier circuit fortified with earth and timber. There are indications, however, that the borough was not truly a *de novo* creation on a virgin site. The odd peripheral position of the parish church of St Mary's relative to the enclosed core of the medieval borough in all probability represents the pre-Norman focus of settlement in the zone of the town later known as Frenchgate, and perhaps the core of the Domesday vill of *Hindrelag*. Other important Norman castles in Yorkshire also exhibit the addition of a planned borough to a pre-urban nucleus. At the honorial *caput* of Knaresborough and the bishop's castle of Northallerton, for instance, regular towns have clearly been grafted onto earlier villages. In 1086 Northallerton was waste and Knaresborough worth only one sixth of its pre-Conquest value, indicating that here as elsewhere in the North, town-planning by new Norman lords was part and parcel of re-building devastated estates. Yet Richmond Castle was not a military site

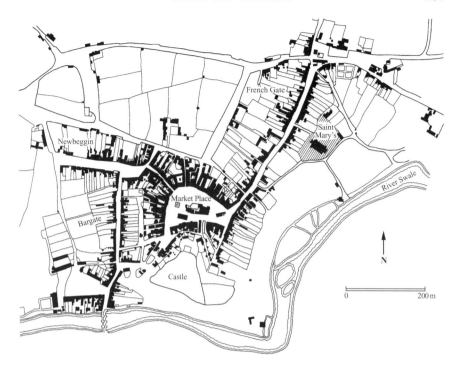

Figure 7.10 Plan of the castle and town of Richmond (North Yorkshire), based on a map of 1773. The semicircular castle borough appears to have been appended to an earlier village that contains the original parish church; other units of settlement to the west indicate later medieval urban expansion.

in the classic sense. Despite its dramatic cliff-edge position, the castle had minimal involvement with military affairs and lay well away from major communications routes in the strategic cul-de-sac of Swaledale. The location of castle and borough at Richmond can only be understood relative to the wider pattern of lordship in the North. As the *caput* of the Honour of Richmond, castle and borough were founded as an integrated unit for economic as much as military reasons. Located at the interface of the arable lowlands of the Vale of York and the pastoral uplands of Swaledale, Richmond served a vast network of estates as a market centre for wool and corn, and later as a centre for industries such as tanning, and lead and copper mining. At a wider scale still, while the eleventh-century castlery as a whole was plainly a strategic statement in opposition to the Scots and a quasi-independent Northumbria (see Chapter 5), the choice of site for the castle-borough was clearly informed by economic factors. At Richmond, as at important Norman honorial *capita* elsewhere, the establishment of a borough was, as much as the foundation of a castle, an essential part of establishing, maintaining and enhancing economic and territorial control.

Castles and town planning

Conzen (1960: 4–5) has suggested that a town-plan comprises an arrangement of three essential elements: street systems; plot boundaries; and buildings. Within such a scheme, castles can themselves be conceptualized as separate and distinct plan units or, indeed, plan 'dominants'. The castle was invariably the social and economic focus of a town and often formed a pre-urban nucleus towards which settlement gravitated, although in certain cases both could be planted contemporaneously. It would be wrong, however, to propose an all-embracing model of castle-town relationships based on town-plan analysis. The dangers of this type of morphogentic explanation – using plan forms as the sole basis for retrogressive analysis of a settlement's development – have been made clear elsewhere (Austin 1985). The sheer variety of castle-town plan forms makes such a model impossible. The physical form taken by a planned medieval town is determined not only by which plan forms were current, but also circumstances of physical topography, local commercial considerations and patronage (Slater 2000: 100). Instead, we may identify a series of broad trends in the physical relationship between castles and urban growth, and relate these to the wider pattern of town development in England after 1066.

Topographical factors frequently conditioned the layout of castle-towns, as at Bungay (Suffolk) and Warkworth (Northumbria) where settlements lay within tight loops of rivers providing naturally defensible sites, and Christchurch (Hampshire), where castle, borough and priory were squeezed together on a natural promontory between the Avon and Stour. In other landscapes the physical location of even a major honorial castle could be completely incompatible with the commercial growth. The borough of Newport (Isle of Wight) planted by the lords of Carisbrooke Castle in *c.* 1177– 84, for instance, lay 1.4 km north-east of the fortress, on the very edge of the parish, where the Downs run down to the Medina estuary (Beresford 1967: 137–8). In those parts of Britain characterized predominantly by non-nucleated forms of rural settlement, a castle and town could also be planned as separate entities yet remain administratively linked, as at Okehampton (Devon). Here the castle and planned borough lie approximately 1 km apart, the former on a prominent spur near a crossing of the West Okemont river, and the latter in a more sheltered position at the confluence of the East and West Okemonts (Higham 1980: 73; 1982a: 110–11). The impractical headland situation of Tintagel meant that when Richard, Earl of Cornwall, received a borough charter in 1253, the town grew up *c.* 1.5 km away from his castle in the old manorial centre of Bossiney, adjacent to a ringwork that represented an earlier focus of lordship in the locality (Rose 1992: 141).

We must make sharp physical and functional distinction between a castle-gate borough of the immediate post-Conquest period and the more fully developed urban institution that could constitute a typical castle-town by the late twelfth or thirteenth century. Plan analysis of castle-towns has indicated an early yet still rather obscure phase of nascent settlement growth at castle gates, and a later trend of formal town planning associated with more sophisticated and economically inspired plan forms. In the early Norman period there may not have been a strict dichotomy between the military community of the castle and the civilian community at the castle gate. It is only later that urban communities asserted their own identities and distanced themselves – often physically as well as metaphorically – from castles, as expressed through charters and urban defences. The late-eleventh-century castle-borough may have been a settlement with little more than urban potential and a specialized economy oriented explicitly to the workings of the castle. As demonstrated by the example of Richmond, the coupling of castle and town was a key tool of territorial expansion in Anglo-Norman England. Early castle-towns would have grown up to sustain the seigneury, their retinues and visitors through the provision of goods and services and, of course, to provide for the garrison. The great problem is that, other than Domesday, there is little documentary evidence for these arrangements in the immediate post-Conquest decades, so it falls to archaeology and topographical analysis to illuminate very early castle-towns. In addition, identification of early phases of settlement within town plans is invariably hindered by later episodes of re-planning that may blur or even eradicate antecedent patterns.

In a pioneering town-plan analysis of Alnwick (Northumbria), Conzen (1960) suggested that the early Norman castle was coupled with a dedicated unit of settlement (termed a *suburbium*). The area of the town known as Bailiffgate has a distinctive plan, comprising a series of short plots disposed symmetrically either side of a central street, widening towards the castle to form Castle Square (Fig. 7.8). Bailiffgate also appears to have been administratively separate from the remainder of the borough: a number of holdings are documented in a late medieval survey as tenements rather than burgesses, and paid rent to the castle reeve (*praepositus castri*), rather than the town reeve (Conzen 1960: 21–3). As a mustering point for troops, a venue for the baronial court, and a place for the entertainment of guests, it is clear that Alnwick Castle was, at times, a focal gathering point for a vast range of miscellaneous personnel, including militia, assorted administrative officials and their retinues, and craftspeople. Bailiffgate in all probability grew up in response to these needs. At Nottingham, too, the Domesday reference to 25 'horsemen's houses' in the newly-established castle-gate borough may indicate accommodation for soldiers, while the 101 houses held by other tenants, including many occupied by merchants, provides the most tentative of hints of a niche economy geared towards the royal castle (Roffe 1997: 37). At Tutbury (Staffordshire), a Domesday castle-borough in the possession of Henry de Ferrers is mentioned with a population of '42 men who live only by their trading', yielding a total of £4 10s. Similar scenarios may have been repeated elsewhere where Domesday specifically mentions a borough in association with a castle, as at Wigmore (Herefordshire). This type of urban growth may well have been spontaneous or even unplanned, with the castle acting as a magnet to settlement that nucleated around the castle gate as a focus of economic activity.

Elsewhere, early phases of nascent settlement growth outside castles took place within embanked precincts appended physically to the seigneurial site (often called *burgus* settlements: e.g. Armitage 1912: 85; King 1983: xix). The best evidence comes from small deserted boroughs whose defences have not been swamped by later growth, particularly those on the Welsh borders (see below). Other physical evidence of enclosures is somewhat elusive, while there is little or no documentary evidence for new urban defences between Domesday and the early thirteenth century (Turner 1970: 21). In addition, it is difficult to differentiate between genuine defensive earthworks, comprising ditches and ramparts formerly topped with palisades, from those serving merely as boundary markers, especially as some of the larger castles associated with enclosed boroughs could themselves have served as communal refuges in times of crisis. In any event, we should not underestimate the symbolic and legal functions of such enclosure works, as all would have emphasized the jurisdiction of a borough. A further issue is whether these enclosures were baileys in the true sense, and thus adjuncts to the castle's defences, or true urban/proto-urban defences, and thus built, at least in part, out of communal interest. There is, unfortunately, no clear answer, although such schemes were doubtless the result of private initiative while, in choosing to embrace a community within an outer precinct, the castle lord was protecting personal interests as much as those of the population. Indeed, it is likely that occupation within some of the larger castle baileys would have resembled small and compact communities of more or less urban appearance. Excavation of approximately one quarter of the castle bailey at Launceston (Cornwall), for instance, has revealed a highly regular grid-plan arrangement not only of halls and kitchens, but other miscellaneous lodgings, perhaps periodically accommodating the holders of knights fees (Saunders 1977: 137). The buildings were aligned either parallel with or at right angles to an axial north–south route through a sub-rectangular bailey measuring approximately 110 × 120 m, giving the overall impression of a town within a town.

At Bridgnorth (Shropshire), a small dependent unit of settlement was clearly planned within an outer bailey attached to the promontory castle. The outline of this feature is indicated by the lines of property boundaries fronting on to East Castle Street and West Castle Street, which form the basis of a ladder-type plan within the sub-rectangular enclosure (Croom 1992: 34; Lilley 1999: 12–14). What makes this example particularly apposite is the documentary evidence that the nucleation was clearly forced by seigneurial hand. In the 1090s the castle lord, Robert de Bellême, is reported to have transplanted part of the civilian population of nearby Quatford to his castle at Bridgnorth, thus mirroring policy on his estates in southern Normandy (Forester 1853: 220; Lilley 1999: 13). A similar site is Castle Acre (Norfolk), where a small settlement, best interpreted as an incipient town, was planted in a massively embanked rectangular precinct embracing a total area measuring *c.* 200 × 250 m, appended to the castle of the de Warenne earls of Surrey (Coad and Streeten 1982: 138).

This unity of castle and enclosed town is reflected especially well by a small number of towns that preserve a semicircular plan focused on the castle. Pleshey (Essex), is the most widely recognized example, the highly appropriate Norman-French place-name being derived from *le plessis* meaning 'enclosure formed by interlaced fencing' (Reaney 1935: 488–9). From the air the almost perfectly semicircular profile of the town defences is immediately apparent (Fig. 7.11), mirroring on a far larger scale those of the imposing motte and bailey, although the settlement did not thrive and has no surviving borough charter (RCHME Essex 1916–23, vol. II: 201–2; Williams 1977: 1–5, 241).

Other castle-towns preserve a semicircular arrangement of streets although

Figure 7.11 Aerial view of Pleshey (Essex), showing the medieval castle and enclosed settlement (Cambridge University Collection of Air Photographs: copyright reserved).

physical evidence of defences is lacking, as at Devizes (Wiltshire), which represents a more developed version of the crescentic castle-town. Here a concentric arrangement of three curving streets focused on the large foreland ringwork (Fig. 6.2) has been interpreted as evidence of the secondary colonization of a former outer bailey by the urban population following a contraction of the castle defences (Aston and Bond 1976: 87; Haslam 1976: 19). But comparison with similar towns suggests rather that the plan indicates two successive episodes of outward expansion (Butler 1976: 45). Also in Wiltshire, the street plan of Trowbridge fossilizes a similar pattern, although forming only one quarter of an arc as opposed to the full semicircle, indicating either a smaller settlement or, more likely, that the remainder has been obliterated by later changes to the town plan (Haslam 1976: 61). Tonbridge (Kent) is another example of a semicircular borough with a similarly decayed street plan. We should not overlook that many of these semicircular castle-towns are also characterized by a main road which runs through the large enclosure and usually near the castle gate, indicating a degree of seigneurial control over the movement of road traffic.

There is tentative evidence that a similar enclosure may have been appended to Tickhill Castle (Fig. 7.8). To the north of the castle a steep V-shaped ditch (*c.* 2.5 m deep and 4 m wide), oriented east–west, and with a stone revetted bank to its south, was shown to pre-date burgage plots in the area and to have silted up entirely during the later medieval period (DOE 1975: 120). In addition, the semicircular arrangement of lanes and property boundaries may also indicate the profile of a large horseshoe-shaped defended enclosure (Magilton 1971–7: 346–7). This feature may account for the unusual peripheral position of the marketplace relative to the castle, and the inter-rupted profile of the burgage plots both north and south of the putative enclosure. Comparable features undoubtedly remain to be identified in other townscapes.

What is clear is that many of these early castle-town complexes represent an early and distinct period of borough foundation when the formation of a castle-gate settlement did not necessarily imply the foundation of a truly urban community, rather an economic support system for the castle (Miller 1968: 196). Parallels for these settlements can be found in eleventh-century Nor-mandy, identified in documents with the terms *bourg*, *burgus* and *burgensis* (Latouche 1966; Miller 1968). As Musset (1960, 1966) has demonstrated, however, the burgess in late-twelfth-century Normandy could be an agri-culturalist, settled deliberately within a settlement having a primarily rural base. This of course begs the question of whether burgesses in Norman England also partook in a mixed economy.

Grid-plan (or bastide-type) town plans are less commonly associated with castles. In general these plans – comprising the chequer-board arrangement of properties typified by New Winchelsea (East Sussex) and Salisbury (Wiltshire) – are characteristic of later medieval urban planning and, as relatively few new castles were founded in England from the thirteenth century, do not usually contain a seigneurial focus. In Wales, however, the grid-iron castle town was exported with great effect, most notably by Edward I to Caernarvon, Conway and Flint, where towns were consistently sited on the most vulnerable sides of castles as an extension to their defences (Butler 1976: 39). Elsewhere it is difficult to distinguish a true embryonic grid from a linear town plan where back lanes have grown up to the rear of burgage plots, as seems to be the case at Bishop's Castle (Shropshire). Where a castle was associated physically with a *de novo* grid-plan town, the seigneurial focus usually lay immediately beyond the grid, so as not to disrupt the uniformity of the plan. This was certainly the case at New Buckenham (Norfolk), where the twinned construc-tion of castle and square gridded town on the edge of the parish c. 1139 (Fig. 7.8) marked the rise of William d'Albini to an earldom, and replaced an earlier honorial *caput* within the village (Rigold 1980: 353). At nearby Castle Rising a late-sixteenth-century map (Fig. 8.7) depicts a grid-plan settlement comprising at least eight 'chequers', with the castle similarly lying beyond the rectilinear plan (Rutledge 1997: 144). A similar topographical relationship is evident between the new grid-iron medieval borough of New Malton (founded c. 1154–73) and Eustace Fitz John's castle, which lay external to the grid within the perimeter of the Roman fort (Robinson 1978: 13–14). A slightly

Figure 7.12   The castle-gate borough at the foot of Corfe Castle (Dorset) (photograph: Oliver Creighton).

more complex variation of the gridded town plan is Ludlow (Shropshire) (Fig. 7.8). Here, the basis of the street plan seems to have been conceived prior to the addition of the castle's large outer bailey in the twelfth century, which expanded over part of the settlement (St John Hope 1908; Conzen 1988). It is unclear whether the part of the town known as Dinham that was disrupted by this alteration originated as a pre-Conquest settlement or as an informal nucleation at the castle gate. It was, however, relegated to the status of a suburb as the focus of urban development shifted to the large marketplace outside the castle gate (Lilley 1999: 14–17; Shoesmith 2000: 12).

Castles and commerce

A marketplace formed the focus for commercial activity outside many castle gates, in the same way that an important ecclesiastical institution might encourage the growth of a market (Slater 1998). The important nunnery of Romsey Abbey (Hampshire), for instance, prompted the nucleation of a small market centre at its gates well before the eventual royal grant of a market and fair and the settlement's legal recognition as a borough (Hughes 1994: 198); comparable examples include Bury St Edmunds (Suffolk), and Battle (East Sussex), which both preserve large open spaces adjacent to monasteries in their town plans. While the multifarious functions of both castles and monasteries would act as a natural focus for commerce, the topographical positions of castles often further encouraged market development, while landlords were doubtless keen to foster markets near their power bases for social and economic reasons. An excellent example of this is Corfe (Dorset), where a small borough grew up at the very foot of the royal castle (Fig. 7.12), at the point

Figure 7.13   Launceston Castle (Cornwall) (photograph: Oliver Creighton).

where two roads from the south converged to run through the narrow Corfe
Gap, with the castle thus overlooking the principal routes between the Isle of
Purbeck and south Dorset (Taylor 1970: 176–8). Those castles sited at key
nodes on the communications grid, and especially at key river crossings, thus
benefited from the volume of passing commerce. Another interesting site in
this regard is the Bishop of Lincoln's castle at Banbury (Oxfordshire). Forming
the economic hub of an extensive barony and the administrative centre for the
hundred and part of the diocese, the castle was located near an important
east–west crossing of the River Cherwell and the north–south route from
Coventry to Oxford. As an archiepiscopal residence, ecclesiastical prison and
place for entertainment, the volume of human concourse attracted to the castle
must have been immense, and a castle-gate market was a natural focus of
activity. This status is reflected in the vast elongated rectangular marketplace
(measuring *c.* 250 × 80 m), immediately south of the castle gates, at the point
where these two routes intersected (Lobel 1969; Rodwell 1976).

   The association of castles and markets in Domesday Book provides further
insight into the ways in which powerful castle lords encouraged commercial
activity at their castles. Most remarkably, the Exon Domesday records the
existence of markets in association with two of the Count of Mortain's castles
in Cornwall (Darby 1967: 339–40; Harfield 1991: 375–6). At Launceston
(Fig. 7.13), the market was said to have been taken away from St Stephen's-
by-Launceston, where it had been under the control of the canons, and
transplanted to the castle. At Trematon, the Count's market was held on a
Sunday, the same day as the bishop of Exeter's, and was said to have reduced
the earlier market at St German's, little more than 4 kilometres distant, to
nothing. While these references are exceptional, the fact that such commercial
rivalry is not mentioned in the folios of Greater Domesday relating to Laun-

ceston and Trematon indicates that other examples may go unmentioned. A parallel case can be identified on William Malet's Suffolk estates, where a Domesday market within the castle at Eye was clearly a rival to the market on the bishop's manor at nearby Hoxne. A later example is Beaudesert, near Henley-in-Arden (Warwickshire). Here in 1141, Thurstan de Montford was granted a charter for a market again to be held within his castle; the present cluster of properties around the ridge-top site and adjacent parish church represent the remnants of the failed commercial enterprise (VCH Warwicks 1904: 355–7; 1945: 45).

Castle-gate marketplaces could take any one of a number of forms depending upon topographical circumstances and, of course, the status and ambitions of the castle lord. The simplest arrangement was a small open marketplace immediately in front of the castle gates, often square (Castleton, Derbyshire) or rectangular (Oakham, Rutland), and sometimes triangular (Egremont, Cumbria), although in all cases later encroachment could blur the original arrangement. The triangular castle-gate marketplace in the modest medieval town of Week St Mary (Cornwall) originally measured *c.* 200 × 170 m, covering an area of 2 hectares, although today only vestiges of this feature remain (Preston-Jones and Rose 1992: 149). At Brinklow (Warwickshire), an unusually shaped early marketplace is represented by an elongated lozenge-shaped green ('The Crescent') that curves around the Norman motte and bailey, indicating a road diversion that must post-date its construction (Lilley 1994: 58). A marketplace curving around the eastern facade of Barnard Castle (Co. Durham) was similarly an early feature of the settlement's topography (Austin 1979: 58). More ambitious arrangements, with larger or extended marketplaces allowing more space for surrounding burgage plots, can be found at Corfe (Dorset) and Ludlow (Shropshire), where rectangular marketplaces were sandwiched between castle and parish church. Elsewhere the need to serve the commercial needs of burgesses was best served by a market focus not adjacent to the castle gate but at another intersection of routes. This factor may well account for the separation of Alnwick Castle from the large triangular marketplace where the three main routes in and out of the town intersect, probably on the site of the original Anglian vill (Conzen 1960: 23–38). At Hereford, William Fitz Osbern's new town (founded *c.* 1067–9) was conceived around a vast funnel-shaped marketplace placed well north of the castle and old Saxon *burh* in order to select the site with optimum commercial potential (Hillaby 1983: 185–90). The town plans of Alnwick and Hereford, among others, indicate that, despite certain advantages, commercial concerns were not necessarily best served by a castle-gate focus. The topographical relationships between castles and marketplaces have, however, received little attention, although considerable potential exists for detailed study. For instance, in an analysis of medieval town plans in Warwickshire and Worcestershire Slater (1982: 189) has suggested a link between triangular marketplaces and monastic sites. Castle sites could provide an interesting parallel, with the perimeter defences and castle gate naturally forming one side of the market, although further regional study, through maps and fieldwork, is required.

The topographical growth of other medieval towns shows that later market settlements were often fostered not immediately adjacent to castles, but developed with an eye for commercial possibilities at a distance from the siegneurial site. A particularly clear example is Downton (Wiltshire), where the new market founded by the Bishop of Winchester in *c.* 1208–9 lay not outside the gate of his castle but on the opposite bank of the River Wyle. The planned market street was grafted onto the earlier manorial core – comprising parish church, Saxon moot and castle – to form a T-junction with the main road to Salisbury in order to take advantage of commercial opportunities presented by changing communications patterns in south Wiltshire (Beresford 1959: 193–5). Similar scenarios are repeated elsewhere, and are especially common in the early thirteenth century. For instance, topographical analysis of the town of Thirsk (North Yorkshire) indicates a number of separate foci either side of Cod Beck. The Mowbray castle is clearly associated with a large rectangular marketplace with slight evidence of former defences, sited near the pre-urban village of Kirkgate ('Church Gate'). What is surprising is that the zone of settlement at the castle gate appears never to have enjoyed urban status, while a third focus, growing up on the east bank was described as a borough in 1145 when its chapel was granted to Newburgh Priory (Beresford 1967: 519; Beresford and Finberg 1973: 189). The long, curvilinear pattern of burgage plots in this area suggests expansion over ridge and furrow and it seems likely that the borough was encouraged here in order to take advantage of commerce generated by traffic on the York–Northallerton road. At Witham (Essex), a small town focused on a triangular marketplace between castle and church (Chipping Witham) fell into decline following the plantation *c.* 1212 of a linear borough (Newland Witham) by the Knights Templar along the main London–Colchester road which ran through the parish (Rodwell 1993: 85–9). Finally, Brough (Cumbria) shows a similar dislocation of a small castle-dependent focus (Church Brough), from a second plantation strung out along the trans-Pennine road (Market Brough) (Beresford and St Joseph 1979: 144–5). All these examples show a clear distinction between a manorial vill associated with the castle and a commercial borough, and reflect the changing circumstances facing lords keen to maximize profits from their estates.

Changing economic conditions could even mean that a town that had grown up around a castle could be transplanted to a fresh site. This process is exemplified by the example of Old Sarum (Wiltshire) (Fig. 3.1), which remarkably demonstrates the full array of forms that the relationship between a castle and an urban community could take through time. The siting of the ringwork (the largest in England) is exceptional in its scale of imposition (alongside a new cathedral) within the late Saxon community that nestled within the former iron-age hillfort, precipitating relocation of elements of the population to the New Portway plantation outside the earthworks (Haslam 1976: 48). The friction between garrison and cathedral clergy, but also the virtually indivisible nature of fortress and town are highlighted in a remarkable poem of Henry d'Avranches, a court poet of the time of Henry III:

> The hill of Sarum was distinguished both for its castle and also for its city, but was unsuitable for either. The city stood in the castle and the castle in the city, so which was the greater and which the less?
>
> (quoted from Torrance 1959: 242)

The poet went on to compare the topographical juxtaposition of fortress and cathedral to having the Ark of the Covenant in the Temple of Baal, commenting on the damp and exposed position of the hilltop, the quality of the soil and lack of reliable water supply as arguments for the cathedral's removal to a fresh site by the meadows of the Avon below. The progressive desertion of the town in favour of the bishop's new plantation of Salisbury from *c.* 1219 thus demonstrates that the initial advantages of a borough site closely associated with a castle could be outweighed by other circumstances.

Deserted boroughs

Despite the benefits that a borough might bring to a lord, we must remember that, overall, only a small proportion of castles spawned towns. On occasion, a settlement associated with a castle may have had market functions but not ever attain the status of a borough, or else not be documented as one. The development of the market village trailing away from the royal castle at Portchester (Hampshire), for instance, was limited not only by the emergence of nearby Portsmouth as an economic rival, but also by circumstances of lordship. In 1231, part of the manor was granted to the Abbot of Titchfield, who, possessing another market at Titchfield, may have further discouraged Portchester's growth (Munby 1985: 292). Mostly, we can assume that the venture of founding a castle-borough was too risky or inappropriate given local circumstances, although many failures can be identified. Indeed, a surprisingly large number of planted castle-boroughs failed to emerge from the medieval period as fully-fledged towns and a proportion survive only as deserted settlements. The study of these sites has two contributions to make to our wider understanding of the castle in the landscape. First, plan analysis of failed plantations can tell us much about the early phases of more successful castle-towns. Second, there is evidence to suggest that many deserted castle-boroughs were not 'typical' in any sense, but small and specialized settlements with little potential to flourish into the late medieval period following the abandonment of the seigneurial site. In many cases it remains uncertain whether these settlements had anything but urban potential, and across Britain, the failure rate for castle-towns is comparatively high. The desire of Norman lords to foster urban communities near their castles undoubtedly meant that sites with limited commercial possibilities could be chosen. Those towns contained within the defences of iron-age hillforts, such as Old Sarum (Wiltshire), were particularly prone to failure, and even where a castle-town survives to the present day, the site may have been marginal. For instance, the *de novo* castle borough of Mountsorrel (Leicestershire) occupied a narrow terrace bracketed by the cliff-top castle of the earls of Leicester to the west, and floodplain of the River Soar to the east. Excavation has revealed parts of the medieval town to overlie a dense network of drainage gullies indicative of an unfavourable and poorly drained site (Lucas 1987). Settlements such as these were nucleations forced by seigneurial agency, initially sustainable under the patronage of a local lord but vulnerable to changing social, political and economic circumstances.

The field evidence for failed castle-boroughs ranges from small clusters of properties marking the position of a severely contracted site (e.g. Skipsea, East Yorkshire), to completely deserted towns where the skeleton of a settlement plan is preserved by earthworks, property boundaries and road alignments (e.g. Castle Carlton, Lincolnshire). It is quite unusual for the plan of a borough to be entirely lost, as at Belvoir (Leicestershire), where the sites of the former town and priory have been completely disrupted by the creation of massive post-medieval garden terraces and other landscaping (Hartley 1987: 5–6). Sometimes, the creation of a borough, while intended, may not have been realized. This seems to have been the case at Kenilworth (Warwickshire), where one of the confirmation charters for the priory mentions that land near the castle had been reserved for a borough that is otherwise unknown to history (Beresford 1967: 128). A further problem is that there is often little in physical terms to differentiate such plantations from deserted villages. At Castle Carlton (Lincolnshire), for instance, the zone of enclosed settlement remains east of the powerful motte and bailey has been identified traditionally as a deserted village (Beresford and Hurst 1971: 193). A recent re-interpretation of the site, however, based on the Wigston manuscript (a fifteenth-century source containing references to earlier manorial documents) suggests that Castle Carlton contained burgesses and enjoyed commercial privileges indicative of borough status by *c.* 1157–8 (Owen 1992: 19). Sited within a pre-existing morphological frame provided by an abandoned Roman fort, the regular, double-row settlement was a small urban appendage to the castle planned by the lord of the manor, Hugh Bardolf I. This case is strengthened by the fact that the same lord is thought to have been actively involved in village planning during the reorganization of his other Lincolnshire estates, as at Riseholme, where the village was re-planned in neat rectangular form over a zone of former arable (Everson *et al.* 1991: 55–9).

Three failed Norman plantations on the Welsh borders (Kilpeck and Richard's Castle, Herefordshire and Caus, Shropshire) are particularly fine examples of deserted castle-boroughs (Fig. 7.14). Roger Fitz Corbet's castle of Caus was founded high on Long Mountain, within a prominent iron-age hillfort overlooking the key route between Shrewsbury and Montgomery. This represented a transferral of lordship from an earlier ringwork and manorial vill at Hawcock's Mount, where the name *Aldescausefield* ('Old Caus Field') is recorded in the fourteenth century (VCH Salop 1968: 303–10). The relocation to a more prominent and defensible position was followed shortly by the foundation of a seigneurial borough crammed into the hillfort defences, extant in 1200 when a weekly market was granted, and with no fewer than 59 burgage tenements by 1349 (Barker 1981: 34). Yet with its exposed position and a physically constricted site hemmed in by the hillfort defences, the borough was virtually doomed to failure '. . . like a prehistoric monster crushed beneath the weight of its own armour' (Beresford 1967: 188).

Although the early phases of the motte and bailey at Richard's Castle are feasibly pre-Conquest in origin (as suggested by Domesday Book), excavation has shown the simple earthen town defences to be an addition of *c.* 1200 and not a re-used hillfort as sometimes previously assumed (Curnow and Thompson 1969: 117–19). Although the plan of the enclosure is more akin to an outer bailey, no less than 103 burgesses are mentioned in 1304 (although not all necessarily lay within the enclosure), and a regular layout of plots

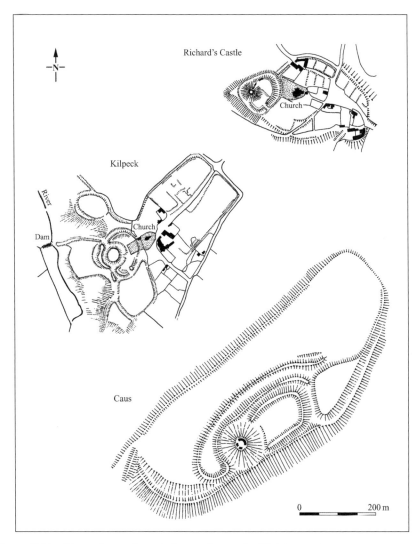

Figure 7.14 Three deserted castle boroughs on the Welsh marches.

survives as earthworks (RCHME Herefords. 1931–4: vol. 3, 172–3; Beresford 1967: 451).

Kilpeck's famous late Romanesque church lies at the heart of perhaps the most remarkable of these three sites, comprising the earthworks of a multiphase motte and bailey, Benedictine priory and an enclosed rectangular settlement (Fig. 7.15). Here the embanked defences, enclosing an area of *c.* 180 × 280 m, are almost independent of the castle, with the church of St David's forming the interface between the zone of lordship and the community. Kilpeck was granted a weekly market and annual fair in 1259, and while never formally recorded as a borough, the regular disposition of earthwork property

Figure 7.15 Aerial view of Kilpeck (Herefordshire). The large rectangular enclosure below the castle contains the earthworks of a deserted borough (Cambridge University Collection of Air Photographs: copyright reserved).

boundaries in two equal parcels seemingly indicates provision for a total of 44 burgage plots (Shoesmith 1992: 205).

As the foci of small Marcher baronies, castle and borough remained important tools of colonization in the border zone long after much of lowland England had been effectively pacified. But by the beginning of the fourteenth century the strategic importance of these tenurial units and their castles was in steep decline, fatally weakening the economic base of associated settlements (Rowley 1972: 178). By 1361 many of the houses in Caus were without tenants; Richard's Castle was ruinous by the sixteenth century and probably earlier; and archaeological evidence at Kilpeck suggests progressive abandonment after 1327, when the castle was no longer occupied by the lords of the manor (Buteux 1996; Dalwood 1996a; 1996b). The adverse social, economic and environmental conditions of the mid-fourteenth century undoubtedly accelerated decay, weeding out those settlements with less potential, and particularly those with niche economies centred on castles.

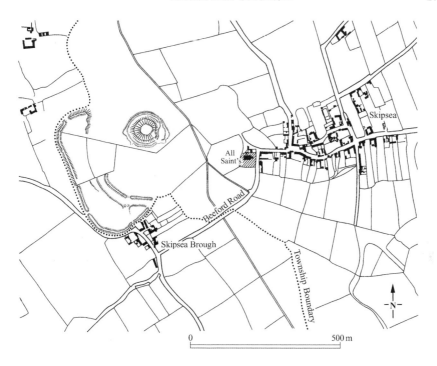

Figure 7.16 Skipsea (East Yorkshire), showing castle, deserted borough ('Skipsea Brough') and village (based on OS First Edition)

Today, all three sites have outstanding archaeological potential and, with the exception of Richard's Castle, have not been exposed to serious archaeological intervention. The lack of significant post-medieval development means that they doubtless hold archaeological evidence relating not only to the layout of castle and settlement, but potentially also to the social and economic relationships between the two. While the decline of castle boroughs such as these examples was attributable to changing political circumstances, environmental factors could also conspire to disadvantage other settlements. Thus in Cornwall, the castle-towns of Tregony (planned around a riverside quay beneath the Pomeroy castle), and Lostwithiel (founded in the late twelfth century by the lords of nearby Restormel), both lost their maritime rôles due to the progressive silting of the Rivers Fal and Fowey, and fell into decline (Halliday 1975: 123; Balchin 1983: 27).

An excellent example of a deserted castle-borough worthy of more detailed analysis is Skipsea Brough (East Yorkshire), planted by the lords of Holderness under the shadow of their honorial castle (Fig. 7.16). The castle-borough is now reduced to an irregular cluster of properties either side of a single route leading from the castle gate (Bail Gate). Here, the First Edition OS 6-inch sheet shows a decayed row of three burgage plots bracketed by the bailey defences and Beeford Road, which has been diverted in a right-angle to form the skeleton of the abortive plantation. The borough was clearly a latecomer to the medieval landscape: while the castle lay within Dringhoe township, Skipsea Brough lay on the opposite side of the boundary within what was formerly

Cleeton. The plantation is first recorded *c* 1160–75 as *burgo castelli de Skipse* (English 1979: 210–11). The borough's failure is charted by the fact that a mere three burgesses were recorded in an extent of 1260, which makes additional reference to a further ten plots which apparently yielded nothing at the *Newhithe* ('new landing place': Beresford 1967: 514). The latter reference must refer to the miniature harbour created within the former mere between motte and bailey. The place-name Skipsea ('isle of the ships') is itself suggestive of harbour functions, and artificial terraces indicative of building platforms and harbour facilities have been recognized within the vast horseshoe-shaped bailey enclosure (Atkins 1988; Youngs *et al.* 1988: 259).

What is especially remarkable is how the specific geographical circumstances of Skipsea Brough's location contributed to its eventual decline and failure. As the *caput* of the great Honour of Holderness, the castle and borough occupied a nodal position within the peninsula, controlling both the main landward approach to the peninsula (otherwise blocked by the marshes of the River Hull), and regional sea-borne trade. The borough was thus clearly sited to take advantage of the commerce generated by the castle's position at this intersection of routes. But Skipsea castle was abandoned *c.* 1221, and the consequent transfer of the administrative centre of Holderness to Burstwick seems to have spelled disaster for the plantation (Illingworth 1938: 103–5). Despite the absence of a rival urban plantation in the vicinity, the castle-borough was clearly not sustainable as a commercial venture. Of the total of three failed seigneurial boroughs in Holderness, the contraction of Hedon was related to the emergence of Kingston upon Hull as a competitor, whilst Ravenserodd was inundated by the sea in the fourteenth century; the decline of Skipsea Brough, in contrast, was attributable to its inherently limited economic rôle as a child of the castle (see Beresford 1967: 286–9, 510–14).

Another castle-borough that failed to flourish due to adverse geographical circumstances is Almondbury (West Yorkshire), where a tiny plantation was squeezed into the opposite end of a remote iron-age hillfort to a castle of the de Lacy family (Fig. 7.17). Two rows of rectangular closes front on to a central hollow-way within the pre-existing enclosure, along with remnants of later ridge and furrow cultivation (Moorhouse 1981; RCHME 1996: 17–18). Here the logical sequence of a defended borough founded shortly after the military site is not borne out by detailed scrutiny of documentary sources. The overall sequence seems to be of a mid-eleventh-century origin for the castle and mid- to late-thirteenth-century origin for the borough (Ahier 1946: 24–31; Manby 1968: 354). Almondbury borough was thus a relatively late initiative, apparently founded when the castle enjoyed a renaissance as a convenient stopping-over point on the route between the de Lacy's main castle at Pontefract and their detached hunting grounds of Marsden to the west (Faull and Moorhouse 1981: 302). These circumstances help explain some of oddities in the socio-economic of profile of the burgesses, including exceptionally low rents and the fact that the tenants appeared to have held substantial tracts of agricultural land in addition to their plots (Faull and Moorhouse 1981: 255). Clearly exceptional arrangements were necessary to temporarily sustain the nucleation of a community in such a location.

Figure 7.17 Aerial photograph of Almondbury (West Yorkshire). The castle has been inserted into one end of an iron-age hillfort. The large enclosure in the foreground contains earthworks that may represent the remains of a small failed borough (© Crown copyright NMR).

Summary

The basic chronological framework of urban castle foundation is now reasonably well established, and if anything more secure than our under-standing of the pattern of town foundation by castle lords. What unites these two processes is that most castles associated with urban settlements were sites of particularly high status, whether they preceded the town or vice versa. Castles founded within late Saxon towns were mainly royal fortresses and it was generally only sites of baronial status that spawned seigneurial boroughs which formed commercial centres within their lordships and hinterlands. The establishment of castles within extant urban centres such as Exeter, Leicester and York was particularly rapid, being confined almost entirely to the two decades after 1066. The growth of nascent towns outside castles such as Devizes, Brinklow and Warkworth was predominantly a slightly later process. Although the precise origins of these settlements are often uncertain, most seem to have been in existence by the middle of the twelfth century, and it is only on the borders and beyond that twinned castle-town units continued to be planted beyond this time. Nonetheless, while the establishment of urban communities at the gates of castles in England was rare from the thirteenth century, many settlements associated with castles expanded, for instance through the extension of marketplaces or the addition of planned units. In many of these cases, growing commercial considerations saw the physical association between castle and settlement weakened. In other contexts, castle-towns withered away as their seigneurial sites declined in significance (e.g. Caus). But while the period during which castle-towns were founded was relatively brief, their impacts on townscapes could be far more enduring, in many cases leaving their imprint on street patterns up to the present day.

8 Castles in the Countryside

Although we often tend to think of castles as élite structures that, in terms of their designs, followed national, and indeed international, trends, we must not overlook the fact that they were built within, and contributed to the development of, medieval landscapes with distinctive regional cultures and character (Jope 1963: 327; Astill and Grant 1988: 224–6). English castles show a close connection with the soil, as recognized by Ella Armitage, who noted the greater density of Norman castles in arable areas (1912: 83). The strong link between the English castle and village is part of a far broader phenomenon. The association of nucleated communities with sites of lordship, both defended and undefended, was a distinctive feature of the European medieval landscape – what has been termed the 'communality of enforcement' (Roberts 1996: 37). Many castles were, however, associated with other types of medieval rural economy and settlement landscape, including areas practising pastoral and mixed forms of agriculture. Castles are also found as isolated settlements as well as within nucleated villages. Indeed, in the medieval countryside the castle was adapted to a remarkable variety of tenurial and social as well as physical geographical circumstances, ranging from the administration of vast tracts of royal forest to the management of relatively small manors. This chapter examines the physical settings of castles within the countryside and assesses their contribution to its development, drawing particular attention to the impact of castles in different types of landscape.

The Norman Conquest

It is important to understand the initial impact of castles on the English countryside within the wider context of the Norman Conquest and colonization. Despite the traumatic historical and political events of 1066 and their aftermath, seen from a strictly archaeological perspective, the Norman victory had little discernible impact on the rural landscape (Rowley 1997: 26–30; Reynolds 1999: 181–2; see also Sawyer 1985). Indeed, it is a tantalizing question as to whether, in the hypothetical absence of documentary sources concerning the Norman Conquest and without preconceptions of its importance in English history, we would be able to detect its impact on the countryside from archaeological evidence alone. For instance, the term 'Saxo-Norman' is conventionally used to describe much indigenous pottery and the transitional ecclesiastical architecture of the late eleventh century – it being practically impossible to distinguish changes as a direct consequence of the Conquest (Austin 1987: 49). The Conquest bought no appreciable change in burial practice, while the system of coinage remained essentially unaltered, despite the obvious change of face on coins. The increase in commercial contacts with the continent, as evident for instance through the growing use of certain types of imported pottery, was also less apparent in the countryside.

Domesday Book does, of course, mark a tenurial revolution in the virtually wholesale replacement of Saxon overlords with Norman tenants-in-chief, including great continental magnates such as the de Warennes and de Clares. That said, detailed studies of Domesday have drawn attention to the survival of many lesser English lords and landowners as successful, and indeed prosperous, sub-tenants and mesne-tenants after the Conquest (Williams 1995: 71–125). In almost every other sphere of everyday rural life the coming of a new order represented no appreciable break with the past, as demonstrated by continuity in agricultural technology and the management of field systems. Other important transformations occurred a century or more later, including, the proliferation of pillow mounds, fishponds, mill mounds and, in rural housing, the replacement of earth-fast building techniques with timber framing.

Studies of the Anglo-Norman impact on landscape and society in Ireland, Scotland and Wales have often stressed that castles were introduced in tandem with a fundamentally different mode of lordship, agricultural system and manorial structure (Edwards 1997: 6; McNeill 1992: 84). Moreover, these introductions were commonly associated with quintessentially 'Norman' forms of settlement; namely the planned village and castle-borough. Some of the numerous castles which acted as catalysts for the nucleation of villages include Piperstown (Co. Louth, Ireland), Rattray (Perthshire, Scotland) and Templeton (Pembrokeshire, Wales) (Barry 2000: 194; Yeoman 1995: 89–95; Kissock 1997: 124–6). In other cases, however, castles must have been added to extant rural settlements. In England, Norman castles were overwhelmingly situated with explicit reference to a well-established pattern of settlement, tenurial geography, administrative sub-division and ecclesiastical topography. Although the precise form and siting of particular castle sites varied depending upon the specific demands of lordship, the sites of Norman castles, many of which were perpetuated by later re-building, were clearly related to the landscape of late Saxon England.

It is within this general framework that we must seek to understand the contribution of castles to the English rural scene. Rather than castles being imported into the countryside as part of a radically new Norman package, many were planted at established central places within the landscape. This is not to say, however, that ambitious and competitive Norman landlords, many of whom rose meteorically as a consequence of the Conquest, did not use castles as a means of tightening control over the countryside and the peasantry in order to strengthen their social and economic positions (Faith 1997: 178–200). Many interesting relationships are evident between castles and other newcomers to the rural landscape, such as deer parks and royal forests, as well as the religious houses that came into being as part of the monastic expansion inspired by new lords. Le Patourel (1976: 28–48) has argued that the Norman Conquest comprised two phases: military action and colonization. Although it may seem surprising, an examination of the relationship between castle and landscape in the late eleventh and twelfth centuries suggests that the castle's rôle in the latter was certainly as significant, if not more so, than in the former.

Manorial resources

The vast majority of castles in the English countryside also functioned as manors, representing part of the machinery of rural lordship. Most castles were also the hubs of extensive and often scattered frameworks of estates and centres for the management of a wide range of agricultural resources. The rural castle has been described a 'mother economic cell' (Chapelot and Fossier 1985: 147) – a central place in the medieval landscape that received agricultural surpluses and distributed work. Castles were also the venues of manorial courts, where matters relating to the economic administration of the manor were dealt with, along with the regulation of labour services owed by tenants. In this context, it is unsurprising to find a close association between the castle and other features of the rural landscape including, most obviously, villages, hamlets, farms and field systems, but also other accoutrements with symbolic connotations of status as well as practical benefits, such as deer parks and dovecotes. Even the medieval farming of rabbits using artificial warrens may have had symbolic connotations rooted in medieval theology and relating to the salvation of humankind by the church (Stocker and Stocker 1996: 265–6). The rural castle was also invariably to be found close to a block of land held directly by the lord (the demesne). The prominent exceptions to this general rule were those expedient fortifications, such as siege-works, raised rapidly during a time of military crisis and rapidly abandoned (see Chapter 3).

The various linkages between a castle and the resources of the countryside are particularly well understood at Portchester (Hampshire), due to the excellent preservation of written records relating to the administration of its associated estate and, in particular, a detailed survey of 1405 (Fig. 8.1) (Munby 1985). But this example may be atypical: the economic structure of medieval Portchester was complicated by dual lordship. Only one-third of the manor belonged to the Crown and supplied the castle with rents, food and other resources; the remainder had been in the hands of Titchfield Abbey since the early thirteenth century, and in the open fields the holdings of the Abbot and the King were intermixed in complex fashion. Other resources in the locality included the King's demesne woodland of *Kingesden* (which contained a warren), the common pasture of Portsdown, and the salt-pans in the reclaimed marsh north of the castle that were again divided between the two manors, while from the fourteenth century the castle's outer bailey and ditch were let out as pasture.

The physical juxtaposition of the earthworks of castles with traces of medieval ridge and furrow is to be expected in those areas where open field systems operated in some form. Some castles have been demonstrated to lie on top of, and therefore clearly post-date, ridge and furrow. This is especially clear at Hen Domen (Powys) and Sandal (West Yorkshire), where plough ridges sealed by occupation levels or defensive earthworks have been excavated (Barker and Lawson 1971; Mayes and Butler 1983). While this evidence would seem to indicate that castle-building caused disruption to, and possibly the reorganization of, the agricultural landscape, environmental evidence from Hen Domen (Fig. 2.1) suggested that the field system had apparently been out of cultivation at the time of castle-building (see Chapter 2). Elsewhere, aerial photography and/or earthwork survey demonstrates earlier ridges and furrows

Figure 8.1   Portchester (Hampshire) as reconstructed from a survey of 1405, showing the relationship between the royal castle and rural resources in the area, including the village and its open fields, and areas of marsh, woodland and common (based on Munby 1985).

to extend directly up to castle earthworks without an intervening headland, as at Sheriff Hutton (North Yorkshire) (Fig. 8.17). Other castle sites are clearly contemporary with, or earlier than, agricultural earthworks in their immediate vicinity. The coastal enclosure castle of Dunstanburgh (Northumberland), for instance, stands in apparent isolation from other settlement, and is adjoined to the south by a miniature field system organized in a herringbone pattern (Fig. 8.2). The existence of ridges and furrows within castle baileys or outer wards, as at Topcliffe (North Yorkshire) probably indicates the maximization of agricultural production at a time following castle abandonment. Some such agricultural features are likely to have been created with the spade, as the constricted nature of a bailey would have given insufficient room to turn a plough. The ringwork and bailey known as Castle Ring, Stanton Lacy (Shropshire) is another castle that clearly lay within a busy agricultural landscape (Fig. 8.3). The site is almost entirely surrounded by the corrugated earthworks of ridge and furrow cultivation running in different directions, some ante-dating and others apparently post-dating the castle earthworks.

As manorial centres, many castles were physically associated with other features representing the paraphernalia of rural lordship, such as milling facilities and rabbit warrens, that might have connotations of authority as well

Figure 8.2 Vertical aerial photograph of Dunstanburgh (Northumberland), showing the position of this large enclosure castle on a remote headland. To the south of the castle (bottom of the photograph) lies an undated field system (BKS Air Survey Ltd: copyright reserved).

as practical uses. Nowhere is this clearer than in a late fourteenth-century poem by the Welsh court poet Iolo Goch, in which he describes the setting of Owain Glyn Dwr's castle and residence at Sycharth (now in Llansilin parish, Clwyd).

> Each side full, each house at court,
> Orchard, vineyard and white fortress;
> The master's rabbit warren;
> Ploughs and strong steeds of great frame;
> Near the court, even finer,
> The deer park within that field;
> Fresh green meadows and hayfields;
> Neatly enclosed rows of grain;
> Fine mill on a smooth-flowing stream;
> Dovecot a bright stone tower;

Figure 8.3　Aerial view of Castle Ring, Stanton Lacy (Shropshire) (Clwyd-Powys Archaeological Trust: copyright reserved).

> A fish-pond, enclosed and deep,
> Where nets are cast when need be,
> Abounding, no argument,
> In pike and splendid whiting;
> His land a board where birds dwell,
> Peacocks, high-stepping herons.
> 　　　　　(quoted from Breeze 1997: 137)

While the poet draws attention to the splendour of the residential structures with details such as their white lime-washed appearance and, elsewhere, the description of features such as tiled roofs and glazed windows, what is notable is that the agricultural setting of the site also had desirable aesthetic qualities. The fact that this élite residence was simultaneously a working rural estate centre (as emphasized by the presence of ploughs, plough-teams and fields) emphasized its rôle as a symbol of prosperity and social order. The poetic form and somewhat sycophantic tone of the account means, however, that we cannot interpret it as an exact description of the castle's setting. Nonetheless, examination of the physical remains of the site has identified the remnants of certain features listed in the poem, most notably the sites of the mill and fishponds visible as earthworks (Hague and Warhurst 1966: 112).

Castles very often represented only one stage in a longer-term sequence of high-status occupation on a given site. On the one hand, a great number of rural Norman castles perpetuated the sites of Saxon manors or other status sites (see Chapter 3). But on the other hand, many early castles also continued to function as seats of manorial administration long after their defensive rôles had been relinquished. This type of post-military reorganization is well represented by the transformation of early castles into manorial compounds through the levelling of ramparts and mottes, and the addition of dependent paddocks, enclosures and fishponds. Good examples of this process include Sapcote (Leicestershire), where a series of large manorial paddocks were appended to the Norman motte and bailey remembered in the place-name 'Toot Close' (Addyman 1960), and Stapleford (Wiltshire) where a large rectangular close with fishpond was added to an earlier, presumably defunct ringwork (Creighton 2000a: 111). Countless other lowland castles were adapted as moated manors, commonly through the conversion of a bailey into a moated enclosure, as at the sites of Aughton and Lockington (East Yorkshire). An alternative scenario is represented at Old Manor Farm, Great Staughton, (Huntingdonshire), where a motte was entirely encompassed by a later quadrangular moat (RCHME Huntingdonshire 1926: 251–2). Elsewhere a castle site was sufficiently constricted or inconvenient for some other reason, and lordship was transferred to a new moated manor built on a fresh in the immediate vicinity. This scenario is well represented in Yorkshire where a number of moated manorial sites are clearly the successors of nearby motte and baileys, including good examples at Bilton (East Yorkshire) and Langthwaite (South Yorkshire) (Le Patourel 1973: 17–20).

Elsewhere, evidence of such demilitarization can be more difficult to distinguish from earthwork remains. For instance, from the air, the earthworks surrounding the motte and bailey at Yielden (Bedfordshire) appear superficially to represent a row of ditched and embanked medieval crofts comprising part of a settlement, into which a Norman castle has been inserted (Fig. 8.4) (Brown 1989: 236). Closer scrutiny of the physical relationship between the motte, baileys and outworks indicates a more complex sequence, however (Fig. 8.5). The castle itself appears to have undergone at least two stages of growth, as indicated by the rather odd profile of the triangular (northern) bailey, which has clearly been appended to an earlier motte with a single bailey. The banks of the surrounding closes also actually abut, and therefore post-date, the castle earthworks, and almost certainly represent a suite of manorial paddocks. Presumably contemporary with these additions, the ditches of the two baileys have been widened and partly filled-in to produce an elongated fishpond supplied by the River Till, probably after the castle ceased to have any real military purpose (Baker 1982c). Here, as is the case with so many other earth and timber castles, even those of substantial size and complex form with apparently long-lived occupation, there is little or no supporting documentary evidence, the site having a single secure documentary reference, in 1361, when it was apparently ruinous (A. E. Brown 1987: 109–10). The earthworks of other Bedfordshire castles reflect a similar process of manorialization, including the sites of at Cainhoe, Bletsoe, Meppershall and Poddington (Baker 1982b: 45–6). Fieldwork and topographical study thus have a vital rôle to play in identifying episodes of re-use as well as the original forms of earth and timber castles. The re-adaptation of castles in this manner may, however, be severely under-represented in the landscape record as the earthworks of, for instance, manorial enclosures have offered less significant obstacles to the plough or bulldozer than more massive defensive features.

Medieval watermills were key instruments of lordship and an important

Figure 8.4   Aerial view of Yielden (Bedfordshire) (Cambridge University Collection of Air Photographs: copyright reserved).

means of income for manorial lords. Most, but by no means all mills were firmly under the jurisdiction of lords who possessed legal rights obliging tenants use the amenity and pay tolls in the form of multure (Holt 1988: 36–53). By physically associating a seat of lordship with a mill, the owner of a castle was further able to exert control over the production of an agricultural surplus (Harfield 1988: 142–3). Castles and mills are juxtaposed countless times in the British landscape, although the precise chronological relationships and spatial patterns are yet to be studied at any level of detail. At Garthorpe (Leicestershire), for instance, a substantial but undocumented motte standing in 'Castle Close' on the edge of the earthworks of a shrunken medieval village lay next to the manorial watermill (Hartley 1987: 9). It is of course difficult to date either feature or prove for certain that they indeed coexisted. The earthworks of other castles preserve mill-races integrated with moats; a good example is the ringwork and bailey at Kingshaugh (Nottinghamshire), where such a channel and other water control features link to the castle ditch. Water

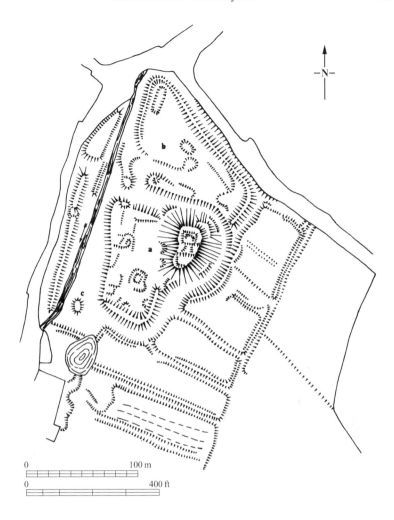

Figure 8.5. Earthwork plan of Yielden Castle (Bedfordshire), showing some of the features depicted in Figure 8.4. A motte and bailey with at least two clear phases appears to have been demilitarized and transformed into a manorial site through the addition of a series of rectangular closes and the excavation of one of its ditches to form a fishpond (Brown 1987).

power would certainly appear to be the type of milling facility preferred by castle lords, although Pounds (1990: 193–4) has traced documentary references to the use of horse mills, hand mills and, exceptionally, wind power in English and Welsh castles. One possible explanation is that watermills tended to occupy the perimeters of castle sites, their feeder systems being commonly integrated with moated defences, rendering an alternative means of grinding essential in the event of prolonged siege. The occurrence of two nearby medieval mill sites at the base of Castle Hill, Corfe (Dorset) can be explained differently. While West Mill was the demesne mill of the castle, the mill on the opposite side of the hill (Boar Mill), although only 300 m away, lay within the separate manor of Rollington (Eldred and Papworth 1998: 63).

We may also suspect that many castle baileys and outer wards would have contained granaries and other buildings associated with agricultural storage, although at present our sample of excavated sites is too limited to confirm or deny this. At Lydford (Devon), the small eleventh- to mid-twelfth-century ringwork was shown through excavation to resemble a fortified granary. A large part of the interior of this compact site was occupied by five earth and timber buildings associated with an enormous deposit of charred cereal (Wilson and Hurst 1967: 263), although it is unclear whether this represented the storage of an agricultural surplus or the supplies of a military force. Some indication of the importance of castles as milling centres is provided by a documentary and topographical study of the Bishop of Lincoln's castle at Sleaford (Lincolnshire). A manorial survey of 1324 makes specific mention of a *grangia* (barn) lying within the outer defences, while a sixteenth-century document mentions a similar feature with a suggested capacity of 300 loads of corn or hay (Pawley 1988: 37). Sleaford Castle was sited on an island surrounded by tributaries of the Slea, at the heart of an area of intense milling activity: immediately to the north lay Dam Mill, a double mill set in a causeway providing access to the castle, while a further eight mills were documented in *Eslaforde* at Domesday. Together, these conditions point to a castle functioning as a fortified centre for the collection, storage and redistribution of agricultural surplus and the control of milling activity in what appears to have been a specialist milling centre serving an extensive archiepiscopal estate.

Medieval fishponds are important indicators of élite consumption and, as such, it is unsurprising to find many closely associated with castles (Aston 1988b). Fishponds associated with élite residences have been relatively poorly studied relative to monastic fisheries, although the available evidence points towards some of the earliest large-scale fishponds being constructed by important secular lords (Currie 1991: 98). Freshwater fish, such as bream, pike and roach, were highly prized and played an important part in medieval aristocratic diet, as indicated by the recovery of substantial volumes of fish bones at, for instance, at Castle Acre (Norfolk) (Lawrance 1982: 287–9). Many fishponds were doubtless intended to provide for domestic consumption, although fish from royal ponds were also distributed as gifts and rewards for service, and some of the larger fisheries were run, at least partly, as commercial operations (Dyer 1988: 28). The field evidence for medieval fishponds found in association with castles varies from single rectangular depressions, slightly detached from the main residential site, that represent simple ponds, to multiple pond units featuring elaborate sluices, dams, feeder leats, islands and breeding tanks. Elsewhere we may suspect that castle moats also functioned as fishponds. The field evidence from the county of Rutland provides some measure of the ubiquity of castle fishponds in a lowland area. Of the county's five recognized castle sites, three have fishponds: the ditch of Oakham's bailey was widened to form a linear series of ponds; Woodhead Castle had at least one outlying rectangular fishpond; and a more complex series of stews (now destroyed) were attached to the moated defences of the ringwork at Essendine (Hartley 1983; Creighton 1999b).

The occurrence of fishponds near castles will be influenced by a wide variety of external factors. Most obvious of these are the circumstances of water supply, but local availability of fish in rivers, lakes and the sea may also be important. Indeed, this may partially explain the general rarity of manorial fishponds in medieval Ireland (O'Conor 1998: 34), and perhaps areas of England such as Devon and Cornwall. The high cost of constructing and maintaining fishponds was clearly a factor that both limited their spread and enhanced their appeal to those able to afford them. Being more affordable than deer parks, fishponds were built by members of the medieval gentry at large rather than only the owners of great castles. Indeed, it is an intriguing possibility that the tradition diffused to the lower levels of the aristocracy through a process of emulation, rather than proliferating due to an increase in demand (Taylor 1988: 466–9), although the immense difficulties in dating fishponds make such a hypothesis difficult to test. What is clear is that water features associated with castles could be both extremely complex and multi-functional, serving social, economic and recreational as well as defensive needs, nowhere more so than at Kenilworth (Warwickshire) (Fig. 6.12; see also Chapter 4). At York, the great artificial pool formed by the damming of the Foss flanked the vulnerable eastern approach to the castle and city, but was stocked with fish and also fed the King's mill before it flowed into the Ouse (Brown *et al.* 1963: 891). Expenditure on other royal fishponds associated with castles and invariably integrated with their moated defences is recorded at Leeds (Kent), Sauvey (Leicestershire) and Windsor (Berkshire), while the pond next to the episcopal castle of Banbury (Oxfordshire) was occasionally put to royal use. Among the most important of all royal fishponds were those of Marlborough Castle (Wiltshire); these served, among other things, as a central reservoir for stocking other ponds, and were substantially enlarged in 1245–51, when the dam was raised and the long, narrow pond enclosed with a hedge (Steane 1988: 60–1).

Hunting resources

Proximity to hunting resources appears to have been an important factor conditioning the location of castles. Important differences existed between those castle sites built within or close to royal forests, and others adjoining seigneurial chases and parks. The forests of medieval England were primarily created and maintained to serve the royal love of hunting but were also managed as economic concerns. Through the jurisdiction of forest law, the venison and the vert could be protected, while wood and venison could be given as prestige gifts by the Crown or sold by royal licence to form an important source of revenue to be maximized in a time of crisis (Young 1979: 114–34). Those castles in or near medieval forests often fulfilled specialized administrative rôles through the settlement of appointed foresters and other officials, as well as providing domestic facilities for the accommodation of hunting parties. Sites such as these tended to occupy isolated and secluded locations remote from other settlements. In contrast, castles with dependent deer parks were more likely to be associated with villages or planted towns, with the zone of parkland often exerting an important topographical influence on plan-form and settlement development. At Sheffield, for instance, the seigneurial deer park lying between the Don, Sheaf and Meersbrook and appended to the de Lovetot castle persisted as a landscape feature that limited expansion of the town east of the Sheaf well into the post-medieval era (Coates 1964–9: 135; Fine 1993: 31).

Royal forests

The link between castle and forest was particularly pronounced in Hampshire, where well over 50 per cent of the shire lay within the bounds of forests when they reached their maximum extent in the late twelfth century (Hughes 1989: 34). Six of the eleven forests recorded in the county by the thirteenth century have early castle sites on their fringes – a pattern that contrasts strongly with the location of hunting lodges deep within the forested areas. The constable of the royal stronghold of Portchester simultaneously held the keepership of the Forest of Bere (also known as the Forest of Portchester), which also contained royal demesne, and within which tenants held grazing rights (Munby 1985: 276). Elsewhere in the shire the ringwork at Godshill, a bailiwick of the New Forest, lay close to the forest bounds, while a network of at least four purpose-built royal hunting lodges covered the interior. Hunting lodges such as these would generally appear to post-date the forest-edge castles and show an intensification of royal forest exploitation, yet with time many forest castles were themselves increasingly maintained as domestic sites rather than fortresses. In neighbouring Wiltshire, the royal castles of Ludgershall and Marlborough were closely related to the distinctively afforested region on the border with Hampshire, including the Royal Forests of Chute and Savernake (Stevenson 1992: 70–1). Similar observations could be made about Pickering (North Yorkshire), Rockingham (Northamptonshire), and even urban royal castles such as Nottingham, Northampton and York, which were all conveniently located for access to forests and their resources.

The extensive area of royal forest on the border between Leicestershire and Rutland contains several excellent examples of isolated forest castles. Sauvey Castle (Leicestershire) lay in the north-west corner of the forest of Leafield, a northern extension of the Forests of Rockingham, and was held, along with the manor of Witchcote, by a series of appointed royal foresters during the thirteenth century (Farnham and Thompson 1921). Sauvey's social and economic functions as a place for gathering hunting parties and managing the forest were clearly best served by a secluded location, as reflected by the Norman-French place-name *Salveé*: 'dark island' (Cox 1971: 198–9). A similar scenario is repeated over the border in Rutland at Beaumont Chase, where a powerful ridge-top motte and bailey was also the seat of an appointed forester (Rut. Loc. Hist. Soc. 1982: 2). The peripheral position of this fortification relative to human settlement is emphasized by its position at the boundary of two parishes (the bailey lies in Uppingham and the motte in Beaumont Chase; Beaumont Chase itself was extra parochial until the eighteenth century) (Creighton 2000b: 419). Higham (1991: 86) makes a similar connection between a scatter of small upland mottes and zones of royal forest in Lancashire, demonstrating that sites such as Castle Hill, Dolphinholme (associated with Wyresdale Forest) and Hall Hill (Forest of Bowland) were built to exert control over these important resources.

Most of these castles lay on the margins of, or immediately beyond, the afforested zone: the three castles in the Exmoor region, for instance, all lay on the fringes of the former royal forest (Holwell Castle, Devon, and Bury Castle and Dunster, Somerset), although none appears to have been royal. The four castles of the Dartmoor region (Hembury, two at Lydford, and Okehampton), were similarly located immediately beyond the high moor and the area of the Forest of Dartmoor, which actually lay within the vast parish of Lydford. The Forest of Dean, containing no fewer than ten castles within its bounds (most of them small mottes and ringworks, including good examples at East Dean, English Bicknor and Little Dean, Gloucestershire), is somewhat of an anomaly in this respect, attributable to the fact this was also a border area. But few large tracts of royal forest were without a castle. Intriguing questions can of course be posed concerning whether castle or forest came first or, as perhaps seems most likely, the two were conceived more or less together. The proximity of early castles to the edges of royal forests also means that many are mentioned, some for the first and only time in documentary history, as relict features during later perambulations of forest bounds. The first direct documentary reference to Castle Neroche (Somerset) occurs in a perambulation of the Forest of Neroche in 1298, over a century after its abandonment, when it is referred to as a 'certain Mons called the Castle of *Rachich*' (Davison 1972: 23). The 'Old Castle of Ansley' (Annesley, Nottinghamshire) remained a landmark and convenient turning point in the second and later perambulations of the Forest of Sherwood long after it had been disused (Stevenson 1918: 84). Other early castles on the fringes of Sherwood Forest include the motte at South Normanton (Derbyshire) and a ringwork at Kingshaugh (Nottinghamshire); both again lay in remote positions and were mentioned in perambulations of the forest boundaries (Crook 1990: 94–5; Speight 1994: 68).

Forest castles were far more than defended hunting lodges and centres of élite consumption. As judicial centres, many provided venues for forest courts and, on occasion, jails for those committing forest offences. The courts of the forest (and manor) of Dartmoor were always held at Lydford, presumably in or near the castle; the infamous castle dungeon, however, was principally for offenders tried in the tinner's court, the castle being a centre of stannary administration, as was Restormel in Cornwall (Saunders 1980: 127–36). But these sites were not alone in their roles as centres for the administration of mineral exploitation. Another excellent example is St Briavels in the Forest of Dean (Gloucestershire), sited typically not within the heart of the royal forest, but on its west fringe, on a site overlooking an important fording point over the Wye. The constable-warden of St Briavels exercised not only overall control of the royal forest, but was charged with responsibility for the area's iron production and armaments industry that centred on the local network of bloomery forges (Curnow and Johnson 1985: 71). The mass production of crossbow bolts in the area is well recorded in the thirteenth and fourteenth centuries, with the castle acting also as a royal arsenal and distribution centre. In 1265, for instance, the constable undertook to produce no less than 25,000 quarrels per annum (VCH Gloucs. 1996: 266). A parallel is Peveril Castle (Derbyshire), which was closely associated with the regulation of lead workings in the Royal Forest of the Peak that are recorded in Domesday Book (Hart 1981: 136, 148).

Close relationships also existed between castles and chases – in effect private forests under the jurisdiction of the higher nobility. Nowhere is this clearer than in the arrangement of eleventh-century mottes around Leicester Forest (actually a chase) to serve the hunting interests of the earls of Leicester (Phythian-Adams 1988: 36). Norman fortifications in the villages of Earl Shilton, Groby and Sapcote (all manors in the hands of Hugh de Grantmesnil in 1086) were apparently raised to secure access to, and act as administrative centres for, the extensive afforested zone of boulder clay recorded in Domesday as *Hereswood* (Fox and Russell 1955: 59; Liddle 1982: 20).

Deer parks and chases

The creation and development of a seigneurial deer park was one particularly important way in which a castle lord could restructure the immediate landscape setting of a castle. The close connection between castles and deer parks was noted by Crawford (1953: 189), commenting that fieldwork and the analysis of historic maps could often reveal the presence of previously unrecognized parks adjacent to fortified medieval sites. Certainly, the majority of castle lords commanding the necessary resources would have built a deer park to accompany their principal residence. In Staffordshire, for instance, of fifteen medieval castles, no fewer than twelve had an attendant park (Cantor 1966: 42). Parks also had undoubted aesthetic qualities, being often skilfully designed to link a castle to its physical surroundings while simultaneously demonstrating its seclusion. But this was a two-way process. While many parks formed stunning physical backdrops for castles and deliberately designed environments from they could be viewed, parks were also doubtless intended to be viewed from the castle itself (see Chapter 4 for full discussion). The use of deer parks in this way is, of course, a fascinating precursor for the better-known designed landscapes of the post-medieval period (Bettey 1993)

The bounds of many of these parks can often be readily reconstructed from the surviving earthworks of park pales, the alignment of roads, property boundaries and parish boundaries, and place-name evidence (Fig. 8.6). Very occasionally a park's boundaries could survive intact as a modern parish: the boundaries of Haverah Park parish, for instance, seem to fossilize the perimeter of a hunting park carved from the Forest of Knaresborough, as indicated by its location at the focus of five surrounding parishes. This earthwork castle was an isolated hunting seat serving the honorial *caput* of Knaresborough (VCH Yorks. 1906: 312). Other early castles that doubled as (or were redeveloped as) hunting lodges serving important baronial castles include Knepp, Sussex (an outpost of Bramber) and Thorne, South Yorkshire (built for the lords of Conisborough).

The most common arrangement was for the park to take the form of a lobe, and to append directly onto one side of the castle (Fig. 8.6). Subsidiary lodges for parkers and occasional visits by hunting parties, by contrast, tended to lie well within the park boundaries, as at Odiham (Hampshire), where the lodge built by Edward III lay approximately at the centre of the royal park (Roberts 1995: 92). The royal park at Odiham was somewhat unusual in its physical separation from the royal castle, partially explained by the fact that the park

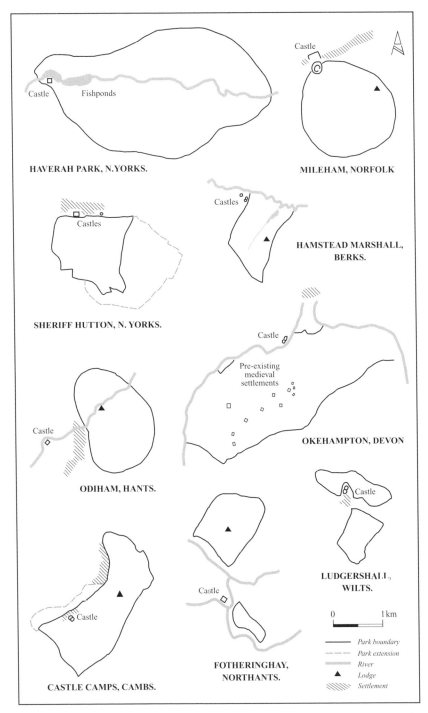

HAVERAH PARK, N.YORKS.

Castle   Fishponds

MILEHAM, NORFOLK

Castle

SHERIFF HUTTON, N. YORKS.

Castles

Castles

HAMSTEAD MARSHALL, BERKS.

Castle

Pre-existing medieval settlements

OKEHAMPTON, DEVON

Castle

ODIHAM, HANTS.

LUDGERSHALL, WILTS.

Castle

CASTLE CAMPS, CAMBS.

Castle

FOTHERINGHAY, NORTHANTS.

0   1 km

Park boundary
Park extension
River
▲ Lodge
Settlement

Figure 8.6 Relationships between deer parks and castles, showing park boundaries, principal park lodges and settlements.

antedated John's castle, begun in 1207, and may feasibly have pre-Conquest origins (MacGregor 1983: 27). The unusual presence of a motte *within* the perimeter of the park at Hamstead Marshall (Berkshire) is explained by the fact that it is probably an unfinished siege-work, constructed on a strong natural site in opposition to one of two motte and bailey castles built *c.* 800m to the west (Bonney and Dunn 1989: 173, 178). Berry Pomeroy 'Castle' (Devon) was also set within (as opposed to on the edge of) a deer park, although here the reasons were quite different; this was a late-fifteenth-century fortified manor house built as a deliberately secluded residence, its site possibly supplanting an earlier hunting lodge (Brown 1996: 4–10).

Where a castle was apparently associated with two or more parks, this seems likely to be a reflection of an original medieval arrangement rather than the dismemberment of one originally larger unit. The available evidence suggests that where two parks are contemporaneous, they might have had distinct functions. In particular, smaller parks closely appended to castles, and in some cases clearly designed to embrace the site, may have functioned as dedicated pleasure parks unsuited to hunting but designed for the staging of other entertainment activities such as tournaments and, perhaps, for aesthetic appeal. This seems particularly likely at Fotheringhay (Northamptonshire), where the 'Little Park' of 12 hectares, associated with an orchard, garden and pond, was clearly designed as an adjunct to the castle, while the 'Great Park' of 120 hectares was detached on the opposite side of the parish (Taylor 1989: 221). The same may be true at Ludgershall, where field names such as 'Bowling Alley Park' and 'Coneygre' suggest the north park may have been the venue for non-hunting activities while a second park in the south of the parish was stocked with deer (Everson *et al.* 2000: 105). Other facilities for aristocratic entertainment that could be provided near castles include jousting paddocks or tournament spaces, one example of which was the 'Turf Close' appurtenant to Brampton Castle (Oxfordshire) (Coulson 1993: 8–9).

We may well often overestimate the importance of seigneurial deer parks as dedicated hunting reserves. As a live larder, a park provided a ready source of fresh venison for the high table, or to bestow in the form of gifts. It has also been long recognized that a well-stocked deer park, as a conspicuous luxury unaffordable for most, could be an important vehicle for social expression by a highly competitive aristocracy (Stamper 1988: 146). Deer parks were clearly the objects of pride, and rights to hunt in them could be granted as gifts, as reflected in the instructions given by Henry III to the constable of Dover, specifying that the visiting French noble Gaucher de Châtillon, upon visiting the castle, should be allowed to hunt in the King's park at Eltham (Coulson 1979: 75).

But possession of a deer park could also bring considerable practical and economic benefits. Birrell (1992) has stressed the intensity of deer management practices within parks and underlined the wide range of other activities that were integrated within park management practices, including the exploitation of timber from managed woodland, and the leasing of rights to turf and pasture. The intensity and diversity of park management is reflected well in the calendared documentation relating to the park of Hadleigh Castle (Essex), first documented in 1235. In addition to providing timber, underwood and meat both for domestic consumption and gifts, the park also contained a fishpond, park lodge and horse rearing facilities, and was progressively sub-divided through assarting (Rippon 1999: 26). A nearby park could certainly provide a convenient resource for fuel wood and building timber; more exceptionally, in 1276, Robert de Sandwich, the castle steward of Odiham (Hampshire) was obliged to provide the King's engineer with six oaks from the castle park for the construction of engines of war (MacGregor 1983: 76).

While the curved profiles of park boundaries probably have owed something to the practicalities of hunting and the economics of maintaining expensive paling, what is certain is that medieval imparkment often had a disruptive effect on the rural landscape, with new parks invariably cutting across the grain of earlier boundaries. In many ways deer parks were miniaturized landscapes of exclusion, reflecting directly the coercive power and status of castle lords. Many medieval parks were carved out of waste and represent a way of maximizing poor quality land (Cantor and Hatherly 1979: 71–2); for instance 'Flitteris Park', closely associated with Oakham Castle (Rutland), means 'brushwood area of disputed ownership', reflecting well its position on the county boundary (Cox 1994: 126). Yet imparkment could also result in the disruption and even displacement of settlement. At Okehampton (Devon), the earls of Devon cleared the area south of their castle of farmsteads and removed the community's rights to other agricultural resources in order to create a vast and conspicuous greenbelt around their seat of lordship in the late thirteenth century (Austin 1978: 195–6; 1990: 73–4). A remarkable document of 1292 records an agreement between Hugh de Courtenay and the burgesses of Okehampton whereby rights to common pasture in the zone later occupied by the park were exchanged for access to wastes and woodland elsewhere on the fringes of Dartmoor, while part of the Courtenay's own demesne was also converted from arable to parkland. Another good example of this process is the deserted village found in direct association with the motte and bailey at Castle Camps (Cambridgeshire) (Fig. 6.5 and 8.6). This settlement was finally overwhelmed by the expansion of the nearby castle park, first recorded in 1263, and the creation of another before 1450, to give a total imparked area in excess of 240 hectares (Way 1997: 64, 229). The settlement may partly have been transplanted to Camps Green, and the present scattered settlement pattern in the parish probably owes something to the vast extent of the seigneurial park. Elsewhere, the former medieval village of Wittenham (Wiltshire) was depopulated to make way for the park of the Hungerfords at Farleigh Hungerford Castle, which lay on the opposite side of the River Frome in Somerset (Aston 1988a: 59). In 1428 Lord Hungerford received a licence to amalgamate the two parishes, thus accounting for the finger-like protrusion of the Somerset county boundary into Wiltshire at this point. The village was entirely deserted, its parish church now surviving only as a series of earthworks at the place known as Holy Green, Rowley. In other settlements a park could provide a physical barrier to settlement expansion and serve to strangle development or else determine the pattern of growth, as at Ludgershall (Stevenson 1992: 78–9; Everson *et al.* 2000: 106).

In many of these cases we may pause to consider whether the abandonment, disruption or relocation of a village was not so much a by-product of imparkment, as part and parcel of the wholesale reorganization of large tracts of landscape for seigneurial needs. Parks were often only one element in the

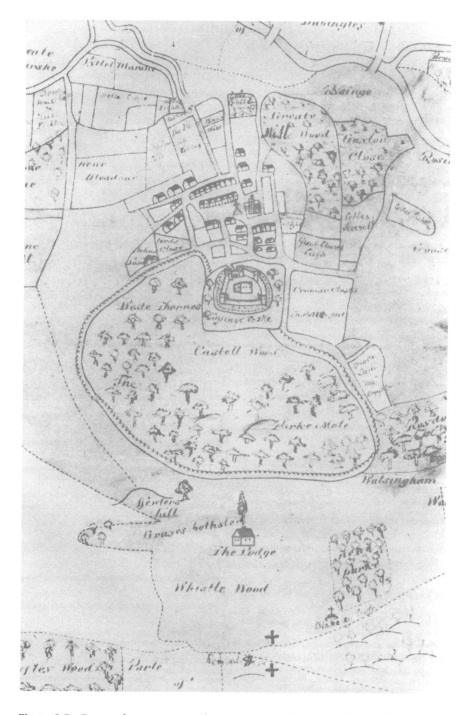

Figure 8.7 Extract from a nineteenth-century copy of a map of Rising Chase, 1588. depicting the relationship between the castle, park and grid-plan town (Norfolk Record Office, Bradfer Lawrence, 71).

restructuring of landscapes surrounding castles, as exemplified by the case of Castle Rising (Norfolk) (Fig. 8.7). The castle park was one of three seigneurial parks embraced entirely by a great chase stretching between the Babingley and Gaywood rivers, with a perimeter of no less than 24 km (Liddiard 2000a: 55). Here the castle was bracketed on the one side by the park and on the other by a planned town – a topographical relationship mirrored at, for instance, Devizes (Wiltshire). The arrangement constituted a carefully contrived land-scape comprising a series of nested spaces, one inside the other, with the castle set at the interface between the community and the privatized, exclusive area of the park.

Rural settlement patterns

In their groundbreaking study of rural settlement evolution in Western Europe, Chapelot and Fossier (1985: 129–33) identified the castle as the most important factor in the nucleation of rural communities between the ninth and the eleventh centuries. Recent archaeological and historical studies in Britain, however, have stressed quite how complex the process of village evolution could be, and how widely it could vary, both spatially and temporally (Lewis *et al.* 1997). Although nucleated villages were already established features of the English landscape well before the eleventh century in areas such as the East Midlands, elsewhere the process of nucleation was only gathering pace by the time of the Conquest, as in much of Yorkshire and County Durham (Taylor 1983b; Roberts 1987). The landscape of other parts of England, such as much of Devon and Cornwall, however, retained a predominantly non-nucleated rural settlement pattern throughout the medieval period. In addition, detailed mapping of settlement patterns demonstrates that even in regions where the nucleated village was apparently the norm, at a local level settlement forms were invariably mixed (Roberts and Wrathmell 2000). It is against this background of complex settlement patterns that we must assess the impact of the castle on rural England. What is particularly important is that the various interrelationships between medieval castles and other forms of medieval set-tlement show a similar level of regional variation, emphasizing the status of the castle as an element within, and contributor to, the kaleidoscopic medieval rural settlement pattern (Creighton 1999a).

Dispersed settlement

Social and economic demands could dictate that in certain landscapes a castle could carry out its functions in a position physically remote from other forms of human settlement. We must, however, bear in mind that a proportion of apparently isolated castle sites may have been associated with medieval set-tlements that have failed and subsequently vanished from the landscape record. In addition, other earthworks mistaken for isolated mottes or ring-works may have alternative origins, such as barrows, mill mounds or prospect mounds (see Chapters 3 and 4). But most isolated castles were part of regional settlement patterns characterized, wholly or partially, by other dispersed forms of rural settlement. In areas such as Devon, where castles are generally remote features in the countryside or else loosely associated with small hamlets or dispersed farmsteads, their distribution can be viewed as part and parcel of the characteristically dispersed regional settlement pattern and its related economy (Higham 1980: 74; Higham 1982b: 106). Some of the many Devon castles that stand in positions remote from other human settlements without being prohibitively inaccessible include the mottes at Durpley, Shebbear and Heywood, Wembworthy, and the ringwork known as Castle Roborough, Loxhore, all of which are located in parishes containing multiple foci of predominantly non-nucleated settlement. In the south west and elsewhere, castles were thus key elements within the workings of manorial economies dominated by mixed or pastoral agricultural practices.

A practical problem for the fieldworker is that the ownership histories of some of these early, isolated rural castles can be difficult to pin down. While a certain proportion of such sites may well be short-term military foundations, in other cases fragmented and complex tenurial geography makes it difficult to demonstrate that a given castle site lay within a certain manor, vill or township. Cainhoe Castle (Bedfordshire) is another excellent example of a motte and bailey that was part of a local settlement pattern without large rural nucleations. In 1973 excavations during road widening failed to recover evidence of structures on adjacent earthworks suspected to be house platforms, documentary evidence recording a number of unoccupied cottages in the manor in 1374 (Taylor and Woodward 1975). Later earthwork analysis has shown the series of eroded earthworks adjacent to the site to be the closes, fishponds and associated water management features of a manorial successor to the castle (Baker 1982a: 32). Here, the castle and late manorial complex on the same site thus seem always to have been discrete elements within a dispersed pattern of human geography.

In the rather different landscape of south-east Lincolnshire, castles again constitute elements of a dispersed settlement pattern (Fig. 8.8). In South Holland, castles predominantly lie in positions isolated from loosely agglomerated villages, or are otherwise isolated forms of settlement in their own right. This pattern mirrors exactly the landscape context of moated manorial sites in this lowland district. Indeed, the low relief of castle earthworks in this part of Lincolnshire, and in particular the low, flat morphology of mottes, may represent a hybrid form combining some of the characteristics of the earth and timber castle and moated manor. These early castles were thus integral components of a regional economy dominated by split manors and a relatively free social structure; the castles followed a settlement pattern where church, settlement and manor were not necessarily conjoined. (Healey 1977: 28; Creighton 1999a: 30). In contrast, medieval lordship sites in neighbouring Kesteven are far more closely integrated with villages, indicating that here, castles and manorial sites were imposed within a fundamentally different type of medieval social and administrative structure.

There is clearly much of interest in the respective distribution of castle and moated site. A morphological continuum – or catena – clearly existed between the motte and moated manor, so that one type of earthwork actually blurs into the other (Le Patourel and Roberts 1978: 47). What is instructive, however, is that the division between the two types of seigneurial residence is increasingly

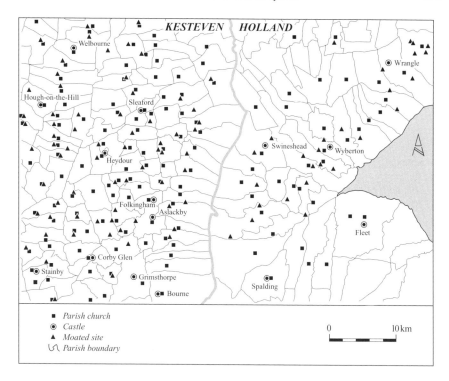

Figure 8.8 Castles, churches and moated manorial sites in part of southern Lincolnshire (based on Healey 1977, with additions).

blurred in certain types of landscape, as in South Holland. The morphology of low moated mounds clearly reflects a compromise between the need to give an appearance of defensive strength in landscapes where the construction of a moat made more sense, presumably at time before the moated site had become accepted culturally as an appropriate capital messuage. Nationwide analysis of the two types of earthwork by Roberts (1964) has highlighted the frequency of moats in areas of later colonization, in contrast to mottes, which tend to occupy the prime cultivable zone. Clearly an integrated understanding of the interrelationships between castle sites and moated sites is a research priority for the future (Aberg 1983: 100). A further indication of the prestige inherent in castle-building is the competitive emulation of castle moats and associated water features by slightly lower ranking members of the medieval rural élite. Many studies of the morphology and settings of medieval moated sites have stressed that the construction of a water-filled ditch around domestic buildings may have been a symbolic gesture by lords anxious to express their status as much as a practical means of defence or drainage. In Cambridgeshire, for instance, Christopher Taylor has suggested that ostentatious mock moated defences of sites such as Cheveley Castle (built 1341) could have provided part of the inspiration behind water features associated with the many moated manors scattered throughout the county (Taylor 1972: 246).

  Although we tend to associate the notion that rural settlement patterns could come into being through deliberate planning with the plantation of

Figure 8.9 Motte at Hockleton, Chirbury (Shropshire): one of a chain of small mottes built in the Vale of Montgomery, probably in the late eleventh century. Like many of the other mottes in the group, the site stands close to an isolated farmstead (photograph: Oliver Creighton).

regulated nucleated villages by medieval lords, an intriguing possibility is that dispersed settlement patterns could also originate as a result of seigneurial initiative. It has been suggested that the impact of lordship on settlement change in dispersed settlement landscapes is likely to be less important due to freer social structures which restricted the ability of lords to intervene (Lewis *et al.* 1997: 209). Limited evidence can, however, be found to give some support to the thesis that dispersed settlement landscapes could also be planned. King and Spurgeon (1965) have demonstrated a link between castle-building and dispersed rural patterning in the Vale of Montgomery, where a dense concentration of twelve mottes was apparently planted in the late eleventh century as a contribution to the re-settlement of a region devastated by a series of cross-border disturbances (Fig. 3.9). What is especially remarkable is the homogeneity of the earthworks' forms and settings: most are conical mottes with small summits and baileys, located adjacent to small farms or hamlets in a manner suggesting a link with agriculture rather than any military strategy (Fig. 8.9). Moreover, there is clear evidence that the mottes, lying in separate townships, were the centres of petty lordships and therefore seats of private individuals. While the precise occasion for this re-settlement remains a matter for debate, what is certain is that the earls of Shrewsbury, who held much of Shropshire almost as a palatinate in the last quarter of the eleventh century, and the lordship of Montgomery in demesne, had the authority to carry out such an ambitious programme. While the scheme is perhaps unique in its scale, due to the extreme socio-political circumstances of a border region,

Figure 8.10   Castle Bolton (North Yorkshire), showing the great quadrangular castle of the Scrope family at the head of a regular village planned around a rectangular green, probably by the castle lords (photograph: Oliver Creighton)

the example does demonstrate an essential point: that planned settlements need not necessarily take the form of nucleated villages. In another important study, Daniels (1990) has suggested that the seigneurial planning of individual farmsteads was an enduring feature of the moorland-fringe landscape of Kilton (North Yorkshire). Here, individual farmsteads or hamlets at Stank House, Buck Rush and Greenhills were apparently laid out in conjunction with the construction of the nearby castle in 1265. Although all lie within 2 kilometres of the castle, there is no obvious morphological link between the different settlement units, while the failed planned village of Kilton was similarly not spatially associated with the cliff-side seigneurial residence. Rather, it is only through painstaking analysis of documentary sources that the link between dispersed settlement and lordly planning can be made. Similar schemes could certainly have accompanied castle-building elsewhere in the highland zone; it is primarily the fact that such schemes do carry that obvious hallmark of planning – regularity – that seigneurial re-orientation of settlement in non-nucleated forms remains so little understood.

Castles and villages

The impact of castle-building on medieval villages, as on towns, could be positive as well as destructive. From one perspective we can see the castle, in its capacity as manor, as an integral part of the social and economic fabric of the village and, on occasions as a focus for nucleation. The range of morphological relationships between castles and village plans of all types – rows and agglomerations of all shapes, sizes and levels of complexity, with and without greens – is immense. Particularly common is the location of the castle at the head of a village whose principal axis is formed by a single street (e.g. Fotheringhay, Northamptonshire) or rectangular green (Castle Bolton, North Yorkshire: Fig. 8.10), although other sites are part of linear villages of more attenuated form (e.g. Edlingham, Northumberland) or attached to the corners of irregular greens (e.g. Ravensworth, North Yorkshire). Arrangements such as these can be related to a wider local or regional pattern of medieval rural settlement, although as a general rule, castles appear to lie in essentially similar positions within village plans as other manor sites (see Roberts 1987: 152–5). The military functions of a castle could, however, attract the ravages of warfare, while the construction of a castle site could sometimes disrupt settlements and their field systems. A fundamental distinction can thus be made between cases where the castle was planted within an *existing* village, and cases where a *secondary* village grew up adjacent to a *primary* castle. Even so, it is often less than abundantly clear whether castle or village came first. For instance, even where a settlement appears to have been planted contemporary to or later than the castle, this could represent the re-orientation of earlier settlement, traces of which may not be apparent within the present landscape.

As Christopher Taylor has pointed out, the nucleation of many villages resulted from the collapse of antecedent scattered settlement patterns (1983b: 131). Although the growth of castle-dependent villages must have impacted on the settlement landscape in precisely this way, the actual process remains largely conjectural due to insufficiently clear archaeological and historical evidence. One intriguing case where the intervention of a castle lord resulted, directly or indirectly, on the depopulation of dispersed settlements is Barry (South Glamorgan). Here, an integrated programme of excavation and field-walking has suggested that the nucleation of a castle-gate settlement in the thirteenth century resulted in the relinquishment of an earlier pattern of scattered farmsteads as part of a policy of manorial consolidation (Thomas and Dowdell 1987: 98–101).

While the lifetimes of medieval castles built in villages could sometimes be short, the consequences of their construction and the impact of the new seigneurial presence might be dramatic and their legacy enduring. The castle at Middleton Stoney (Oxfordshire), for instance, was a transient feature of the local scene, being established by the de Camvilles in the mid twelfth century on the site of an earlier hall but pulled down by the orders of King John in 1216 (Rahtz and Rowley 1984: 11–15). But in this time the new residence was furnished with a deer park and the village layout totally re-designed following the grant of a market. The construction of the castle also resulted in the obliteration and re-routing of an important road between Oxford and Brackley, and was also closely associated with the foundation of a new parish church. All these types of change represent not only the impact of the castle on the landscape but also the presence of a puissant aristocratic force in the district.

Imposition of rural castles

As the excavation of countless castles has shown, the external appearance of earthworks, while often superficially simple, can be extremely misleading. The surface morphology of an earthwork can be radically altered by multiple disturbances and episodes of re-use, sometimes decades or centuries after its original abandonment. In addition, by stratigraphically sealing antecedent phases of activity, castle earthworks can conceal far more than they reveal (Higham and Barker 1992: 196). Indeed, it is usually only through the total excavation of a castle site that physical evidence of earlier occupation may be recovered,

Figure 8.11 Aerial view of Burwell (Cambridgeshire). The earthworks immediately above the castle site represent a line of medieval village properties disrupted by its construction (Cambridge University Collection of Air Photographs: copyright reserved).

which, given the massive nature of castle earthworks can be an inordinately time-consuming and expensive operation. It is only very rarely, and due to exceptional conditions of preservation, that fragments of pre-existing settlements or other earlier features therefore survive as visible earthworks.

The clearest evidence for the construction of castles over village remains comes from two important sites in Cambridgeshire that represent remarkable Anarchy-period royal campaign fortresses. The earthworks of Burwell Castle, begun in 1143 and left unfinished in 1144, are interesting in demonstrating how a mid-twelfth-century castle was constructed, but also for preserving evidence of earlier domestic occupation on the site (Fig. 8.11). Projecting from beneath the irregular spoil heap on the north side of the uneven, unfinished ditch can be identified croft enclosures representing at least three and possibly as many as five separate holdings, while to the east lie the earthworks of two abandoned long houses (RCHME Cambs. 1968–72: vol. 2, 41–2). Excavation on the site has also recovered sherds of Stamford Ware from deposits beneath the castle mound, presumably derived from the earlier settlement (Lethbridge 1936: 127–9; Hurst 1958: 37). The contemporary castle earthworks at Rampton take a similar form, comprising a partly-formed rectangular castle mound associated with earthen ramps built for the removal of spoil from the ditch. Here, detailed earthwork survey has again demonstrated the castle mound to overlie, and thus post-date, the southern parts of at least three rectangular embanked closes and the east side of a fourth, larger, feature (Brown and Taylor 1977: 97–9). Two similar enclosures lie to the west, forming a linear arrangement of croft enclosures clearly disrupted by the insertion of the castle. The similarity in the topographical settings as well as the physical forms of these two castles underlines that they were elements within a coordinated royal strategy of castle-building aimed at containing the raiding activities of Geoffrey de Mandeville, and built with apparently little concern for the disruption they would cause to nearby settlements. In neither case, however, is it absolutely clear that the earlier settlement was occupied immediately before the construction of the castle.

Another excellent example of rural castle imposition is Alstoe Mount, near Burley (Rutland) (Fig. 8.12). A complex of multi-phase earthworks centred on a small medieval motte and bailey includes at two roughly parallel rows of toft and croft earthworks aligned either side of a hollow-way that formerly continued further to the south, where it has been ploughed out (Brown 1975: 5). The comparative profile of the motte and bailey relative to the settlement earthworks is again suggestive of secondary imposition within an extant medieval community, almost certainly part of the lost medieval hamlet of *Alsthorpe* (Creighton 1999a: 27). This hypothesis is supported further by the fact that part of the castle was also raised over an area of former open field agriculture, as indicated by the block of cultivation ridges and furrows to the south of the motte, which were clearly truncated by its construction. Despite limited excavation on the site, the erection of the motte cannot be dated more closely than some time prior to the mid-twelfth century, although the site is not incompatible with an Anarchy-period foundation (Dunning 1936: 402). Comparable evidence comes from Braybrooke (Northamptonshire), where earthwork remains of the settlement of West Hall, including hollow-ways, crofts and associated ridge and furrow, partially underlie another undocumented castle (RCHME Northants. 1975–84: vol. 2, 11–13).

More dramatic still is the evidence of a settlement displaced by castle-building at Eaton Socon (Cambridgeshire), where the castle's imposition over a church with associated cemetery and the private buildings of a late Saxon settlement has been identified through excavation. The north ward was constructed over at least 40 Saxon burials belonging to a cemetery, itself partially covered by a rubble layer indicating a levelled church (Lethbridge and Tebbutt 1952). In addition, the castle rampart stratigraphically sealed a timber building destroyed by fire, representing part of an extensive Saxon village lying under the castle; another excavated Saxon house lay just outside the defences (Addyman 1965). The destruction of the houses cannot, however, be dated any more closely than *c.* 1050–1150, and it remains hazardous and difficult to relate the sequence to a documented context, such as, for instance, William I's

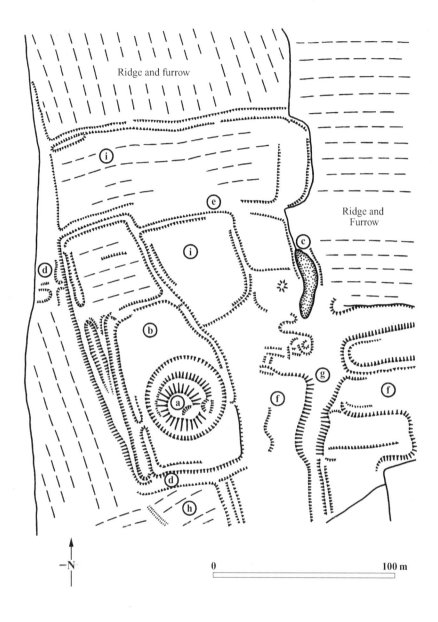

Ridge and furrow

Ridge and
Furrow

Figure 8.12 Plan of motte and bailey and associated earthworks at Burley (Rutland), showing the insertion of a Norman castle into a medieval community. Key to lettering: a, motte; b, bailey; c, spring-fed pond; d, bailey ditch; e, (later?) manorial enclosure; f, house platforms of the medieval village; g, hollow-way; h, ridge and furrow ante-dating the castle earthworks; i, enclosures built over ridge and furrow (based on Hartley 1983, with additions and amendments).

fenland campaign, or the Anarchy. The obvious explanation for the sequence at Eaton Socon would seem to be that the necessity of controlling a strategic crossing of the Ouse during a military campaign or a time of crisis resulted in the sweeping away of the village. It is equally possible, however, that the settlement's removal (and re-foundation on a fresh site) was a deliberate scheme of seigneurial aggrandisement involving the enlargement of the castle and re-planning of the village as an assertion of lordly status (Bigmore 1979: 99). Yet castle-building was not the only activity which resulted in the removal and re-siting of entire medieval communities. In particular, the requirement to build the religious houses of the more austere monastic orders in secluded settings could result in the wholesale displacement of a village, as at Pipewell (Northamptonshire) or, perhaps more commonly, the forced abandonment of farmsteads and hamlets, as at Witham (Somerset) (Taylor 1983b: 169; Aston 2000: 81). But the construction of non-defended secular buildings could also have a similar impact. For instance, excavations beneath Northolt Manor (Middlesex) revealed the late-thirteenth-century manor house to have been raised over a village, and subsequently re-located to a fresh site (Hurst 1961: 214), while Henry VIII's palace of Nonsuch (Surrey) was built over Cuddington church and village (Keevill 2000: 162).

These examples probably represent a tiny fraction of the total number of instances where castle-building caused disruption to existing villages. Nonetheless, with the limited amount of evidence available, Anarchy-period castles seem to have caused particular disruption to villages. Elsewhere we may suspect that similar sequences are repeated. For instance, the enclosure of a Saxon church within the bailey of a Norman castle may suggest disruption of adjacent settlement, as may castle-building on the site of an earlier manorial seat (see Chapter 6). Finally, castle-building in areas ravaged by warfare or subject to scorched earth policies, may have resulted in the displacement of settlement (see Chapter 3), although in all these cases physical evidence remains elusive.

Village planning

The characteristic hallmarks of medieval village planning include the regular disposition of equally sized peasant tenements at right angles to a street network that also shows evidence of regularity, particularly through the provision of equally sized pockets of tofts and crofts delimited by back lanes. Village plans which exhibit such physical characteristics must have resulted from one or more episodes of deliberate and conscious planning. What is important is that such settlements demonstrate a rigorous structuring and definition of social space, and that the regularity of a planned nucleated village associated with a castle or other high-status site could be a physical manifestation of the power of medieval lordship (Saunders 1990: 18–94). This is not to say, however, that all planned settlements contain lordship sites. Commonly, the castle forms a 'plan dominant' (Roberts 1987: 151), with the village taking an axial form in relation to the site of lordship. The format of an outer bailey or ward was another feature that often structured village plans, in the same way that a monastic precinct or manorial enclosure might condition growth.

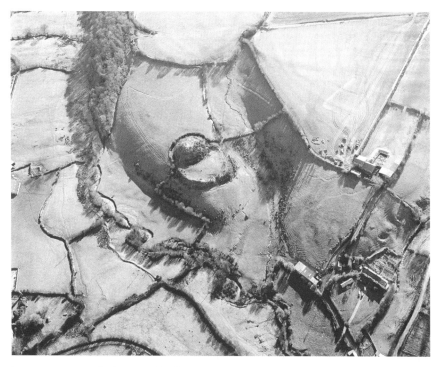

Figure 8.13 Aerial photograph of Parracombe (Devon), showing the isolated position of the motte and bailey (Photograph by F.M. Griffith, Devon County Council: copyright reserved).

Occasionally, entire settlements are embraced within castle-baileys, although most are planned immediately beyond, but relative to, the enclosure.

This importance of the castle as a nucleation point is particularly clear at Pulverbatch (Shropshire), where the existence of two nucleated settlements within a kilometre of one another within the same parish seems to have been a direct result of castle building. The builder of this motte and bailey castle avoided the existing village, choosing instead a site that commanded routes of communication between the hill country and the Severn Valley. Here a regular settlement with back lanes (although the plan is now decayed) grew up adjacent to the new seigneurial centre, being recorded as *Castell* Pulverbatch from the late thirteenth century in order to differentiate it from the earlier nucleus thereafter known as *Chyrche* Pulverbatch (VCH Salop. 1968: 131; Gelling and Foxall 1990: 246). A possible comparable case can be found on the north-west fringes of Exmoor, where a substantial and impeccably preserved motte and bailey known as Holwell Castle (Fig. 8.13) is one of several settlement foci in the parish, including a green-based nucleation that contained the parish church of St Petrocks's (Churchtown), and a large nucleation (Parracombe) on lower ground beneath the Norman castle. Sited at the tip of an interfluvial ridge near the terminus of the narrow Heddon Valley that winds its way up to the North Devon coast, the castle appears to have little strategic or tactical military value, and a manorial explanation may be entirely appropriate. An intriguing possibility is that the present village of Parracombe, nestled under the castle at a river crossing, was a latecomer to this settlement landscape, drawn towards the new seigneurial focus some time after the Norman Conquest, either through piecemeal settlement shift or deliberate planning (Higham 2000: 445). The lack of clearly planned elements suggests that it was not envisaged as a small borough, despite the large size of the nucleation for the region.

The impact of castles on village nucleation must, however, be related to the wider debate within medieval settlement studies concerning the rôle of seigneurial authority in settlement change (see Aberg 1988). Scholars have differed in their judgement of whether landlords were the agents of village planning. On the one hand, Dyer (1985) has emphasized that mechanisms of local custom and the social remoteness of medieval landlords will have been key factors limiting their ability to plan settlements, implying perhaps that communities themselves may have been the agents of change. In contrast, Harvey (1989) has suggested that, while manorial custom may be important in negotiation between lords and individual tenants, that at the level of an entire community, the vill was powerless in the face of lordly interest. One of the key reasons for these differences of opinion is clearly epistemological. On the one hand, archaeologists, examining medium- and long-term processes of change through physical evidence, have interpreted the regularity of field systems and villages as manifestations of lordship in the landscape. On the other hand, historians, examining temporally cross-sectional documentary sources, have emphasized the complexity of everyday social relations between lord and community. The debate has more recently been refined by the increasing realization that lordship will operate differently nucleated, mixed and non-nucleated landscapes (Lewis *et al.* 1997: 204–10).

Although many castles form broadly datable features within village plans, it is extremely hazardous to use the presence of a castle as a means of dating the settlement itself. Nonetheless, in some cases the presence a castle within a settlement can provide an additional key to unravelling village origins, if studied in conjunction with other topographical and historical data. A major shortcoming in any model seeing castle lords as the key agents of village planning is the fact that many early castles were sited in the vicinity of established estate centres. Where Norman castles overlay Saxon manorial sites, it is difficult to choose between an Anglo-Saxon and post-Conquest context for the planning. It is only where castles occupied fresh sites, or were sited within settlements of little prior significance, that we can draw a firmer link between castle lords and settlement change.

In England only quite rarely do nucleated villages on fresh sites appear to have come into being as the foundations of castle lords, in contrast to boroughs (see Chapter 7). One clear case is the village of Bowes (North Yorkshire). The absence of a related entry in Domesday suggests that the linear street-village post-dates, or was planned out in conjunction with, the Norman castle, which is itself inserted into the Roman fort of *Lavatrae*. The castle and adjacent church occupy the southern part of the plan, immediately adjacent to a marked broadening of the village street representing a market place; on the opposite side of the street can be identified a single regular row of long tofts of likely planned origin. Far more commonly we may suspect that castle lords will have re-planned extant settlements or else have been responsible for planned additions to earlier villages. At Barwick-in-Elmet (West Yorkshire), for instance, the de Lacy castle is closely associated with a village comprising an irregular core centred on the parish church and a regular extension to the south planned over open fields, as indicated by the curvilinear profiles of the toft plots (Fig. 8.14). The likely sequence is that this addition was created shortly after the castle was built in the twelfth century, when Barwick became the hub of a large demesne estate and the administrative centre for the eastern part of the Honour of Pontefract (Faull and Moorhouse 1981: 257). Kirkby Malzeard (North Yorkshire) (Fig. 8. 14) was similarly a place of little administrative significance prior to the erection of the Mowbray castle, which followed the family's receipt of local estates from the Crown. Here, castle-building was commensurate with the manor's elevation to an important honorial centre at the heart of a territory stretching from Great Whernside in the west to the fringes of Ripon in the east, and incorporating the great chase of Nidderdale (Gowland 1936–8: 351–2). Roberts (1987: 40) has suggested that the regular double-row settlement expanded from an initial church core, in a manner analogous to Barwick-in-Elmet. Charter evidence makes it clear that the castle lord Nigel d'Aubigny was actively engaged in the economic development of Mowbray estates around Thirsk in the period *c.* 1107–18, (Greenway 1972: xxiii–iv), and there is no reason why his other rural estates in the region should not have received the same attention.

Aston has raised the intriguing possibility of a correlation between the distribution of villages in Somerset showing evidence of *solkifte* ('sun division') – a system by which medieval open field systems and settlements could be planned in regular form – and castles known or suspected to have seen action during the Anarchy (1985: 93–5). Quite possibly, the devastation resulting from war and sieges provided the opportunity for landlords to subsequently reorganize settlements, as was certainly the case in late-eleventh-century Yorkshire, where many planned villages lay in close association with the castles of new Norman tenants. Nonetheless, such hypotheses remain to be tested more widely.

In areas of the countryside characterized by villages with less regular plans, a castle could form a manorial focus in a plan comprising several formerly discrete units that have coalesced to form what is now a single settlement. These composite settlements, often termed 'polyfocal villages' (Taylor 1977), could form through the natural expansion of population; however, there is also evidence that deliberate planning could sometimes play a rôle. At Culworth (Northamptonshire)(Fig. 8.15), the present village appears to have formed from two originally discrete settlements – Culworth and Brime – that were linked together by the creation of a marketplace immediately adjacent to a small ringwork castle (Taylor 1982: 26). More complex sequences are apparent at Cawood (North Yorkshire) and Ashby-de-la-Zouch (Leicestershire), where the planning of fortified sites resulted in the coalescence of two earlier settlement foci to form composite plans. At Ashby the large precinct around the fortified Hastings manor linked two previously discrete villages as an act of seigneurial promotion (Hillier 1984: 13–14), while a scheme of twelfth-century archiepiscopal planning at Cawood resulted in a similar arrangement (Blood and Taylor 1992: 98–102).

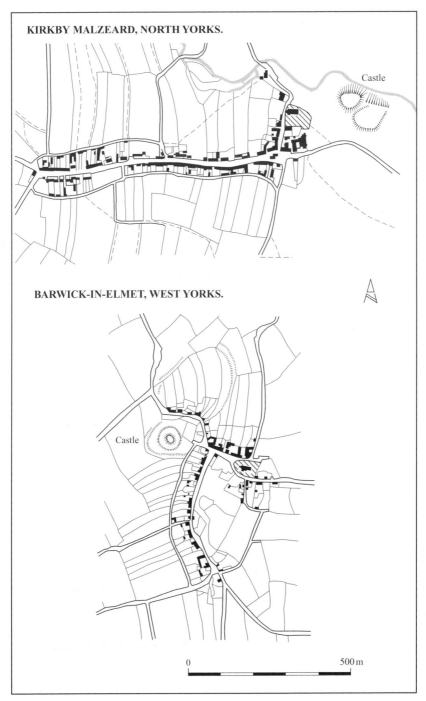

Figure 8.14 Examples of castles and planned villages in Yorkshire. Both settlements show evidence of regularity and may have been planned or re-planned in conjunction with the castles.

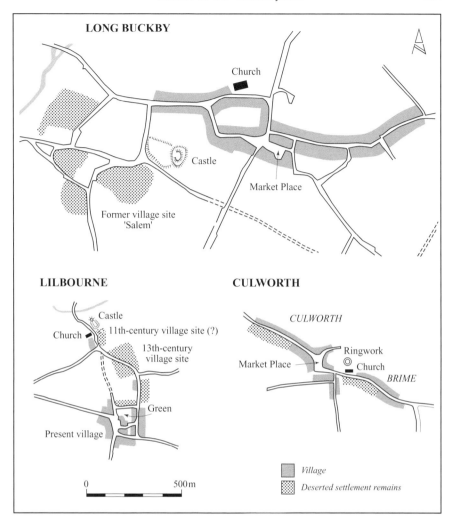

Figure 8.15 Castles and changes in village topography in Northamptonshire. Topographical study of these three villages suggest that Culworth was formed by the coalescence of two foci bought about by the construction of a marketplace adjacent to the castle, while the plans of both Long Buckby and Lilbourne appear to have shifted and migrated away from the seigneurial focus (based on Taylor 1979; 1983b, with additions).

Lordship and the rural landscape: case study of Laxton, Nottinghamshire

One of the clearest examples of the influence of castle lords on rural settlement planning is Laxton (Nottinghamshire), a village famous for its still substantially non-enclosed field system and remarkable seventeenth-century estate plan by Mark Pierce. To the north of the village lie the earthworks of a large motte and bailey castle (Fig. 4.12), later remodelled as a non-defended manorial residence, which functioned for much of its life as the centre of a local barony and the administrative centre of Sherwood Forest. While the peculiar survival of Laxton's open fields has meant that the place has frequently been portrayed as the quintessential English medieval village, the specific character of Laxton's lordship, as manifested in the development of the castle, meant that the village was, paradoxically, atypical (Rowley 1978: 110–11).

The estate plan of 1635 depicts the village as somewhat contracted from its original form, showing shrinkage from its medieval heyday. The powerful motte and bailey lay on the northern fringe of the settlement, embraced on the remaining three sides by the demesne. Estimated at 650 acres in 1635 and running along the entire northern edge of the settlement, this zone formed a buffer that limited any expansion of the village to the north (Chambers 1964: 12). As well as the seigneurial pleasure park recorded from the thirteenth century, the demesne also contained a suite of fishponds, first mentioned in a charter of 1232, in addition to rabbit warrens, enclosures for horses and a jousting paddock, as suggested by field names (Cameron 1980: 224). This zone thus appears to have been dedicated to the support and amusement of the castle seigneury and visiting dignitaries, as opposed to agricultural usage; additional demesne resources for this purpose were, certainly by the thirteenth century, scattered within the open fields (Orwin and Orwin 1967: 76–80).

The line of a back lane (Hall Lane), backed by a substantial embankment, forms a seam between this zone of lordship and the rest of the village plan, creating part of a morphological frame that conditioned its development (Fig. 8.16: top). The regularity of the northern (east-west) row of the village is striking. Here, long tofts of remarkably similar width reach back to the back lane, while excavation on an open site near the Vicarage, south of the main east-west row has recovered evidence of medieval boundary features, perhaps echoing the formalized arrangement of the north side (Challis 1995: 21–2). The southern (north-south) block of settlement appears distinct, characterized by plots set back from the street. A tentative suggestion has been made by Cameron (1980: 222), that a sinuous route running parallel to this street formed the axis of the original settlement. Careful analysis of the Pierce map suggests, however, that this route cut through existing property boundaries, while excavations of two abandoned plots within the north row which recovered a volume of residual middle to late Saxon wares provide limited evidence of antecedent occupation predating the planned village (Challis 1994: 30). The likely scenario thus appears to be a core settlement unit, planned on an east–west alignment immediately south of the castle, which later expanded to the south. Certainly, natural topography ensured that the more usual plan of a castle-village, that of the castle at the head of a linear settlement, was not an option here, due to the marshy low-lying area of ground to the south of the east–west row.

Furthermore, the documentary record of Laxton's changing status as a settlement means that it is possible to draw a correlation between the *process* of planning a regulated settlement and the *mechanism* of lordship. Vitally, the documentary record shows that Laxton only gained status as a key estate centre from the period around the foundation of the castle, when it became *catput* of the de Caux family, hereditary foresters of Sherwood. With the coming of the de Caux family, Laxton emerged not only as a fortified centre but a venue for forest courts and other status activities. Documentary sources

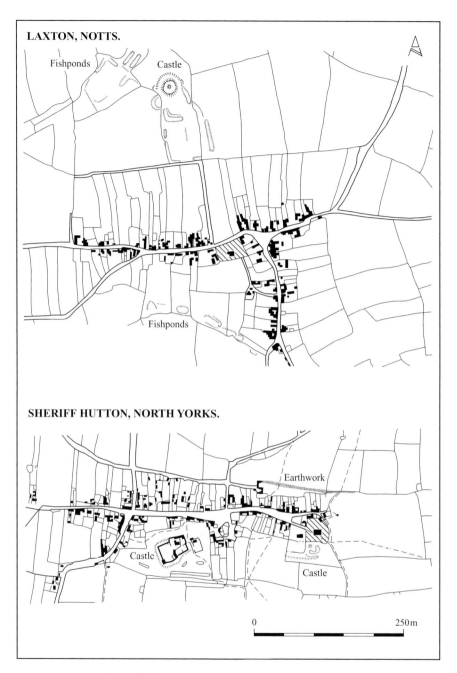

LAXTON, NOTTS.

Fishponds

Castle

Fishponds

SHERIFF HUTTON, NORTH YORKS.

Earthwork

Castle

Castle

0   250m

Figure 8.16 Castles and planned villages. Laxton seems to have been planned or re-planned as a market village associated with a substantial motte and bailey. The village plan of Sheriff Hutton is closely related to two successive castle sites.

suggest that Laxton became a favoured stopping point on royal itineraries from Henry II to Edward I (Beckett 1989: 11), and must have served and accommodated huge retinues and hunting parties requiring accommodation, sustenance and generating revenue. This would certainly have meant the presence of salaried officials operating outside the agricultural workings of the village, and the presence of individuals of such status within the settlement is reflected in tax returns (Cameron 1980: 223–5). Laxton was thus clearly a settlement with social and economic functions that distinguished it from other villages in the region. In this sense, a triangular widening of the street at the hub of the village plan adjacent to the parish church of St Michael may indicate the presence of a small rural market.

Laxton's decline, as indicated by the abandoned plots on Pierce's map, may be partially a product of the declining influence of lordship. The castle was downgraded significantly to a site of manorial status only by the late thirteenth century, in line with a reduction of the area under Forest Law in 1227 to exclude Laxton (Beckett 1989: 11). We may also note Robert de Everingham's ultimate loss of the keepership of Sherwood Forest in 1286 and relocation of the family seat to an undefended site at Everingham which put an end to the castle as a focus of economic activity (Speight 1994: 59). Limited excavation within Laxton demonstrates vacant plots within the present village to be deserted well before the fifteenth century (Challis 1994: 31).

Castles and village planning: case study of Sheriff Hutton, North Yorkshire

The village plan of Sheriff Hutton (North Yorkshire) (Fig. 8.16: bottom) contains not one but two castle sites: a denuded motte and bailey at the eastern extremity of the settlement, and, in the centre of the village, an impressive late-fourteenth-century quadrangular castle. The dating of the first castle site is, however, uncertain. Although it is commonly held to be a foundation of the Anarchy, being first documented when besieged c. 1140 (King 1983: 525, 528), the site may equally have origins as the estate centre of Aschetil de Bulmer, who received the manor before c. 1100 from the Domesday sub-tenant (L'Anson 1913: 378). Aschetil was Sheriff of Yorkshire from c. 1115, and as such, Sheriff Hutton may have emerged as an administrative centre within a small yet relatively compact, Yorkshire-based lordship with satellites in Durham. The manor passed to the Neville family through marriage before 1194, and it was under their lordship that the second castle was built. Here, the duplication of castles thus reflects the transferral of lordship from one site to another, although it is unclear whether they were occupied successively or there was a break in occupation. What is important, however, is that each site is related to different episodes of village growth.

The motte, raised at the eastern extremity of a low natural spur, lies adjacent to the parish church of St Helen and the Holy Cross, and is closely associated with a compact focus of settlement characterized by short toft plots and centred on a small triangular green. The alignment of outworks associated with the castle, property boundaries and substantial boundary earthworks recognized as cropmarks in aerial photographs, all suggest that this unit of the village was formerly enclosed and linked to the castle (Winton 1993).

Figure 8.17   Aerial view of Sheriff Hutton (North Yorkshire), showing the two castle sites within the village. The earthworks of an early castle lie near the top of the photograph, surrounded by ridge and furrow; the later quadrangular castle of the Neville family lies in the foreground and stood within a large moated enclosure (Cambridge University Collection of Air Photographs: copyright reserved).

Furthermore, the castle clearly post-dates the zone of ridge and furrow in the fields immediately to the south and east, into which it evidently intrudes. This ridge and furrow is oriented east–west, unlike that backing on to the village tofts, which is aligned exclusively north–south (Fig. 8.17). The likely implication is thus that the present arrangement of castle and settlement represents the re-orientation of an earlier plan.

   In the fourteenth century, the upward mobility of the lords of Sheriff Hutton ensured a policy of residential aggrandisement, as manifested in the great palatial castle licensed to Sir John de Neville of Raby in 1382. The new castle was built on a less restricted site within a large moated precinct, which is itself probably an ornamental feature, and incorporates walkways and terraces (Dennison 1997: 296). Within the space of four years of the licence being granted, Lord Neville received a market charter (VCH NR Yorks. 1923:

172–97). This event seems to have resulted in the addition to the village plan of a square market green immediately north-east of the Neville castle, although the space is now substantially in-filled by later settlement. At around this time a second major plan unit, characterized by longer, more regular plots than the primary nucleus, and framed to the north by a back lane, was added to the village plan.

A further factor in the evolution of Sheriff Hutton was the castle park (Fig. 8.6). This feature was in existence by 1282/3, when it may have been associated with the first castle site, and extended in 1334/5 when Ralph de Neville obtained licence for free warren (Beresford 1957: 221–2). In the following decades Sheriff Hutton is noted as a hunting seat as well as regional administrative centre, especially following its acquisition by the Crown from the Nevilles in 1471 (Beresford and St Joseph 1979: 155). The foundation of the new castle was associated closely with the enlargement of the park, which enclosed a significant proportion of the open fields of the deserted village of East Lilling, and, between 1471 and 1485, expanded over the remainder of the weakened settlement (Swan *et al.* 1990: 108). At its greatest extent, the park embraced more than half of the total perimeter of Sheriff Hutton village, forming something of a seigneurial green belt that greatly influenced its form and growth.

Defended villages

Very few rural castles were built explicitly as a means of property protection, although the tiny motte at Knapwell (Cambridgeshire) is a rare example. Standing at the eastern end of a deserted village overlooking the point where the road between Alsworth and Boxworth crosses a ford, the motte may well have been built by the abbot of Ramsey, who owned Knapwell, as a means of protecting their property during the turbulent years of 1143–44 (RCHME Cambs. I 1968–72: vol. 2, 160–3; Taylor 1979: 127–8). While medieval towns without castles could sometimes be enclosed or walled (e.g. Bath, Coventry and Kingston upon Hull), the same was not true of villages – a very rare exception of an embanked medieval village being Wellow (Nottinghamshire) (Barley 1957). Other examples of enclosed rural settlements are associated with castles. The clear implication is of seigneurial authority being the driving force behind the decision to enclose a settlement, reflecting a desire for increased local control and even an element of ostentation and display. The perimeters of deserted medieval villages, particularly in Midland England are commonly delimited by pronounced ditches and banks topped with hedges (Chapelot and Fossier 1985: 133), both as a symbolic and quasi-legal means of demarcation, and as a practical means of separating open field agriculture and stock from the community. Nonetheless, the strength and predominantly regular plans of settlement enclosures appended to castles, combined, vitally, with seigneurial influence, mark these sites out as different entities.

The clearest evidence for a rural castle being built for the defence of a community relates to the small and unfinished Anarchy-period motte and bailey at Therfield (Hertfordshire). Here, a bank and ditch system appended to the earthwork castle forms a rectangle around the western part of the village

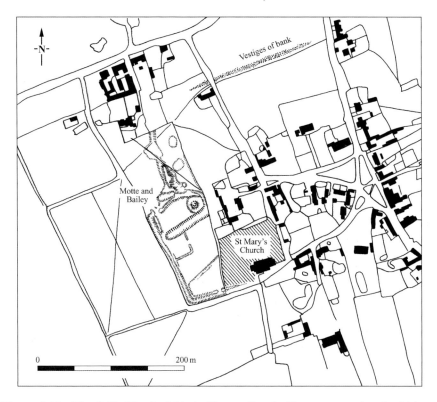

Figure 8.18 Therfield (Hertfordshire). The medieval village was enclosed within a large rectangular earthwork enclosure attached to a small motte and bailey (based on Biddle 1964, with additions).

(Fig. 8.18). Excavations across these defences revealed the profile of the rampart and ditch to match the bailey defences, although both were left partially completed, the motte being a mere 6 ft (*c.* 1.8 m) tall (Biddle 1964: 65). Therfield was part of the lands of Ramsey Abbey, and a likely historical context for the castle's construction was Geoffrey de Mandeville's plundering of the locality in 1143–4, when it was perhaps hurriedly built by Abbot Walter, or conceivably by a sub-tenant, as a means of protecting his assets. The topographical setting of the castle supports this contention, as it occupies a 'reverse slope' position, protecting the village, but with a view towards the important Icknield Way blocked. Hertfordshire has something of a concentration of castles with attached village enclosures; other good examples can be identified at Anstey, Pirton and possibly Great Wymondley (Renn 1971). An embanked village seems also to have been attached to the impressive motte and bailey at Bytham (Lincolnshire) (Fig. 5.6). We may also wonder how many outer enclosures appended to castles could have served at some stage as temporary refuges for tenants and portable wealth in the form of stock. Such a function is well documented for the great border fortresses of Northumbria and a use to which the large *base-courts* of Channel Island castles such as Mont Orgueil (Jersey) were frequently put.

A programme of rescue excavation at the site of Boteler's (or Oversley)

Castle, a large motte and bailey surviving largely as a cropmark site south of Alcester, Warwickshire, has offered further evidence for the layout of a small enclosed castle village (Jones *et al.* 1997). Between 1992 and 1993, an archaeological evaluation in advance of the construction of a bypass included the excavation of eight open areas along a north–south corridor through a large sub-rectangular outer enclosure of five hectares appended to the east of the motte and bailey (Fig. 8.19). The settlement formed a planned ladder-type arrangement based around two parallel east–west tracks running between the main castle complex and the Roman road of Ryknild Street, which the outer enclosure embraced, along with the site of a church and small cemetery. The excavated pattern of boundary gullies suggested the orientation of a series of long, thin plots at right angles to the tracks, although less than half the sampled plots showed evidence of habitation, suggesting, perhaps, that the village was not settled to its intended capacity. It is far from clear, however, whether this was a genuinely rural community as opposed to a failed market settlement promoted by the Boteler family. While no documentary evidence exists for a medieval market at Oversley, the settlement may well have been deserted before such arrangements were formalized, and the excavations have produced evidence of material culture that, while a limited sample, provides evidence of an economic base that was not wholly agricultural. In particular, age profiles derived from the assemblage of animal bones indicate a 'consumer' as opposed to 'producer' economy, while craftworking activities represented include textile finishing, horn working, and, possibly, steel manufacture. In addition, the settlement's desertion in the early thirteenth century, at a time of rural settlement expansion elsewhere in the region, points towards a settlement serving a niche economy dependent upon the castle, which was downgraded to a manorial complex, and perhaps slighted, at around this time (Jones *et al.* 1997: 94).

Settlement change

Much of the foregoing discussion has examined the influence of castle lords on the nucleation of villages. But modern archaeological studies of English medieval rural settlement have shown how fluid the form of a village could be. Far from being stable features of the landscape, as once thought, it is now widely recognized that the location and morphology of villages could change radically throughout the medieval period and beyond (Taylor 1978: 1983b). Medieval villages could metamorphose in any one of a number of complex ways, such as through phases of planned or unplanned growth, contraction, or even gradual migration or 'shift' to another site. Naturally, many castles lay in villages subject to changes such as these.

Nowhere in England is the process of settlement migration better represented than in East Anglia and, in particular Norfolk. In this county many castle sites, including Horsford, Hunworth and Weeting lay on common edges, and were part and parcel of a highly fluid pattern including the drift of settlement that often left parish churches as isolated features within the landscape (Liddiard 2000a: 105, 123). The contraction or movement of a village could, on occasion, also leave a castle physically isolated in the present

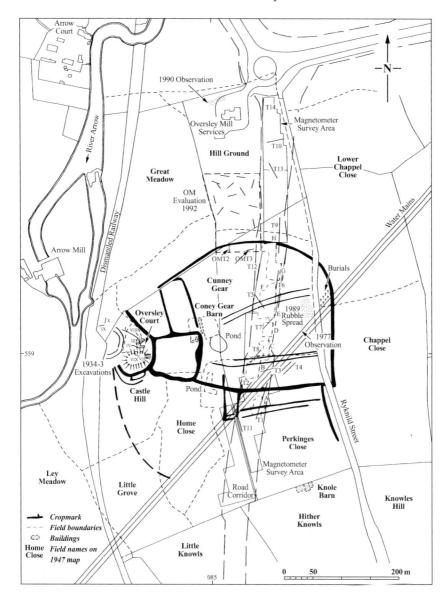

Figure 8.19 General site plan of Boteler's Castle (Warwickshire), showing location of excavations and the plan of earthworks and cropmarks associated with the motte and bailey (Jones *et al.* 1997).

landscape, where it was once part of village topography, as at Lilbourne (Northamptonshire) (Fig. 8.15). Settlement earthworks adjacent to this substantial motte and bailey suggest that the village has migrated away from the focus of lordship, leaving the castle and church as isolated features. Although the present village, clustered around a rectangular green, lies 400 m south of the castle, a complex of settlement earthworks laid out over ridge and furrow between the two features suggests at least two distinct phases of settlement shift (RCHME Northants. 1975–84: vol. 2, 125–8; Taylor 1983b: 160). Another clear example of a village migrating away from an earlier focus closely associated with an early castle is Lingen (Herefordshire) (Higham and Barker 1992: 230).

The village plan of Bolingbroke (Lincolnshire) preserves not only multiple settlement foci, but also multiple castles that together constitute a complex and fascinating settlement landscape (Fig. 4.8). The original settlement core seems to have been located in the vicinity of the parish church, which is overlooked by Dewy Hill, the site of an eleventh- and twelfth-century for-tification that pre-dated the hexagonal castle built *c*. 1220–30 on a low-lying site immediately to the south. The large wedge-shaped marketplace to the east marked an addition to the earlier manorial centre, and was apparently in existence in 1086, when the 'new market' was recorded in Domesday Book (Thompson 1966; Beresford and St Joseph 1979: 150–2).

Conversely, settlement could expand or even migrate from an earlier focus to become closely associated with a castle. At Segenhoe (Bedfordshire), earthwork evidence suggests that the village migrated uphill to a new position adjacent to the castle (Taylor 1983b: 162–5). Mileham (Norfolk) is another village that seems to have evolved through a series of shifts to become closely associated with a seigneurial site. The settlement moved from an initial Saxon focus near the parish church to adopt a regular east–west plan stretching away from the castle by the eleventh century, as suggested by field walking (Wade Martins 1975: 147–9). It is extremely difficult to prove, however, that the existence of the castle was a contributory factor to such changes, which may occur for a variety of other social, economic or environmental reasons. Indeed it is often uncertain whether episodes of settlement expansion or contraction were contemporaneous with the functional lifetime of the castle.

A more complex sequence of development is evident at Long Buckby (Northamptonshire) (Fig. 8.15), where the establishment of a market by the castle lord conditioned a major re-planning of settlement topography. The castle was originally built immediately east of, and overlooking, a late Saxon focus of settlement in the area of the village now known as Salem. This settlement was superseded and deserted when the present village was planned around a regular marketplace to the east of the castle when Henry de Lacy obtained the grant of a weekly market and two annual fairs in his manor of Buckby in 1280 (Taylor 1979: 137–9; RCHME Northants. 1975–84: vol. 2, 131–5). The addition of the 'Long' element to the place-name reflects the expansion of the settlement, in linear fashion, away from the area of the castle and original Saxon village. Other examples of composite village plans con-taining possible evidence of village shift or re-planning can be found in Lei-cestershire. At Gilmorton and Shawell in the south of the county, motte and bailey castles are once again closely associated with small areas of deserted settlement earthworks and parish churches. In both cases these units of medieval settlement are curiously dislocated from the main village plan, sug-gesting either that a once larger village has been partially deserted or, more likely, that a process of shift has taken place away from an initial magnate core settlement (Winter 1978; Creighton 1997). Other village plans in the East Midlands that might indicate similar sequences include Lockington (East Yorkshire) and Lowdham (Nottinghamshire).

Deserted medieval villages

A surprising number of castles lay within or adjacent to medieval villages that were completely abandoned. Where conditions of preservation are favourable, a castle might form one part of an extensive earthwork site including the winding hollow-ways of former village streets and the sites of deserted peasant tofts and crofts, as at More, Lydham (Shropshire). Elsewhere, only vestiges of such earthworks might survive, as at Tothill (Lincolnshire) and Givendale (North Yorkshire), while occasionally physical traces of a village have been totally obliterated by agriculture but its presence known from documentary or place-name evidence, as at Langthwaite (South Yorkshire). Castles can also lie in or near shrunken settlements, such as Pilsbury (Derbyshire), where the present cluster of three farmsteads marks the vestiges of a more extensive hamlet that previously extended along the hollow-way running along the valley floor and up to the bailey ramparts (Fig. 3.10) (Barnatt 1991). In all these examples, the castle formed a clear seigneurial focus within the village plan; an exception is found at Ingarsby (Leicestershire), where a motte ('Monk's Grave') directly overlooked the village (which contained another lordship site in the form of a substantial manorial enclosure) from the slopes on the opposite side of Ingarsby Hollow, some 250m distant (Hoskins 1956: 46–7).

Where castle and appended deserted village are juxtaposed in the present landscape, a likely explanation is that the village had initially been drawn to the castle by economic and protective advantages, and that when the castle was disused such advantages no longer existed, prompting desertion or re-siting. Yet such a deduction may be premature, it is extremely hazardous to causally link castle and settlement desertion in the absence of sufficiently detailed archaeological or historical data. A medieval village could be deserted due a myriad of socio-economic circumstances, and the desertion of the seigneurial focus might be only a single factor (Beresford 1954; Beresford and Hurst 1971). Once established, a castle-village could expand and develop along an economic trajectory that made it increasingly less dependent on the castle. Nonetheless, where village desertion has occurred, we may often suppose that it took place subsequent to the disuse of the castle. We may also indicate a number of sites where desertion was an entirely post-medieval process attributable to the remodelling of estates into formal gardens or landscape parks. Castle Howard (North Yorkshire) is a clear example where the castle retained its position as a focus of high status residence. Here, the castle and church formerly occupied a central position within the medieval village of *Hinderskelfe*, which was swept away wholesale in a radical programme of estate transformation when the castle was superseded by a mansion in the late seventeenth century (Beresford 1951–5: 300; Barley 1978). Hornby (North Yorkshire) shows a parallel process yet on a smaller scale; in 1517 William, Lord Conyers 'caste down forty husbandries' in order to remodel the environs of Hornby Castle as a formal garden (VCH NR Yorks. 1914: 313); the core of the displaced settlement lay *c.* 300 m east of the castle in the vicinity of the eleventh-century parish church of St Mary's (Beresford 1948–51: 352).

The earthworks east of Whorlton Castle (North Yorkshire) (Fig. 8.20)

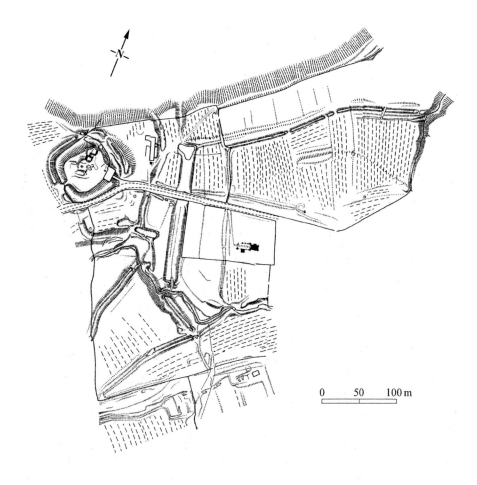

Figure 8.20　An earthwork survey of Whorlton Castle (North Yorkshire). East of the castle lie the earthworks of a former medieval village and those of a later ornamental landscape (© Crown copyright NMR).

represent a multi-phase amalgamation of military, ornamental and settlement earthworks demonstrating the conversion of a former village into a designed landscape by the castle lords, the Meynell family (RCHME 1990; Everson 1998). In all probability these developments took place when the castle was radically remodelled in the late fourteenth century and a magnificent new gatehouse constructed (Corbett 1994). Facing the castle from a low natural knoll to the east of the bailey defences, the parish church of the Holy Cross represents the core of the deserted village of Whorlton. A settlement was recorded from Domesday but in decline by 1301 when 17 households were re-taxed, whilst fewer than 10 were documented in the last known listing of Whorlton in 1428. The vestiges of this weakened settlement may well have been transplanted to the village's present site when the landscape around the castle was remodelled. While the vestiges of hollow-ways and house platforms remain, in addition to boundary earthwork that divided it from the seigneurial deer park, other physical traces of the village are confused by the area's conversion into a large formal garden incorporating terraces and water features, with the church as their focus. Features from this phase of development include the large flat-bottomed linear ditch in front of the castle (Fig. 4.7). Cutting across earlier banks that were evidently part of the hollow-way formerly linking castle and settlement, and supplied with water from a nearby stream via an elaborate sluice and dam system, this feature appears to have been an integral part of the formal garden and not a defensive feature.

But often physical traces of former villages known to have been associated with castles can be more elusive. At Castle Camps (Cambridgeshire), for instance, the remains of a small dependent settlement remained unrecognized prior to a detailed earthwork survey (Taylor 1973: 41–2; 1983b: 146). Only a small pocket of damaged settlement earthworks survived, although these, in association with a spread of medieval pottery in the plough soil, were sufficient to indicate an approximately horseshoe-shaped settlement lying entirely beyond the site's defences (Fig. 6.5).

A striking example of a deserted medieval village with a highly regular plan that incorporates an early castle is Kingerby, Osgodby (Lincolnshire). The settlement earthworks have been planned in detail by the RCHME (Fig. 8.21), and provide excellent evidence for the intervention of castle lords in village planning (Everson *et al.* 1991: 146–9). A twelfth-century castle of the Amunderville family, comprising a large and partially levelled ringwork between two baileys, appears to have been inserted within an extant settlement, resulting in the diversion of the major east–west thoroughfare to skirt the north edge of the castle defences. At a subsequent stage of the settlement's development, two extremely regular blocks of peasant tenements, each appearing to originally consist of ten toft and croft units of equal frontage, have been added on the north and west sides of the original village. The net result is a regulated and closed plan form that is clearly related to the seigneurial focus. While the Royal Commission's survey of West Lindsey has shown that village planning by secular and ecclesiastical lords was not an uncommon feature of the high medieval landscape (Everson *et al.* 1991: 14–16), at Kingerby the link between the process of planning and agent of change is particularly apparent.

How can we judge whether a castle site constituting an isolated element in the present landscape was similarly isolated from settlement during its functional lifetime? An important case study of early Devonshire castles has not located deserted settlements in conjunction with apparently isolated castle sites (Higham 1982b: 106). It may be significant that many Devon castles were, however, integrated components within a wider regional settlement pattern dominated by non-nucleated forms. In regions of Britain where the nucleated village was the characteristic form of medieval rural settlement, however, some apparently isolated castles were once associated with deserted villages for which little or no physical evidence survives. A good example of this is Woodhead Castle, in Great Casterton parish (Rutland). Although the present field monument, comprising a sub-rectangular ringwork, is apparently an isolated feature, the castle appears to have spawned a dependent hamlet or

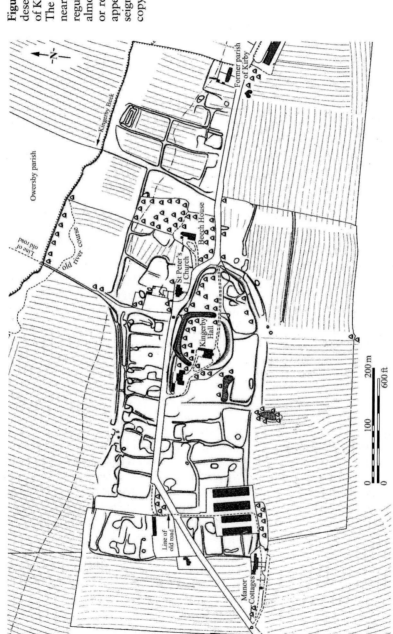

Figure 8.21 Plan of the deserted medieval village of Kingerby (Lincolnshire). The castle/manor site lies near the east end of the regular village, which was almost certainly planned or re-planned as an appendage to the seigneurial site (© Crown copyright NMR).

Owersby parish

Kingerby Beck

Line of old road

old river course

St Peter's Church

Beech House

Kingerby Hall

Line of old road

Manor Cottages

Former parish of Kirby

0   100   200 m

0   600 ft

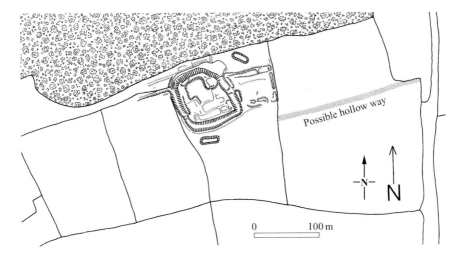

Figure 8.22 Woodhead Castle (Rutland), showing ringwork and bailey and adjacent closes, as depicted in an estate map of 1798.

settlement. In 1286–7 a toft and croft at Woodhead are specified in the endowment of a chapel here (Irons 1917: 50–1; VCH Rutland 1935: 235), and in 1684 the antiquarian Wright mentions 'Woodhead, formerly a village and chapelry, now only one house, and that in ruins' (1684: 36). The precise location and plan of this settlement remains obscure, yet a 1798 estate plan of Bridge Casterton (Fig. 8.22) depicts four sub-rectangular enclosures in line to the south of the castle earthworks which are associated with the field-name *Woodhead Closes*. These features may well indicate a series of amalgamated peasant crofts, subsequently overlain by ridge and furrow cultivation, whilst a superficial depression leading east from the castle may indicate a former hollow-way.

Summary

This chapter has attempted to reconcile two conflicting ways of understanding the contribution of castles to the making of the rural landscape. On the one hand, castles were part and parcel of wider rural landscapes and components within local and regional settlement patterns. On the other hand, however, they possessed certain characteristics that in some ways elevated them above the rural scene. The status of rural castles as manorial centres is particularly evident in their close association with other characteristic features of rural lordship. While the common juxtaposition of castle and parish church perpetuated an established tradition of association between high-status private residence and ecclesiastical site, the development of fishponds and deer parks as appendages to seigneurial residences appears to have been largely a post-Conquest phenomenon. But only rarely did castles in England bring entirely new rural settlements into existence. Far more commonly, castle lords were involved in the re-orientation of village plans, or the addition of planned extensions to earlier cores (e.g. Sheriff Hutton). The limited evidence available for the clearance of rural property to make way for castles suggests that this was a short-lived product of the Anarchy (e.g. Burwell). Most other eleventh- and twelfth-century castles form a manorial focus within village plans and many embraced dependent settlements or were in some way located to bring communities under tighter control. Castles also existed as dispersed settlements in non-nucleated landscapes, and many later castles were intended as isolated lordship sites that were deliberately removed from the tenantry. What is essential is that these patterns and processes are not seen in isolation, but understood within the wider context of regional economies and landscapes.

9 Overview

This study has re-examined an old and established focus of scholarly enquiry – the medieval castle – using the more modern interdisciplinary approaches of landscape archaeology and landscape studies. It has had as its principal aim the re-integration of castles into their contemporary surroundings in order to further a more holistic understanding of their functions and place in the medieval landscape. To move towards this objective it is necessary to sweep away many of our preconceptions about medieval castles, especially those ultimately derived from the Romantic movement, and to appreciate their truly multifarious functions as estate centres, status symbols and residences, as well as fortresses. In economic terms, medieval castles were central places in the medieval landscape; socially, they were badges of wealth and status that proclaimed the status and coercive power of their owners to the surrounding population. It has been demonstrated that past academic failure to view castles in this way was often based on a misreading of the functions of these sites and a marked unwillingness for truly integrated analysis. In particular, traditional studies of castles based on military and architectural analysis but bereft of the context of land tenure, settlement patterns and regional geography, seriously overlook their important contribution to the development of the English landscape.

This study certainly raises questions that are, at present, difficult or impossible to answer; there is undeniably much still to be learnt about castles and their landscapes. If fundamental questions still remain concerning the contribution of monasticism to the landscape (Bond 2000: 72), then, given the comparative sluggishness with which castellologists have embraced the theories and methodologies of landscape study, even more elementary questions remain unanswered concerning the impact of castles on the landscapes and townscapes of Britain. Perhaps most glaring of all are some basic uncertainties concerning chronology; in particular, we have remarkably little idea of when the vast majority of earth and timber fortifications were built or for how long they functioned. Constant difficulties also arise in attempting to correlate developments in the landscapes around castles – such as the planning of settlements or field systems, or the creation of gardens and fishponds with the initial construction of the seigneurial site, changes in ownership or episodes of remodelling. Some of the theories contained in this book will certainly be challenged and probably overturned, as would be perfectly normal in a vibrant field of study. It is hoped, however, that this work has established a broad framework for applying a 'landscape approach' to castles that will encourage further study. This short overview brings together some issues of particular significance and makes some recommendations for future research.

As well as underlining that castles were instruments of administration and tools of lordship, this study has emphasized the complexity of castle siting and the variety of impacts the presence of castles and the policies of their lords could have on their surroundings. The impact of castles on the development and topography of other human settlements has been identified as particularly important. In the towns and in the countryside, the building of a castle could have disastrous consequences for settlements, with properties levelled and streets occasionally obliterated and re-routed so that the new site could occupy the most favourable position. The construction of an appending castle park could have similar effects. These impacts were, however, short-lived, and we can also identify the more important positive influence that castles exerted on the evolution of settlement as their lords took an active interest in the development of associated estates. Thus we see the creation and expansion of towns, villages and other forms of settlement closely linked to castles. All these changes to the physical topography of settlements must also have had deep psychological impacts on the human community. But while archaeological excavations and related settlement plan analyses underline so clearly the immense coercive power of castle lords, these sequences must also conceal a level of dialogue between castle lord and community in these contested landscapes. Objections or resistance to castle lords and their often grandiose schemes of settlement planning must have occurred, but we are so far unable, or remain unwilling, to detect this in the physical evidence available to us.

The various interrelationships between medieval castles and their settings have been examined at a number of different scales of analysis and from various perspectives. One way of understanding the place of the castle in the landscape is as a dot on a map or as a feature on a scaled plan, another is as the backdrop in a painting or manuscript illustration, while another is as a site viewed vertically or obliquely from the air. While each of these points of view can offer us different insights, none alone is adequate and, more importantly, none tells us enough about how medieval society perceived its own castles. An holistic view of the castle must thus take account of these perspectives and others. In addition, a castle did not necessarily stand in the centre of its particular landscape. Indeed, a recurrent theme has been that many castles from the Norman period onwards actually lay at the edge of different types of landscape. Numerous are the cases where a castle was sited between zones of upland and lowland. At a more localized scale, the arrangement of a castle bracketed by a planted borough or planned village on one side and a seigneurial deer park on the other was also common. These élite landscapes were often further structured by the location of a church at the junction between castle and community and a suite of gardens or pleasure grounds that projected into the parkland. In addition, those castles formed of successive enclosures, one inside the other, constituted miniature landscapes of exclusion and negotiation in their own right. The frequency with which a combination of these different elements coincides raises the intriguing question of whether medieval lords had in mind a hypothetical 'ideal' landscape moulded to particular local circumstances.

Castle studies and the landscape: directions for future research

Studies of symbolism in castle architecture and of the usage and manipulation of social space within their designs demonstrate one important way in which

castle studies can be made more accessible to a wider audience. Yet analysis of
the material remains of castles needs to be framed within a broader understanding of the context and significance of these sites within their wider
landscapes. What is vital, of course, is that these two modes of enquiry are not
severed from one another. Detailed analyses of the physical fabric of castles
have a continued rôle to play, alongside broader studies of their social and
political contexts, and the most profitable future research projects will
doubtless combine both approaches. While recent work has shown glimpses of
what can be achieved by examining castles in a more holistic way, much still
remains to be done. Archaeological studies of castles will certainly advance if
the recommendations of the Society for Medieval Archaeology concerning the
excavation of fortified sites are heeded in future research designs: 'All such
sites need to be studied within their contemporary setting, and the most useful
will be those that reveal a place's interaction with its hinterland' (Hinton
1987: 6). But how, in practical terms, can future research come more closely
to grips with the complex interrelationships between castles and their
surroundings?

Of foremost importance is the need to integrate fully and effectively a wide
range of data sources. This study has necessarily adopted an interdisciplinary
approach and has cut across traditional boundaries – most notably between
history and archaeology – but also included contributions from the fields of
historical geography and architectural study. The widespread failure of
archaeology to contextualize medieval castles within their landscapes is, to an
extent, a reflection of a failure to exploit fully the variety of data sources
available. For instance, we have noted a reluctance to integrate the findings of
environmental contributions within excavation reports and highlighted the
under-exploited potential of combining the excavation of a castle site with
fieldwork in its environs. The critical issue here is that truly multifaceted,
interdisciplinary research into medieval landscapes must cross-fertilize
between data sources rather than subsuming one type of enquiry within an
inflexible framework provided by another. In this sense, castle studies can be
best served through long-term interdisciplinary research projects. The benefits
of reflection, re-assessment, and flexibility facilitated by this type of study are
exemplified within medieval settlement studies (Aston 1993; Beresford and
Hurst 1990). Integration can be achieved at two levels. First, castle studies
deserve greater integration within medieval archaeology as a whole, so that
future projects may see the study of castles – as part of the panoply of lordship
sites – integrated within studies of medieval rural and urban settlements, rural
resources and territories. Second, other specialists besides architectural and
documentary historians clearly have important rôles to play, including historical geographers and environmental historians.

From another perspective, settlement studies must give greater recognition
to the fact that castles did not exist above and beyond the medieval settlement
pattern, but were embedded within it and contributed to its evolution. We
must, however, also be aware that, sometimes, settlements associated with
castles may have had atypical social and economic structures and distinctive
plan-forms due to the presence of seigneurial sites. The excavation of castles
within settlements, meanwhile, can have immense significance for medieval
settlement studies in general. In particular, urban castle sites may well seal

some of the best-preserved stratigraphy – particularly for the late Saxon period – in modern British towns and cities (Schofield and Vince 1994: 46). As excavations at Colchester, Newark, Norwich and Winchester have demonstrated, castles can seal remarkable evidence of antecedent activity, including high-status secular and ecclesiastical occupation, as well as more typical properties and street frontages. The targeted excavation of urban castle baileys potentially may provide important windows into the economies of medieval towns and, especially, into the seigneurial influence on trade and commerce.

Archaeological examination of castle baileys generally is a clear priority for the future. Higham and Barker's survey of archaeological excavations of earth and timber castles (1992: 244–325) has highlighted the comparative wealth of archaeological information regarding the superstructures of mottes and the interior buildings of ringworks relative to the data set concerning bailey interiors. Certainly fundamental changes in archaeological sampling strategies are essential if we are to clarify some of the cultural activities potentially centralized within baileys and outer wards, which remain almost totally obscure (Harfield 1988: 137–8). We are thus urgently in need of a broader data set, including sites from varied regional and social settings, with which to supplement the remarkable findings from Hen Domen (Powys). As a borderland fortress, this site probably gives little idea of what went on in the baileys of rural castles in more settled districts. The potential range of activities contained within castle baileys is enormous and will doubtless have varied greatly; what is certain is that bailey interiors have much to tell us about the economic lives of castles and their linkages with surrounding hinterlands. The purposes of outer baileys remain even more enigmatic, due to a basic lack of archaeological attention and often poor conditions of preservation. The geophysical survey of the interiors of baileys or outer wards would certainly seem to hold potential, although few studies have been conducted to date – examples being the resistivity survey of outer baileys at Hamstead Marshall (Dorset) and Wigmore (Herefordshire) (Redhead 1990; Keevill and Linford 1998: 14).

A further potentially fruitful avenue for future research is the analysis of castle sites within large areas of territory. While county studies of castles are valuable, other analyses of castle siting and distribution, based perhaps on units of lordship, regions or other topographical zones are needed. Certainly, the inventorizing, categorization and sub-categorization of surface remains alone will do little to push forward the field archaeology of castles. Those studies completed to date have nonetheless demonstrated interesting patterns of variation in terms of castle siting and relationships with settlement patterns and regional economies. It is only through further comparative studies, however, that the true extent and meaning of these variations will become any clearer.

Future studies will also no doubt pay greater attention to the ways in which castles and their surroundings were perceived and experienced by contemporaries. Certainly the detailed reconstruction of castles through illustration or model-making can stimulate thought, but the tools with most potential for the future are undoubtedly GIS (Geographical Information Systems) and virtual reality technologies. Alongside these innovative methods, however, more traditional source material also demands greater attention. In particular, the value of contemporary literary and pictorial material has often been under-appreciated, and their study presents many exciting opportunities for examining further the impact of castles and castle building on cognitive landscapes.

But while this study has highlighted some important lines of enquiry for future research, two sobering conclusions can be drawn from the material discussed. First, many of the case studies can only be offered as tentative hypotheses with necessarily limited shelf-lives, underlain and informed by current academic trends and personal perspectives. Modern studies of medieval landscapes have always been marked by constant reappraisal (e.g. Taylor 1992), and there is no reason for this study to be any different. Second, most of the issues discussed here are not specific to the landscapes that surrounded castles. Rather, all of the examples and case studies can and must be related to wider debates within medieval studies, both general and specific. For instance, it would be manifestly wrong to discuss the foundation of castle boroughs in the eleventh and twelfth centuries without reference to their context within a wider upsurge in urbanism, just as it would be misleading to examine those deserted villages appended to castles in isolation from the wider phenomenon of rural depopulation. This provides a further reminder of quite how interconnected medieval landscapes were; no single element, not least the castle, is explicable without reference to wider issues of lordship, power, community, economy and environment.

Figure 9.1 Restormel Castle (Cornwall). Now managed as a heritage site, the castle is as popular and appealing for its dramatic scenery as for the physical fabric of the medieval structure. Formerly lying within one of the largest medieval deer parks in Cornwall, the site commands spectacular views over the countryside around the Fowey estuary (photograph: Oliver Creighton).

A final point that emerges is that many of the landscapes discussed have obviously changed immeasurably since the medieval period. Many castle towns have expanded to obscure original plan-forms and sometimes obliterate or encroach upon the site of lordship that originally bought them into existence. Elsewhere, agriculture and other forms of development endanger the earthworks of adjacent deserted settlements or threaten areas of woodland or other landscape features that form part of castles' historic settings. Far greater recognition is now given to conserving the integrity of landscapes around sites and monuments than in the past. One of the most important and pressing challenges for the future remains, however, the need to conserve and preserve not only the physical fabric of medieval castles, but also something of what remains of their settings and context within the landscape (Fig. 9.1).

Glossary

advowson: the patronage of an ecclesiastical office

assart: zone of arable land cleared from waste or common

aula: hall

bailey: dependent enclosure of a motte or ringwork

berwick: outlying place attached to a manor

burgus: unit of settlement annexed physically to a castle through the provision of an enclosing earthwork

caput: head manor

carucate: a unit of land measurement sometimes used for the purposes of tax assessment in Domesday Book

castle-guard: a term of garrison duty performed by a tenant at a lord's castle

ceorl: class of Anglo-Saxon peasant defined by 'free' status

crossing: the area of a church where the chancel, nave and transepts meet

croft: zone of enclosed arable land attached to a toft

Danelaw: area of England subject to Danish control and law in the ninth and tenth centuries

demesne: land owned and administered directly by a lord rather than being let to tenants

eigenkirche: private ecclesiastical foundation, often neighbouring a manor or castle

fief or *fee:* an estate of land

five boroughs: a series of urban or quasi-urban fortified centres (Derby, Leicester, Lincoln, Nottingham and Stamford), forming the basis of the ninth-century Danish confederacy known as the Danelaw

glebe-land: land attached to the rectory of a church in order to supplement income

graveship: an administrative unit describing a grouping of demesne vills or townships within an extensive fee. The local administration of a graveship was the responsibility of the grave.

honour: a group of estates held by a tenant-in-chief of the crown, and often named after the lord's principal castle

hollow-way: a sunken track-way, often marking the course of a medieval road

hundred: an administrative district within a shire, whose representatives met monthly, usually at a moot

incastellamento: the fortification or creation of a defended upland site, usually comprising a castle and associated village

messuage: a house with associated land

moot: the assembly point of a hundred

motte: artificial mound, usually of earthen construction, providing the basis for a fortified superstructure

multiple estate: a territorial unit defined by a central manor (*caput*), associated with a series of outlying dependencies

multure: a fee paid for the use of a lord's mill

open field system: large tracts of non-enclosed arable land, divided into strips and held individually

parochia: an area dependent ecclesiastically upon a minster church

porticus: chapels contained within the sides of Anglo-Saxon church

prospect mound: an artificial mound forming a platform for the viewing of formal gardens

ridge and furrow: curvilinear agricultural earthworks characteristic of the open field system

ringwork: fortification comprising a bank and external ditch, and enclosing a series of internal structures or buildings

Stamford ware: a type of Saxo-Norman pottery manufactured in Stamford *c.* 850–1250

tenant-in-chief: a feudal magnate holding land directly from the Crown

thegn: Anglo-Saxon lord

toft: a house plot

vicus: small Roman civilian settlement, usually attached to a military establishment

viewshed: the area of a landscape intervisible with a specific point

vill: a unit used to assess taxation in Domesday Book, in many cases forming the basis of a civil parish

Bibliography

Aberg, F. A. (1983) The Moated Sites Research Group. In D. A. Hinton (ed.), *Twenty-five Years of Medieval Archaeology*. Sheffield: Department of Prehistory and Archaeology, 97–101.

Aberg, F. A. (1988) MSRG Annual Conference at Manchester 1–2 April 1989: Lordship and Settlement, a précis of the papers presented. *Medieval Settlement Research Group Annual Report* 3: 5–7.

Adams, C. (1999) Medieval administration. In K. Leslie and B. Short (eds), *An Historical Atlas of Sussex*. Chichester: Phillimore, 40–1.

Addy, S. O. (1913) *Castle and Manor: A Study in English Economic History*. London: Alien.

Addyman, P. V. (1960) Excavations at a moated site in Sapcote, 1958. *Transactions of the Leicestershire Archaeological and Historical Society* 36: 1–5.

Addyman, P. V. (1965) Late Saxon settlements in the St Neots area I: The Saxon settlement and Norman castle at Eaton Socon, Bedfordshire. *Proceedings of the Cambridgeshire Antiquarian Society* 58: 38–73.

Addyman, P. V. and Priestley, J. (1977) Baile Hill, York: a report on the Institute's excavations. *Archaeological Journal* 134: 115–56.

Ahier, P. (1946) *The Story of Castle Hill, Huddersfield Throughout the Centuries, BC 200–AD 1945*. Huddersfield: Advertiser Press.

Airs, M., Rodwell, K. and Turner, H. (1975) Wallingford. In K. Rodwell (ed.), *Historic Towns in Oxfordshire: A Survey of the New County*. Oxford: Oxfordshire Archaeological Unit, 155–62.

Albarella, U. and Davis, J. M. (1994) Mammals and birds from Launceston Castle Cornwall: decline in status and the rise of agriculture. *Circaea* 12.1: 1–56.

Alcock, L. (1987) Castle-studies and the archaeological sciences: some possibilities and problems. In J. R. Kenyon and R. Avent (eds), *Castles in Wales and the Marches: Essays in Honour of D. J. Cathcart King*. Cardiff: Cardiff University Press, 5–22.

Aldsworth, F. G. (1979) 'The mound' at Church Norton, Selsey, and the site of St Wilfrid's church. *Sussex Archaeological Collections* 117: 103–07.

Alexander, J. W. (1970) New evidence on the Palatinate of Chester. *English Historical Review* 85: 715–29.

Andrews, G. (1984) Archaeology in York: an assessment. In P. V. Addyman and V. E. Black (eds), *Archaeological Papers Presented to M. W. Barley*. York: York Archaeological Trust, 173–207.

Armitage, E. S. (1912) *The Early Norman Castles of the British Isles*. London: Murray.

Astill, G. (1978) *Historic Towns in Berkshire: An Archaeological Approach*. Reading: Berkshire Archaeological Committee.

Astill, G. (1984) The towns of Berkshire. In J. Haslam (ed.), *Anglo-Saxon Towns*. Chichester: Phillimore, 53–86.

Astill, G. and Grant, A. (eds) (1988) *The Countryside of Medieval England*. Oxford: Blackwell.

Aston, M. (1985) Rural settlement in Somerset: some preliminary thoughts. In D. Hooke (ed.), *Medieval Villages: A Review of Current Work*. Oxford: Oxford University Committee for Archaeology Monograph No. 5: 81–100.

Aston, M. (ed.) (1988a) *Aspects of the Mediaeval Landscape of Somerset and Contributions to the Landscape History of the County*. Taunton: Somerset County Council.

Aston, M. (ed.) (1988b) *Medieval Fish, Fisheries and Fishponds*, 2 vols. Oxford: BAR British Series No. 182.

Aston, M. (1993) Report on the Shapwick project, 1993. *Medieval Settlement Research Group Report* 8: 15–17.

Aston, M. (2000) *Monasteries in the Landscape*. Stroud: Tempus.

Aston, M. and Bond, C. J. (1976) *The Landscape of Towns*. London: Dent.

Aston, M. and Bond, C. J. (1998) Warwickshire fishponds. In M. Aston (ed.), *Medieval Fish, Fisheries and Fishponds*, 2 vols. Oxford: BAR British Series No. 182: 417–34.

Aston, M. and Burrow, I. (eds) (1982) *The Archaeology of Somerset, a Review to 1500 AD*. Taunton: Somerset County Council.

Aston, M. and Leech, R. (1977) *Historic Towns in Somerset: Archaeology and Planning*. Gloucester: Committee for Rescue Archaeology in Avon, Gloucestershire and Somerset.

Aston, M. and Rowley, T. (1974) *Landscape Archaeology: An Introduction to Fieldwork Techniques on Post-Roman Landscapes*. Newton Abbot: David and Charles.

Atkin, M. (1991) Gloucester's Norman castle rediscovered. *Fortress* 9: 20–3.

Atkins, C. (1983) 'The Castles', Barrow-on-Humber. *Lincolnshire History and Archaeology* 18: 91–3.

Atkins, C. (1988) *Skipsea Castle. North Humberside: A Survey of the Earthworks, 1987/88*. Unpublished report, Humberside SMR.

Audouy, M., Dix, B. and Parsons, D. (1995) The tower of All Saints' church. Earl Barton, Northamptonshire: its construction and context. *Archaeological Journal* 152: 73–94.

Austin, D. (1978) Excavations in Okehampton deer park, Devon, 1976–1978. *Proceedings of the Devon Archaeological Society* 36: 191–239.

Austin, D. (1979) Barnard Castle, Co. Durham. First interim report: excavations in the town ward, 1974–6. *Journal of the British Archaeological Association* 132: 50–72.

Austin, D. (1980) Barnard Castle, Co. Durham. Second interim report: excavations in the inner ward. *Journal of the British Archaeological Association* 133: 74–96.

Austin, D. (1984) The castle and the landscape. *Landscape History* 6: 70–81.

Austin, D. (1985) Doubts about morphogenesis. *Journal of Historical Geography* 11: 201–9.

Austin, D. (1987) The archaeology of the Domesday vill. In W. R. S. Erskine (ed.), *Domesday Book Studies*. London: Alecto Historical Editions, 48–55.

Austin, D. (1990) The 'proper study' of medieval archaeology: a case study. In D. Austin and L. Alcock (eds), *From the Baltic to the Black Sea: Studies in Medieval Archaeology*. One World Archaeology Series No. 18. London: Unwin Hyman, 43–78.

Ayers, B. (1985) *Excavations within the North-east Bailey of Norwich Castle, 1979*. Dereham: East Anglian Archaeology Report No. 28.

Ayers B. (1994) Norwich. In P. Wade-Martins (ed.), *An Historical Atlas of Norfolk*, 2nd edn. Norwich: Norfolk Museums Service, 74–5.

Balchin, W. G. V. (1983) *The Cornish Landscape*. London: Hodder and Stoughton.

Baker, D. (1973) Bedford Castle: some preliminary results from rescue excavation. *Château Gaillard* 6: 15–22.

Baker, D. (1982a) Cainhoe Castle. *Archaeological Journal* 139: 32–4.

Baker, D. (1982b) Mottes, moats and ringworks in Bedfordshire: Beauchamp Wadmore revisited. *Château Gaillard* 9–10, 35–54.

Baker, D. (1982c) Yielden Castle. *Archaeological Journal* 139: 17–18.

Ballard, A. (1910) Castle-guard and barons' houses. *English Historical Review* 25: 712–15.

Barker, P. A. (1981) Caus Castle and Hawcock's Mount. *Archaeological Journal* 138: 34.

Barker, P. A. (1987) Hen Domen revisited. In J. R. Kenyon and R. Avent (eds), *Castles in Wales and the Marches: Essays in Honour of D. J. Cathcart King*. Cardiff: Cardiff University Press, 51–4.

Barker, P. A. and Higham, R. A. (1982) *Hen Domen Montgomery: A Timber Castle on the Welsh Border*. London: Royal Archaeological Institute.

Barker, P. A. and Lawson, J. (1971) A pre-Norman field system at Hen Domen, Montgomery. *Medieval Archaeology* 15: 58–72.

Barley, M. W. (1951) Cuckney church and castle. *Transactions of the Thoroton Society of Nottinghamshire* 4: 26–9.

Barley, M. W. (1957) Cistercian land clearance in Nottinghamshire: three deserted villages and their moated successors. *Nottingham Medieval Studies* 1: 75–89.

Barley, M. W. (1969) Nottingham. In M. D. Lobel (ed.), *Historic Towns*, Vol. 1. London: Lovell Johns – Cook, Hammond and Kell, 1–8.

Barley, M. W. (1976) Town defences in England and Wales after 1066. In M. W. Barley (ed.), *The Plans and Topography of Medieval Towns in England and Wales*. London: CBA Research Report No. 14: 57–71.

Barley, M. W. (1978) Castle Howard and the village of Hinderskelfe, N. Yorkshire. *Antiquaries Journal* 58: 358–60.

Barley, M. W. and Waters, F. (1956) Newark Castle – excavations 1953–56. *Transactions of the Thoroton Society of Nottinghamshire* 60: 20–33.

Barnatt, J. (1991) Pilsbury Farm, Hartington Town Quarter. Derbyshire Archaeological Survey 1991. Unpublished report: Derbyshire Sites and Monuments Record.

Barnatt, J. and Smith, K. (1997) *The English Heritage Book of the Peak District: Landscapes through Time*. London: Batsford/English Heritage.

Barry, T. (2000) The chronology and development of medieval rural settlement in Munster. *Journal of the Cork Historical and Archaeological Society* 105: 191–8.

Bartley, D. D. (1976) Palaeobotanical evidence. In P. H. Sawyer (ed.), *Medieval Settlement*. London: Edward Arnold, 226–35.

Barton, K. J. and Holden, E. W. (1977) Excavations at Bramber Castle, Sussex. *Archaeological Journal* 134: 11–79.

Bassett, S. R. (1982) *Saffron Walden: Excavations and Research 1972–80*. London: CBA Research Report No. 45.

Bassett, S. R. (1985) Beyond the edge of excavation: the topographical context of Goltho. In H. Mayr-Harting and R. I. Moore (eds), *Studies in Medieval History Presented to R. H. C. Davis*. London: Hambledon, 21–39.

Bearman, R. (1994) *Charters of the Reavers Family and the Earldom of Devon, 1090–1217*. Exeter: Devon and Cornwall Record Society New Series, Vol. 37.

Beaumont, E. (1997) Waiting for an editor: the cartulary of Castle Acre Priory. *Medieval Life* 7: 10–13.

Beaumont James, T. (1997) *English Heritage Book of Winchester*. London: Batsford/English Heritage.

Beckett, J. V. (1989) *A History of Laxton: England's Last Open Field Village*. Oxford: Blackwell.

Beeler, J. (1956) Castles and strategy in Norman and early Angevin England. *Speculum* 31: 581–601.

Beeler, J. (1966) *Warfare in England 1066–1189*. Cornell: Cornell University Press.

Bell, M. (1982) Land molluscs. In R. A. Higham, J. P. Allan and S. R. Blaylock, Excavations at Okehampton castle, Devon, part two – the bailey. *Proceedings of the Devonshire Archaeological Society* 40: 145–6.

Bell, M. (1989) Environmental archaeology as an index of continuity and change in the medieval landscape. In M. Aston and C. Dyer (eds), *The Rural Settlements of Medieval England*. Oxford: Blackwell, 269–86.

Bennett, P., Frere, S. S. and Stow, S. (1982) *The Archaeology of Canterbury Castle*. Maidstone: Kent Archaeological Society.

Beresford, G. (1975) *The Medieval Clay-Land Village: Excavations at Goltho and Barton Blount*. London: Society for Medieval Archaeology Monograph No. 6.

Beresford, G. (1977) The excavation of the deserted medieval village of Goltho, Lincolnshire. *Château Gaillard* 8: 47–68.

Beresford, G, (1981) Goltho manor, Lincolnshire: the buildings and their surrounding defences, *c*. 850–1150. *Proceedings of the Battle Conference on Anglo-Norman Studies* 4: 13–36.

Beresford, G. (1987) *Goltho: The Development of an Early Medieval Manor c. 850–1150*. London: HMSO.

Beresford, M. W. (1948–51) Glebe terriers and open fields, Yorkshire. *Yorkshire Archaeological Journal* 37: 325–68.

Beresford, M. W. (1951–5) The lost villages of Yorkshire, parts II, III and IV. *Yorkshire Archaeological Journal* 38: 44–70, 215–40, 280–309.

Beresford, M. W. (1954) *The Lost Villages of England*. London: Lutterworth Press.

Beresford, M. W. (1957) *History on the Ground*. London: Lutterworth.

Beresford, M. W. (1959) The six new towns of the Bishops of Winchester, 1200–55. *Medieval Archaeology* 3: 187–215.

Beresford, M. W. (1967) *New Towns of the Middle Ages*. London: Lutterworth Press.

Beresford, M. W. and Finberg, H. P. R (1973) *English Medieval Boroughs: A Handlist*. Newton Abbott: David and Charles.

Beresford, M. W. and Hurst, J. G. (1971) *Deserted Medieval Villages*. London: Lutterworth Press.

Beresford, M. W. and Hurst, J. G. (1990) *English Heritage Book of Wharram Percy*. London: Batsford/English Heritage.

Beresford, M. W. and St Joseph, J. K. S. (1979) *Medieval England: An Aerial Survey*, 2nd edn. Cambridge: Cambridge University Press.

Berg, D. (1994) The animal bone. In J. Manley, Excavations at Caergwrle Castle, Clwyd, North Wales: 1988–1990. *Medieval Archaeology* 38: 125–6.

Bettey, J. H. (1993) *Estates and the English Countryside*. London: Batsford.

Biddle, M. (1964) The excavation of a motte and bailey Castle at Therfield, Herts. *Journal of the British Archaeological Association* 27: 53–91.

Biddle, M. (ed.) (1976) *Winchester in the Early Middle Ages: An Edition and Discussion of the Winton Domesday*. Oxford: Clarendon Press.

Biddle, M. (1986) Archaeology, architecture and the cult of saints in Anglo-Saxon England. In L. A. S Butler and R. Morris (eds), *The Anglo-Saxon Church*. London: CBA Research Report No. 60: 1–31.

Biddle, M. and Hill, D. (1971) Late Saxon planned towns. *Antiquaries Journal* 51: 70–85.

Bigmore, P. (1979) *The Bedfordshire and Huntingdonshire Landscape*. London: Hodder and Stoughton.

Binns, A. (1966) Scarborough in 1066. In M. Edwards (ed.), *Scarborough 966–1966*. Scarborough: Scarborough and District Archaeological Society: 17–23.

Birch, J. (1980a) Bailey Hill, Bradfield. *Archaeological Journal* 137: 457–8.

Birch, J. (1980b) Castle Hill, Bradfield. *Archaeological Journal* 137: 458–9.

Birrell, J. (1992) Deer and deer farming in medieval England. *Agricultural History Review* 40(2): 112–26.

Bishop, T. A. M. (1948) The Norman settlement of Yorkshire. In R. W. Hunt, W. A. Pantin and R. W. Southern (eds), *Studies in Medieval History Presented to Fredrick Maurice Powicke*. Oxford: Clarendon Press: 1–14.

Blair, J. (1981) William Fitz Ansculf and the Abinger motte. *Archaeological Journal* 138: 146–8.

Blood, N. E. and Taylor, C. C. (1992) Cawood: an archiepiscopal landscape. *Yorkshire Archaeological Journal* 64: 83–102.

Bond, C. J. (1987) Anglo-Saxon and medieval defences. In J. Schofield and R. Leech (eds), *Urban Archaeology in Britain*. London: CBA Research Report No. 61: 92–115.

Bond, J. (1986) The Oxford region in the middle ages. In G. Briggs, J. Cook and T. Rowley (eds), *The Archaeology of the Oxford Region*. Oxford: Oxford University Department for External Studies, 135–59.

Bond, J. (2000) Landscapes of monasticism. In D. Hooke (ed.), *Landscape, the Richest Historical Record*. Society for Landscape Studies Supplementary Series No. 1: 63–74.

Bonney, D. J. and Dunn, C. J. (1989) Earthwork castles and settlement at Hamstead Marshall, Berkshire. In M. Bowden, D. Mackay and P. Topping (eds), *From Cornwall to Caithness: Some Aspects of British Field Archaeology. Papers Presented to Norman V. Quinnell*. Oxford: BAR British Series No. 209: 173–82.

Bourne, J. (1988) Some Anglo-Saxon multiple estates. In C. Phythian-Adams (ed.), *The Norman Conquest of Leicestershire and Rutland: A Regional Introduction to Domesday Book*. Leicester: Leicestershire Museums, Art Galleries and Records Service, 13–16.

Bowden, M. (1998) The conscious conversion of earlier earthworks in the design of parks and gardens. In P. Pattison (ed.), *There by Design*. Oxford: BAR British Series No. 267: 23–6.

Bowden, M. (ed.) (1999) *Unravelling the Landscape: An Inquisitive Approach to Archaeology*. Stroud: Tempus.

Bradbury, J. (1992) *The Medieval Siege*. Woodbridge: Boydell Press.

Breeze, A. (1997) *Medieval Welsh Literature*. Dublin: Four Courts Press.

Brooks, F. W. (1966) *Domesday Book and the East Riding*. Kingston upon Hull: East Yorkshire Local History Series No. 21.

Brooks, N. P. (1965–6) Excavations at Wallingford Castle, 1965: an interim report. *Berkshire Archaeological Journal* 62: 17–21.

Brooks, N. P. (1971) The development of military obligations in eighth- and ninth-century England. In P. Clemoes and K. Hughes (eds), *England before the Conquest – Studies in Primary Sources Presented to Dorothy Whitelock*. Cambridge: Cambridge University Press, 69–94.

Brooksbank, J. H. (1929) Castleton: its traditions, sayings, place-names, etc. *Transactions of the Hunter Archaeological Society* 3: 34–51.

Brown, A. (ed.) (1999) *The Rows of Chester: The Chester Rows Research Project*. London: English Heritage Archaeological Report No. 16.

Brown, A. E. (1975) *Archaeological Sites and Finds in Rutland, a Preliminary List*. Leicester: Leicester University Press.

Brown, A. E. (1987) *Fieldwork for Archaeologists and Local Historians*. London: Batsford.

Brown, A. E. (ed.) (1991) *Garden Archaeology*. London: CBA Research Report No. 78.

Brown, A. E. and Taylor, C. C. (1977) Cambridgeshire earthwork surveys, II, Rampton: Giant's Hill. *Transactions of the Cambridgeshire Antiquarian Society* 67: 97–9.

Brown, R. A. (1952) Framlingham Castle and Bigod. *Proceedings of the Suffolk Institute of Archaeology* 25: 127–48.

Brown, R. A. (1954) *English Medieval Castles*. London: Batsford.

Brown, R. A. (1976) *English Castles*. London: Batsford.

Brown, R. A. (1985) *The Normans and the Norman Conquest*, 2nd edn. Woodbridge: Boydell Press.

Brown, R. A. (1987) The castles of the Conquest. In W. R. S. Erskine (ed.), *Domesday Book Studies*. London: Alecto Historical Editions, 69–74.

Brown, R. A. (1989) *Castles from the Air*. Cambridge: Cambridge University Press.

Brown, R. A., Colvin, H. M. and Taylor, A. J. (1963) *The History of the King's Works, Volumes I and II: The Middle Ages*. London: HMSO.

Brown, S. (1996) Berry Pomeroy Castle. *Proceedings of the Devon Archaeological Society* 54 (dedicated volume).

Browne, S. (2000) The animal bones. In R. A. Higham and P. A. Barker, *Hen Domen, Montgomery. A Timber Castle on the English-Welsh Border: A Final Report*. Exeter: University of Exeter Press, 126–34.

Buckley, R. and Lucas, J. (1987) *Leicester Town Defences: Excavations 1958–1974*. Leicester: Leicestershire Museums, Art Galleries and Records Service.

Bu'Lock, J. D. (1970) Churches, crosses and mottes in the Lune Valley. *Archaeological Journal* 127: 291–2.

Bur, M. (1983) The social influence of the motte and bailey castle. *Scientific American* 248.(5): 132–8.

Buteux, V. (1996) *Archaeological Assessment of Caus, Shropshire: The Central Marches Historic Towns Survey*. Unpublished report, Shropshire Sites and Monuments Record.

Butler, L. A. S. (1976) The evolution of towns: planted towns after 1066. In M. W. Barley (ed.), *The Plans and Topography of Medieval Towns in England and Wales*. Oxford: BAR British Series No. 14: 32–48.

Butler, L. A. S. (1992) The origins of the Honour of Richmond and its castles. *Château Gaillard* 16: 69–80.

Cameron, A. (1980) Laxton before 1635. *East Midlands Geographer* 7.6: 219–26.

Cameron, K. (1961) *English Place-Names*. London: Batsford.

Cantor, L. M. (1966) The medieval castles of Staffordshire. *North Staffordshire Journal of Field Studies* 6: 38–46.

Cantor, L. M. (1978) The medieval castles of Leicestershire. *Transactions of the Leicestershire Archaeological and Historical Society* 53: 30–41.

Cantor, L. M. and Hatherly, J. (1979) The medieval parks of England. *Geography* 64: 71–85.

Carrington, P. (1994) *English Heritage Book of Chester*. London: Batsford/English Heritage.

Carver, M. O. H. (1979) Three Saxo-Norman tenements in Durham City. *Medieval Archaeology* 23: 1–80.

Carver, M. O. H. (1987) *Underneath English Towns: Interpreting Urban Archaeology*. London: Batsford.

Castle Studies Group (1987) Statement of intent. *Castle Studies Group Newsletter* 1: 2.

Chalkley Gould, I. (1907) Some Nottinghamshire strongholds. *Journal of the British Archaeological Association* (New Series) 13: 51–64.

Challis, K. (1994) Trial excavation at Top Lane, Laxton, Nottinghamshire. *Transactions of the Thoroton Society of Nottinghamshire* 98: 24–31.

Challis, K. (1995a) Recent excavations at Laxton, Nottinghamshire. *Medieval Settlement Research Group Report* 10: 20–3.

Chambers, J. D. (1964) *Laxton: The Last English Open Field Village*. London: HMSO.

Chapelot, J. and Fossier, R. (1985) *The Village and House in the Middle Ages*. Berkeley: University of California Press.

Charles, M., Halstead, P. and Jones, G. (1996) The archaeology of fodder: an introduction. *Environmental Archaeology* 1: i–ii.

Cherry, J. (1992) *Imago Castelli*: the depiction of castles on medieval seals. *Château Gaillard* 15: 83–90.

Chibnall, M. (ed.) (1969) *The Ecclesiastical History of Orderic Vitalis*, Vol. 2. Oxford: Clarendon.

Chitty, L. (1949) Subsidiary castle sites west of Shrewsbury. *Transactions of the Shropshire-Archaeological Society* 53: 83–90.

Clark, G. T. (1884–5) *Mediaeval Military Architecture in England*, 2 vols. London: Wyman.

Clark-Maxwell, W. G. and Hamilton Thompson, A. (1927) The college of St Mary Magdalene, Bridgnorth, with some account of its deans and prebendaries. *Archaeological Journal* 84: 1–87.

Clay, C. T. (1949) *Early Yorkshire Charters: Vol. 8, the Honour of Warenne*. Huddersfield: Yorkshire Archaeological Society.

Coad, J. G. (1994) Medieval fortifications and post-medieval artillery defences: developments in post-war research and future trends. In B. Vyner (ed.), *Papers Celebrating 150 Years of the Royal Archaeological Institute*. London: Royal Archaeological Institute, 215–27.

Coad, J. G. (1995) *English Heritage Book of Dover Castle*. London: Batsford/English Heritage.

Coad, J. G. and Streeten, A. D. F. (1982) Excavations at Castle Acre Castle, Norfolk, 1972–77: country house and castle of the Norman earls of Surrey. *Archaeological Journal* 139: 138–301.

Coates, B. E. (1964–9) Parklands in transition: medieval deer park to modern landscape park. *Transactions of the Hunter Archaeological Society* 9: 132–50.

Collingwood, W. G. 1914–18: Anglian and Anglo-Danish sculpture in the West Riding. *Yorkshire Archaeological Journal* 23: 129–299.

Colvin, H. M. (1951) *The White Canons in England*. Oxford: Clarendon Press.

Colvin, H. M., Brown, R. A. and Taylor, A. J. (1963) *The History of the King's Works*, Vol. 2. London: HMSO.

Colyer, C. (1975) *Lincoln: The Archaeology of an Historic City*. Lincoln: Lincolnshire Archaeological Trust.

Conzen, M. R. G. (1960) *Alnwick, Northumberland: A Study in Town-Plan Analysis*. London: Philip.

Conzen, M. R. G. (1988) Morphogenesis, morphological regions and secular human agency in the historic townscape, as exemplified by Ludlow. In D. Denecke and G. Shaw (eds), *Urban Historical Geography*. Cambridge: Cambridge University Press, 253–72.

Corbett, G. S. (1994) *Whorlton Castle Gatehouse, Whorlton, N. Yorks*. Unpublished report, National Monuments Record Centre.

Coulson, C. (1979) Structural symbolism in medieval castle architecture. *Journal of the British Archaeological Association* 132: 73–90.

Coulson, C. (1982) Hierarchism in conventual crenellation: an essay in the sociology and metaphysics of medieval fortification. *Medieval Archaeology* 26: 69–100.

Coulson, C. (1990) Bodiam castle: truth and tradition. *Fortress* 10: 3–15.

Coulson, C. (1992) Some analysis of the castle of Bodiam. *Medieval Knighthood* 4: 51–107.

Coulson, C. (1993) Specimens of freedom to crenellate by license. *Fortress* 18: 3–15.

Coulson, C. (1994a) Freedom to crenellate by licence – an historiographical revision. *Nottingham Medieval Studies* 38: 86–137.

Coulson, C. (1994b) The castles of the Anarchy. In E. King (ed.), *The Anarchy of Stephen's Reign*. Oxford: Clarendon Press, 67–92.

Coulson, C. (1994c): The French matrix of the castle-provisions of the Chester-Leicester conventio. *Proceedings of the Battle Conference on Anglo-Norman Studies* 17: 65–86.

Coulson, C. (1996) Cultural realities and reappraisals in English castle study. *Journal of Medieval History* 22.2: 171–208.

Counihan, J. (1990) Ella Armitage, castle studies pioneer. *Fortress* 6: 51–9.

Cownie, E. (1998) Conquest, lordship and religious patronage in the Sussex rapes 1066–1135. *Sussex Archaeological Collections* 136: 111–22.

Cox, B. (1971) The Place-Names of Leicestershire and Rutland. Unpublished PhD thesis, University of Nottingham.

Cox, B. (1994) *The Place-Names of Rutland*. Nottingham: English Place-Name Society Vols 67–9.

Crawford, O. G. S. (1953) *Archaeology in the Field*. London: Dent.

Creighton, O. H. (1997) Early Leicestershire castles: archaeology and landscape history. *Transactions of the Leicestershire Archaeological and Historical Society* 71: 21–36.

Creighton, O. H. (1999a) Early castles in the medieval landscape of Rutland. *Transactions of the Leicestershire Archaeological and History Society* 73: 19–33.

Creighton, O. H. (1999b) Early castles and rural settlement patterns: insights from Yorkshire and the East Midlands. *Medieval Settlement Research Group Annual Report* 14: 29–33.

Creighton, O. H. (2000a) Early castles in the medieval landscape of Wiltshire. *Wiltshire Archaeological and Natural History Magazine* 93: 105–19.

Creighton, O. H. (2000b) The medieval castles of Rutland: field archaeology and landscape history. *Rutland Record* 20: 415–24.

Cronne, H. A. (1970) *The Reign of Stephen, 1135–54: Anarchy in England*. London: Weidenfeld and Nicolson.

Crook, D. (1990) The forest between the Erewash and the Derwent, 1154 to 1225. *Derbyshire Archaeological Journal* 110: 93–104.

Croom, J. N. (1992) The topographical analysis of medieval town plans: the examples of Much Wenlock and Bridgnorth. *Midland History* 17: 16–38.

Cruden, S. (1960) *The Scottish Castle*. Edinburgh: Nelson.

Crummy, P. (1981) *Aspects of Anglo-Saxon and Norman Colchester*. London: CBA Research Report No. 39.

Cunliffe, B. W. (ed.) (1976) *Excavation at Portchester Castle: Vol. II, Saxon*. London: Report of the Research Committee of the Society of Antiquaries of London No. 33.

Cunliffe, B. W. (ed.) (1977) *Excavation at Portchester Castle: Vol. III, Medieval, the Outer Bailey and Its Defences*. London: Report of the Research Committee of the Society of Antiquaries of London No. 43.

Cunliffe, B. W. and Munby, J. (eds) (1985) *Excavation at Portchester Castle: Vol. IV, Medieval, the Inner Bailey*. London: Report of the Research Committee of the Society of Antiquaries of London No. 43.

Curnow, P. and Johnson, E. A. (1985) St Briavels Castle. *Château Gaillard* 12: 91–114.

Curnow, P. E. and Thompson, M. W. (1969) Excavations at Richard's Castle, Herefordshire, 1962–1964. *Journal of the British Archaeological Association* (3rd Series) 32: 105–27.

Currie, C. K. (1991) The early history of the carp and its economic significance in England. *Agricultural History Review* 39.2: 97–107.

Dalton, P. (1994) *Conquest, Anarchy and Lordship: Yorkshire, 1066–1154*. Cambridge: Cambridge University Press.

Dalwood, H. (1996a) *Archaeological Assessment of Kilpeck, Hereford and Worcester*. Unpublished report, Central Marches Historic Towns Survey, Herefordshire and Worcester County Council.

Dalwood, H. (1996b) *Archaeological Assessment of Richard's Castle, Hereford and Worcester*. Unpublished report: Central Marches Historic Towns Survey, Herefordshire and Worcester County Council.

Daniels, R. (1990) Kilton: a survey of a moorland fringe township. In B. Vyner (ed.), *Medieval Rural Settlement in North-east England*. Durham: Architectural and Archaeological Society Research Report No. 2: 33–57.

Daniels, R. (1995) The church, the manor and the settlement: the evidence from Cleveland. In B. Vyner (ed.), *Moorland Monuments: Studies in the Archaeology of*

North-east Yorkshire in Honour of Raymond Hayes and Donn Spratt. CBA Research Report No. 101: 79–90.

Darby, H. C. (1967) *The Domesday Geography of South-west England*. Cambridge: Cambridge University Press.

Darby, H. C. (1977) *Domesday England*. Cambridge: Cambridge University Press.

Darlington, J. and Jecock, M. (2001) Historical summary. In J. Darlington (ed.), *Stafford Castle: Survey, Excavation and Research 1978–98, Volume I – The Surveys*. Stafford: Stafford Borough Council, 9–20.

Darvill, T. (1988) Excavations on the site of the early Norman castle at Gloucester, 1983–84. *Medieval Archaeology* 32: 1–49.

Davies, R. H. C. and Chibnall, M. (eds) (1998) *The Gesta Guillelmi of William of Poitiers*. Oxford: Clarendon.

Davison, B. K. (1972) Castle Neroche: an abandoned Norman fortress in south Somerset. *Transactions of the Somerset Archaeological and Natural History Society* 116: 16–58.

Davison, B. K. (1977) Excavations at Sulgrave, Northamptonshire, 1960–76: an interim report. *Archaeological Journal* 134: 105–14.

Delano-Smith, C. and Kain R. J. P. (1999) *English Maps: A History*. London: British Museum, Studies in Map History, Vol. 2.

Denholm-Young, N. (1934) The Yorkshire estates of Isabella de Fortibus. *Yorkshire Archaeological Journal* 31: 389–420.

Dennison, E. (1997) Sheriff Hutton Castle. *Archaeological Journal* 154: 291–6.

Department of the Environment (DOE) (1975) *Archaeological Excavations, 1975*. London: HMSO.

Dixon, P. (1990) The donjon of Knaresborough: the castle as theatre. *Château Gaillard* 14: 121–39.

Dixon, P. (1998) Design in castle-building: the controlling of access to the lord. *Château Gaillard* 18: 47–57.

Dixon, P. and Marshall, P. (1993) The great tower in the twelfth century: the case of Norham castle. *Archaeological Journal* 150: 410–32.

DOE, *see* Department of the Environment.

Doel, F., Doel, G. and Lloyd, T. (1998) *Worlds of Arthur: King Arthur in History, Legend and Culture*. Stroud: Tempus.

Donaldson, A. M., Jones, A. K. G. and Rackham, D. J. (1980) A dinner in the great hall: report on the contents of a fifteenth-century drain. In D. Austin, Barnard Castle, Co. Durham second interim report: excavation in the inner ward 1976–8: The later medieval period. *Journal of the British Archaeological Association* 133: 86–96.

Donel, L. (1992) Lincoln Castle. *Current Archaeology* 129: 380–1.

Drage, C. (1987) Urban castles. In J. Schofield and R. Leech (eds), *Urban Archaeology in Britain*. London: CBA Research Report No. 61: 117–32.

Drage, C. (1989) Nottingham Castle: A Place Full Royal. *Transactions of the Thoroton Society of Nottinghamshire* 93 (dedicated volume).

Drew, J. H. (1963) Notes on the water system at Kenilworth Castle. *Transactions of the Birmingham and Warwickshire Archaeological Society* 81: 74–7.

Drewett, P. L. (1992) Excavations at Lewes Castle, East Sussex 1985–1988. *Sussex Archaeological Collections* 130: 69–106.

Drury, P. J. (1982) Aspects of the origins and development of Colchester Castle. *Archaeological Journal* 139: 302–419.

Dulley, A. J. F. (1966) The level and port of Pevensey in the middle ages. *Sussex Archaeological Collections* 104: 26–45.

Dunning, G. C. (1936) Alstoe Mount, Burley, Rutland. *Antiquaries Journal* 16: 396–411.

Dyer, C. C. (1985) Power and conflict in the medieval village. In D. Hooke (ed.),

Medieval Villages: A Review of Current Work. Oxford: Oxford University Committee for Archaeology Monograph No. 5: 27–32.

Dyer, C. C. (1988) The consumption of fresh-water fish in medieval England. In M. Aston (ed.), *Medieval Fish, Fisheries and Fishponds*, 2 vols. Oxford: BAR British Series No. 182: 27–38.

Eales, R. (1990) Royal power and castles in Norman England. *Medieval Knighthood* 3: 49–78.

Eaton, T. (2000) *Plundering the Past: Roman Stonework in Medieval Britain*. Stroud: Tempus.

Eddy, M. R. (1983) A Roman settlement and early medieval motte at Moot-Hill, Great Driffield, North Humberside. *East Riding Archaeologist* 7: 40–51.

Edwards, N. (1997) Landscape and settlement in medieval Wales: an introduction. In N. Edwards (ed.), *Landscape and Settlement in Medieval Wales*. Oxford: Oxbow Monograph No. 81: 1–12.

Eldred, K. and Papworth, M. (1998) West Mill, Corfe Castle. *Proceedings of the Dorset Natural History and Archaeological Society* 120: 63–8.

Ellis, P. (ed.) (1993) *Beeston Castle, Cheshire: Excavations by Laurence Keen and Peter Hough, 1968–85*. London: Historic Buildings and Monuments Commission for England, Archaeological Report No. 23.

Ellis, P. (ed.) (2000) *Ludgershall Castle, Wiltshire: A Report on the Excavations by Peter Addyman, 1964–1972*. Devizes: Wiltshire Archaeological and Natural History Society Monograph No. 2.

English, B. (1979) *The Lords of Holderness 1086–1260: A Study in Feudal Society*. Oxford: Oxford University Press.

Ervynck, A. (1991) Medieval castles as top-predators of the feudal system: an archaeozoological approach. *Château Gaillard*, 151–9.

Evans, J. G. (1972) The environment of the inner bailey ditch. In T. Rowley, First report on the excavations at Middleton Stoney castle, Oxfordshire, 1970–71. *Oxoniensia* 37, 129–36.

Everitt, A. (1977) River and wold: reflections on the historical origin of the region and *pays*. *Journal of Historical Geography* 3.1: 1–19.

Everitt, A. (1979) Country, county and town: patterns of regional evolution in England. *Transactions of the Royal Historical Society* (5th Series) 29: 79–108.

Everson, P. (1988) What's in a name? 'Goltho', Goltho and Bullington. *Lincolnshire History and Archaeology* 23: 93–9.

Everson, P. (1990) The problem of Goltho. *Medieval Settlement Research Group Report* 5: 9–14.

Everson, P. (1996a) Bodiam Castle, East Sussex: a fourteenth-century designed landscape. In D. Morgan Evans, P. Salway and D. Thackray (eds), *'The Remains of Distant Times', Archaeology and the National Trust*. London: Occasional Papers of the Society of Antiquaries of London, 66–72.

Everson, P. (1996b) Bodiam Castle, East Sussex: castle and designed landscape. *Château Gaillard* 16: 70–84.

Everson, P. (1998) 'Delightfully surrounded with woods and ponds': field evidence for medieval gardens in England. In P. Pattison (ed.), *There by Design*. Oxford: BAR British Series No. 267: 32–8.

Everson, P., Brown, G. and Stocker, D. (2000) The castle earthworks and landscape context. In P. Ellis (ed.), *Ludgershall Castle, Wiltshire: A Report on the Excavations by Peter Addyman, 1964–1972*. Devizes: Wiltshire Archaeological and Natural History Society Monograph No. 2: 97–119.

Everson, P. and Jecock, M. (1999) Castle Hill and the early medieval development of Thetford in Norfolk. In P. Pattison, D. Field and S. Ainsworth (eds), *Patterns of the Past: Essays in Landscape Archaeology for Christopher Taylor*. Oxford: Oxbow, 97–106.

Everson, P., Taylor, C. C. and Dunn, C. J. (1991) *Change and Continuity: Rural Settlement in North-west Lincolnshire*. London: HMSO.

Everson, P. and Williamson, T. (1998) Gardens and designed landscapes. In P. Everson and T. Williamson (eds), *The Archaeology of Landscape*. Manchester: Manchester University Press, 139–65.

Fairclough, G. (1992) Meaningful constructions – spatial and functional analysis of medieval buildings. *Antiquity* 66: 348–66.

Faith, R. (1997) *The English Peasantry and the Growth of Lordship*. London: Leicester University Press.

Farmer, P. G. (1988) Early medieval settlement in Scarborough. In T. G. Manby (ed.), *Archaeology in Eastern Yorkshire: Essays in Honour of T. C. M. Brewster*. Sheffield: Department of Archaeology and Prehistory, 124–48.

Farnham, G. F. and Thompson, A. H. (1921) Notes on the history of the manor of Withcote. *Reports of the Associated Architectural Society* 36: 127–31.

Faulkner, P. A. (1963) Castle planning in the fourteenth century. *Archaeological Journal* 120: 215–35.

Faull, M. L. and Moorhouse, S. A. (1981) *West Yorkshire: An Archaeological Survey to AD 1500*, 4 vols. Wakefield: West Yorkshire Metropolitan City Council.

Fawcett, R. (1998) Castle and church in Scotland. *Château Gaillard* 18: 87–92.

Field, D., Brown, G. and Crockett, A. (2001) The Marlborough Mount revisited. *Wiltshire Archaeological and Natural History Magazine* 94: 195–204.

Fine, D. (1993) *Sheffield: History and Guide*. Stroud: Sutton.

Flight, C. and Harrison, A. C. (1978) Rochester Castle, 1976. *Archaeologia Cantiana* 94: 27–60.

Forester, T. (1853) *The Ecclesiastical History of England and Normandy by Ordericus Vitalis; Translation with Notes*, Vol. III. London: H.G. Bohn.

Fox, H. S. A. (1989) The people of the wolds in English settlement history. In M. Aston and C. Dyer (eds), *The Rural Settlements of Medieval England*. Oxford: Blackwell, 77–101.

Fox, L. and Russell, P. (1955) *Leicester Forest*. Leicester: Edgar Backus.

Freeman, J. (2000) Survey of the pre-castle plough-soil surface. In R. A. Higham and P. A. Barker, *Hen Domen, Montgomery. A Timber Castle on the English-Welsh Border: A Final Report*. Exeter: University of Exeter Press, 137–40.

Fulford, M. (1985) Excavations on the sites of the amphitheatre and forum-basilica at Silchester, Hampshire: an interim report. *Antiquaries Journal* 65: 39–81.

Gaimster, D. R. M., Margeson, S. and Hurley, M. (1990) Medieval Britain and Ireland in 1989. *Medieval Archaeology* 34: 162–252.

Gale, A. (2000) *Britain's Historic Coast*. Stroud: Tempus.

Gelling, M. (1978) *Signposts to the Past: Place-Names and the History of England*. London: Dent.

Gelling, M. and Foxall, H. D. G. (1990) *The Place-Names of Shropshire: Part One, the Major Names of Shropshire*. Nottingham: English Place-Name Society Vol. 62.

Gem, R. (1986) Lincoln Minster: *Ecclesia Pulchra, Ecclesia Fortis. Transactions of the British Archaeological Association Conference* 8: 9–28.

Gem, R. (1988) The English parish church in the eleventh and early twelfth centuries: a great rebuilding? In J. Blair (ed.), *Minsters and Parish Churches: The Local Church in Transition, 950–1200*. Oxford: Oxford University Committee, 21–30.

Glassby, W. J. J. (1893) *Memorials of Old Mexboro*. Sheffield: Fillingham.

Goddard, E. H. (1930) The mount at Great Somerford. *Wiltshire Archaeological Magazine* 45: 88–9.

Golding, B. (1980) The coming of the Cluniacs. *Proceedings of the Battle Conference on Anglo-Norman Studies* 3: 65–77.

Golding, B. (1994) *Conquest and Colonization: The Normans in Britain, 1066–1100*. New York: St Martin's Press.

Gover, J. E. B., Mawer, A., and Stenton, F. M. (1939) *The Place-Names of Wiltshire*. London: Cambridge University Press, English Place-Name Society Vol. 16.

Gowland, T. S. (1936–8) The honour of Kirkby Malzeard and the chase of Nidderdale. *Yorkshire Archaeological Journal* 33: 349–96.

Graham, A. H. and Davies, S. M. (1993) *Excavations in Trowbridge, Wiltshire, 1977 and 1986–1988*. Salisbury: Wessex Archaeology Report No. 2.

Graham, B. (1988) The town in the Norman colonisations of the British Isles. In D. Denecke and G. Shaw (eds), *Urban Historical Geography*. Cambridge: Cambridge University Press, 37–52.

Grant, A. (1977) The animal bones: mammals. In B. Cunliffe, *Excavations at Portchester Castle: Vol. III, Medieval*. London: Report of the Research Committee of the Society of Antiquaries No. 34: 213–33.

Grant, A. (1984) Medieval animal husbandry. In C. Grigson and J. Clutton-Brock (eds), *Medieval Animal Husbandry: The Archaeozoological Evidence*. Oxford: BAR British Series No. 227, 179–86.

Grant, A. (1988) Animal resources. In G. Astill and A. Grant (eds), *The Countryside of Medieval England*. Oxford: Blackwell, 149–87.

Greene, J. P. (1992) *Medieval Monasteries*. London: Leicester University Press.

Greenway, D. E. (1972) *Charters of the Honour of Mowbray, 1107–1191*. London: British Academy Records of Social and Economic History.

Greig, J. R. A., Girling, M. A. and Skidmore, P. (1982) The plant and insect remains. In P. Barker and R. A. Higham, *Hen Domen, Montgomery: A Timber Castle on the Welsh Border*. London: Royal Archaeological Institute, 60–71.

Griffith, N. J. L., Halstead, P. L. J., MacLean, A. C. and Rowley-Conwy, P. A. (1983) Faunal remains and economy. In P. Mayes and L. Butler, *Sandal Castle Excavations 1964–1973: A Detailed Archaeological Report*. Wakefield: Historical Publications, 341–8.

Hadley, D. (2001) *Death in Medieval England: An Archaeology*. Stroud: Tempus.

Hague, D. B. and Warhurst, C. (1966) Excavations at Sycharth Castle, Denbighshire, 1962–63. *Archaeologia Cambrensis* 115: 108–27.

Hale, J. R. (1983) Tudor fortifications: the defence of the realm, 1485–1558. In *Renaissance War Studies*. London: Hambledon Press, 63–97.

Hall, R. A. and Whyman, M. (1996) Settlement and monasticism at Ripon, North Yorkshire, from the 7th to the 11th centuries A.D. *Medieval Archaeology* 40: 62–150.

Halliday, F. E. (1975) *A History of Cornwall*. London: Duckworth.

Hamilton Thompson, A. (1912) *Military Architecture in England During the Middle Ages*. Oxford: Oxford University Press.

Hamilton Thompson, A. (1917) Notes on colleges of secular canons in England. *Archaeological Journal* 74: 139–239.

Hamilton Thompson, A. (1931) The church and parish. In A. Rowntree (ed.), *The History of Scarborough*. London: Dent.

Harbottle, B. (1982) The castle of Newcastle-upon-Tyne. *Château Gaillard* 9–10: 407–13.

Harbottle, B. and Ellison, M. (1981) An excavation in the castle ditch, Newcastle-upon-Tyne. *Archaeologia Aeliana* (5th Series) 9: 75–250.

Harfield, C. G. (1988) Control of recourses in the medieval period. In J. Gledhill, B. Bender and M. T. Lawson (eds), *State and Society: The Emergence and Development of Social Hierarchy and Political Centralisation*. London: Unwin Hyman, 137–45.

Harfield, C. G. (1991) A hand-list of castles recorded in the Domesday Book. *English Historical Review* 106: 371–92.

Hart, C. R. (1981) *The North Derbyshire Archaeological Survey to AD 1500*. Chesterfield: Derbyshire Archaeological Trust.

Hartley, R. F. (1983) *The Medieval Earthworks of Rutland, a Survey.* Leicester: Leicestershire Museums, Art Galleries and Records Service.

Hartley, R. F. (1987) *The Medieval Earthworks of North-east Leicestershire.* Leicester: Leicestershire Museums, Art Galleries and Records Service.

Harvey, A. (1911) *The Castles and Walled Towns of England.* London: Methuen.

Harvey, J. (1981) *Medieval Gardens.* London: Batsford.

Harvey, M. (1982) Irregular villages in Holderness, Yorkshire: some thoughts on their origin. *Yorkshire Archaeological Journal* 54: 63–72.

Harvey, P. D. A. (1989) Initiative and authority in settlement change. In M. Aston and C. Dyer (eds), *The Rural Settlements of Medieval England.* Oxford: Blackwell, 31–43.

Haslam, J. (1976) *Wiltshire Towns: The Archaeological Potential.* Devizes: Wiltshire Archaeological and Natural History Society.

Hassall, T. G. (1976) Excavations at Oxford Castle, 1965–1973. *Oxoniensia* 41: 232–308.

Hayes, P. P. and Lane, T. W. (1992) *The Fenland Project, No. 5: Lincolnshire Survey. The South-west Fens.* Sleaford: East Anglian Archaeology Report No. 55.

Healey, H. (1977) Moated sites in south Lincolnshire. *South Lincolnshire Archaeology* 1: 28–9.

Heslop, T. A. (1991) Orford Castle, nostalgia and sophisticated living. *Architectural History* 34: 36–58.

Heslop, T. A. (1994) *Norwich Castle Keep: Romanesque Architecture and Social Context.* Norwich: Centre of East Anglian Studies.

Hey, D. (1979) *The Making of South Yorkshire.* Ashbourne: Moorland.

Hey, D. (1980a) Tickhill Church. *Archaeological Journal* 137: 420.

Hey, D. (1980b) Tickhill Town. *Archaeological Journal* 137: 418–19.

Hey, D. (1986) *Yorkshire from AD 1000.* New York: Longman.

Hickman, T. and Tew, D. (1989) *Throsby Revisited.* Wymondham: Witmehá Press.

Higham, M. C. (1991) The mottes of North Lancashire, Lonsdale and South Cumbria. *Transactions of the Cumberland and Westmorland Antiquarian and Archaeological Society* 91: 79–90.

Higham, R. A. (1980) Castles in Devon. In S. Timms (ed.), *Archaeology of the Devon Landscape.* Exeter: Devon County Council, 71–80.

Higham, R. A. (1982b) Early castles in Devon, 1068–1201. *Château Gaillard* 9–10: 102–15.

Higham, R. A. (1987) Public and private defence in the medieval South West: town, castle and fort. In R. Higham (ed.), *Security and Defence in South-west England before 1800.* Exeter: Exeter Studies in History No. 19.

Higham, R. A. (2000a) Castles, fortified houses and fortified towns in the Middle Ages. In R. Kain and W. Ravenhill (eds), *Historic Atlas of the South-West.* Exeter: Exeter University Press, 136–43.

Higham, R. A. (2000b) Parracombe. *Archaeological Journal* 157, 445–8.

Higham, R. A., Allan, J. P. and Blaylock, S. R. (1982) Excavations at Okehampton Castle, Devon, part two – the bailey. *Proceedings of the Devon Archaeological Society* 40: 19–151.

Higham, R. A. and Barker, P. A. (1992) *Timber Castles.* London: Batsford.

Higham, R. A. and Barker, P. A. (2000) *Hen Domen, Montgomery. A Timber Castle on the English-Welsh Border: A Final Report.* Exeter: University of Exeter Press.

Higham, R. A., Goddard, S. and Rouillard, M. (1985) Plympton Castle, Devon. *Proceedings of the Devon Archaeological Society* 43: 59–75.

Higham, R. A. and Saunders, A. (1997) Public and private defence in British medieval towns. *IBA Bulletin 50* (Actes des Réunions du Comiteé Scientifique), 117–28.

Hill, C. and Klemperer, W. (1985) The deserted medieval settlement at Stafford Castle. *Medieval Village Research Group Report* 33: 19–22.

Hill, F. (1965) *Medieval Lincoln*. Cambridge: Cambridge University Press.

Hillaby, J. (1983) The Norman new town of Hereford: its street pattern and its European context. *Transactions of the Naturalists' Field Club of Herefordshire* 44: 181–95.

Hillier, K. (1984) *The Book of Ashby-de-la-Zouch*. Buckingham: Barrowden.

Hillier, W. and Hanson, J. (1984) *The Social Logic of Space*. Cambridge: Cambridge University Press.

Hinton, D. A. (1977) *Alfred's Kingdom: Wessex and the South 800–1500*. London: Dent.

Hinton, D. A. (ed.) (1987) Archaeology and the Middle Ages: Recommendations by the Society for Medieval Archaeology to the Historic Buildings and Monuments Commission for England. *Medieval Archaeology* 31: 1–12.

Hinton, D. A (1990) *Archaeology, Economy and Society: England from the Fifth to the Fifteenth Century*. London: Seaby.

Hodges, R. (1980) Excavations at Camp Green, Hathersage (1976–77) – a Norman ringwork. *Journal of the Derbyshire Archaeological and Natural History Society* 100: 25–34.

Hodges, R. (1988) Origins of the English castle. *Nature* 333: 112–13.

Holden, E. W. (1967) The excavation of a motte at Lodbridge Mill, Lodsworth. *Sussex Archaeological Collections* 105: 103–25.

Holden, E. W. (1975) New evidence relating to Bramber bridge. *Sussex Archaeological Collections* 113: 104–17.

Holdsworth, P. (1984) Saxon Southampton. In J. Haslam (ed.), *Anglo-Saxon Towns*. Chichester: Phillimore, 331–43.

Holland, J. (1826) *The History, Antiquities, and Description of the Town and Parish of Worksop, in the County of Nottingham*. Sheffield: Blackwell.

Holmes, R. (1883–4) Discovery of a fragment of a Saxon cross in the tower of Kippax church. *Yorkshire Archaeological Journal* 8: 377–80.

Holt, R. (1988) *The Mills of Medieval England*. Oxford: Blackwell.

Hooke, D. (ed.) (2000) *Landscape, the Richest Historical Record*. Birmingham: Society for Landscape Studies Supplementary Series No. 1 .

Hope Taylor, B. (1950) The excavation of a motte at Abinger in Surrey. *Archaeological Journal*, 107: 15–43.

Hope Taylor, B. (1953) *Report on the Excavation of Lowe Hill, Wakefield*. Wakefield: Wakefield Historical Society.

Hopkinson, M. F. (2000) Living in defended spaces: past structures and present landscapes. *Landscapes* 1.2: 53–73.

Hoskins, W. G. (1955) *The Making of the English Landscape: An Illustrated History of the Leicestershire Landscape*. London: Hodder and Stoughton.

Hoskins, W. G. (1956) Seven deserted village sites in Leicestershire. *Transactions of the Leicestershire Archaeological and Historical Society* 32: 36–51.

Hoskins, W. G. (1970) *Leicestershire: A Shell Guide*. London: Faber and Faber.

Hudson, W. (1912) The ancient Deaneries of the Diocese of Chichester. *Sussex Archaeological Collections* 55: 109–22.

Hughes, M. (1976) *The Small Towns of Hampshire*. Southampton: Hampshire Archaelogical Committee.

Hughes, M. (1989) Hampshire castles and the landscape: 1066–1216. *Landscape History* 2: 26–59.

Hughes, M. (1994) Towns and villages in medieval Hampshire. In M. Aston and C. Lewis (eds), *The Medieval Landscape of Wessex*. Oxford: Oxbow Monograph No. 46: 195–212.

Hull, M. R. (1958) *Roman Colchester*. Oxford: Oxford University Press.

Hull, P. L. (1971) *The Caption of Seisin of the Duchy of Cornwall, 1337*. Torquay: Devon and Cornwall Record Society.

Hunt, J. D. (1992) *Gardens and the Picturesque: Studies in the History of Landscape Architecture*. Cambridge, MA: MIT.

Hunter-Blair, C. (1944) The early castles of Northumberland. *Archaeologia Aeliana* (4th Series) 22: 116–70.

Hurst, H. (1984) The archaeology of Gloucester castle: an introduction. *Transactions of the Bristol and Gloucestershire Archaeological Society* 102: 73–128.

Hurst, J. G. (1958) Saxon-Norman pottery in East Anglia. *Proceedings of the Cambridgeshire Antiquarian Society* 51: 37–65.

Hurst, J. G. (1961) The kitchen area of Northolt Manor, Middlesex. *Medieval Archaeology* 5: 211–99.

Hutcheson, A. (2000) The French borough. *Current Archaeology* 170: 64–8.

Illingworth, J. L. (1938) *Yorkshire's Ruined Castles*. London: Burrow.

Irons, E. A. (1917) Woodhead Castle. *Fifteenth Annual Report of the Rutland Archaeological and Natural History Society*, 50–1.

Ivens, R. J. (1984) Deddington Castle, Oxfordshire, and the honour of Odo of Bayeux. *Oxoniensia* 49: 101–19.

Jecock, M. and Corbett, G. (1997) Stafford Castle, Staffordshire, NMR Number SJ 92SW2 Request Survey. Unpublished report, National Monuments Record Centre.

Johnson, M. (1996) *An Archaeology of Capitalism*. Oxford: Blackwell.

Johnson, M. (1999) Reconstructing castles and refashioning identities in Renaissance England. In S. Tarlow and S. West (eds), *The Familiar Past: Archaeologies of Later Historical Britain*. London: Routledge: 69–86.

Johnson, S. (1980) Excavations at Conisborough Castle 1973–1977. *Yorkshire Archaeological Journal* 52: 59–88.

Jones, C., Eyre-Morgan, G., Palmer, S. and Palmer, N. (1997) Excavations in the outer enclosure of Boteler's Castle, Oversley, Alcester, 1992–3. *Transactions of the Birmingham and Warwickshire Archaeological Society* 101: 1–98.

Jones, G. R. J. (1983) The pre-Norman field system and its implications for territorial organisation. In P. Mayes and L. Butler, *Sandal Castle Excavations 1964–1973: A Detailed Archaeological Report*. Wakefield: Historical Publications, 70–1.

Jones, M. J. (1993) *Lincoln: History and Guide*. Stroud: Alan Sutton.

Jones, R. (1999) Castles and other defensive sites. In K. Leslie and B. Short (eds), *An Historical Atlas of Sussex*. Chichester: Phillimore, 50–1.

Jones, R. T. (1997) The animal bones. In B. Morley and D. Gurney, *Castle Rising Castle, Norfolk*. Norfolk: East Anglian Archaeology Report No. 81: 123–31.

Jones, R. T. and Ruben, I. (1987) Animal bones, with some notes on the effects of differential sampling. In G. Beresford, *Goltho: The Development of an Early-Medieval Manor*. London: HMSO, 197–206.

Jones, T. L. (1985) *Ashby-de-la-Zouch Castle*. London: English Heritage/HMSO.

Jope, E. M. (1952–3) Late Saxon pits under Oxford Castle. *Oxoniensia* 17–18: 77–111.

Jope, E. M. (1963) The regional cultures of medieval Britain. In I. L. L. Foster and L. Alcock (eds), *Culture and Environment: Essays in Honour of Sir Cyril Fox*. London: Routledge and Kegan Paul, 327–50.

Jope, E. M. and Threlfall, R. I. (1946–7) Recent medieval finds in the Oxfordshire district. *Oxoniensia* 11–12: 165–71.

Jope, E. M. and Threlfall, R. I. (1959) The twelfth-century castle at Ascot Doilly, Oxfordshire: its history and excavation. *Antiquaries Journal* 39: 127–31.

Kapelle, W. E. (1979) *The Norman Conquest of the North: The Region and Its Transformation, 1100–1135*. London: Croom Helm.

Keats-Rohan, K. S. B. (1986) The devolution of the Honour of Wallingford, 1066–1148. *Oxoniensia* 65: 311–18

Keen, L. (1967) Excavations at Old Wardour Castle, Wiltshire. *Wiltshire Archaeological and Natural History Magazine* 62: 67–78.

Keene, D. J. (1976) Suburban growth. In M. W. Barley (ed.), *The Plans and Topography of Medieval Towns in England and Wales.* CBA Research Report No. 14: 71–82.

Keene, D. (1985) *Survey of Medieval Winchester,* 2 vols. Oxford: Clarendon Press (Winchester Studies No. 2).

Keevill, G. D. (2000) *Medieval Palaces: An Archaeology.* Stroud: Tempus.

Keevill, G. D. and Linford, N. (1998) Landscape with gardens: aerial, topographical and geophysical survey at Hamstead Marshall, Berkshire. In P. Pattison (ed.), *There by Design.* Oxford: BAR British Series No. 267, 13–22.

Kendall, H. P. (1926) The forest of Sowerbyshire. *Papers of the Halifax Antiquarian Society,* 85–126.

Kenyon, J. R. (1990) *Medieval Fortifications.* Leicester: Leicester University Press.

Kenyon, J. R. and Thompson, M. W. (1994) The origins of the word 'keep'. *Medieval Archaeology* 38: 175–6.

King, D. J. C. (1956) The castles of Cardiganshire. *Ceridigion* 3: 50–69.

King, D. J. C. (1961) The castles of Breconshire. *Brycheiniog* 7: 71–94.

King, D. J. C. (1972) The field archaeology of mottes in England and Wales: Eine kurze Ubersicht. *Château Gaillard* 5: 101–12.

King, D. J. C. (1983) *Castellarium Anglicanum,* 2 vols. London: Kraus.

King, D. J. C. (1988) *The Castle in England and Wales: An Interpretative History.* Beckenham: Croom Helm.

King, D. J. C. and Alcock, L. (1969) Ringworks of England and Wales. *Château Gaillard* 3: 90–127.

King, D. J. C. and Spurgeon, J. (1965) Mottes in the Vale of Montgomery. *Archaeologica Cambrensis* 114: 69–86.

Kinsley, A. G. (1993) Excavations on the Saxo-Norman town defences at Slaughter House Lane, Newark-on-Trent, Nottinghamshire. *Transactions of the Thoroton Society of Nottinghamshire* 97: 14–63.

Kissock, J. (1997) 'God made nature and men made towns': post-Conquest and pre-Conquest villages in Pembrokeshire. In N. Edwards (ed.), *Landscape and Settlement in Medieval Wales.* Oxford: Oxbow Monograph No. 81, 123–38.

Knocker, G. M. (1966–9) Excavations at Red Castle, Thetford. *Norfolk Archaeology* 34: 119–86.

Knowles, D. and Hadcock, R. N. (1971) *Medieval Religious Houses.* London: Longman.

Landsberg, S. (1996) *The Medieval Garden.* London: British Museum Press.

L'Anson, W. M. (1897) Skipsea Castle. *Yorkshire Archaeological Journal* 24: 258–62.

L'Anson, W. M. (1913) The castles of the North Riding. *Yorkshire Archaeological Journal* 22: 303–99.

Latouche, R. (1966) Un aspect de la vie rurale dans la Maine au XI et au XII siècle. In R. Latouche (ed.), *Etudes Médiévales.* Paris, 133–43.

Lawrance, P. (1982) Animal bones. In J. G. Coad and A. D. F. Streeten, Excavations at Castle Acre Castle, Norfolk, 1972–77, country house and castle of the Norman earls of Surrey. *Archaeological Journal* 139: 275–96.

Lawrance, P. (1987) Animal bones. In J. G. Coad, A. D. F. Streeten and R. Warmington, Excavations at Castle Acre Castle, Norfolk, 1975–1982: the bridges, lime kilns and eastern gatehouse. *Archaeological Journal* 144: 297–302.

Leach, P. (ed.) (1984) *The Archaeology of Taunton, Excavations and Fieldwork to 1980.* Gloucester: Western Archaeological Trust Excavation Monograph No. 8.

Leech, R. H. (1989) Aspects of the medieval defences of Bristol: the town wall, the castle barbican and the Jewry. In M. Bowden, D. Mackay and P. Topping (eds), *From Cornwall to Caithness: Some Aspects of British Field Archaeology, Papers Presented to Norman V. Quinnell*. Oxford: BAR British Series No. 209: 235–50.

Le Maho, J. (1976) L'apparition des seigneuries châtelaines dans le Grand Caux à l'époque deucale. *Archéologie Médiévale* 8: 223–33.

Le Patourel, H. E. J. (1971) The Norman Conquest of Yorkshire. *Northern History* 9: 1–21.

Le Patourel, H. E. J. (1973) *The Moated Sites of Yorkshire*. London: Society for Medieval Archaeology Monograph No. 5.

Le Patourel, H. E. J. (1976) *The Norman Empire*. Oxford: Clarendon Press.

Le Patourel, H. E. J. and Roberts, B. K. (1978) The significance of moated sites. In A. Aberg (ed.), *Medieval Moated Sites*. London: CBA Research Report No. 17: 46–55.

Lethbridge, T. C. (1936) Excavations at Burwell Castle, Cambridgeshire. *Proceedings of the Cambridgeshire Antiquarian Society* 36: 121–33.

Lethbridge, T. C. and Tebbutt, C. T. (1952) Excavations on the castle site known as 'The Hillings' at Eaton Socon, Bedfordshire. *Proceedings of the Cambridgeshire Antiquarian Society* 4: 48–61.

Lewis, C. (1989) Paired mottes in East Chelborough, Dorset. In M. Bowden, D. Mackay and P. Topping (eds), *From Cornwall to Caithness: Some Aspects of British Field Archaeology, Papers Presented to Norman V. Quinnell*. Oxford: BAR British Series No. 209: 159–73.

Lewis, C., Mitchell-Fox, P. and Dyer, C. (1997) *Village, Hamlet and Field: Changing Medieval Settlements in Central England*. Manchester: Manchester University Press.

Liddiard, R. (2000a) *'Landscapes of Lordship': Norman Castles and the Countryside in Medieval Norfolk, 1066–1200*. Oxford: BAR British Series No. 309.

Liddiard, R. (2000b) Population density and Norman castle building: some evidence from East Anglia. *Landscape History* 22: 37–46.

Liddle, P. (ed.) (1982) *Leicestershire Archaeology, The Present State of Knowledge. Vol. 2: The Anglo-Saxon and Medieval Periods*. Leicester: Leicestershire Museums, Art Galleries and Records Service.

Liddle, P. (ed.) (1989) Archaeology in Leicestershire and Rutland 1988. *Transactions of the Leicestershire Archaeological and Natural History Society* 63: 105–20.

Lilley, K. D. (1994) A Warwickshire medieval borough: Brinklow and the contribution of town-plan analysis. *Transactions of the Birmingham and Warwickshire Archaeological Society* 98: 51–60.

Lilley, K. D. (1999) Urban landscapes and the cultural politics of territorial control in Anglo-Norman England. *Landscape Research* 24(1) 5–23.

Lilley, K. D. (2000) 'Non urbe, non vico, non castris': territorial control and the colonization and urbanization of Wales and Ireland under Anglo-Norman lordship. *Journal of Historical Geography* 26(4) 517–31.

Lobel, M. D. (ed.) (1969) *Historic Towns*. London: Lovell Johns – Cook, Hammond and Kell.

Loughlin, N. and Miller, K. (1979) *A Survey of Archaeological Sites in Humberside*. Hull: Humberside Libraries and Amenities for Humberside Joint Archaeological Committee.

Loyn, H. (1989) Rayleigh in Essex: its implications for the Norman settlement. In C. Harper-Bill, C. J. Holdsworth and J. L. Nelson (eds), *Studies in Medieval History Presented to R. Allen Brown*. Woodbridge: Boydell Press, 235–40.

Lucas, J. (1987) Excavations in a medieval market town: Mountsorrel, Leicestershire. *Transactions of the Leicestershire Archaeological and Historical Society* 61: 1–7.

Lyle, M. (1994) *English Heritage Book of Canterbury*. London: English Heritage/ Batsford.

McCarthy, M. R., Summerson, H. R. T. and Annis, R. G. (1990) *Carlisle Castle: A Survey and Documentary History*. London: HMSO.

MacGregor, P. (1983) *Odiham Castle 1200–1500, Castle and Community*. Gloucester: Alan Sutton.

McLean, T. M. (1981) *Medieval English Gardens*. London: Collins.

McNeill, T. E. (1992) *English Heritage Book of Castles*. London: Batsford/English Heritage.

McNeill, T. E. (1997) *Castles in Ireland: Feudal Power in a Gaelic World*. London: Routledge.

McNeill, T. E. and Pringle, M. (1997) A map of mottes in the British Isles. *Medieval Archaeology* 41: 220–2.

Magilton, J. R. (1971–7) Tickhill: the topography of a medieval town. *Transactions of the Hunter Archaeological Society* 10: 344–9.

Magilton, J. R. (1977) *The Doncaster District: An Archaeological Survey*. Doncaster: Doncaster Museums and Arts Service.

Mahany, C. (1977) Excavations at Stamford Castle, 1971–6. *Château Gaillard* 81: 223–45.

Mahany, C., Burchard, A., and Simpson, G. (1982) *Excavations in Stamford, Lincolnshire 1963–1969*. London: Society for Medieval Archaeology Monograph No. 9.

Mahany, C. and Roffe, D. (1982) Stamford: the development of an Anglo-Scandinavian borough. *Proceedings of the Battle Conference on Anglo-Norman Studies* 5: 197–219.

Maltby, M. (1982) Animal and bird bones. In R. A. Higham, J. P. Allan and S. R. Blaylock, Excavations at Okehampton-castle, Devon, part two – the bailey. *Proceedings of the Devon Archaeological Society* 40: 114–35.

Manby, T. G. (1968) Almondbury Castle and hill fort. *Archaeological Journal* 125: 352–4.

Marples, B. (1976) The animal bones. In T. G. Hassall Excavations at Oxford Castle. *Oxoniensia* 41: 302–4.

Marshall, G. (1938) The mottes of the Golden Valley. *Transactions of the Woolhope Naturalists' Field Club, Herefordshire* 30: 141–58.

Marshall, P. and Samuels, J. (1994) Recent excavations at Newark castle, Nottinghamshire. *Transactions of the Thoroton Society of Nottinshamshire* 98: 49–57.

Marshall, P. and Samuels, J. (1971) *Guardian of the Trent: The Story of Newark Castle*. Newark: Newark Castle Trust.

Martin, G. H. (1987) The Domesday boroughs. In W. R. S. Erskine (ed.), *Domesday Book Studies*. London: Alecto Historical Editions, 56–60.

Martindale, J. (1992) Monasteries and castles: the priories of St-Florent de Saumur in England after 1066. In C. Hicks (ed.), *England in the Eleventh Century: Proceedings of the 1990 Harlaxton Symposium*. Stamford: Watkins, 135–56.

Mason, J. F. A. (1963) Roger de Montgomery and his sons. *Transactions of the Royal Historical Society* (5th Series) 13: 1–28.

Mason, J. F. A. (1964) The rapes of Sussex and the Norman Conquest. *Sussex Archaeological Collections* 102: 68–93.

Mason, J. F. A. (1968) The 'Honour of Richmond' in 1086. *English Historical Review* 78: 703–4.

Mathieu, J. R. (1998) A new interpretation of Caernarfon Castle. *Medieval Life* 9: 11–15.

Mathieu, J. R. (1999) New methods on old castles: generating new ways of seeing. *Medieval Archaeology* 43: 115–42.

Matthew, D. (1962) *The Norman Monasteries and Their English Possessions*. London: Oxford University Press.

Mayes, P. and Butler, L. (1983) *Sandal Castle Excavations 1964–1973, a Detailed Archaeological Report*. Wakefield: Wakefield Historical Publications.

Miles, T. J. (1986) The excavation of a Saxon cemetery and part of the Norman castle at North Walk, Barnstaple. *Devon Archaeology Society Proceedings* 44: 59–84.

Miller, E. (1968) Review of M. W. Beresford, 'New Towns of the Middle Ages: Town Plantation in England, Wales and Gascony'. *Northern History* 3: 193–7.

Moorhouse, S. A. (1979) Documentary evidence for the landscape of the manor of Wakefield during the Middle Ages. *Landscape History* 1: 44–58.

Moorhouse, S. A. (1981) The medieval pottery industry and its markets. In D. W. Crossley (ed.), *Medieval Industry*. CBA Research Report No. 40: 96–125.

Moorhouse, S. A. (1986) The Harewood landscape project. *CBA Forum* (1985), 10–15.

Morillo, S. (1994) *Warfare under the Anglo-Norman Kings 1066–1135*. Woodbridge: Boydell Press.

Morley, B. M. (1976) Hylton Castle. *Archaeological Journal* 133: 118–34.

Morley, B. M. (1977) Farleigh Hungerford Castle, Somerset. *Archaeological Journal* 134: 356–8.

Morley, B. M. (1983) Corfe Castle. *Archaeological Journal* 140: 55–7.

Morley, B. M. and Gurney, D. (1997) *Castle Rising Castle. Norfolk*. Norfolk: East Anglian Archaeology Report No. 81.

Morris, R. K. (1989) *Churches in the Landscape*. London: Dent.

Mortimer, R. (1978) Religious and secular motives for some English monastic foundations. *Studies in Church History* 15: 77–86.

Muir, R. (2000) *The* New *Reading the Landscape: Fieldwork in Landscape History*. Exeter: Exeter University Press.

Müller-Wille, M. (1966) *Mittelalterliche Burghügel ('Motten') im Nördlichen Rheinland*. Cologne: Bonner Jahrbücher, Band 16.

Munby, J. (1985) Portchester and its region. In B. Cunliffe and J. Munby (eds), *Excavation at Portchester Castle: Vol. IV, Medieval, the Inner Bailey*. London: Report of the Research Committee of the Society of Antiquaries of London No. 43: 270–95.

Murphy, P. (1987) Mollusca. In J. G. Coad, A. D. F. Streeten and R. Warmington. Excavations at Castle Acre castle, Norfolk, 1975–1982: the bridges, lime kilns and eastern gatehouse. *Archaeological Journal* 144: 302–3.

Musset, L. (1960) Recherches sur les bourgs et les bourgs ruraux du bocage Normand. *Le Pays bas-Normand* 53: 86–94.

Musset, L. (1966) Peuplement en bourgage et bourgs ruraux en Normandie du Xe au XIIIe siècle. *Cahiers de Civilisation Medievale* 9: 177–93.

Myres, J. N. L., Steer, K. A. and Chitty, A. M. H. (1959) The defences of *Isurium Brigantum* (Aldborough). *Yorkshire Archaeological Journal* 40: 1–77.

Neaverson, E. (1947) *Medieval Castles in North Wales: A Study of Sites, Water Supply and Building Stones*. Liverpool: Liverpool University Press.

Nenk, B. S., Margeson, S. and Hurley, M. (1994) Medieval Britain and Ireland in 1993. *Medieval Archaeology* 38: 184–293.

Newman, P. (2000) *The Town and Castle Earthworks at Lydford, Devon*. Unpublished English Heritage Survey Report.

Noddle, B. A. (1975) A comparison of the animal bones from eight medieval sites in southern Britain. In A. T. Clason (ed.), *Archaeozoological Studies*. Papers of the Archaeological Conference 1974, held at the Biolisch-Archaeologisch Institut of the State University of Gronigen, 248–60.

O'Conor, K. D. (1998) *The Archaeology of Medieval Rural Settlement in Ireland*. Dublin: Discovery Programme Monograph No. 3.

Oman, C. (1979) Security in English churches, A.D. 1000–1548. *Archaeological Journal* 136: 90–8.

Orwin, C. S. and Orwin, C. S. (1967) *The Open Fields*, 3rd edn. Oxford: Clarendon Press.

Owen, A. E. B. (1992) Castle Carlton: the origins of a medieval 'new town'. *Lincolnshire History and Archaeology* 27: 17–22.

Owen, L. V. D. (1945) The borough of Nottingham, 1066 to 1284. *Transactions of the Thoroton Society of Nottinghamshire* 49: 13–27.

Owen, L. V. D. (1946) The borough of Nottingham 1284–1485. *Transactions of the Thoroton Society of Nottinghamshire* 50: 25–35.

Padel, O. J. (1988) Tintagel in the twelfth and thirteenth centuries. *Cornish Studies* 16: 61–6.

Painter, S. (1935) English castles in the early middle ages: their number, location and legal position. *Speculum* 10: 321–32.

Palliser, D. M. (1992) An introduction to the Yorkshire Domesday. In A. Williams and R. W. H. Erskine (eds), *The Yorkshire Domesday*. London: Allecto Historical Editions, 1–38.

Palliser, D. M. (1993) Domesday Book and the 'Harrying of the North'. *Northern History* 29: 1–23.

Palliser, D. M. (1995) Town defences in medieval England and Wales. In A. Ayton and J. L. Price (eds), *The Medieval Military Revolution: State, Society and Military Change in Medieval and Early Modern Europe*. London: Tauris, 105–20.

Parker, M. S. (1986) Morthen reconsidered. *Yorkshire Archaeological Journal* 58: 23–9.

Pawley, S. (1988) Grist to the mill: a new approach to the early history of Sleaford. *Lincolnshire History and Archaeology* 23: 37–41.

Penn, K. J. (1980) *Historic Towns in Dorset*. Dorchester: Dorset Natural History and Archaeology Society.

Pevsner, N. and Harris, J. (1989) *The Buildings of England, Lincolnshire*, 2nd edn. London: Penguin.

Phythian-Adams, C. (ed.) (1988) *The Norman Conquest of Leicestershire and Rutland: A Regional Introduction to Domesday Book*. Leicester: Leicestershire Museums, Art Galleries and Records Service.

Platt, C. (1995) *The Parish Churches of Medieval England*. London: Chancellor.

Poole, A. L. (1955) *From Domesday Book to Magna Carta*. Oxford: Clarendon.

Potter, K. R. (ed.) (1976) *Gesta Stephani*. Oxford: Clarendon.

Pounds, N. J. G. (1989) Nottingham and its region. In N. H. Cooper (ed.), *The Nottingham Area*. Supplement to the *Archaeological Journal* 146: 7–13.

Pounds, N. J. G. (1990) *The Medieval Castle in England and Wales: A Social and Political History*. Cambridge: Cambridge University Press.

Pounds, N. J. G. (1991) The chapel in the castle. *Fortress* 9: 12–20.

Preston-Jones, A. and Rose, P. (1992) Week St Mary, town and castle. *Cornish Archaeology* 31: 143–53.

Price, G. (1996) Castle ownership: politics and power in high medieval England. *Medieval Life* 4: 11–17.

Proudfoot, B. (1959) Report on soil samples from Lismahon, Ballykindler Lower TD, Co. Down. In D. M. Waterman, Excavations at Lismahon, Co. Down. *Medieval Archaeology* 3: 171–13.

Putter, A. (1995) *Sir Gawain and the Green Knight and French Arthurian Romance*. Oxford: Clarendon.

Rackham, O. (1986) *The History of the Countryside*. London: Orion.

Rackman, D. J. and Wheeler, A. (1977) The faunal remains. In P. V. Addyman and J. Priestley, Baile Hill, York: a report on the Institute's excavations. *Archaeological Journal* 134: 146–53.

Radford, C. A. R. (1955) Leicester: Church of St Mary de Castro. *Archaeological Journal* 112: 156–8.

Radford, C. A. R. (1970) The later pre-conquest boroughs and their defences. *Medieval Archaeology* 14: 83–103.

Rahtz, S. and Rowley, T. (1984) *Middleton Stoney: Excavation and Survey in a North Oxfordshire Parish 1970–1982*. Oxford: Oxford University Department for External Studies.

RCHME, *see* Royal Commission on Historical Monuments for England.

RCHMW, *see* Royal Commission on Historical Monuments for Wales.

Reaney, P. H. (1935) *The Place-Names of Essex*. London: Cambridge University Press, English Place-Name Society, Vol. 12.

Reaney, P. H. (1960) *The Origins of English Place-Names*. London: Routledge.

Redhead, N. (1990) Wigmore castle – a resistivity survey of the outer bailey. *Transactions of the Woolhope Naturalists' Field Club. Herefordshire* 46: 423–31.

Redmonds, G. and Hey, D. (2001) The opening up of Scammonden, a Pennine Moorland valley. *Landscapes* 2.1: 56–73.

Remfry, P. (1994) Five castles in Clun lordship. *Herefordshire Archaeological News* 61: 15–23.

Renn, D. (1959) Mottes: a classification. *Antiquity* 33: 106–12.

Renn, D. (1968) *Norman Castles in Britain*. London: John Baker.

Renn, D. (1971) *Medieval Castles in Hertfordshire*. Chichester: Phillimore.

Renn, D. (1993) Burhgeat and gonfanon: two sidelights from the Bayeux tapestry. *Proceedings of the Battle Conference on Anglo-Norman Studies* 16: 177–98.

Reynolds, A. (1999) *Late Anglo-Saxon England: Life and Landscape*. Stroud: Tempus.

Richardson, H. G. (1960) *The English Jewry under Angevin Kings*. London: Methuen.

Rigold, S. (1965) *Portchester Castle, Hampshire*. London: Department of the Environment, Ancient Monuments and Historic Buildings.

Rigold, S. (1980) New Buckenham Castle. *Archaeological Journal* 137: 353–5.

Riley, H. and Wilson-North, R. (2001) *The Field Archaeology of Exmoor*. Swindon: English Heritage.

Rippon, S. (1999) The Rayleigh Hills: patterns in the exploitation of a woodland landscape. In L. S. Green (ed.), *The Essex Landscape: In Search of Its History*. Chelmsford: Essex County Council, 20–8.

Roberts, B. K. (1964) Moats and mottes. *Medieval Archaeology* 8: 219–22.

Roberts, B. K. (1987) *The Making of the English Village: A Study in Historical Geography*. Harlow: Longman.

Roberts, B. K. (1996) *Landscapes of Settlement, Prehistory to the Present*. London: Routledge.

Roberts, B. K. and Wrathmell, S. (2000) *An Atlas of Rural Settlement in England*. London: English Heritage.

Roberts, E. (1995) Edward III's lodge at Odiham, Hampshire. *Medieval Archaeology* 39: 91–106.

Robinson, J. F. (1978) *The Archaeology of Malton and Norton*. Leeds: Yorkshire Archaeological Society.

Rodwell, K. A. (1976) Excavations on the site of Banbury Castle. *Oxoniensia* 41: 90–147.

Rodwell, W. (1993) *The Origins and Development of Witham, Essex: A Study in Settlement and Fortification, Prehistoric to Medieval*. Oxford: Oxbow Monograph No. 26.

Roffe, D. (1997) The Anglo-Saxon town and the Norman Conquest. In J. Barrett (ed.), *A Centenary History of Nottingham*. Manchester: Manchester University Press, 24–42.

Roffe, D. and Mahany, C. (1986) Stamford and the Norman Conquest. *Lincolnshire History and Archaeology* 21: 5–9.

Rogerson, A. (1994) Castles. In P. Wade-Martins (ed.), *An Historical Atlas of Norfolk*, 2nd edn. Norwich: Norfolk Museums Service, 68–9.

Rollason, D. W., Gore, D. and Fellows-Jensen, G. (1998) *The Archaeology of York, Volume 1: Sources for York History to AD1100*. York: York Archaeological Trust.

Rose, P. (1992) Bossiney Castle. *Cornish Archaeology* 31: 138–42.

Rose, P. (1994) The medieval garden at Tintagel Castle. *Cornish Archaeology* 33: 170–82.

Roth, C. (1964) *A History of the Jews in England*, 3rd edn. Oxford: Clarendon.

Round, J. H. (1902) Castle Guard. *Archaeological Journal* 59: 144–59.

Round, J. H. (1907) The origin of Belvoir castle. *English Historical Review* 22: 508–10.

Rowley, T. (1972) *The Shropshire Landscape*. London: Hodder and Stoughton.

Rowley, T. (1978) *Villages in the Landscape*. London: Orion.

Rowley, T. (1997) *The English Heritage Book of Norman England*. London: Batsford/ English Heritage.

Royal Commission on Historical Monuments for England (RCHME) (1916–23) *An Inventory of the Historic Monuments in Essex*, 3 vols. London: HMSO.

RCHME (1926) *An Inventory of the Historic Monuments in Huntingdonshire*. London: HMSO.

RCHME (1931–34) *An Inventory of the Historic Monuments in Herefordshire*, 3 vols. London: HMSO.

RCHME (1952–75) *An Inventory of the Historic Monuments of Dorset*, 5 vols. London: HMSO.

RCHME (1962) *EBVRACUM: Roman York*. London: HMSO.

RCHME (1968–72) *An Inventory of the Historical Monuments of Cambridgeshire*, 2 vols. London: HMSO.

RCHME (1972) *York: The Defences*. London: HMSO.

RCHME (1975–84) *An Inventory of the Historical Monuments in the County of Northampton*, 6 vols. London: HMSO.

RCHME (1977) *The Town of Stamford*. London: HMSO.

RCHME (1990) Whorlton Castle, Holy Cross Church, Whorlton Village and environs, Hambleton District, North Yorkshire. Unpublished report, National Monuments Record Centre.

RCHME (1996) Castle Hill, Almondbury, West Yorkshire, NMR Nos. SE 11 SE, 24, 25, 26, and 28: Archaeological Survey Report. Unpublished report, National Monuments Record Centre.

Royal Commission on Historical Monuments for Wales (RCHMW) (1991) *An Inventory of the Ancient Monuments in Glamorgan*, Vol. 3, Part 1a. London: HMSO.

Ruckley, N. A. (1990) Water supply of medieval castles in the United Kingdom. *Fortress* 7: 14–27.

Rudling, D. R. (1983) The archaeology of Lewes: some recent research. *Sussex Archaeological Collections* 121: 45–77.

Rutland Local History Society (1982) *Uppingham in Rutland*. Stamford: Speigl.

Rutledge, P. (1980) New Buckenham. *Archaeological Journal* 137: 352–3.

Rutledge, P. (1997) Appendix III: the settlement pattern of Castle Rising. In B. M. Morley and D. Gurney (eds), *Castle Rising Castle, Norfolk*, Norfolk: East Anglian Archaeology Report No. 81: 144–5.

Ryder, P. (1979) Ravensworth Castle, North Yorkshire. *Yorkshire Archaeological Journal* 51: 81–100.

Ryder, P. (1980) All Saint's church, Laughon-en-le-Morthen. *Archaeological Journal* 137: 426–9.

Ryder, P. (1982) *Saxon Churches in South Yorkshire*. South Yorkshire County Council County Archaeology Monograph No. 2.

Ryder, P. (1993) *Medieval Churches of West Yorkshire*. Wakefield: West Yorkshire Archaeology Service.

St John Hope, W. H. (1908) The ancient topography of Ludlow, in the county of Salop. *Archaeologia* 61(1): 257–328.

St Joseph, J. K. (1950) Castles of Northumbria from the air. *Archaeologia Aeliana* (4th Series) 28: 7–17.

Salzman, L. F. (1931) The origin of the Sussex rapes. *Sussex Archaeological Collections* 72: 20–9.

Saunders, A. D. (1977) Excavations at Launceston Castle 1970–76: interim report. *Cornish Archaeology* 16: 129–37.

Saunders, A. D. (1980) Lydford Castle, Devon. *Medieval Archaeology* 24: 123–86.

Saunders, A. D. (1989) *Fortress Britain: Artillery Forts in the British Isles and Ireland*. Liphook: Beaufort.

Saunders, T. (1990) The feudal construction of space: power and domination in the nucleated village. In R. Samson (ed.), *The Social Archaeology of Houses*. Edinburgh: Edinburgh University Press, 181–96.

Sawyer, P. H. (1985) The Anglo-Norman village. In D. Hooke (ed.), *Medieval Villages: A Review of Current Work*. Oxford: Oxford University Committee for Archaeology Monograph No. 5: 3–6.

Schofield, J. and Vince, A. (1994) *Medieval Towns*. London: Leicester University Press.

Shepherd, E. (1997) Recent excavations at Norwich Castle. In G. De Boe and F. Verhaeghe (eds), *Military Studies in Medieval Europe: Papers of the Medieval Europe Brugge 1997 Conference*. Volume 11: 187–1

Shepherd, E. (2000) Norwich Castle. *Current Archaeology* 170: 52–9.

Shirley, W. W. (1866) *Royal and Other Historical Letters Illustrative of the Reign of Henry III, Vol. II: 1236–1272*. London: Rolls Series No. 27.

Shoesmith, R. (1982) *Hereford City Excavations. Volume 1, Excavations on and Close to the Defences*. CBA Research Report No. 46.

Shoesmith, R. (ed.) (1992) Excavations at Kilpeck. Herefordshire. *Transactions of the Woolhope Naturalists' Field Club, Herefordshire* 47: 162–209.

Shoesmith, R. (1996) *A Guide to Castles and Moated Sites in Herefordshire*. Almeley: Logaston Press.

Shoesmith, R. (2000) Ludlow town. In R. Shoesmith and A. Johnson (eds), *Ludlow Castle: Its History and Buildings*. Almeley: Logaston Smith.

Simpson, W. D. (1949) *Castles from the Air*. London: Country Life Ltd.

Slade, C. F. (1960) Wallingford Castle in the reign of Stephen. *Berkshire Archaeological Journal* 58: 33–43.

Slater, T. R. (1982) Urban genesis and medieval town plans in Warwickshire and Worcestershire. In T. R. Slater and P. J. Jarvis (eds), *Field and Foci: An Historical Geography of Warwickshire and Worcestershire*. Norwich: Geo.

Slater, T. R. (1998) Benedictine town planning in medieval England: evidence from St Albans. In T. R. Slater and G. Rosser (eds), *The Church in the Medieval Town*. Aldershot: Ashgate, 155–76.

Slater, T. R. (2000) Understanding the landscape of towns. In D. Hooke (ed.), *Landscape, the Richest Historical Record*. Society for Landscape Studies Supplementary Series No. 1: 97–108.

Smith, A. H. (1961a) *The Place-Names of the West Riding: Part I, Lower and Upper Strafforth and Staincross Wapentakes*. London: Cambridge University Press, English Place-Name Society, Vol. 30.

Smith, A. H. (1961b) *The Place Names of the West Riding: Part II, Osgoldcross and Asbrigg Wapentakes*. London: Cambridge University Press, English Place-Name Society, Vol. 31.

Speight, S. (1994) Early medieval castle sites in Nottinghamshire. *Transactions of the Thoroton Society of Nottinghamshire* 98: 58–70.

Speight, S. (1995) Four more early medieval 'castle' sites in Nottinghamshire. *Transactions of the Thoroton Society of Nottinghamshire* 99: 65–72.

Speight, S. (2000) Castle warfare in the *Gesta Stephani*. *Château Gaillard* 19: 269–74.

Spurgeon, J. (1965–6) The castles of Montgomeryshire. *Montgomeryshire Collections* 59: 1–59.

Spurgeon, J. (1987a) Mottes and castle ringworks in Wales. In J. R. Kenyon and R. Avent, (eds), *Castles in Wales and the Marches: Essays in Honour of D. J. Cathcart King*. Cardiff: Cardiff University Press, 23–49.

Spurgeon, J. (1987b) The castles of Glamorgan: some sites and theories of general interest. *Château Gaillard* 13: 203–26.

Spurrell, M. (1995) Containing Wallingford Castle, 1146–1153. *Oxoniensia* 60: 257–70.

Squires, A. (1995) A provisional list of the medieval woodlands of Leicestershire (excluding Rutland) *c.* 1200 – *c.* 1530. *Transactions of the Leicestershire Archaeological and Natural History Society* 69: 86–96.

Stamper, P. [A.] (1988) Woods and parks. In G. Astill and A. Grant (eds), *The Countryside of Medieval England*. Oxford: Blackwell, 128–48.

Stamper, P. A. (1984) Excavations on a mid-twelfth century siege castle at Bentley, Hampshire. *Proceedings of the Hampshire Field Club and Archaeological Association* 40: 81–9.

Steane, J. (1988) The royal fishponds of medieval England. In M. Aston (ed.), *Medieval Fish, Fisheries and Fishponds*, 2 vols. Oxford: BAR British Series No. 182: 39–68.

Steane, J. (1999) *The Archaeology of the Medieval English Monarchy*, 2nd edn. London: Routledge.

Stenton, F. M. (1932) *The First Century of English Feudalism, 1066–1166*. Oxford: Clarendon Press.

Stevenson, J. H. (1992) The castles of Marlborough and Ludgershall in the Middle Ages. *Wiltshire Archaeological and Natural History Magazine* 85: 70–9.

Stevenson, W. (1918) Topographical and other early notes about Nottingham. *Transactions of the Thoroton Society of Nottinghamshire* 22: 51–74.

Stocker, D. (1989) Review of G. Beresford, 'Goltho: The Development of an Early Medieval Manor *c.* 850–1150'. *Archaeological Journal* 14: 627–9.

Stocker, D. (1992) The shadow of the general's armchair. *Archaeological Journal* 149: 415–20.

Stocker, D. and Stocker, M. (1996) Sacred profanity: the theology of rabbit breeding and the symbolic landscape of the warren. *World Archaeology* 28.2: 265–72.

Stocker, D. and Vince, A. (1997) The early Norman castle at Lincoln and a re-evaluation of the original west tower of Lincoln Cathedral. *Medieval Archaeology* 41: 223–33.

Stone, B. (1959) *Sir Gawain and the Green Knight*. London: Penguin.

Strickland, M. (1992) Securing the North: invasion and the strategy of defence in twelfth-century Anglo-Scottish warfare. In M. Strickland (ed.), *Anglo-Norman Warfare: Studies in Late Anglo-Saxon and Anglo-Norman Military Organization and Warfare*. Woodbridge: Boydell Press, 208–29.

Strickland, M. (1996a) Military technology and conquest: the anomaly of Anglo-Saxon England. *Proceedings of the Battle Conference on Anglo-Norman Studies* 19: 353–82.

Strickland, M. (1996b) *War and Chivalry: The Conduct and Perception of War in England and Normandy, 1066–1217*. Cambridge: Cambridge University Press.

Swan, V. G., Mackay, D. A. and Jones, B. E. A. (1990) East Lilling, North Yorkshire: the deserted medieval village reconsidered. *Yorkshire Archaeological Journal* 62: 91–109.

Symonds, J., Webster, J., Cooper, T. and Badcock, A. (1995) A Review of the Area of Archaeological Interest in Old Bolsover. Unpublished report for ARCUS, Derbyshire Sites and Monuments Record.

Tait, J. (1904) *Medieval Manchester and the Beginnings of Lancashire*. Manchester: University of Manchester History Series No, 1.

Taylor, A. and Woodward, P. (1975) Cainhoe Castle excavations 1973. *Bedfordshire Archaeological Journal* 10: 41–52.

Taylor, A. J. (1985) *Studies in Castles and Castle Building*, London: Hambledon.

Taylor, C. C. (1970) *Dorset*. London: Hodder and Stoughton.

Taylor, C. C. (1972) Medieval moats in Cambridgeshire. In P. J. Fowler (ed.), *Archaeology and the Landscape: Essays for L. V. Grinsell*, London: John Baker, 237–48.

Taylor, C. C. (1973) Cambridgeshire earthwork surveys: motte and bailey castle and deserted village, Castle Camps. *Proceedings of the Cambridgeshire Antiquarian Society* 64: 38–43.

Taylor, C. C. (1974) *Fieldwork in Medieval Archaeology*. London: Batsford.

Taylor, C. C. (1977) Polyfocal settlement and the English village. *Medieval Archaeology* 21: 189–93.

Taylor, C. C. (1978) Aspects of medieval village mobility in medieval and later times. In S. Limbrey and J. G. Evans (eds), *The Effects of Man on the Landscape: The Lowland Zone*. London: CBA Research Report No. 21: 126–34.

Taylor, C. C. (1979) *Roads and Tracks of Britain*. London: Dent.

Taylor, C. C. (1982) Medieval market grants and village mobility. *Landscape History* 4: 21–8.

Taylor, C. C. (1983a) *The Archaeology of Gardens*. Aylesbury: Shire.

Taylor, C. C. (1983b) *Village and Farmstead: A History of Rural Settlement in England* London: Philip.

Taylor, C. C. (1988) Problems and possibilities. In M. Aston (ed.), *Medieval Fish, Fisheries and Fishponds*, 2 vols. Oxford: BAR British Series No. 182: 465–73.

Taylor, C. C. (1989) Somersham Palace, Cambridgeshire, a medieval landscape for pleasure? In M. Bowden, D. Mackay and P. Topping (eds), *From Cornwall to Caithness: Some Aspects of British Field Archaeology, Papers Presented to Norman V. Quinnell*. Oxford: BAR British Series No. 209: 211–24.

Taylor, C. C. (1992) Medieval rural settlement: changing perceptions. *Landscape History* 14: 5–17.

Taylor, C. C. (1996) The archaeology of gardens and designed landscapes. In D. Morgan Evans, P. Salway and D. Thackray (eds), *'The Remains of Distant Times', Archaeology and the National Trust*. London: Occasional Papers of the Society of Antiquaries of London, 59–65.

Taylor, C. C. (1998a) From recording to recognition. In P. Pattison (ed.), *There by Design*. Oxford: BAR British Series No. 267: 1–6.

Taylor, C. C. (1998b) *Parks and Gardens of Britain*. Edinburgh: Edinburgh University Press.

Taylor, C. C. (2000) Medieval ornamental landscapes. *Landscapes* 1(1): 38–55.

Taylor, C. C., Everson, P. and Wilson-North, W. R. (1990) Bodiam Castle, Sussex. *Medieval Archaeology* 34: 155–7.

Thomas, H. J. and Dowdell, G. (1987) A shrunken medieval village at Barry, South Glamorgan. *Archaeologica Cambrensis* 136: 94–137.

Thompson, K. (1997) Lords, castellans and dowagers: the rape of Pevensey from the 11th to the 13th century. *Sussex Archaeological Collections* 135: 209–20.

Thompson, M. W. (1964) Reclamation of waste ground for the Pleasance at Kenilworth Castle. *Medieval Archaeology* 8: 222–3.

Thompson, M. W. (1965) Two levels of the Mere at Kenilworth Castle. *Medieval Archaeology* 9: 156–61.

Thompson, M. W. (1966) The origins of Bolingbroke Castle, Lincolnshire. *Medieval Archaeology* 10: 152–8.

Thompson, M. W. (1977) *Kenilworth Castle, Warwickshire*. London: Historic Buildings and Monuments Commission for England.

Thompson, M. W. (1986) Associated monasteries and castles in the Middle Ages: a tentative list. *Archaeological Journal* 143: 305–21.

Thompson, M. W. (1987) *The Decline of the Castle*. Cambridge: Cambridge University Press.

Thompson, M. W. (1989) The Green Knight's castle. In C. Harper-Bill, C. J. Holdsworth and J. L. Nelson (eds), *Studies in Medieval History Presented to R. Allen Brown*. Woodbridge: Boydell Press, 317–26.

Thompson, M. W. (1991) *The Rise of the Castle*. Cambridge: Cambridge University Press.

Thompson, M. W. (1994) The military interpretation of castles. *Archaeological Journal* 151: 439–45.

Thompson, M. W. (1997) Castles. In D. Brewer and J. Gibson (eds), *A Companion to the Gawain Poet*. Cambridge: Cambridge University Press, 119–30.

Tilley, C. (1994) *A Phenomenology of Landscape*. Oxford: Berg.

Torrance, W. J. (1959) A contemporary poem on the removal of Salisbury Cathedral. *Wiltshire Archaeological Magazine* 57: 242–6.

Toulin Smith, L. (ed.) (1907) *The Itinerary of John Leland in or About the Years 1535–1543, Parts I–III*. London: George Bell and Sons.

Toy, S. (1933) The round castles of Cornwall. *Archaeologia* 83: 203–26.

Trezise, S. (2000) *The West Country as a Literary Invention: Putting Fiction in Its Place*. Exeter: Exeter University Press.

Turner, H. L. (1970) *Town Defences in England and Wales*. London: John Baker.

Twycross-Raines, G. F. (1920) Aldbrough church, Holderness. *East Riding Antiquarian* 23: 28–33.

Tyler, A. (1976) *Richmond: An Archaeological Study*. Richmond: Richmondshire District Council.

VCH (1904) *Victoria History of the County of Warwick*, Vol. I. London: Archibald Constable.

VCH (1906) *Victoria History of the County of Lincoln*, Vol. II. London: Archibald Constable.

VCH (1906) *Victoria History of the County of York*, Vol. I. London: Archibald Constable.

VCH (1908) *Victoria History of the County of Buckingham*, Vol. II. London: Archibald Constable.

VCH (1908) *Victoria History of the County of Warwick*, Vol. II. London: Archibald Constable.

VCH (1910) *Victoria History of the County of Nottingham*, Vol. II. London: Archibald Constable.

VCH (1911) *Victoria History of the County of Suffolk*, Vol. I. London: Archibald Constable.

VCH (1914) *Victoria History of the County of York, North Riding*. Vol. I. London: Constable and Company.

VCH (1935) *Victoria History of the County of Rutland*, Vol. II. London: St Catherine Press.

VCH (1945) *Victoria History of the County of Warwick*, Vol. III. Oxford: Oxford University Press/University of London Institute of Historical Research.

VCH (1948) *Victoria History of the County of Cambridge and the Isle of Ely*, Vol. II. Oxford: Oxford University Press/University of London Institute of Historical Research.

VCH (1964) *Victoria History of the County of Leicester*, Vol. V. London: Oxford University Press/University of London Institute of Historical Research.

VCH (1968) *The Victoria History of the County of Shropshire*, Vol. VIII. London: Oxford University Press/University of London Institute of Historical Research.

VCH (1984) *Victoria History of the County of Sussex*, Vol. IV. London: Dawsons/ University of London Institute of Historical Research.

VCH (1984) *Victoria History of the County of York, East Riding*, Vol. V. Oxford: Oxford University Press/University of London Institute of Historical Research.

VCH (1996) *Victoria History of the County of Gloucestershire*, Vol. V. Oxford: Oxford University Press/University of London Institute of Historical Research.

Vince, A. (1990) *Saxon London: An Archaeological Investigation*. London: Seaby.

Wade-Martins, P. (1975) The origins of rural settlement in East Anglia. In P. J. Fowler (ed.), *Recent Work in Rural Archaeology*. Bradford-on-Avon: Moonraker Press.

Walker, J. (1939) *Wakefield: Its History and People*, 2 vols, 2nd edn. Wakefield: privately printed.

Walker, D. (1967) William Fitz Osbern and the Norman settlement in Herefordshire. *Transactions of the Woolhope Naturalists' Field Club. Herefordshire* 39: 402–12.

Watson, B. (1992) The Norman fortress on Ludgate Hill in the City of London, England, recent excavations 1986–1990. *Château Gaillard* 15: 335–45.

Warren Hollister, C. (1989) The campaign of 1102 against Robert of Bellême. In C. Harper-Bill, C. J. Holdsworth and J. L. Nelson (eds), *Studies in Medieval History Presented to R. Allen Brown*. Woodbridge: Boydell Press, 193–202.

Watson, B. (1992) The Norman fortress on Ludgate Hill in the city of London. *Château Gaillard* 15, 335–45.

Way, T. (1997) *A Study of the Impact of Imparkment on the Social Landscape of Cambridgeshire from c1080 to 1760*. Oxford: BAR British Series No. 258.

Weaver, J. (1987) *Beeston Castle*. London: English Heritage/HMSO.

Welldon Finn, R. (1971) *The Norman Conquest and Its Effects on the Economy: 1066–1086*. London: Longman.

Welfare, H., Bowden, M. and Blood, K. (1999) Fieldwork and the castles of the Anglo-Scottish borders. In P. Pattison, D. Field and S. Ainsworth (eds), *Patterns of the Past: Essays in Landscape Archaeology for Christopher Taylor*. Oxford: Oxbow, 53–60.

West Yorkshire Archaeological Service (WYAS) (1991) The Parlington Estate, West Yorkshire: Preliminary Archaeological Potential. Unpublished report, West Yorkshire Sites and Monuments Record.

Whitehead, D. (1995) Some connected thoughts on the parks and gardens of Herefordshire before the age of landscape gardening. *Transactions of the Woolhope Naturalists' Field Club, Herefordshire* 48: 193–223.

Whitelock, D., Douglas, D. C. and Tucker, S. I. (eds) (1961) *The Anglo-Saxon Chronicle*. London: Eyre and Spottiswoode.

Wightman, W. E. (1962) The Palatine Earldom of William Fitz Osbern in Gloucestershire and Worcestershire (1066–1071). *English Historical Review* 77: 6–17.

Wightman, W. E. (1966) *The Lacy Family in England and Normandy*. Oxford: Clarendon Press.

Wilkinson, M. (1982) Fishbones. In R. A. Higham, J. P. Allan and S. R. Blaylock, Excavations at Okehampton castle, Devon, part two – the bailey. *Proceedings of the Devonshire Archaeological Society* 40: 135–8.

Williams, A. (1992) A bell-house and a *burhgeat*: lordly residences in England before the Norman Conquest. *Medieval Knighthood* 4: 221–40.

Williams, A. (1995) *The English and the Norman Conquest*. Woodbridge: Boydell Press.

Williams, D. (1992) Plant macrofossils. In K. W. B. Lightfoot, Rumney Castle, a ringwork and manorial centre in South Glamorgan. *Medieval Archaeology* 36: 155–6.

Williams, F. (1977) *Pleshey Castle, Essex (XII–XVI Century): Excavations in the Bailey 1959–1963*. Oxford: BAR British Series No. 42.

Williamson, F. (1942) Old Derby street names. *Journal of the Derbyshire Archaeological and Natural History Society* 63: 1–27.

Wilmott, T. (1985) Excavations at Tanner's Row, Pontefract, an interim report. *Bulletin of the CBA Churches Committee* 20: 18–20.

Wilmott, T. (1986) Excavations at Tanner's Row, Pontefract: second interim report. *Bulletin of the CBA Churches Committee* 21: 20–1.

Wilmott, T. (1987a) Pontefract. *Current Archaeology* 106: 340–4.

Wilmott, T. (1987b) Tanner's Row, Pontefract, West Yorkshire. *Bulletin of the CBA Churches Committee* 22: 20.

Winton, H. (1993) *Sheriff Hutton Project*. Unpublished Aerial Photographic Interpretation Report, National Monuments Record Centre.

Wilson, B. (1976) The animal bones. In K. A. Rodwell, Excavations on the site of Banbury Castle, 1973–4. *Oxoniensia* 41: 144–7.

Wilson, D. M. and Hurst, D. G. (1965) Medieval Britain in 1964. *Medieval Archaeology* 91: 170–220.

Wilson, D. M. and Hurst, D. G. (1966) Medieval Britain in 1965. *Medieval Archaeology* 10: 168–219.

Wilson, D. M. and Hurst, D. G. (1967) Medieval Britain in 1966. *Medieval Archaeology* 11: 262–319.

Wilson-North, W. R. and Dunn, C. J. (1990) 'The Rings', Loddiswell: a new survey by the Royal Commission on the Historic Monuments of England. *Proceedings of the Devon Archaeological Society* 48: 87–100.

Winchester, A. J. L. (1987) *Landscape and Society in Medieval Cumbria*. Edinburgh: John Donald.

Winter, M. J. (1978) Gilmorton. *Medieval Settlement Research Group Report* 26: 8.

Winwood, H. H. (1879) Report of the Pen Pits Exploration Committee. *Proceedings of the Somersetshire Archaeological and Natural History Society* 25: 7–17.

Winwood, H. H. (1884) The results of further excavations at Pen Pits. *Proceedings of the Somersetshire Archaeological and Natural History Society* 30: 149–52.

Woodward, S. (1984) *The Landscape of a Leicestershire Parish: The Historical Development of Groby*. Leicester: Museums, Art Galleries and Records Service.

Wrathmell, S. (1994) Rural settlement in medieval England: perspectives and perceptions. In V. Vyner (ed.), *Papers Celebrating 150 Years of the Royal Archaeological Institute*. London: Royal Archaeological Institute, 178–94.

Wright, J. (1684) *The History and Antiquities of the County of Rutland*. London.

Wright, R. P. and Hassall, M. W. C. (1971) Roman Britain in 1970. *Britannia* 2: 243–304.

Wright, T. (ed.) (1863) *The Historical Works of Giraldus Cambrensis*. London: H. G. Bohn.

WYAS, *see* West Yorkshire Archaeological Service.

Yeoman, P. (1995) *Medieval Scotland, an Archaeological Perspective*. London: Batsford/Historic Scotland.

Young, C. R. (1979) *The Royal Forests of Medieval England*. Leicester: Leicester University Press.

Young, R. (1980) An inventory of barrows in County Durham. *Transactions of the Durham and Northumbria Architectural and Archaeological Society* 5: 1–13.

Youngs, S. M., Clark, J. and Barry, T. (1987) Medieval Britain and Ireland in 1986. *Medieval Archaeology* 31: 110–91.

Youngs, S. M., Gaimster, D. R. M. and Barry, T. (1988) Medieval Britain and Ireland in 1987. *Medieval Archaeology* 32: 225–314.

Index

Note: page numbers in **bold** denote a figure or table.